# IN THE MIDST OF THE PEOPLE

*by*

*Valerie Bonham*

Valerie Bonham

Frontispiece

The Revd. Canon T.T. Carter, Rector of Clewer, 1844 - 80.
Photographed in 1900

Errata

p.34 para. 5 - "A Victorian Rubbish heap". These articles are now in the Clewer History Museum.

p.43 para. 4 line 7 - "Eton College" should read "Eton Cottage".

p.78 line 6 - Should read "In 1912 the first edition of the English Missal..."

p.94 para. 5 line 10 -"Internment" should read "interment".

p.101 para. 5 line 2 - Should read "and there was a Requiem at St. Agnes..."

p.103 para. 4 line 4 - "Internment" should read "interment".

p.113 para. 3 line 9 - Should read "At 11.55 p.m. tonight..."

p.113 para. 5 line 6 - Should read "Since the Coronation in 1911..."

p.142 para. 5 line 10 - "Miss Hackamore" should be spelt 'Hakoumoff' and her pets were two grey cats.

p.143 para. 5 line 14 - Should read "Assisted by Mr. & Mrs. Ham..."

p.144 - Last line should read "...we can enter 1948 with gratitude in our hearts to God for his blessing..."

P.148 para. 2 line 2 - "Canon Pike..." Minor Canons are not addressed as Canon.

p.152 Last line should read "Bought on loan in 1950; and our bills for necessary repairs... must be met.."

P.156 para. 5 - Alan and Barbara Bridges were married in All Saints' Frances Road, the bride having resided in Windsor parish.

p.160 para. 1. In fact the first Confirmation at St. Agnes was on Sept. 27th 1945. See page 141.

p.160 bottom line. The first wedding took place on Sept. 7th 1957 not Aug. 7th.

This book is dedicated to the Greater Glory of God, and in thanksgiving for the Life and Work of Thomas Thellusson Carter, Rector of Clewer, 1844 - 80, Founder and Benefactor of Saint Agnes', Spital; and to the Priests and People of St. Agnes', past, present and future, in thanks giving for the past, and in the hope of a still more glorious future.

CONTENTS

Preface Page 8

Acknowledgements Page 9

List of Illustrations Page 10

Forword Page 11

Introduction I. Carter of Clewer

Early years; early ministry; Rector of Clewer; condition of Clewer Church and attempts to restore it; Foundation of the Clewer Sisters; Clewer St. Stephen; the 'Clewer Case'; resignation; death. Page 12

Introduction II. Clewer Close-up

A perambulation of the Parish in the 1870's. Page 17

Chapter I. In Our End is Our Beginning. (Mid-1850's - 1876)

Poverty in Clewer and Windsor parishes; Cemetery Acts 1852 and 1853; use of Cemetery Chapel for Sunday worship; Revd S. J. Stone and the 'Churchs' One Foundation'; Stone requests improvements to Cemetery Chapel; letter in Windsor Express complaining of 'Popery' in Cemetery Chapel; opening of St Agnes'; Revd G. H. Swinny; St Agnes' 'peculiar' status; Swinny's later ministry and death. Page 20

Chapter II. In the Midst of the People (1877 - 1893)

Revd Roland Errington, Rector of Clewer; Revd Henry Ley at St Agnes'; Rector's wedding; Interior of St Agnes' in 1880's; social activities; Mission Rooms built 1884; services and ceremonial; finances; people and pastimes; Bishop Hornby's visit, 1893; Smallpox at Clewer; Henry Ley's departure. Page 29

Chapter III. Music, Missions and a Royal Jubilee. (1894 - 1900)

Revd George Jones at St Agnes'; services, Guilds and gifts; building of gallery; Reservation of the Blessed Sacrament; parish Mission; musical matters; Queen Victoria's Diamond Jubilee; Church Army; departure of Rector Errington; departure of Revd George Jones. Page 36

Interlude: Spital Village in 1900

A perambulation from Bolton Road to Clewer Green. Page 43

Chapter IV. Passing Shadows (1900 - 1904)

Revd A. T. C. Cowie, Rector of Clewer; Relief of Mafeking; Revd H. B. Hunt at St. Agnes'; Patronal Festival, 1901, and death of Queen Victoria; death of Canon Carter; redecoration of church and Mission Rooms; Coronation of King Edward VII; breakdown and departure of Hunt; Revd W. S. Hulme at St Agnes'; Hulme's departure. Page 45

Chapter V. Edwardian Summer (1904 - 1907)

Revd Charles Farr at St Agnes'; Concerts and Socials; wealthy benefactors and where they lived; Spital people; Christmas treats, 1905; St. Agnes' Dramatic Society; Clewer Horticultural Show; first visit of Fr. Stanton; death of Sir Francis Tress Barry. Page 50

Chapter VI. Without Let or Hindrance (1907 - 1909)

Need for a church extension; fund-raising; summer outings; building operations; enlarged church dedicated January, 1908; St. Agnes' legal status; gifts of vestments; plays, dances and excursions; visiting preachers; visit of Fr. E. F. Russell. Page 56

Chapter VII. A few Farewells (1910 - 1911)

St. Agnes-tide 1910; 'A Midsummer Night's Dream'; Death of King Edward VII; death of Edward King, Bishop of Lincoln and the Revd. S. K. Tahourdin; further extension planned; Norman Font dedicated;Coronation of King George V and Queen Mary; departure of Revd. Charles Farr. Page 63

Chapter VIII. Cloud-capped Towers (1911 - 1913)

Revd. Marsh Kirkby at St. Agnes'; finances; departure of Mrs Carpenter Rowe; acquisition of organ 1912; Kirkby's ambition to build a larger church; death of Fr. Stanton; departure of Revd. M. Kirkby. Page 69

Chapter IX. The Last of the Old World (1913 - 1914)

Revd. William Brook at St. Agnes'; spiritual matters; social events; last weeks of peace; War; the 'War Effort' in Clewer. Page 77

Chapter X. A Time for War ... (1915 - 1917

National Day of Prayer, January 3rd, 1915; The 'War Effort' at Clewer Green School and elsewhere in the Parish; Imperial Service College; Miss Lack; Spital men who gave their lives; death of Oscar Fenner; National Mission of Repentance and Hope, 1916; War Shrines; War Memorial dedicated; death of 'Squire' Foster. Page 83

Chapter XI. ... and a Time for Peace 1918 - 1919

Spanish 'flu; Armistice; deaths - William Clark, Revd. G. S. Cuthbert, and Victor Biddulph; Peace celebrations. Page 90

Chapter XII. Stability, Station Days and the Golden Jubilee (1920 - 1924)

Loss of benefactresses - Lady Arran and Lady Dalton Fitzgerald; death of Arthur William Weston; Imperial Service College; Anglo-Catholic Congresses; P.C.C. Decisions; Guild of Servants of the Sanctuary; 'Fiery Cross' Pilgrimage; St. Agnes' Golden Jubilee; Retirement of Rector Cowie. Page 94

Chapter XIII. Hail and some more Farewells (1925 - 1929)

Revd. William Elwell as Rector; Death of Queen Alexandra; General Strike; Finances; Coral League; Death of Revd. A. T. C. Cowie; Death of George and Emma Uglow. Page 100

Chapter XIV. The Old Order Changeth (1930 - 1935)

St. Agnes' Cottages; resignation and later ministry of Revd. William Elwell; memorial pulpit dedicated; Revd. G. G. Payne-Cook, Rector; death of Revd. G. D. Nicholas; Oxford Movement Centenary; St. Agnes' Diamond Jubilee; declining health of Revd. Wm. Brook; resignation and death. Page 105

Chapter XV. All Things New (1935 - 1939)

Revd. R. E. Beer at St. Agnes'; Mr and Mrs G. Bridges; death of King George V; death of Mrs Beer; Abdication; Miss Thorne and Miss Hearmon; re-ordering of Sanctuary and redecoration of the Church; Coronation of King George VI and Queen Elizabeth; social activities; departure of Revd. R. E. Beer. Page 112

Interlude: Spital on the Brink of War.

A perambulation from the Stag and Hounds to Imperial Road in 1939. Page 120

Chapter XVI. Winds of Change (1939 - 1942)

Revd. H. Thornton Trapp at St. Agnes'; death of Constance Rodwell; War declared; Spiritual observances for the war; Innovations in the church services; the local 'War Effort'; Battle of Britain and the Blitz; ME 109 down behind Stag Meadow; bomb on St. Leonard's Hill; death of Patience Payne-Cook; War Weapons Week 1941; death of Lady Edward Spencer-Churchill; departure and later life of Fr. Trapp. Page 122

Chapter XVII. Hornets Nests and Doodle Bugs (1942 - 1945)

Resignation of Revd. G. G. Payne-Cook; Revd. Cyprian Dymoke-Marr, Rector of Clewer; Revd. Alban Howard at St. Agnes'; death of Mrs Mosscockle; controversy concerning Canon Carter's Centenary; V-1 Flying Bomb at Dedworth; death of Miss Boycott; Clewer fete; proposals for Post-War development; 'Three Half Crowns'; Peace Celebrations; Departure of Fr. Alban Howard. Page 131

Chapter XVIII. Plough Shares into Pre-Fabs (1946 - 1949)

Revd. Edward Dixon at St. Agnes'; Worshippers at St. Agnes'; Floods; death of Revd. G. G. Payne-Cook; 'Pearly Pearls'. Page 142

Chapter XIX. Rot and Rose Petals (1949 - 1955)

Revd. W. A. Pike at St. Agnes'; death of Miss Hearmon; cottage obtained for priest-in-charge; Revd. M. W. Hickin at St. Agnes'; restoration of Lady Chapel floor; death of King George VI; Coronation of Queen Elizabeth II; death of Mrs Brook; Clewer Rectory; departure of Fr. Hickin; Fr. Brian Elliott-Smith at St. Agnes'; deteriorating health and resignation. Page 148

Chapter XX. Sundry and Manifold Changes (1955-1959)

Revd. A. E. Wood at St. Agnes'; New Services in Holy Week, 1956; introduction of 9.30 Parish Communion; Young Wives and Scouts; New Presbytery completed; Dedworth becomes a Conventional District but St. Agnes' does not; St. Agnes' licensed for Marriages; death of Sister Dorothy Ellen; first evening Eucharist; departure of Fr. Wood. Page 156

Chapter XXI. Boilers, Blowers and Bank Balances (1959 - 1963)

Revd. F. J. Prebble at St. Agnes'; Christian Stewardship Campaign; Finance; some deaths; worshippers at St. Agnes'; Ordination of Norman Knibbs; departure of Fr. Prebble. Page 165

Chapter XXII. Stewardship and a Spot of D.I.Y. (1963 - 1967)

Revd. R. G. Hayne at St. Agnes'; Stewardship; finances; organ; death of Fr. J. A. Wynne; some deaths at St. Agnes'; youth work; George Kelsey's Golden Jubilee as organist; Church redecorated by Congregation; Stewardship again; Series II Holy Communion introduced; departure of Fr. Hayne. Page 169

ChapterXXIII. Full Circle (1967 - 1974)

Revd. G. A. Friend at St. Agnes'; Rector's Silver Jubilee; Restoration of Hall; 'Westward Position ' Experiment; Stewardship; Fr. Cyprian's retirement; Revd. Dennis Shaw, Rector; roof repaired; Series III Holy Communion introduced; Centenary Celebrations; departure of Fr. Friend. Page 177

Chapter XXIV. To Arrive Where we Started (1975 - 1982)

Revd. F. T. Bonham at St. Agnes'; Saturday markets; church roof repaired; church rewired; windows restored; floor rot discovered - restored - church redecorated; David Saunders; organ re-build; Sunday School; Seekers Week; deaths since 1975; memorials; bequests; social activities. Page 184

Appendix I. Torpor and Torrent

State of Church of England in early 19th century; Keble's Assize sermon, 1833; Tracts for the Times; the Ornaments Rubric and the Six Points; Rise of the Church Association; Public Worship Regulation Act, 1874; The Lincoln Case. Page 193

Appendix II

Rectors of Clewer since 1844; Priests-in-charge of St. Agnes'. Page 196

## PREFACE by the Rector of Clewer

Valerie Bonham has produced, in this excellent book, a remarkable piece of work. Her patience, her industry, her persistence in tracking down information - coupled with an extraordinary flair for sensing where it might be found - have been put to use, over a period of six years, to produce what must surely be the most comprehensive account of the history of any Church in the land.

The rich and loving detail with which her story is told, however, gives something more than a history of St. Agnes' Church. There emerges from these pages a vivid picture of what life was like for average, 'ordinary' people throughout the period covered. The effect of national and international events on life at this level is faithfully shown, as also is the influence of major movements and changes of thought in the Church of England.

Mrs Bonham's account, then, of the life and worship of the people of St. Agnes' Church, Spital, is a microcosm of the history of our church and nation.

And - if all that were not enough - she has recreated for Spital that separate identity, as a place in its own right, which was rapidly being forgotten.

She has put all who care about our Windsor local history in her debt, but I venture to prophesy that, in years to come, writers on Church History and Social History, at the national level, will consider this book a gold-mine.

For me, personally, there is certainly a vein of pure gold which runs right through the book. Mrs Bonham makes it clear that, in every generation, through the many vicissitudes of the years, there have been men and women at St. Agnes' Church who have said, from their hearts:

"We love the place, O God,

Wherein thine Honour dwells.."

-and who have proved it by their lives.

Denis Shaw.

## ACKNOWLEDGEMENTS

I am indebted to many people and organisations for information, photographs, personal memories and other assistance. My first thanks must be to my husband, the Revd. Frederick Bonham, not only for checking each successive chapter, but also, during the past six years, for living with St. Agnes' of the past as well as the present. The Revd Dennis Shaw, Rector of Clewer, has provided much of the source material and a good deal of the inspiration for this book.

From the very start Mr Maurice Bond has given me much encouragement and without his valued assistance, I would have been denied access to much important source material.

The following have helped me in many and varied ways:

Mr & Mrs R. P. Garner; the late Miss Daisy Wilkins; Mrs A. Chandler; the late Mr Charles Wilkins; Mrs J. Paternoster; the Revd. Mother Superior C. S. J. B.; The United Society for the Propagation of the Gospel, for allowing me to reproduce the photograph of the Revd G. H. Swinny; Mrs E. Clarke; the late Mr E. Howells; the late Mr G. G. Simpson; Mrs J. Kidby; Miss B. Fowler; the Revd P. R. L. Morgan, Headmaster of Haileybury Junior School; the late Mr J. Uglow and Mrs Uglow; Mr and Mrs A. Bridges; the late Mrs L. V. Bridges; Mr and Mrs Digby; Mrs E. Drury; Mr and Mrs G. Tyrell; Mr Reader; the late Mrs M. Pert; Mrs E. Jefferies; Mr A. W. Green; the Revd D. N. Griffiths, Rector of Windsor; Mr Gordon Cullingham and fellow members of the Windsor Local History Publications Group; Mr and Mrs K. Harland; Mrs H. MacTiffen and staff, Windsor Public Library; the Chapter Librarian, Windsor Castle; the Revd C. Dymoke-Marr; the Revd A. C. M. Howard; the Revd E. A. Dixon; the Revd A. E. Wood; the Revd and Mrs F. J. Prebble; the Revd and Mrs R. G. Hayne; Mr D. Armstrong of the Church Commissioners; Mrs J. Fletcher; Mr R. Fletcher; Mrs Rosemary Young; Mrs M. M. Cramer; The Editor of the Windsor & Eton Express for allowing me to quote from the files; Mrs King; Mrs R. Gray; Miss E. Cuthbert; Dr Molly Barratt of the Department of Western MSS, Bodleian Library; the Right Revd Dom Wilfred Weston, O. S. B., Abbot of Nashdom; Mr and Mrs Keeler; Mrs J. Eagle; Mr Angus MacNaghten; the Berkshire Record Office; Mrs J. Hunter; Mr Leslie Barker; Mr J. Roderick; Mrs Valerie Eliot/Faber & Faber for permission to quote from the 'Four Quartets' by the late T. S. Eliot; Mr John Saunders; Miss D. Hornagold; Miss I. Bayley; Kingsley Jones Studios.

Regarding the production of the book, I must thank my father, Mr Horace Dean for the line drawing of the interior of St. Agnes' taken from Mr Tyrell's wartime photograph. Without the patience and hard work of Miss Dulcie Green my manuscript would never have been typed. Mr Roger Cullingham has steered me through the minefield of printing processes and it is thanks to his expertise that the book has finally been produced. Lastly I would like to thank all those who have made loans or given grants and donations, without which financial help the book could not have been produced; the St. Andrew's Clewer District Church Council; the St. Agnes' Spital District Church Council; the Trustees of the Royal Albert Institute; and a number of individuals who wish to remain anonymous.

# ILLUSTRATIONS


Frontispiece. The Revd Canon T. T. Carter.

| | | |
|---|---|---|
| Plate 1. | The Revd G. H. Swinny, the first priest of St. Agnes' | Page 197 |
| Plate 2. | St. Agnes' Spital in 1907 before the extension was added. | Page 198 |
| Plate 3. | Mothers' outing at Boulter's Lock, June 1909. | Page 198 |
| Plate 4. | Choir and Servers in 1911. | Page 199 |
| Plate 5. | Memorial Card from the Mission of December 1912. | Page 200 |
| Plate 6. | Choir and Servers c.1914. | Page 201 |
| Plate 7. | 5th Windsor (Clewer St. Andrews) Scouts in the early 1920s | Page 202 |
| Plate 8. | Scouts outing, early 1920s. | Page 203 |
| Plate 9. | Mothers' outing, early 1920s. | Page 203 |
| Plate 10. | St. Agnes' interior before 1937 restoration | Page 204 |
| Plate 11. | St Agnes' as it was from 1937 until 1973. (Drawing by H.Dean from photograph taken by Mr G. Tyrell) | Page 205 |
| Plate 12. | Pert's Bakery, Spital, c.1905. | Page 206 |
| Plate 13. | The 'Stag and Hounds', Spital, 1918 or just after. | Page 206 |
| Plate 14. | The 'Royal Standard', Spital, V. E. Day, 1945. | Page 207 |
| Plate 15. | Clewer Lodge, Spital, when it was the Headmaster's House, Imperial Service College. | Page 207 |

## FOREWORD

"Remember the days of old, consider the years that are past; ask your father and he will show you, ask your elders and they will tell you." Deuteronomy Ch. 32. V.7

I first 'discovered' St Agnes' Spital on Low Sunday, 1970. At the time, I had just left college and had come to live in Windsor. A friend, who lived in London and had known St. Agnes' many years previously, paid me a visit and took me 'out to Spital'. Upon my first glimpse inside I was entranced ...... Time passed ..... I married and left Windsor, but in September 1975 my husband was appointed Curate of Clewer, in charge of St. Agnes'.

There had been an interregnum lasting a year which unfortunately coincided with the Centenary of the Church's dedication. I decided it would be a good idea to write a history of St. Agnes', and set about searching the Service Registers and Parish Magazines. However, I soon found that this small, rather undistinguished-looking Church had a great past, and that some of the leading figures in the Anglo-Catholic revival had been here to preach, or had shown a benevolent interest in the Church. Furthermore the clergy and people began to 'emerge' from the magazines as more than just 'names'; and as I began listening to the reminiscences of local people it became apparent that many still love and respect their memory. Finally, no church can be separated from its parish, and my curiosity was ever more aroused by the question of what Spital village was like in those far off days a century ago.

Therefore, a certain amount of local history has been included but this is by no means exhaustive and there is ample scope for further research. I hope this will make some contribution to local studies; there is a great wealth of material available on Windsor, but very little research has been done on Clewer. Whilst the emphasis here is on Spital, it must be remembered that most of the village is part of the larger Parish of Clewer which until 1982 also included Dedworth. Thus some of the events which are herein recalled are of importance to the Parish as a whole, and likewise so are many of the people.

We live in an age where it is fashionable to look back to a halcyon period before 1914 when life was simpler, the pace was slower, and people had a different sense of values from our modern, noisy way of life. It is very easy to over emphasise this side of the picture at the expense of the hardship and poverty, and thus to over-sentimentalise. I hope I have escaped this trap - the Parish Magazines are in themselves a commentary on life before the emergence of the Welfare State. However, the past is too easily brushed to one side and forgotten in the hubbub of modern life, and whilst we at St. Agnes' must not rest on our laurels but go forward in the service of God and His Church, I feel that we need and indeed ought to remember the years that are past, and the people who lived, worked and worshipped in Spital.

Valerie Bonham

January 1983.

# INTRODUCTION

## I. Carter of Clewer.

Thomas Thellusson Carter, the son of the Revd Thomas Carter, for many years Vice-Provost of Eton, and his wife, Mary, daughter of Henry Proctor, was born at Eton on March 19th, 1808. After an Eton education he went to Christ Church, Oxford in 1826. There he was surrounded by men who were to be famous in their time -in 1820 Dr Pusey was Hebrew Professor and living in Tom Quad; W. E. Gladstone was in the year behind Carter; Newman was at Oriel, and later Vicar of St Mary's, the University Church. Later Carter wrote, "We were at the time of leaving Oxford, on the very verge of the Tractarian Movement, but as yet there was .....no sign of its approach". He passed his exams in 1831, six months later than was intended due to an attack of jaundice. After this he stood for a fellowship at Oriel - and failed. (For an explanation of the Tractarian Movement, see Appendix I: Torpor and Torrent.)

Thomas Carter had always intended his son for Holy Orders,and indeed Thomas Thellusson Carter himself "never had any other thought." Therefore he was ordained Deacon on Sunday, October 21st, 1832, by Bishop Burgess in Salisbury Cathedral and went to serve as curate at St. Mary's, Reading, which was at the time in the Salisbury Diocese. As in many other Parishes, spiritual life was at a low ebb and upon Carter's arrival, the Rector went away for a six week holiday leaving the parish in the hands of the young deacon. In 1833, Carter's father became Vicar of Burnham and Thomas, who was unhappy at Reading, for there was little spiritual life and much socialising, became his father's curate. Sunday, December 22nd, 1833, saw his ordination to the Priesthood at Buckden by Dr Kaye, Bishop of Lincoln, in which diocese Buckinghamshire was at the time. The Burnham curacy was a very happy time and it was here that Thomas Thellusson Carter evolved his habit of parish visiting. He later described the impact made by the Oxford Tracts, "At that time we were at a great loss as to parish work, without training and without guidance .... There was an equally entire want of guidance as to what books or what lines of theolgy one should adopt. This want of guidance ran throughout. It was while we were thus floating without authority to guide us, that the Oxford Tracts appeared. It is impossible to exaggerate the immediate effect. In reading them as they came out, one felt a sense of interest and earnestness in religious doctrines one had not known before .... The Church, its Priesthood, and Sacraments acquired a reality unfelt before ....."

In 1838 T. T. Carter was presented by his father to the living of Piddlehinton in Dorset, in the gift of Eton College. The clergy around were largely unaffected by the Oxford Tracts and many were parsons of the hunting and shooting type. Upon hearing that the new Rector neither shot nor fished one of them is reported to have said, "What will he find to do?"

The Parish had been neglected and the most earnest people were Wesleyans. Carter raised money for the restoration of the Church and the work was duly accomplished. The Dorset climate was a great trial to Carter's health and he spent two Winters at Weymouth for that reason. In 1842, after living at Piddlehinton for four years, he obtained leave of absence and returned to Burnham as his father's curate where he remained for two years.

In the Spring of 1844 Thomas Thellusson Carter resigned Piddlehinton for the living of Clewer in the gift of Eton College. His predecessor, William Henry Roberts (Rector from 1827-1844), was the first Rector appointed by Eton College who was not also a

Fellow. He was also the first Rector for many years to reside in the parish, (possibly, because he was not a Fellow of Eton), and indeed he took most of the services himself instead of delegating to a curate. Roberts ceased ministering in the Parish in 1840 and the living was put under sequestration. Thomas Thellusson Carter's biographer, W. H. Hutchings, states that the sequestration was due to Roberts' "intemperate habits". For the last two years of Robert's incumbency there was a "locum tenens", the Revd. Robert Gould, Carter's brother-in-law. Hutchings' statement, whilst no doubt true, was also rather unsympathetic to a Priest who was at least living and ministering in his parish for most of the time of his incumbency, at a time when non-residence was the generally accepted standard. He was pre-Tractarian in outlook, unlike Carter, who was influenced by the new Movement from the beginning; and although, as we shall see, Carter found the church in a disgraceful state and the people with barren spiritual lives, it was all part of the disease of the time - the last vestiges of the ailing Eighteenth Century Church which the Oxford Movement succeeded to a large degree in healing.

Meanwhile, other changes were taking place in the Parish at about this time. The Parish of Clewer was large and diverse including as it did a considerable part of the town of Windsor and also rural hamlets. Two curates of Windsor Parish, the Revd. Stephen Hawtrey and the Revd. George Selwyn (who was also at Eton tutor and was later to become Bishop of New Zealand, and later of Lichfield) had been doing pastoral work among the town population of Clewer Parish. A well-known local builder, Mr. Bedborough, gave some land for a new church, the foundation stone of which was laid in April 1842. The church was consecrated in July 1844 and was dedicated to the Holy Trinity. A new parish was formed from the town part of Clewer Parish and the Revd. Stephen Hawtrey became the first incumbent.

At this time the outlying hamlet of Dedworth belonged to Windsor Parish, even though it was separated from it by Clewer. Mr. Selwyn and Mr. Hawtrey had succedded in building a school-chapel at Dedworth, and Hawtrey would take a choir on Sundays and pass the whole day there, resting between services in a cottage, or in the fields. When Clewer lost some it its territory to form Holy Trinity Parish, Dedworth was 'transferred' to Clewer Parish. All Saints' Church, Dedworth was built by the Revd. Henry Tudor, curate of Clewer, in 1863.

In 1844 the fabric of Clewer Church was in an appalling condition - some of the pillars had been cut away and the walls were held up with iron clamps. In the middle of the church was a stove around which people gathered before the start of the service and made noisy conversation. The font was filled with hats. Seating consisted of tall box pews for which the wealthy paid a fee. Music was provided by a barrel-organ. T. T. Carter would often sit in his stall in his surplice before the service began in an attempt to quell the chatter. One of the worst practices which had arisen was that of the Churchwardens having half the alms and giving them to those who came regularly to Holy Communion. This had the effect of repelling people from the Sacrament, and those who came were looked upon with contempt as beggars by those who stayed away. Later Carter wrote, "It took long to root out this most unhappy state of feeling, though the Churchwardens kindly gave up to me their share of the alms."

T. T. Carter set about restoring order and decency into worship - the Eucharist was celebrated regularly; Mattins was said daily, often with an address; house to house visiting was begun; evening meetings were held in cottages. A benefit society was established; part of the glebe was given for allotments; and in an attempt to stem the drink problem which was rife, a Temperance Society was started. In order to raise money to repair the chancel Carter acted for two years as Organising Secretary for the Society for the Propagation of the Gospel.

In 1853 Carter's health broke down due to overwork and he was forced to recuperate at Folkestone. Upon his return he set about the restoration of the fabric of Clewer Church. A proposal was made to build a new church in a more central position and leave the old one for a Cemetery chapel - such was the state of the building. However, the decision was made against this and the chancel was restored first of all, followed by the nave. The barrel-organ had been disposed of, and the mixed choir (surpliced choirs in those days were hardly ever seen in village churches) was taken in hand by Mrs.

Carter. In 1859 a hymn-book was especially compiled for the use of Clewer parishioners (this was used until the publication of 'Hymns, Ancient and Modern'). By the 1860's a surpliced choir gradually supplanted the mixed choir. This was accompanied by a string orchestra - an organ was not introduced until much later.

Alongside the work of restoring the parish church and pastoral duties, Thomas Thellusson

Carter had been engaged in a great work for which he will ever be remembered -the foundation of the Community of St. John the Baptist.

For sometime there had been general concern in the Church about the increasing problem of prostitution. In a garrison town such as Windsor it was particularly acute. In 1849 the Revd. C. Wellington Johnson, tutor at Eton, had been doing part-time pastoral work in the area called Clewer Fields, and he managed to "rescue" some of these fallen women. Mrs. Mariquita Tennant, a lady of Spanish origin, who was the widow of an English clergyman, agreed to take them into her home, 'The Limes' near Clewer Church. Within three months she had eighteen girls living there and, having later moved to Clewer Hill, she decided that she must found a permanent House of Mercy. For health reasons she gave the work up to other voluntary helpers in 1851.

One of the direct results of the Oxford Movement was the revival of the Religious Life in the English Church - communities of women (later of men) living together under vows, dedicated to God, living lives of prayer and meditation, often with some "active" work at the same time. Upon Mrs. Tennent's withdrawal from the penitentiary work, the Rector decided to form a Sisterhood with this as the main external activity. It was about this time that the recently widowed Harriet Monsell came to Clewer to stay with her brother-in-law, the Revd. the Hon. C. A. Harris, curate of Clewer, who was involved in the penitentiary work. So it was that Harriet Monsell offered herself for the work of the House of Mercy with a view to forming a Sisterhood. On Ascension Day 1851, Mrs. Monsell was clothed as a Sister, and on St. Andrew's Day 1851, she made her profession in the presence of Samuel Wilberforce, Bishop of Oxford, who installed her as first Superior of the new Community.

In this way began a Religious community which by the early years of the present century had over forty branch houses in Great Britain and India. Later the work was extended to include care of orphans, the elderly, convalescent patients and educational work. The original House of Mercy building was demolished in 1855, and in its place arose a vast range of red brick buildings designed by Henry Woodyer. Some of these are still in use such as the main Conventual buildings, but others, such as St. John's Home which later became St. Anne's House now stand empty and forlorn , and still others such as St. Andrew's Hospital have been demolished. With the emergence of the Welfare State much of the welfare work of the Community has been taken over and the Sisters nowadays are chiefly engaged in Retreat work, parish work, the care of the elderly, and the making of vestments and altar breads. The life of prayer and dedication to God is, needless to say, unchanged and goes on unceasingly.

(St. Anne's House has recently been sold, and has subsequently been restored and converted into office accommodation)

In Lent 1868 services were begun in a cottage in Clewer Fields and the Clewer Sisters began working in the district. In July 1868 the foundation stone of St. Stephen's Mission was laid and a mission house and school were built. On October 28th 1868, St. Stephen's Mission and temporary chapel was solemnly blessed by the Rector who was assisted by the Revd. G. D. Nicholas and the Revd. R. J. Ives, curates, and a choir consisting of boys from "Bell Farm", a prep. school in the parish. There were forty Communicants.

In 1871 the Rector was taken seriously ill partly through overwork and partly as the result of grief following the death of his wife a year previously. Following his recovery he convalesced for almost two years, mostly in Italy, before he was strong enough to resume active parish work. During his absence the Revd. George Davenport Nicholas, senior curate, was left in charge of the Parish. On July 15th 1871 the new church of St.

Stephen was opened for worship with the dedication of the chancel, although it was not until 1874 that the church was completed. Thomas Thellusson Carter had by then returned to Clewer and on December 22nd 1874 Bishop Mackarness of Oxford consecrated the new church. St. Stephen's became a separate parish with the Revd. G. D. Nicholas as the first Vicar. From the very start the services at St. Stephen's were conducted with far more ceremonial than at St. Andrew's where even as late as 1865 Carter still wore the black preaching gown in the pulpit rather than a surplice, and whilst he would wear a white stole, he had not 'advanced' to the use of coloured ones.

During the next few years Carter began to introduce more 'advanced' ceremonial into Eucharistic worship which can be generally summed up as the "Six Points" and which are all practices to be found widely in the Church of England today. (See Appendix 1: Torpor and Torrent).

In 1877 some parishioners initiated a campaign against Carter's 'ritualistic' practices and the caption "Look out for High Mass at Clewer Church" was daubed on the walls of the Tithe Barn in Parsonage Lane. In July 1878 Dr. Frederick Guilder Julius, who was technically a parishioner but did not attend Clewer Church, and indeed resided abroad for most of the year, was persuaded by the Church Association to complain to the Bishop about these practices. The Bishop refused to take any legal action pointing out that the majority of parishioners agreed with their Rector, and also that he was an aging priest who was loved and respected by many people. In February 1879 Dr. Julius took proceedings in the Queen's Bench Division and invoked the Church Discipline Act of 1840 in order to force the Bishop to bring a prosecution. Julius contended that the wording of the Act placed the Bishop under duty to prosecute, but the Bishop contended that he had a discretion as to whether he should take action or not. Julius won his case but the Bishop appealed to the Court of Appeal which reversed the Queen's Bench decision by finding in the Bishop's favour. In March 1880 Dr. Julius appealed to the House of Lords who upheld the Court of Appeal's decision.

The Bishop had finally won his case and the Lords' decision meant that the Episcopal right of veto would not be questioned again. However, John Fielder Mackarness, Bishop of Oxford, was no ritualist, and Carter knew full well that although the Bishop had given him his protection it was from a purely pastoral motive and was not a sign of Episcopal approval of ritualism. At the same time Carter was faced with a dilemma, for he had strict views on submission to the Episcopal authority but could not abandon these same practices of which the Bishop so strongly disapproved. Therefore, in 1880 he resigned the living of Clewer and retired to be resident Warden of the Community which he had founded. He was succeeded as Rector of Clewer by the Revd. Roland Errington.

St. John's Lodge, Hatch Lane, was built for Carter and succeeding Wardens of the Community of St. John the Baptist. Carter, who had been made a Canon in 1880, resided there for the remaining twenty years of his life. During this time he led a full and active life and did much visiting of the scattered branch houses of the Community. To the end of his days he maintained an interest in Clewer Parish, but only once was persuaded to take the pulpit at the Parish Church, although he sometimes did so at the daughter Churches.

Thomas Thellusson Carter died on 28th October 1901; he had been ailing for some time but had still managed a fair amount of work. His body was laid at St. John's Lodge for two days and many people came to pay their last respects to a great man and a beloved Pastor. His body was clad in full vestments, with chalice and paten in his hands. Among those who filed past were boys from St. Augustine's Home, and one of them, now an elderly gentleman, still vividly remembers this solemn occasion. (He has died since this was written.)

At 8.00 p.m. on the eve of the funeral the body was brought into the Chapel of the House of Mercy and a vigil was kept all night by relays of Sisters. The funeral took place next day, the Eve of All Saints. There was a Solemn Requiem at the House of Mercy, the celebrant being Dr. William Carter, Bishop of Zululand, Canon Carter's nephew. This was followed by a quarter of a mile-long procession to St. Andrew's

Church. The Revd. Roland Errington, read the opening sentences of the Burial Service, The Lesson was read by the Revd. G. D. Nicholas, and the Committal by the Venerable Archdeacon W. H. Hutchings, former Sub-Warden and later Canon Carter's biographer. The final blessing at the graveside was given by the Bishop of Oxford. Also present were the Bishop of Reading, and the Deans of Lichfield, Windsor and Chichester. It was estimated that there were one hundred clergy and one hundred and fifty Sisters present. The pall-bearers were Fr. R. M. Benson of the Society of St. John the Evangelist (the Cowley Fathers); the Revd. R. J. Suckling, Vicar of St. Alban's, Holborn; Viscount Halifax; and Colonel The Honourable Hay-Drummond.

Thus was laid to rest one of the most distinguished Priests of the nineteenth century. Thomas Thellusson Carter was a link betwen the old order and the new. He was ordained in the year before the start of Tractarianism, a movement which he embraced wholeheartedly; he had been present at the beginnings, at the first stirrings of the new awakening; he stood firm with Keble and Pusey in the dark days of the 1840's and fifties when all seemed to be deserting the cause and everything seemed lost; he mingled with the younger more 'extreme' men, indeed was himself persecuted as a 'ritualist', and yet throughout was loyal to the Church of his Baptism and to the authority of his Bishop -he resigned his living rather than compromise his principles or disobey his Bishop. He was both intensely spiritual and yet eminently practical; it was for such as he to show the way to an often bewildered Church at a time when it was shaking off the torpor of the preceding century and awakening to its true heritage and tradition.

## II. Clewer Close-up

"I never think of Spital as a village", someone said to me quite recently, and indeed a stranger would be hard pressed to see any village characteristics nowadays. Yet it was a village until not so long ago - the late 1940's and early 1950's, when post-war building took over and Spital became absorbed into the suburbs of Windsor. Therefore, it may be well to take an imaginery walk around Spital, and indeed Clewer Parish generally, to see what it was like in the 1870's when St. Agnes' was built. (The name 'Spital' is thought to be derived from the Medieval leper Hospital of St. Peter which stood in the vicinity of the present day King Edward VII Hospital - well away from the main settlement of New Windsor. This is fully dealt with in 'The Changing Face of Windsor - The Beginnings', by Judith Hunter and published by Windsor Local History Publications Group.)

An early map of the district, (dated 1812 but taken from a survey of the Vansittart estate of 1711) shows the village green extending from the Stag and Hounds right along Clewer Hill Road to the present Kenton's Lane. Parts of this long narrow green were still in existence in the 1870's, especially along Clewer Hill Road. The settlement of Clewer Green was quite separate from Spital in medieval times, but by the mid-Nineteenth Centry the division was by no means so clear-cut, although the two names are retained on maps of the period.

All the eastern part of Spital roughly up to the Stag and Hounds was, and still is, in Windsor parish, not Clewer. The whole of the parish of Clewer was outside the Municipal Borough until 1920, but that part of Spital belonging to Windsor parish was within it. Clewer village and Clewer New Town were within the Parliamentary Borough, as was the part of Spital on the Cemetery side of Spital Road from The Hermitage to the Windsor parish boundary.

The main road through Spital, now called St. Leonard's Road, was then called Spital Road all the way into Windsor. Most of the houses along Spital Road, between Bourne or Bone Lane, now called Bolton Road, and the Cemetery gates were not built until the 1890's, and there were very few houses on the Park side of the road.

The village 'Smithy' was roughly where the turning down to the modern Gardeners' Hall is now situated. Here also was a lane lined with trees with a row of cottages alongside, at right angles to Spital Road. Continuing along Spital Road up the hill, there was a terrace of houses on the Park side which must have been demolished to make way for the 'new' houses in the early 1890's. There were a few houses on the opposite side, most of which have been replaced. Most of the dwellings in Spital were at the top of the hill between the Stag and Hounds and Clewer Green, although only a few of the older houses remain today: the Sixteenth Century Stag and Hounds is the oldest; Eton Cottage was built in 1874; Myrtle Cottage; and Wellington Place, the second terrace before the present day traffic lights. A veritable conglomeration of cottages stood near where the Church now stands, most of which have been demolished: Park Place, of which four remain; Homelee Cottages and Knowles Cottages, the latter of which came to be known as St. Agnes' Cottages. The site occupied by the Church was a vacant plot.

A small white cottage on the corner of the modern road called Peel Close is all that remains to tell the stranger of the existence of Clewer Lodge. The small cottage was the gate lodge to Clewer Lodge (also known as Clewer Villa), for many years the Country home of Captain Thomas Bulkeley, Director of the Great Western Railway 1850-1855 and from 1857 until his death in 1882. He was one of the original promotors of the Great Western Hotel at Paddington and was a great friend of Sir Daniel Gooch. The house was situated at the end of a long tree-lined drive roughly where the cul-de-sac end of Upcroft is now. Parts of the house dated back to the Fifteenth Century and it was reputed to have been the Dower House to the original Clewer Manor.

The grounds of Clewer Lodge were separated from those of Clewer Manor by a twisting tree-lined lane known as Lovers Walk, the line of which is now roughly followed by the busy Imperial Road. At this time the Manor of Clewer was in the hands of the Fosters, but it was much older, having been mentioned in Domesday. In 1713, Lord Lansdowne sold the Manor to Colonel Arthur Vansittart of Shottesbrook, and the family held it until 1812. In that year, Richard Foster rented the Manor from Vansittart as a copyholder, and in 1842 his son Edmund, became Lord of the Manor. It was he who built the present house which is now Haileybury Junior School. In 1882 he was succeeded by his son, Edmund Benson Foster, who is still remembered as 'Squire' Foster.

Continuing along Spital Road, we come to Clewer Green. A room in a large house called The Hermitage had, since 1810, provided the local Roman Catholics with a chapel, until in 1868 St. Edward's Church was built in Alma Road. St. John's Chapel, as it was called, was then secularised and became the chief drawing room of the house. The Hermitage later became the residence of Dr. F. G. Julius, who as we have seen was the principal agitator in the ritualism campaign against T. T. Carter. The Hermitage has now been divided into three separate residences, but for many years was known as 'Chapel House'.

Further along the main road in the direction of Winkfield were the Country seats of the local landed gentry. St. Leonard's Hill was formerly called Gloucester Lodge and was the residence of the Harcourt family until it was bought in 1872 by Mr. (later Sir) Francis Tress Barry who became M. P. for the Borough, and was a benefactor of St. Andrew's Clewer. Barry virtually rebuilt the house in 1876, the new mansion by C. H. Howell being based on a French chateau. This in turn was partly demolished following the dispersal of the estate upon Lady Barry's death in the 1920's. The house is now a sad ruin, but the Dower House known as St. Leonard's Dale is still there. Nearby was St. Leonard's, the seat of Sir Theodore Brinckman. It was acquired in 1932 by Mr. Horace Dodge the American motor magnate who almost completely rebuilt it, and it is now the Headquarters of the Windsor Safari Park. Other mansions in the area included St. Leonard's Lodge, (only the gate lodge remains on Winkfield Road and this is crowded in by new houses) and Forest Hill Park. (For details of the Hermit of St. Leonard's see Judith Hunter's book 'The Changing Face of Windsor'.)

We now turn back towards Clewer Green, the rural character of which is now completely lost due to heavy traffic, road junctions, traffic lights and a mini roundabout. Clewer Hill Road had very few houses and was the main link between the hamlets of Spital and Dedworth. Most of the houses were at the Clewer Green end, but generally it was a rural lane bounded by the estates of the St. Leonard's Hill area on the one side and Clewer Manor on the other. The neighbouring fields provided grazing for the horses belonging to Clewer Manor - these fields may have been the last remnants of the village green. Further up Clewer Hill there was farmland, (St.Leonard's Farm, later called Manor Farm which belonged to the Foster's); and another large Country house known as Clewer Hill House.

Dedworth was a small hamlet connected to Windsor by means of New Road opened in 1833, (now Dedworth Road and part of Clarence Road). All Saints' Church was in roughly the same position as the present new building. Again there was a great deal of farmland, and Dedworth Manor and its estate occupied a large area bounded by Surly Hall Road (now Maidenhead Road) and Smith's Lane.

Hatch Lane was a winding country lane connecting Clewer Hill Road with New Road. Still standing in Hatch Lane is the lodge to Clewer Manor which bears the date 1851. Just opposite was the Harcourt Charity School now known as Clewer Green School. This was started in the early 1800's under the auspices of the Revd.Charles Jervis, Curate of Clewer. It was formally endowed in 1815 by Colonel and Lady Harcourt.

Further on and bordering the grounds of Clewer Manor were the grounds of the House of Mercy and St.John's Home for Girls. Roughly opposite St.John's Home on the other side of the road was St.Andrew's Convalescent Hospital.

There was little housing development along New Road, but going towards Windsor, there was a large house called The Lawns, now a Nursery School, and next to it St.Katherine's Infant School, which has since been demolished. Between The Lawns and the House of Mercy was Clewer New Town which was connected to Windsor by Green Lane.

The continuation of Hatch Lane was Parsonage Lane and this led past the Tithe Barn, now demolished, and Clewer Rectory which was demolished in 1963, and over the junction with Surly Hall Road to Clewer Village. Here were a number of 'desirable residences' but principally Clewer Park, the Country seat of Sir Daniel Gooch. Gooch had trained as an engineer under George Stephenson's son Robert. He later became Chairman of the Great Western Railway Board, and an M. P. for twenty years. The mansion was demolished shortly after World War 11 and modern houses now occupy the site.

Next to St.Andrew's Church was The Limes where Mrs.Tennant began her rescue work among young women in moral danger, and this house still survives. This timber-framed building was the medieval Rectory.

The vast area between New Road and Spital Road which is now completely built up was agricultural land in the 1870's. At the turn of the century there was still practically nothing in the way of buildings between Spital Road at the Stag and Hounds and the River Thames at Clewer.

## Chapter I

### In our end is our beginning

St. Agnes' Spital opened in 1874, but in order to trace the sequence of events which led to its opening, it is necessary to go back to the 1850's.

One of the great social problems affecting both the parishes of Clewer and Windsor was that of poverty. In his answers to the Bishop of Oxford's 1854 Visitation questionnaire, T. T. Carter stated that, "There is a long disuse of Church-going and great poverty so that a very large number have no good clothes. . . . . The Parish is the scattered outskirt of a town which in its lower part is greatly demoralised and there is no aid or practical influence from the higher classes. . . ."

The Vicar of Windsor, the Revd. Henry J. Ellison, was also deeply concerned about the poor, and in particular the fact that pew rents at the parish Church prevented many from attending because they could not afford a seat. Of the 1,700 seatings less than 200 were free and unappropriated. He therefore decided to overcome the problem by building a new Church which eventually led to the opening of All Saint's Frances Road.

A further problem, and one which affected Spital in particular, was 'diversity'. Both parishes were large and the Spital residents were a long way from either parish Church.

As a temporary solution to the problem of Church accommodation for his poor parishioners, Mr. Ellison obtained permission to use the Cemetery Chapel for Sunday worship. The Cemetery Acts of 1852 and 1853 had made it possible for Councils to create new public Cemeteries on the edges of towns. Accordingly, by an Order in Council of December 11th 1854, burials in the parish Churchyards of Old and New Windsor and the William Street Chapel were to be discontinued, and as from July 1st 1855, the burial grounds and Churchyards of the same, and on Bachelors Acre were to be closed. In fact the Town Council had so much difficulty choosing a site that the old burial grounds were not finally closed until early in 1858 when the new Cemetery was Consecrated. Five acres of ground at Spital were purchased from Mr. John Stroud of Clewer Green at £300 per acre. The Cemetery was enlarged in 1874. Windsor parish clergy acted as Chaplains but the Cemetery was actually in Clewer Parish.

It is uncertain exactly when Mr. Ellison applied to the Town Council for permission to use the Anglican Chapel in the Cemetery - there is no record in any of the Hall Books or in the Minute Books of the Burial Board Committee. The Chapel was in regular use by April 1860, for at that time, Mr. Ellison stated in the Bishop's Visitation questionnaire that there was "1 full service each week in the Cemetery Chapel at 3." That it was only a temporary measure is borne out by his answer to the question, "Does the congregation at the parish Church bear a fair proportion to the population of the parish?". Answer: "Yes, but many are prevented attending by the existing pew system. Another Church where the sittings were unappropriated would soon be filled. This I hope may be built as soon as our new Schools are completed."

In 1862, the Revd. Samuel John Stone was appointed curate of Windsor parish, and sometime afterwards was given charge of the services at the Cemetery Chapel. It was during his Windsor curacy that Stone wrote the series of hymns which includes 'The Church's One Foundation'. There is an oral tradition that he composed the hymns to illustrate a series of sermons which he preached in the Cemetery Chapel. There is no firm evidence to support the story except for Stone's own words in the preface to the first edition of the hymns which were published in 1866 under the title 'Lyra Fidelium'; "Most clergymen are aware how many of their parishioners among the poor especially, say the Creed in their private prayers. And they cannot but feel how this excellent use,. . . . is too often accompanied by a very meagre comprehension of the breadth and depth of meaning contained in each Article of the confession of Faith. Such a feeling first suggested to the Author the probable usefulness of a simple and attractive explanation of the Creed in the popular form of a series of Hymns, such as might be sung or said in private devotion, at family prayer, or in public worship. . . . .There can be little doubt but that the poetical form is more likely to be effectual in securing an abiding place in the general mind. . . To this end, the Author set about the composition of the following hymns. . . ." So it would seem that even if Stone did not preach a series of sermons on the Creed, the needs of the poor were uppermost in his mind when deciding to write the hymns, and as he had charge of the Cemetery Chapel at about this time it may well be that Spital has the strongest claim!

There are other theories concerning 'The Church's One Foundation.' Julian's Dictionary of Hymnology' states that the chief impetus for writing the collection of hymns was the impression made upon Stone by Bishop Gray of Capetown's defence of the Faith against Bishop Colenso of Natal. (Between 1861 and 1863, Colenso had written various Biblical works which were held to be heretical. As a result of the controversy which shook the Anglican Church to its very roots, Colenso was deposed and excommunicated by the South African Bishops). This may well be so as many clergy were moved to expound the Faith anew in the light of this scandal and it is easy to imagine Stone making his stand in this way. It does not contradict Stone's motives as explained by him in the preface to 'Lyra Fidelium', although it is somewhat unusual that he makes no reference to the controversy if we are to believe that it played a major part in his decision to write the hymns.

There is also a local legend that 'The Church's One Foundation' was written for the Consecration of All Saints' Frances Road on November 21st 1864. There is no evidence to support this, indeed the lengthy account in the Windsor and Eton Express (Nov.26), gives full details of all the hymns and psalms, but there is no mention of this hymn. Neither was it sung a year previously, when the Foundation Stone was laid on November 21st 1863. (Unfortunately, the compilers of the Order of Service for the laying of the Foundation Stone of Christchurch United Reformed Church have repeated the story without checking its authenticity).

The exact date of the writing of the hymns is uncertain, though a reasonable guess would be sometime between 1863 and 1865, and they were published in 1866. The other hymns in the collection have been largely forgotten except perhaps 'Weary of Earth and Laden with my Sin'. Nowadays it is customary to associate 'The Church's One Foundation' with S. S. Wesley's well known tune 'Aurelia', but in fact, this tune was not used for the hymn until 1872 when it was specially chosen for the thanksgiving service in St. Paul's Cathedral to mark the Prince of Wales' recovery from serious illness. Prior to this date, 'Aurelia' had always been used with the Hymn 'Jerusalem the Golden'. The tune which was originally recommended for use with 'The Church's One Foundation' was number 142 in the first edition of 'Hymns Ancient and Modern'. Hymn number 142 was in three parts, and it is an odd coincidence that today part of it is used with 'Jerusalem the Golden'.

Stone took a deep interest in the spiritual welfare of the Spital people, and was anxious to make the Cemetery Chapel as accommodating and conducive to worship as a regular church would be. He therefore, wrote to the Mayor of Windsor late in 1864 with a list of requirements and suggested additions to the Chapel. This was discussed at a meeting of the Burial Board Committee on January 3rd 1865 and was as follows:-

1. A stove and chimney;
2. Harmonium;
3. Matting for the cold tiled floor;
4. Kneeling hassocks for ditto;
5. Additional seats with backs, part of the seats being new plain forms;
6. Some lighting apparatus;
7. Coals and wood and a place for them;
8. The stoppage of draught from the ill-fitting windows;
9. A small fund from which a weekly gratuity may be given to those who have the care, cleaning and arrangement of the Church;
10. Some ornamentation of the bare, cold wall;
11. Kneeling cushion for the altar rail.

The outcome was that the Burial Board Committee recommended to the Council that items 1 and 8 be carried out at the expense of the Board, and that the rest should be carried out by Mr. Stone at his own expense, subject to the approval of the Council. The Committee also moved that the Council should be recommended not to assist in the ornamentation of the walls. These recommendations by the Burial Board Committee were subsequently adopted by the Town Council.

Despite the opening of All Saints' Church, the Vicar of Windsor seemed to be in no hurry to relinquish the Cemetery Chapel. It was retained by Windsor parish until 1866 when it seems that the Rector of Clewer expressed the desire to use it himself.

At the quarterly meeting of the Town Council on April 5th 1866, the following letter, from the Vicar of Windsor, was read:-

"My dear Sir, dated 5th April 1866

It may be within your knowledge that the Rector of Clewer has recently urged the increasing spiritual necessities of that part of his Parish immediately adjacent to the Cemetery, as a reason for wishing to be allowed the use of the Chapel for Sunday Services.

His wish has been accompanied by an intimation from the Bishop to myself that the law would not permit him to continue his license to me to officiate there, if the consent of the Rector of the Parish in which the Chapel happens to be situated were withdrawn.

This has led me to reconsider the circumstances under which I received permission from the Council to hold services there; and I am bound to say that since the completion of All Saints' Church, the necessity for such an adjunct to the parochial machinery of Windsor no longer exists.

I shall be glad, therefore, to transfer the services of my Curate to other and more needed work in the Parish, and to resign the charge of the Chapel in about six weeks from the present time.

In doing so, I must beg you to convey to the Town Council my own thanks personally, and I am sure I may add those of the Parishioners at large, for the great boon which the free use of the Chapel has conferred on the residents of Spital. The crowded state of the Services will best testify to the estimation in which they have been held; and which, so far as the Inhabitants of Windsor Parish are concerned, their attendance will, I trust be transferred to All Saints' Church. I should be sorry to think that the Inhabitants of Clewer should lose the privilege to which they have been so long accustomed.

I am, my dear Sir, very faithfully yours,

HENRY J. ELLISON."

It was moved that this letter be suitably acknowledged and that in future the Chapel be reserved for mortuary purposes only.

A few weeks later, on May 24th 1866, a special meeting of the Council was held to take into consideration the following letter from the Rector of Clewer:-

"Gentlemen, Clewer Rectory. May 3rd.

I have heard from Mr. Ellison that he has communicated to the Board his intention to relinquish the Services which have been held in the Cemetery Chapel, after Whit Sunday next.

These services have been most valuable to a considerable body of my parishioners who by distance are hindered from attending our own or either of the Windsor Churches. I have not infrequently expressed to Mr. Ellison and Mr. Stone my sincere thankfulness for the great benefits which my Parishioners have derived from these services, and I am glad of this opportunity of certifying to the Board the same feelings of gratitude for their kindess in allowing them to be held.

But my object in writing is to state to the Board how very serious the loss of these services will be, and one which will necessarily be all the more keenly felt, because of the blessings so long enjoyed. The loss will of course fall mainly on the poor and the aged. The greatest anxiety is now being felt among them, and those interested in their welfare, lest the congregation which has been gathered should be left destitute of any similar services for the future.

It is a case of very urgent need, which I feel sure the Board will kindly conceive, and which with their kind aid I should desire to meet to the best of my ability. I, therefore, respectfully request the Board to allow me the use of the Chapel to hold similar services to those which have been hithero held. I hope and trust the Board will kindly grant to me permission. Yet I would add that, in case of any objection arising to the permanent use of the Chapel for the purpose, I should esteem it a great favour and a valuable boon to my poor parishioners to allow me to continue those services for a limited period, till I am able to make some provision to supply the want which otherwise will be so extensively and so keenly felt.

I have the honour, Gentlemen, to be your faithful and obedient Servant,

T. T. CARTER."

At the same meeting a letter from the Revd. S. J. Stone was also read:-

"To the Burial Board, Windsor. Windsor. May 15th 1866.

My dear Sir,

As after next Sunday my duty as the Curate in charge of the Services of the Cemetery Chapel comes to a close, may I, as one not only greatly interested in whatever concerns that Church but as the originator of the attempt to make its interior more adapted for the services, be allowed to urge a reason for their continuance in case an application should be made from the Parish in which the Cemetery lies. The personal friends and others who so kindly contributed to those improvements of course did so under the belief that the result of their liberality would be permanently useful, and I therefore feel bound in their name to express the hope, which has been urgently expressed to me as well as earnestly entertained on my own part, that these services may be still carried on. I would also allude to the crowded Sunday congregations, the considerable attendance on Thursday evenings and at the celebrations of Holy Communion as furnishing an indication of the great loss which many of the Church people of that part of the two Parishes, more especially the old and infirm, will sustain if the doors of the little Church so much loved by them remain closed.

I am, my dear Sir, faithfully yours,
S. J. STONE "

No doubt Stone's letter assisted Mr. Carter's cause, for although Stone was only a curate he would not have acted without the knowledge and approval of his Vicar. Windsor Parish Church was a bastion of Civic respectability and the Town Council would have been loath to cross swords with the Vicar of Windsor. Clewer, on the other hand, whilst senior to Windsor in antiquity, had allied itself with the Tractarian cause. Carter's religion was "too High" to brook any favours with the Establishment. The resolution that in future the Cemetery Chapel should be reserved for mortuary purposes only was clearly an attempt by the Council to prevent the Clewer clergy from officiating there. No doubt Mr. Carter sensed the Council's hostility, hence his request for the use of the Chapel for "a limited period". It was therefore with a certain reluctance that the Council passed the following rather haughtily phrased resolution:- "This Council as the Burial Board for the Borough is desirous of doing all in its power to promote the Spiritual Welfare of the Inhabitants of Spital and therefore accedes to the request contained in the letter of the Revd. T. T. Carter, the Rector of Clewer and will permit him to use the Episcopal Mortuary Chapel for public worship upon the condition that the services are conducted as at the present time in accordance with the usual Simplicity of the Church of England." A further resolution was passed thanking Mr. Stone "for the manner in which he has conducted the Services at the Mortuary Chapel."

The Clewer parish clergy commenced duty at the Cemetery Chapel without an interregnum. T. T. Carter noted in the Bishop's Visitation questionnaire of August 1866 that the Services were: Evensong and Sermon every Sunday at 3 p.m; Holy Communion occasionally at 8.30 a.m.; and Evensong and Sermon on Thursdays at 7 p.m. A Service Register dating from Septuagesima Sunday 1867 is in existence, and it would seem that there were good numbers at Evensong but rarely more than 10 at Holy Communion. It sems that Carter did not put anyone in particular in charge of the Chapel but sent different curates at different times.

One or two signatures in the Register are illegible, but others in 1867 include, Francis Furze Vidal (Conduct of Eton 1867-81 and Curate of Clewer); William Lane Hardisty and Edward Daniel Stone (Assistant Masters at Eton); Robert James Ives (Curate of Clewer 1867-74; later to become famous at St. German's Roath, Cardiff); William Henry Hutchings (Sub-Warden, Clewer House of Mercy 1865-84 and later Archdeacon of Cleveland). At this time, Eton masters frequently served as curates of Clewer, and similarly the clergy attached to the House of Mercy also assisted in the Parish, thus accounting for what seems an endless number of curates. Carter's own signature is in the Register in the early days, although later he was abroad, convalescing from a serious illness.

By 1870, with the exception of W. H. Hutchings, there were different officiating clergy - John Wilson Pickance, George Whitlaw and Edward Dunkin Harrison (Curates of Clewer); and W. F. Rose (Curate of Holy Trinity, Windsor 1867-73 and Assistant Conduct of Eton 1873-74). In addition to Holy Communion and Evensong the Cemetery Chapel was also used for Holy Baptism, and there was still a font there in recent years, although it was, of course, no longer used. Amongst the Register entries for Baptisms are the following - John Frederic (baptised April 5th 1868), and Alfred William (baptised July 2nd 1871), sons of Joseph and Fanny Shipton of Clewer Green; Fanny Elsie (baptised December 7th 1873), son of William Richard and Ann Bampton. All these families were later faithful supporters of St. Agnes'. (The font is now in the Clewer Museum.)

A glance at the entries in the Register reveals that the chief occupations of the Spital men were bricklaying, plumbing, carpentry and gardening. There was also a coppersmith (Mr. Bampton). Other occupations listed included policeman, park keeper, soldier, brewer's drayman and horse-dealer.

T. T. Carter was well aware of the temporary nature of the use of the Cemetery Chapel. People had responded well to the provision of services and there was obviously a need for something more permanent. Also he had intimated his intention to the Town Council of providing a permanent place of worship. However, early in 1871 he was taken desperately ill and there were fears for his life. Following his recovery, Carter was forced to spend almost two years convalescing in Italy, and it was not until July 1873 that he was able to resume full-time work. During this time, as we have seen, the Revd. G. D. Nicholas, senior curate, was left in charge of the Parish, and he was in constant touch with the Rector on parochial matters. Uppermost in everyone's mind was the building of St. Stephen's Church, but T. T. Carter had not forgotten Spital even though it was impossible to do anything until his return. In a letter to G. D. Nicholas from the Hotel de Milan in Florence, dated November 13th 1871, Carter stated, "I am afraid nothing can be done more for Spital till a centre in the shape of a School-Chapel is got there. This I have long had in my mind, and trust to carry it out as soon as possible after my return." It will be remembered that a school-chapel had been the first stage in the provision of a Church at Dedworth, although this chapel was built before Dedworth was amalgamated into Clewer Parish.

There is no indication in the Register as to the amount of ceremonial used at the Cemetery Chapel although often in "missionary districts" a more 'advanced' ceremonial was used than at the Mother Church, as was the case with the new church of Clewer St. Stephen. All that we have to go by is a letter to the "Windsor and Eton Express" of February 1st 1873 from an irate parishioner complaining of "popery" in the Cemetery Chapel.

> "Extraordinary Conduct of one of the Curates of Clewer."
> To the Editor of the Windsor & Eton Express."
>
> Sir,
> I desire to publish by means of your valuable journal the following outrage against all decency and propriety lately committed by one of the curates of Clewer.
>
> A Sunday or two ago the rev. gentleman alluded to, appeared at the 8.o'clock morning service at the Cemetery Chapel, habited as a monk, and styling himself "Father Thomas." Now, Sir, I am not aware of the existence of any order of monks within the Established Church. If this is so, unless the rev. gentleman comes forward and explains his strange behaviour, we must conclude that he is a member of some order of monks in the Roman Catholic Church, and being a Romish priest, has been officiating in a Protestant Church.
>
> I feel, Sir, that this is too great a scandal to be allowed to pass by without notice. And, Sir, I trust Parliament will without delay adopt the only means of doing justice to the Protestant laity by disestablishing a Church, a large proportion of whose clergy have for a long time preached Romish doctrines, and now do not hesitate to outrage our Protestant feelings by officiating at our services in the dress of the Romish priesthood.
>
> I, Sir, feel for one that the Church of England has failed in the high mission entrusted to her. She takes our tithes and our church rates to support a Protestant Establishment, she gives us in return Romish doctrines and Romish ceremonies.
>
> Let us petition Parliament at once to free us from such an anomaly - a crying injustice to the laity, an eternal disgrace to the clergy.
>
> I remain, Sir, your obedient servant.
>
> A RATEPAYER OF CLEWER"

The irate parishioner was misinformed on one or two points. For some years there had been attempts to restore the Religious Life for men in the Church of England, chiefly by Fr. Ignatius of Llanthony. On a less flamboyant scale, and one which has endured where many other attempts failed, was the foundation of the Society of St. John the Evangelist (the "Cowley Fathers") in 1865. One of the founder members was a former curate of Clewer, Simeon Wilberforce O'Neill. From its very beginning the S.S.J.E. met with the approval of Bishop Samuel Wilberforce of Oxford, and his successor, Bishop Mackarness, became the first Episcopal visitor. T. T. Carter had a great interest in the S.S.J.E. and exercised some influence in its earliest days.

Secondly, it is out of the question to imagine that 'Father Thomas' was a Roman Catholic priest. The Roman Catholic Church took a far less charitable view of Anglicans in those days than at present, and no Roman Catholic priest would have entered an Anglican place of worship to conduct a service. Furthermore, Carter would never have entertained the idea of a Roman Catholic priest taking a service, for to all followers of the Oxford Movement, the Church of England represented the 'true Church, Catholic and Reformed.' This is why secessions to the Roman Church were met with such feelings of outrage and betrayal. It is difficult to understand this in these ecumenical days when all sections of Christianity have moved so much closer towards mutual agreement and understanding; but a hundred years ago there was no love lost between Rome and Canterbury.

This still leaves the question, "Who was Father Thomas?", and I regret the mystery remains unsolved. Although the writer of the letter states that the priest was a curate of Clewer, they are all well documented, and although several of them went on to well-known Anglo-Catholic Churches, none of them were members of a Religious Community, or were called 'Thomas'. They were - Charles Hardy Little (1870-74, he later became well-known as Vicar of St. Martin's, Brighton); Sydney Malet Scroggs (formerly curate to John Keble at Hursley, Hants 1860-63, Curate of Clewer 1871-73 and Chaplain Clewer House of Mercy 1873-80); George Seigneley Cuthbert (Clewer 1873-75, Sub-Warden Clewer House of Mercy 1884-1902 and Warden 1902-12); Andrew Lewis Jukes (Clewer 1873-80; later achieved fame at Hackney); also W. H. Hutchings; Edward Dunkin Harrrison; and George Whitlaw. The only other signature in the Register at that time occurred on Advent Sunday 1872 when the Revd. R. J. Simpson, former Curate of Windsor, officiated at 8.0. a.m. I doubt whether he was the offending clergyman, but who knows? It was the 8 o'clock service which aroused the complaint, and he only officiated once. However, it is unlikely that he was "Father Thomas", though it is possible that he may have had 'Tractarian Sympathies' for he started the original subscription towards the building of All Saints', Frances Road and indeed raised £3,000 of the £4,600.

It seems as if "Father Thomas" must remain a mystery if indeed he existed at all. The writer does not actually claim to have been present, but merely infers it. If it was 'hearsay' then the facts may not have been completely accurate, and it is a sad fact that "Protestant Agitators" were not always too concerned about accuracy - a bold statement some might say, but many accounts of the Ritualist controversies of the last century will bear me out. See especially REYNOLDS, M. Martyr of Ritualism (Fr. Mackonochie) COOMBS, JOYCE. Judgement on Hatcham (Fr. Tooth)

Another point is that it was most unusual for a priest, however extreme in his ritualism, to style himself 'Father' at this time. Even famous 'ritualists' as Tooth and Mackonochie were still known as 'Mr'. It was not for a number of years that the term 'Father' came to be used.

As to the so-called "Monkish habit"; it could have been anything from a simple cassock to a surplice and stole, but is more likely to have been the Eucharistic vestments as the 8'clock service was a Celebration.

I have searched the files of the "Windsor Express", but can find no further comments or correspondence concerning the letter of February 1st 1873. It will be noted that the irate parishioner lacked the courage to sign his name. The matter seems to have died down, but it was to erupt in a more virulent form against the Rector, T. T. Carter, for so-called ritualistic practices at the Parish Church within a few years.

Whether the foregoing controversy had any part in the final decision to build St. Agnes' is unknown. Oral tradition has it that the Town Council withdrew permission for the celebration of the Eucharist at Cemetery Chapel, but although this is not beyond the realms of posibility, I have found no suggestion of this in the local records.

There is, however, a letter from T. T. Carter which was read at a Council Meeting on November 3rd 1874:-

My dear Mr. Mayor, Clewer Rectory. October 29th.

I will thank you to communicate to the Burial Board what I mentioned to you in conversation a few days ago - that I no longer need the use of the Cemetery Chapel for a parish service. I desire to thank the Members of the Board very sincerely for their kind permission to me to make use of it so long - but I have now a School Chapel built in the midst of the people which will be more convenient, I believe, for the purpose. I propose to open the School Chapel next week, so that I shall not need the Cemetery Chapel after Sunday next - again expressing my obligations to the Board for their kindness.

Believe me very truly yours,
T. T. Carter."

The tone of the letter does not suggest that the Rector had been served with a 'notice to quit'. It is interesting to note that Carter refers to his new church as a 'School Chapel', the same term which he used in his letter to the Revd. G. D. Nicholas in 1871. There is apparently no record of the mission church of St. Agnes' being under construction. It was built a couple of years before planning permission had to be sought and in any case this part of Spital was outside the Borough of Windsor. There were no Parish Magazines at the time; the local newspaper was more concerned with Windsor news than with Clewer; and there is no mention in Carter's correspondence or in the Diocesan records. Indeed the identity of the architect is not absolutely proven but the church is generally thought to have been the work of Stephen Wyborn. He was a minor Victorian architect who was working in Windsor in the 1870's.

Whilst the church was being built the services continued at the Cemetery Chapel and 1874 sees two new signatures in the Register - John Hyde (curate 1874-80), and George Hervey Swinny. G.H.Swinny was remembered in later years as the first priest of the Spital district and so presumably he was given charge of St. Agnes'. He came from a clerical family. His father, Henry Hutchinson Swinny, became Principal of Cuddesdon in 1859. (Cuddesdon Theological College had been founded five years earlier by Bishop Wilberforce). Edward King, later Bishop of Lincoln, had been Chaplain of Cuddesdon since 1858, and upon H.H.Swinny's sudden death in 1863, succeeded him as Principal. Thus was forged a friendship between King and the Swinny family, and when G.H.Swinny came to Clewer, Edward King took a benevolent interest in St. Agnes' which was to last until King's death. When H.H.Swinny died Bishop Wilberforce wrote that he had "nobleness of spirit....true and tender sympathy....rare singleness of purpose....and increasing saintliness," attributes which were also shared by his son, George. G.H.Swinny's name first appears in the Cemetery Chapel Register about six weeks before the final entry, on All Saints' Day (November 1st) 1874. The date of the final Register entry is consistent with the date proposed for the opening of the Church by Carter in his letter to the Mayor. However, there has always been an 'oral tradition' that September 9th 1874 was the date of the Church's dedication, and indeed the Golden and Diamond Jubilees were observed on September 9th. (So too was the Centenary, but this followed the precedent already established, whereas the Golden Jubilee would have been just within living memory). What is the answer? The Church would not have been dedicated before its completion, and Canon Carter stated quite clearly that he proposed to open the School Chapel "next week". The idea that it was dedicated on September 9th 1875 is a possibility but a very unlikely one. Indeed during the 1880's the Dedication Festival was kept in combination with St. Agnes'-tide (January 21st). In the Bishop's Visitation questionnaire for February 1875 Carter refers to the 'School Chapel' at Spital which suggests that it was still not dedicated. If it had been, one would have expected Carter to have called it St. Agnes'. So it would seem that the evidence weighs against the 'oral tradition', for there is no doubt that Sunday services at the Cemetery Chapel ceased on November 1st, and commenced at St. Agnes' on Sunday, November 8th 1874. The Register comes to an abrupt end with no mention of the transfer to the new Church.

T. T. Carter built St. Agnes' at his own expense and made no attempt to have it incorporated into the Diocesan system as a daughter church of St. Andrew's, Clewer. It was never Consecrated (presumably Carter dedicated it himself) and there is no evidence in the Diocesan Records of it ever being licensed for public worship! (It was licensed for weddings in 1957). Legally it remained the personal property of Canon Carter even after he ceased to be Rector. By a deed of Conveyance dated June 17th 1901 Canon Carter made over to the Rector of Clewer and his successors, St. Agnes' Chapel, Cottage and Mission Rooms. Thus St. Agnes' remains to this day the private chapel of the Rector of Clewer.

The Church was built next to the Spital Road and bordering the grounds of Clewer Lodge, home of Captain Bulkeley. Most of the land around the church belonged to Captain Bulkeley. A photograph of St. Agnes' taken in 1907 shows the church much as it would have looked when first built - a simple rectangular building with small bell turret and round west window. (See Plate 2). The east window was a triple lancet, and in the photograph the windows in the South wall are practically obliterated by creeper. At first only the church was built - the Mission Room was not built until 1884. There is very little information about G.H.Swinny's ministry at St. Agnes', for despite there being a detailed Register of the Cemetery Chapel there is nothing for St. Agnes' until 1883 long after Swinny had left. The first existing register at St. Agnes' is very haphazard, the first pages recording services only on major festivals. After holding weekly services at the Cemetery for so many years I am sure that the use of St. Agnes' would not have been so irregular. The only information about the services during Swinny's time is recorded by T.T.Carter in the Bishop's Visitation questionnaire for February 1875, and it is rather ungrammatical at that! "School Chapel Spital, Holy Communion twice month. Sunday afternoon and evening services with sermons."

George Hervey Swinny left Clewer in 1876 and went to the Society of St. John the Evangelist at Cowley, but his real vocation lay in the missionary field. He left Cowley, and in 1878 became Chaplain of St. George's Mission with charge of Newlands in Cape Colony. He stayed there until 1882 when he went to work for the Universities Mission to Central Africa at Kwamagwaza in Zululand. He married Ann Mackenzie, sister of Bishop Mackenzie of Zululand, and she joined him in pioneering work in Nyasaland.

In 1885, Swinny, his wife and their baby, Mary, went to the island of Likoma on Lake Nyasa which they chose as their headquarters and here the child died. Late in 1886 G. H. Swinny became ill with fever and was nursed by the Scottish missionaries at Bandawé, but on Sexagesima Sunday 1887 he died and was buried at Bandawé on the West shore of Lake Nyasa. He was forty two years old.

Swinny's sister, Charlotte, later wrote to Canon Carter and quoted parts of a letter she had received from Swinney's widow:-

> ". . . . . our brother's spirit passed away at 5.15 that Sunday evening -Evensong was ever his favourite hour of the day. He heard the voice of his little child calling him, suddenly he opened his eyes quite wide and so bright - looked straight up - and never again turned them. We could feel he was really looking right <u>into</u> the land to which he was going and I could just catch the words twice repeated, 'There is the land which we have so long desired. All our loved ones are there. . .' - no-one could for a moment doubt but that he saw all clearly."

"He was", said Miss Swinny, "quite the light and blessing of our home when amongst us".

His wife continued the work, saying, "Where my two dear ones are resting must always be most like Home to me - till my time comes too". Her time was not long in coming - at Easter 1888, she was invalided home and set sail for England, but died en voyage. Thus in the course of two years the whole family had given its life for God's work in Africa. Their work was not in vain though, for in 1903 the Foundation Stone of St. Peter's Cathedral was laid on Likoma Island on the spot where witches had once been burned.

G. H. Swinny was survived by his mother, sister Charlotte and brother Dawnay John Charles Swinny who was ordained priest in 1872 and lived until 1939 when he would have been 95 years old.

## Chapter 11

### In the midst of the people

After the departure of G. H. Swinny, responsibility for St. Agnes' was presumably transferred to one of the other curates, unless they all shared in the work. From 1877-80 the curates were Sydney Malet Scroggs; Andrew Lewis Jukes and John Hyde; all Cemetery Chapel veterans, and in addition, C. J. Duthie and A. W. H. Edwards. As it was normal procedure for the curates to resign when there was a change of incumbent, they all left when T. T. Carter resigned the benefice in 1880. The new Rector was the Revd. Roland Errington who was ordained priest in 1871 and had been a contemporary of G. H. Swinny at Oxford. He was no stranger to the Windsor area having served his first curacy at Stoke Poges (1870-75) and had been Conduct of Eton College (1876-80). Errington was thirty four years old when he came to Clewer Rectory and was unmarried.

The first two years of Errington's incumbency were beset by staff changes which meant upheavals both at Spital and Dedworth. 1881 had seen the appointment of a deacon, the Revd. Gerard Hanley Ball, but ill-health forced his resignation in 1882, shortly before he was to have been ordained priest. There are indications that he would have had charge of Spital had he stayed. (In fact, he was 'priested' in 1883 having recovered away from the unhealthy Thames Valley. After various curacies, Ball became Chaplain of St. Raphael's Home, Torquay, a convalescent home for women run by the Clewer Sisters. He held this post from 1889 until his death in 1929 or 30)!

Despite staff shortages, the work at St. Agnes' had continued to make progress. By 1882, the new Rector had started the Clewer Parish Magazine, and in the early issues we learn that St. Agnes' had a choir, that "Hymns, Ancient and Modern" was in use, and that the Church was open daily from 9.0. a.m. to 4.0. p.m. for Private Prayer.

On December 21st (St. Thomas' Day) 1882, a young Cornish man, named Henry Ley, was ordained deacon, and came to Clewer as curate in charge of St. Agnes'. He took up residence at 1, Manor Terrace, Clewer Green, the home of Mr. & Mrs. Kamester. (Manor Terrace is a terrace at the Clewer Green end of Clewer Hill Road.) He was twenty four years old.

Ley had trained for the Ministry at Cuddesdon after graduating from Cambridge, and he soon became well loved by the Spital people. Sunday Services followed the already familiar pattern - Holy Eucharist twice a month at 8.0. a.m; Evensong and Sermon weekly; and a well attended Children's Service and Catechism on alternate Sunday afternoons. On special Festivals, there was Choral Evensong.

Improvements were made to the Church, both inside and out, particularly in the Sanctuary. We are told that at harvest Evensong, Te Deum was sung as a special act of thanksgiving, and that the altar with its brass candlesticks and rich new hangings made by some of the women, looked very beautiful. Mr. Ley was ordained to the priesthood on St. Thomas' Day 1883.

Before leaving the year 1883 behind, mention must be made of the wedding on April 4th of the Rector to Miss A. J. Hibbert at Chalfont St. Peter. The bridal procession was preceded by a chorister strewing Primroses along the aisle. The Marriage Service was Choral and was followed by a Choral Eucharist at which bride and groom communicated. The couple returned to Clewer on April 27th and upon nearing the Rectory the horses were taken from the carriage and the latter was drawn up to the house by a party of men. Before alighting, bouquets were presented to Mrs. Errington by Miss Hutchings and by one of the smallest children from St. Katherine's Infant School, Nellie Green. Other presents were received including one from the people of Spital - two tablets and a letter clip. This was presented at a special tea meeting at which Mr. Joseph Shipton made the presentation on behalf of the subscribers.

By 1884, Henry Ley's labours at St. Agnes' were beginning to be rewarded and there was a marked increase in the number of Communicants on major Festivals. The Dedication Festival was at this time, observed on St. Agnes' Day (January 21st).

Improvements continued to be made to the Church fabric with the distempering of the interior by Mr. Brewer of Clewer Green. He was one of the 'pillars' of the Church at this time and was a member of the choir. The Sunday School children began a fund to present a stained glass window. The cost was £8 and the children made their weekly offerings, penny by penny. The design chosen to be placed in the central lancet of the East window was that of St. Agnes. The work was done by the Royal Stained Glass Works of Old Windsor, which was connected with the Windsor Tapesty Works. The main figure is till there although the original patterned glass which surrounded it has been replaced by plain frosted glass. Shortly before this, the church interior was photographed by Hills & Saunders of Eton, but I have been unable to trace a copy.

However, it is not difficult to imagine the church interior in 1884. The building was a simple rectangular structure with a small porch over the South door, and another entrance on the North side. The vestry on the North side of the Church was much smaller than the present one. Inside, the main difference from the present church was that there was no gallery. The South wall had four windows, the North had none. The Sanctuary was smaller than at present; the original limit was at the edge of the encaustic tiles, and there are still marks showing the original position of the altar rail. The doorway into the vestry also has tell-tale hinge marks, for when the Sanctuary was enlarged, the door had to be re-hung. It is not certain when the Sanctuary was enlarged, but was most likely either when the gallery was constructed, or when the extension was built on the South side of the church in 1907. The original altar is now in the Lady Chapel and it still retains its beautifully painted panels depicting Our Lady and the Holy Child in the centre, St. Catherine with her wheel in the left-hand panel, and St. Agnes with palm and lamb in the right-hand panel. The altar originally stood on three steps above the Sanctuary. The roof above the Sanctuary was decorated with sacred monograms (which are still there), whilst the rest of the roof was plain. There was no full sized font until 1911, after which time the original small 'font' was used as a holy water stoup, until salt corrosion rendered it useless.

By this time St. Agnes' was beginning to be the social centre of Spital, for clubs and societies were growing up connected with the life of the church. For instance, the Sunday School was flourishing and growing all the time; Mr. Ley had recently formed a boys' Bible Class; and a Cricket Club had been started for men and boys of the district. On a wider parochial basis there was the Mothers' Meeting, the Church of England Temperance Society and Band of Hope. There was also the newly formed Guild of St. Agnes' for girls and young women of the Parish. This met at St. John's Home, the object being 'to help its members in the path of Christian purity and modesty.'

There was, however, nowhere in Spital for these groups to meet and so Mr. Ley resolved to build a recreation room. This was duly completed in 1884 at a cost of £500 which was met by Mr. Ley. The building, together with a cottage for a caretaker, was situated behind the church. It was blessed by Canon Carter at St. Agnes' - tide 1885 and the account in the Parish Magazine describes it as follows:- "The Dedication Festival commenced on Tuesday evening (the eve of St. Agnes') with a full Evensong and Address by the Revd. Canon Carter. The little church was crowded, and we were glad to note, what is not a common fact, that a very large proportion of the congregation were working men, who took a hearty part in the singing and responses....At the close of his address, Canon Carter gave a solemn blessing to the congregation, and then went in procession to the rooms, which were dedicated by him with prayer. At the close of this service the working men of the district came forward, and in their name the Rector, in a very hearty and sympathetic speech, made a presentation to the Revd. H. Ley of a very handsome timepiece and illuminated address as a mark of respect, affection and appreciation, from the working people of the St. Agnes' district. This gift, the result of subscriptions exclusively of the Spital people was a most agreeable surprise to Mr. Ley, who expressed his gratitude in a few simple words, which evidently came from his heart.....The Rector preached on St. Agnes' Day to a large and attentive congregation. After the service a meeting of men was held, at which it was resolved to form a Working Men's Club."

The Club was duly formed and was called the 'Clewer St. Agnes' Working Men's Institute'. It was open every night except Sundays from 7.00 p.m. to 10.30 p.m. There was sixpence entrance fee and a monthly subscription of eightpence. Prospective members were to be nominated and seconded by a member of the Committee. Later a lending library was started. There was also a Lads' Club which met twice a week for boys under seventeen years living in Spital, Clewer Green and Clewer Hill, the area for which Mr. Ley was responsible. Games were provided and there was an opportunity to learn netting and fretwork.

St. Agnes' does not seem to have had many wealthy benefactors in the early years. There were a few people who made a regular 'subscription' to the Church's upkeep, such as the Hon. Captain Dalrymple of St. Leonard's Dale, and Mrs. MacDonald, but generally the attempts to improve the fabric were the results of hard saving. Appeals were made for stained glass for the four windows in the South wall, and promises were received for three of them. Also, at about this time two ladies gave money towards a "white dossal and wings", i.e. altar hangings.

By the late 1880's there is evidence that St. Agnes' was fairly 'advanced' in ceremonial. Although the word 'confession' was not used it was made known that the Priest would be in church to help any who needed it. Writing about the observation of Lent in 1888, Mr. Ley said that there had been "a greater seriousness in the preparation for Communion - hitherto the Sacrament of Penance has by most....been put very wrongly in the background."

By the beginning of 1887 there was an early Celebration every Sunday, and the Harvest Festival (October 9th) saw the introduction of the weekly Choral Communion (Missa Cantata) at 11.00 a.m. Thus from these early days the Eucharist was established as the main Sunday Service. At the Parish Church and at Dedworth the chief choral service continued to consist of Mattins, Litany and Sermon for many years. It is not known whether the Eucharistic vestments were worn at St. Agnes' at this time though it is likely. Certainly altar candles were used and also wafer bread - as shown in the church accounts, and the 'Eastward' position was taken by the Celebrant at the altar.

The Service book in use at St. Agnes' at this time was 'The Priest to the Altar: or Aids to the Devout celebration of Holy Communion chiefly after the ancient English use of Sarum' published in its third edition in 1879. This was basically the Book of Common Prayer with additional devotional material. There had been a revival of the 'Sarum' or 'English Use' in recent years and many Anglo-Catholic churches used this instead of anything more akin to the Roman Use, which would have seemed to many like betraying the Church of England. In fact there was little difference between the two usages, but when the 'English Missal' was published in 1913 many churches, including St. Agnes', which had formerly followed the Sarum use, abandoned it in favour of the Missal. (The English Missal was the English translation of the Roman Missal adapted for Anglican use by the addition of material from the Prayer Book, notably the Prayer of Consecration in the Eucharist).

It was during this period that many priests were being persecuted under the Public Worship Regulation Act*. One such priest was James Bell Cox, of St. Margaret's, Liverpool who was sent to prison from May 5th to May 21st 1887. The English Church Union set up a 'Defence Fund' to assist in the legal costs of such cases, and on Sunday May 15th the collections from services at St. Agnes' amounting to £1:8:9d were sent to this Fund. Two years later, on February 12th 1889 Bishop King of Lincoln was tried before Archbishop Benson, and a Eucharist was celebrated at St. Agnes' on his behalf. *(See Appendix 1)

Henry Ley was a wealthy young man, whose father had been a Cornish landowner. Besides paying for the building of the Mission Rooms, Henry Ley was at this time paying for their upkeep and also keeping the church finances solvent. At one time, in 1888, there was a deficit of £17.00 owing to him, a large sum in those days. Most of the supporters of the church were working class people and, as we have seen, there were but few wealthy subscribers. Most of the men were poorly paid, often desperately so, and there was in many cases, a large family to support. Many of the women took in washing to supplement the meagre income. There was little left over for the church collection, but generally speaking people gave generously in proportion to their income. By 1889, the debt had been cleared, but finance was to be a problem for many years to come, and one from which the Church is still not free.

In addition to the ministration of Henry Ley, there are other signatures in the Service Registers at this time. Among them was the Rector; Revd. Robert Blythe (Chaplain St. Mark's School, Windsor 1871-1887 and Curate, Holy Trinity, Windsor 1889-1890); Revd. Erasmus Austin Ommanney (Priest-in-Charge of Dedworth 1886-1888); Revd. Charles Gordon Browne (Curate, Clewer 1880-1882, Chaplain Clewer House of Mercy 1882-1888); Revd. James Edward Swallow (Chaplain, Clewer House of Mercy 1876-1892); Revd. Richard Tahourdin (Minor Canon of St. George's Chapel 1874-1888); and his brother the Revd. Stephen King Tahourdin, Minor Canon of St. George's Chapel 1881-1910. Stephen King Tahourdin was to be a 'mainstay' to St. Agnes' in times of illness and staff shortages. We have already seen that the clergy attached to the House of Mercy often acted as honorary curates, and at this time there were at least four of them. Similarly clergy attached to St. George's Chapel were sometimes honorary curates in the Windsor and Clewer parishes.

In 1887, Oscar Thomas Fenner became organist and choirmaster at St. Agnes', although at this time there was only an harmonium. He was to hold the position for twenty-nine years.

In 1888, Clewer Lodge changed hands. Captain Thomas Bulkeley had died in May 1882, but the house had remained within his family, in the possession of Colonel Charles Bulkeley. In 1888, it was taken by Colonel Hornby and his family and they were to prove great benefactors of St. Agnes'.

With the dawning of the new decade, the work at St. Agnes' was growing steadily despite some disappointments. Early in 1890 Mr. Ley had been repenting of ever starting the Working Men's Institute, for some members mis-used it, and support was generally poor. However, the threat of closure was enough to re-kindle the spark of interest. Likewise many people failed to attend church and one can detect a note of disillusionment in Mr. Ley's Magazine comments.

A problem was also highlighted which has only been resolved in the last twenty-five years or so - namely, accommodation for the Priest-in-Charge. Mr. Ley had been living in Manor Terrace at the Clewer Green end of Clewer Hill Road; late in 1890 he moved to number 6, Bexley Villas. (These were some tall Victorian villas on New Road, now Clarence Road. They are now faced by Trevelyan School and are flanked by the large roundabout connecting Imperial Road with the Relief Road). Despite assurances that the new abode was only twelve minutes away from the church and would make no difference to his work, it must indeed have done so, and by early 1892, Mr. Ley had moved into the upper part of the Mission Room. He may have also had a room in the caretaker's cottage for there is a connecting door between the cottage and the top of the hall stairs. Seeing the upper hall today, it is difficult to imagine how anyone could have lived in it, but he did so until the end of his ministry at St. Agnes'.

Despite these problems of parish life there were encouraging signs. Inside the church, Mr. Brewer continued his efforts to beautify the fabric by painting a text over the altar. The Sunday School was thriving with about one hundred and fifty children on the roll. They were taught in the Mission Room and accommodation must have been something of a problem.

The Mother's Meeting also met in the Mission Room and at one such meeting in June 1890 Miss Charlotte Swinny, sister of the late Revd. G. H. Swinny, came to talk to the assembly. By this time, she, together with her mother and surviving brother, were living at Hadleigh House, Sheet Street. She brought with her a photograph of G. H. Swinny and his child and promised to have it framed and to present it to the Mother's Meeting. The Clewer Magazine tells us that "those. . . .present. . . .who knew Mr. Swinny were most gratified at the visit. They were glad to have remembrance of former days, when Mr. Swinny so affectionately ministered to them, recalled."

A new venture in the Mission Room in 1890 was the introduction of Penny Readings. Everyone paid one penny admission and then readings, recitations, monologues, songs, etc., were performed. They were an immediate success - this was after all still the age of parlour games and musical evenings and most people had a repertoire of suitable contributions.

Another popular entertainment of this period was the "magic lantern" and occasionally such shows were given in the Mission Room. However, these were not always simply for leisure but were sometimes used as an early form of "visual aid" to devotion. Thus on Good Friday 1890 at 7.0. pm. in church there were Stations of the Cross illustrated with "dissolving views". This medium was later used for Mission Services particularly during Lent, although the 'lantern' was often extremely temperamental.

The Winter of 1890-1891 was very severe with frost and snow for about eight weeks. At one time, the River Thames was frozen between the bridges and there were four to five hundred people playing and skating on the ice. However, the poor and labouring classes were hit very severely for the extreme weather meant no work for many men. Soup kitchens were set up at points in the parish and coals and other necessities distributed. Mr. Ley took responsibility for the needs of the poor at Spital; Lady Mary Currie of Clewer Hill did likewise for Dedworth; and relief was also given at the House of Mercy and the Rectory.

Attendance during Holy Week 1891 was greater than in previous years and we are told that on Good Friday at the Passion Service the "Chapel was closely packed". There were fifty Communicants at three Celebrations on Easter Day (but the Choral Celebration would, at this time, have been 'non-Communicating'). A white cope was borrowed from Dedworth, and worn for the procession - the first time such a vestment had been worn at St. Agnes'. Mr. Ley went to great lengths in the Clewer Magazine to explain that he was acting according to the Rubrics of the Prayer Book - "The Rector gave us permission to have it . . . . Somebody must present one to St. Agnes'. We can't have processions without the proper vestment . . . .the Cope is the vestment ordered by the Church to be worn by the priest in procession. It is not, therefore, an innovation to have used a Cope at St. Agnes', but simply . . . . .obeying the plain directions of the Church".

The Census return of 1891 is worth noting. It listed for Clewer 632 inhabited houses; 32 uninhabited; and seven in the course of building. There were 1,455 adult males and 1,926 adult females, making a total of 3,381. The total population of Clewer in 1881 was 2,830. According to the Parish Magazine, the Spital part of Clewer parish consisted at this time of all from the Cemetery to Clewer Hill, and all one side of Hatch Lane. (This was simply the Rector's interpretation of 'Spital territory' for the purpose of running the parish. This was the area of Ley's responsibility at this time).

Christmas services for 1892 were well supported and were an improvement on other years. We are told that the "Chapel looked very pretty and the decorations were exceedingly tasteful". The altar was dressed by Miss Dann of St. Leonard's Dale Cottage, a faithful supporter of St. Agnes'. Other decorations were provided by Colonel and Miss Margaret Hornby of Clewer Lodge. On the Wednesday in Christmas week the choir and other church workers, numbering about thirty in all, met together for dinner.

The Accounts for 1892 were once again "in the red" with a deficit of £4.17.3d. This was indeed depressing, for urgent work was needed for the four South facing windows. The opening sections on all four had more than once fallen down, and in one case, the stained glass had been smashed to pieces. New frames were urgently needed but there was no money to spare.

By 1893 there was a daily Celebration of the Holy Eucharist and daily Evensong. Confession was also advertised after Evensong any day. A new set of Stations of the Cross was given in 1893 by a Mr. Montague Brown to replace the original set. He also gave two thuribles for incense, "which", stated Mr. Ley, "we hope will soon be in use".

Sexagesima, 1893 was a Red Letter Day at St. Agnes', for it marked the first visit of a Bishop. Wilfrid Bird Hornby, Bishop of Nyasaland celebrated at 8.0 a.m and preached at Evensong. I have gone to great lengths to find out whether there was any family connection between Bishop Hornby and the family at Clewer Lodge, and similarly with Dr. James Hornby, Headmaster, later Provost, of Eton, but without success. However, I should think there was some connection between the Bishop and the occupants of Clewer Lodge for it would explain why a Colonial Bishop with no apparent connections with Clewer Parish should come to a small chapel such as St. Agnes'. Anyway, there can be no doubt that his visit gave a tremendous boost to the morale of the congregation of the little church. (The diocese of Nyasaland was created in 1892 and the Revd. W. B. Hornby Vicar of St. Columba's, Sunderland was chosen as first Bishop. He had been a Founder Member of the Oxford Mission to Calcutta where he had spent six years. He was consecrated on December 21st 1892; after a short time was invalided home, and in 1894 was obliged to resign his diocese after only about eight months work there. Following his return to England he took a living, first in Norwich, then in Northumberland, and in 1904 became Bishop of Nassau until 1919. He died on June 5th 1935.)

Some of the clergy who assisted at St. Agnes' from time to time during this period were the Revd. G. D. Nicholas (Vicar, Clewer St. Stephen); Revd. Walter Marshall and Revd. Charles Albert Treherne (Minor Canons of St. George's Chapel); Revd. Edward Bate (Chaplain, Clewer House of Mercy 1892-1894); Revd. Henry Fortescue Ostrehan (Curate, Clewer St. Stephen's 1889-1906); Revd. Vernon Staley (Chaplain, Clewer House of Mercy 1888-95; Curate of Ascot Heath 1895-1897; Vicar of South Ascot 1895-1901). Vernon Staley was also a well-known author of religious books, the best known of which was "The Catholic Religion", which is still available today. Assistance was also given by G. S. Cuthert and S. K. Tahourdin, who have already been mentioned.

1893 saw the outbreak of Smallpox at Clewer. The lack of an isolation hospital necessitated the erection of hospital tents and the Rector allowed the use of the glebe land near Clewer Rectory. The epidemic lasted from May until August, and equipment and nursing staff came from St. Andrew's Hospital. Recently crockery, including a vinegar bottle containing coal-tar used in the epidemic, has been excavated in the garden of the present Rectory. (A "Victorian Rubbish Heap" excavated by Nicholas and Michael Shaw in 1978 and exhibited at Clewer Rectory.)

Chief amongst those involved in the care of the victims was the Rector himself. A few weeks after the recovery of the last patient there was a public presentation to the Rector of silver dessert dishes in recognition of his "self-sacrifice and courage, and prompt and noble action".

November 1893 saw the departure after eleven years of the Revd. Henry Ley. The Rector wrote in the the Parish Magazine, "It is well known how he loved the place, and how much time and money he expended upon making it really beautiful, as the House of God should be. It is therefore a terrible wrench for him to leave all this, and will be difficult to take up new work elsewhere with zeal and energy . . . .". On November 17th a ceremony took place when Mr. Ley was presented with an illuminated address, and a purse of nearly seventy sovereigns. The presentation was made by the Rector, and Mr. Shipton who was Mr. Ley's right-hand man at St. Agnes' said a few words. Mr Ley replied with suitable sentiments.

Mr Ley was to have gone to Bovey Tracey in Devon as Curate to the Revd. and Hon. Charles Leslie Courtenay, Vicar since 1849, and also a Canon of Windsor since 1859. However, Canon Courtenay died just about the time when Ley should have taken up the appointment and so the arrangement fell through. We next hear in the Clewer Magazine of May 1894 that Mr. Ley was going to work in the Parish of St. Catherine, Liverpool, as curate to the Revd. J. W. Leary, but presumably this also met with a hitch, for 'Crockford' lists instead a curacy at Christ Church, Doncaster. By 1895, Mr. Ley had returned South, to London, where he served curacies at St. Mark, Marylebone 1895-1898 and St. Saviour, Pimlico 1899-1900. He finally seems to have found his 'niche' at St. Matthias, Earls Court where he served as curate from 1900-1919. All these churches were bastions of Anglo-Catholicism, particularly St. Matthias, Earls Court. Alas it is no more, for it was demolished following damage in World War II. The Parish was then amalgamated with that of its famous daughter, St. Cuthbert's, Philbeach Gardens.

Henry Ley's ministry at St. Agnes' is just outside living memory - the earliest personal memories which I have been given date back to 1900. A few years ago however, an old lady told a later priest of St. Agnes' (Fr. Wood), about her childhood in the 1880's. She recalled that her mother was a poor washerwoman, and when the girl was asked by Mr. Ley whether she would like to be Confirmed, she declined knowing that her mother could not have afforded to buy her the white dress. She never told the priest the reason why, "If only I had", she said, "He would have given me one, for oh, he was a kind man". Then she added, "but you couldn't see across the Church for incense!" So it would seem that the two thuribles given in 1893 were indeed put to good use!

Henry Ley served the whole of his ministry as a curate, which might seem unusual nowadays, but was common in his day. He retired back to his native Cornwall and died at Penzance on September 17th 1926, aged 68 years.

## Chapter III

## Music, Missions and a Royal Jubilee

After Henry Ley left St. Agnes' the work was undertaken by another curate, the Revd. Ernest W. Vaughan, assisted at times by the Revd. C. A. Treherne. Vaughan was not given charge of Spital. It was merely a case of Sunday duty except on the major festivals. Dedworth too had its staff problems at this time, there having been a succession of priests since 1890. January 1894 saw the appointment of the Revd. F. S. Stoney as curate, in succession to Ley, although in fact he took charge of Dedworth, and Vaughan continued at Spital. Church life at St. Agnes' kept 'ticking over', but, as with all periods of interregnum, there was no moving forward, and indeed, Communicant numbers dropped due to the reduction of services. However, we cannot blame Vaughan, for a flock without a permanent shepherd soon scatters.

Ernest Vaughan left Clewer to return to his native Lincolnshire late in 1894. Another departure, and one which was to cause some financial hardship to St. Agnes', was that of Colonel Hornby of Clewer Lodge. Writing in the Parish Magazine the Rector said: "The keeping up of the services at St. Agnes', Spital, is a considerable expense to us. We have lost a generous supporter in Colonel Hornby, and no-one has taken his place. May we ask for a few pounds from the affluent?".

The Revd. George Jones took up office at St. Agnes' on November 1st 1894. Ordained priest in 1882, George Jones was 37 years old and had served several curacies before coming to Clewer, including St. Giles, Camberwell 1884-1886, and St. Mary Magdalene, Paddington 1886-1889, both of which were strongholds of Anglo-Catholicism. In common with the Rector, he had a great interest in music, and this was to be put to good purpose during his ministry in Spital. Unlike former clergy at St. Agnes' he was married. He took up residence at 2, Bexley Villas, and in addition to Spital, was also responsible for Clewer New Town.

Mr. Jones embarked on his new work with enthusiasm, and Church life revived both spiritually and socially. Regular Sunday services were restored and there was also a Eucharist on about four weekdays. Sunday Services at this time (late 1894) were:-

| | |
|---|---|
| 8.00 a.m | Holy Communion |
| 10.30 a.m. | Matins (1st and 3rd Sundays said, 2nd and 4th Choral and Sermon) |
| 11.00 a.m. | Holy Communion (1st and 3rd Sundays and Festivals, Choral) |
| 3.15 p.m. | Children's Service |
| 6.30 p.m. | Evensong and Sermon |

With the increase in services, Communicant numbers again increased, although the 11.00 a.m. service was still, as in most churches at this time, non-Communicating. The Sunday School continued to flourish with over 100 children enrolled. This was, of course, the heyday of the Sunday School movement.

1895 saw the establishment of two new Guilds - the Guild of the Holy Childhood, for children who had regularly attended Sunday School for at least three months; and the Guild of St. Mary the Virgin, for young confirmed women of fourteen years upwards, with the object of improving their Christian lives and to promote greater devotion to the Blessed Sacrament. Such guilds were often formed in Anglo-Catholic churches at this time (indeed these were not the first at St. Agnes') and they gave their members added encouragement and solidarity in the Christian life. A disadvantage of Guilds at parish level was that they often floundered when their "priest-founder" moved on. Other Guilds which had 'universal' Church membership, such as the Confraternity of the Blessed Sacrament (founded by T. T. Carter), the Guild of All Souls, the Guild of

Servants of the Sanctuary and several others, survived and still flourish to this day.

St. Agnes'-tide 1895 was described in the Clewer Magazine as being of a "very bright and hearty character". On the Eve, there was a Festal Evensong and Sermon; and on the Day itself, two Celebrations of the Eucharist, the 11.00 a.m. being choral. Evensong and Sermon brought the Day to a close, the preacher being the Revd. G. S' Cuthbert. January 24th witnessed the St. Agnes' Supper at which about eighty people were present. This was to become a highlight of the social life of the village during the next few years. We are told that "thanks to the kindness of Mr. & Mrs. Jones, Miss Dann, the House of Mercy, Mrs. Barry and others, a sumptuous repast was provided, abundant in quantity, unimpeachable in quality and rich in variety". After the supper there were speeches and then a concert followed in which Mr. & Mrs. Jones and other local people performed songs and duets.

Like Henry Ley, George Jones was anxious to beautify the church, and soon after his arrival we hear of a gift of a brass cross and six brass candlesticks for the altar -the cross having been given by members of the congregation and the candlesticks by a friend of Mr. and Mrs. Jones. Other acquisitions, which were mostly saved for, penny by penny, were a new carpet for the Sanctuary costing £5.12.6d, and a red vestment (presumably a chasuble) and vestment chest.

Miss Dann, a staunch worker and benefactor of St. Agnes' for the previous seven years or so, left the district in May 1895, and at a ceremony in the Mision Room she was presented with two silver candlesticks, a silver penholder, and a piece of carving done by Mr. Moss the church caretaker.

The end of the year saw the church accounts still "in the red" to the sum of £13.16.7d. There is a slightly familiar ring about this announcement in the Parish Magazine that there would be a Sale in aid of Church Funds - or perhaps it just goes to show that there is nothing new under Heaven! At any rate, the sale raised £11.18.0d, which was considered a good result, but we are also told that bad weather kept many away.

The Church may have been poor, but this did not dampen the spirits of either clergy or people for long, and the Patronal Festival of 1896 "was kept with becoming joy". Canon Carter preached at the Choral Eucharist - "the little church looked lovely in its Festival apparel . . . . the service was bright and hearty . . . . . and the Sermon very simple, yet deeply spiritual". In the evening about eighty people sat down for the St. Agnes' Supper and with typical Victorian understatement, we are told that "it was rather a close fit". Two welcome guests were the Revd. Henry Ley, who had also attended the services that day, and Miss Dann, who was received with an ovation. There were speeches by Mr. Jones, the Rector, Mr. Shipton and the Revd. Henry Ley, followed by songs and recitations.

The problem of space was not confined to the Mission Room - it was becoming increasingly serious in church especially on festivals when there was a large congregation. At the 1896 Harvest Festival, Mr. Kelsey senior managed to pack ninety-five adults in the church and the remaining children were squeezed into the vestry! Also, the Choir was growing in numbers and it was difficult to accommodate them.

In January 1896 Mr. Jones' father offered to donate £10.0.0d towards the timber for a gallery if the men of the congregation would do the work. The plans were prepared by Mr. T. B. Carter (Canon Carter's grandson), and the work was undertaken by Mr. Moss the Church caretaker as working foreman, assisted by Mr. Weston and Mr. Alf Beal. Mr. G. Kelsey senior offered to do the ironwork and Mr. Shipton to do anything he could. (Mr. A. W. Weston lived at 1, Bryn Terrace, St. Leonard's Road, where he kept a General Store. Later he moved to Vine Cottages just opposite the church. The Beal family were long standing members of the church. Both Mr. Kelsey and Mr. Shipton had worshipped at the Cemetery Chapel and at St. Agnes' since the earliest days). Although it was hoped that the gallery would be finished by Ascension Day, in fact, the work took a good deal longer.

The Church services continued to be well supported and Communicant numbers continued to rise, so that by the end of the year (1896) 1,336 acts of Communion had been made, an increase of three hundred on the previous year. Services during Lent had been fairly well attended, and Good Friday Services had more support than in the previous year. At least no-one could say there wasn't a service at a suitable time on Good Friday 1896:-

| | |
|---|---|
| 8.00 a.m | Ante-Communion |
| 9.00 a.m | The Reproaches |
| 10.00 a.m | Matins and Sermon |
| 11.00 a.m | Children's Service |
| 12.00 to 3.00 p.m | Three Hours Devotion (first introduced in 1895) |
| 6.00 p.m | Stations of the Cross |
| 8.00 p.m | Evensong and Sermon |

It is not clear from the records whether the Blessed Sacrament was permanently reserved in St. Agnes' at this time. As St. Agnes' was a 'private chapel' it would not have been necessary to obtain a 'Faculty' for this, unlike the other churches. During 1896 Mr. Montague Brown gave £1.0.0d for a tabernacle - this sum would not have bought a tabernacle even in those days, so it was either towards the cost of one, or towards the upkeep of an existing one. Certainly it would not be surprising to find permanent reservation here at this time, for by 1896 the main choral service was again the Eucharist every Sunday, and there was a celebration on most weekdays. It has already been noted that the various Guilds held devotion to the Blessed Sacrament among their aims. Such festivals as Corpus Christi were observed by this time, and on All Soul's Day (November 2nd) the offerings were always sent to the Guild of All Souls. Eucharistic vestments were worn at all celebrations and there were two servers at Choral celebrations.

November 1896 was a stirring time in Clewer for, from 21st to the 30th, there was a parochial Mission. Each district of the parish had its own Missioner. The chief missioner at St. Andrew's was the Revd. Cyril Bickersteth, Rector of Radley near Oxford, a founder member of the Community of the Resurrection, which is nowadays based at Mirfield, Yorkshire. The Spital district had for its missioner the Revd. J. Frank Buxton, Curate of Christchurch, St. Leonards, and it is interesting to note that a Fellow Curate at St. Leonards was a man named William Brook, who seventeen years later became priest-in-charge of St. Agnes'. St. Stephen's parish was also included in the Mission, and their missioner was the Revd. A. T. C. Cowie, who a few years later became Rector of Clewer.

The mission programme was rigorous, as they tended to be in those days. In addition to the usual Sunday services there was a Mission Service and Instruction in the evening. On weekdays there was:-

| | |
|---|---|
| 7.00 a.m | Holy Communion |
| 5.30 p.m | Children's Service |
| 8.00 p.m | Mission Service |
| 9.00 p.m | Instruction |

Also, there were services for women only on two days, and similarly for men. There were nearly fifty at these services, but we are told that all the services were well supported.

So 1896 closed with what we hope was the fervent aftermath of the Mission. On the more secular side of parish life, members of the Mother's Meeting could look back to their summer outing to Regent's Park Zoo and Gardens. "A most agreeable surprise" in the form of a visit from Miss Dann and Mr. Ley added to the Mother's enjoyment of their 'day off' - for many of them their only day off in the whole year.

George Jones had a great love of music, and during his ministry at St. Agnes' the choral side of worship immproved greatly. Money was saved for a new American organ - it took a tremendous effort to do this, for, as we have seen, funds were short and the people were poor, but partly through laborious saving and partly through the proceeds of a Rummage Sale, the debt was cleared by mid-1898. The total cost was something in the region of £38.0.0d The organist, Oscar Fenner, wrote a special setting of the Eucharist which he called the 'Missa de Sancta Agnete', and dedicated it to Mr. Jones. This was a full scale setting with parts, and it was first performed on St. Agnes' Day 1897. Very much a product of its time, it is no longer used as there is no choir today and it has been superseded by other settings written for the modern liturgy. It was published in 1898 and was used on special festivals for many years (for as long as there was a proper choir in fact). The printed copies are still in existence.

The Patronal Festival of 1897 was quite an occasion, for besides Mr. Fenner's new composition there was also a sermon from Canon Carter. The usual Supper followed in the evening and the Choirboys and Servers were invited to come and clear up the left-overs on the Saturday night following the feast!

A festival which was always enthusiastically kept in the early years of St. Agnes' was Harvest. Nowadays, whilst still giving thanks, harvest is not kept with the same zeal; but in the 1890's Spital was, as we have seen, very much a rural area, and although some of the open spaces were Royal Parklands as now, there were also cornfields where there are now Council houses. The church must have looked rather like Covent Garden for "children were seen on the Saturday morning flocking towards St. Agnes' laden with flowers, fruit and vegetables, some even being compelled to use clothes baskets to bring their offerings in." The music, except for the hymns, was Mr. Fenner's, and "very beautiful and reverent it was too, worthy of being rendered in a larger and more important church than ours." The edible things were sent to St. Andrew's Hospital and the collections divided between the former and the Convalescent Hospital at Folkestone, which like St. Andrew's was run by the Clewer Sisters.

The Clewer Sisters seemed to be 'everywhere', and indeed at this time there were branch houses in many towns and cities in this Country and overseas. All three churches in Clewer Parish had a Sister who helped with pastoral care and work around the church. Sister Agnes was 'attached' to Clewer Parish Church from 1877 until 1920. She was a particularly talented artist. The Sister working at Spital during Mr. Jones' ministry was Sister Frances Harriet.

The Working Men's Club seems to have died out after Henry Ley left, but the Mission Room was still put to good use. The Mother's Meeting flourished at this time, presided over by Mrs. Jones, and it must have made a welcome break from the drudgery of domestic life. The Penny Bank was held on Saturday mornings to enable subscribers to save a little, and later there were similar facilities in the shape of a Clothing Club, Boot Club and even a Turkey and Goose Club, the latter to enable the provision of some Christmas fare. The Mission Room was also used for the Sunday School. By 1898 there were one hundred and forty children enrolled and it took all the facilities of Church, Vestry and Mission Room to accommodate them, so much so that Mr. Jones was saying how useful it would be to have an 'iron room'.

We cannot leave 1897 behind without some mention of Queen Victoria's Diamond Jubilee. On the evening of Wednesday, June 23rd, the Queen returned to Windsor from London amidst much jubilation from her subjects. The route through Eton was decorated with triumphal arches, and as Her Majesty crossed Windsor Bridge the Royal Standard was hoisted on the Round Tower and the bells of St. George's and the Parish Church rang out. By 7.00pm the procession had reached Her Majesty's Statue where it halted before the Reception Committee. After the Town Clerk had read the loyal address members of the Committee, including the Revd. Roland Erringon, were presented to the Queen. The National Anthem followed and, as the Queen passed by, three thousand local children sang heartily.

The children's entertainment took place in the Home Park on Friday, June 25th, at which six thousand were present. The Clewer contingent "marched down with their teachers, headed with banners most beautifully worked or painted by Sister Agnes. Every child on arriving had a bun and glass of milk, then they dispersed to play . . . . . At 4.30 they were drawn up in the form of a horse-shoe outside the tents to receive the Queen . . . Her Majesty arrived at 5.30 . . . she drove round the inside of the horse-shoe while the children sang and then cheered lustily, waving their programmes. Tea followed. . . and then more games, the return home commencing at 7.30 pm. Every child wore a medal presented by the Queen".

On June 30th there was a similar tea entertainment in the Home Park for the aged poor. After dinner there was an outdoor entertainment consisting of conjuring, juggling, comic songs and ventriloquism, followed by tea. Soon after 7.00 pm the Queen arrived. "Her Majesty drove very slowly twice up and down the line, so that everyone was gratified by a good look at her. As the cheers died away the Queen departed and this was the signal for a general break-up of the party".

The chief achievement of 1898 was the completion of the structural work on the gallery. It still required painting but the decision was made to wait until after the church had been repainted. This task urgently needed doing, but as usual money was the obstacle.

Church life generally continued to flourish during the last part of the decade. A men's club was started in the Mission Room at the end of 1898 and met nightly except on Mondays. There was a weekly subscription of 2d and no-one under eighteen was admitted. There was to be no alchohol or gambling. Two daily London newspapers were provided; cards and games were allowed, and so was smoking.

The choir still flourished and on special festivals was sometimes augmented by a small orchestra. In addition to Mr. Fenner's Missa de Sancta Agnete', Mr. Jones had composed a setting of the Eucharist and this was first performed at Harvest 1898.

A slight variation on the Mission theme took place in Clewer Parish during March 1899, with a visit from the Church Army Van. The Rector was at great pains to make it clear in the Parish Magazine that the Church Army was a "Church Organisation under the patronage of the Bishop of the Diocese. This is quite a different thing from the Salvation Army." Although the latter organisation has now won the respect and admiration of most Christian denominations, this was certainly not the case at the beginning, when ridicule and persecution, together with mistrust and misunderstanding of the Army's methods and motives, had to be endured. However, some Evangelical clergy realised that this particular brand of 'revivalism' could be harnessed to the Church and they set up a number of Church Salvation Armies. Mainly through the efforts of the Revd. Wilson Carlile, these groups were united in 1882 and became known as the Church Army. At first Salvation Army methods were copied, even to the point of producing a weekly paper called the 'Battleaxe'. Bishop Mackarness of Oxford gave his support and did much to persuade his fellow Bishops to grant their approval. Eventually a system of evangelising was evolved by sending horse-drawn vans, usually inscribed with largely painted texts, round the villages. By the end of the 1890's there were about fifty of these vans, and one such came to Clewer in March 1899. Starting in Clewer New Town, services were held in all parts of the Parish. On Friday, March 10th, there was an open-air service at Spital followed by a Lantern Service at St. Agnes'. There was an address to the children at St. Agnes' on Sunday afternoon, and one for the adults after Evensong. Finally, on the Monday there was another open-air evening service followed by a Lantern Service in church. There were three missioners led by a Captain Bennett.

November 1899 saw the departure from Clewer of the Revd. Roland Errington, who had accepted the living of Warden with Newborough in Northumberland. Errington had been in a peculiar position regarding St. Agnes' for, although as Rector he appointed the assistant clergy, the Chapel of St. Agnes' still belonged to Canon Carter. I have no evidence to suggest that this caused any practical difficulties, and I am sure that Canon Carter would never have interfered with Mr. Errington over any policy concerning the Parish. However, St. Agnes' was always much more 'advanced' in ceremonial than the Parish Church in Errington's time, and I wonder whether things would have been different if St. Agnes' had been solely under Errington's control. Errington was no 'ritualist' and, while holding and teaching the Catholic Faith of the Church of England, he was very 'moderate' in outward ceremonial. Indeed he may have been appointed to Clewer to 'tone it down' after Canon Carter, for at his Induction ceremony Bishop

Mackarness expressed his hope that there would henceforth be 'compromise on both sides'.

Errington had the right sort of middle-class background to appeal to the Protestant landed gentry of Clewer such as the Foster's, the Barry's and the Gooch's who had been alienated from Clewer Church in the 'ritualism' troubles. ("A good thing for the Parish," Sir Daniel Gooch had written in his diary, concerning Canon Carter's resignation). These families, together with their wealth, returned to Clewer Church during Errington's incumbency.

Roland Errington was in many ways a typical Victorian clergyman - an earnest and devout pastor, a man of culture (he had a great appreciation of music), and 'good breeding'. He was an ardent crusader for social justice especially when it affected his own people. We have already noted his efforts during the smallpox epidemic, and no-one fought harder than he for the provision of a decent drainage system for Clewer. Similarly he continued Canon Carter's efforts to restore the Parish Church and to maintain dignity in the services. It was mainly through his efforts and no small expense on his part that the Clewer Hall was built in Parsonage Lane. In the Parish Magazine he often wrote with what today would be regarded as an over-bearing and Imperialistic style, but it was the style of the time - the halcyon days of the British Empire - and our world today is totally different.

Errington stayed at Warden until 1905, and then returned South to become Rector of East Tisted in the diocese of Winchester, a living which he held until his retirement in 1921. Mrs. Errington died in 1919, and after his retirement Mr. Errington resided in Winchester. He died in 1926 aged eighty years.

During the interregnum the Revd. G. Jones and the Revd. John Kinchin Smith (Dedworth) were left in charge of the Parish. The Rector had stated that "the Churchwardens' duty is to see that the Statutory Services go on as usual; that is to say Celebration, Mattins and Evensong at the two Consecrated Churches, St. Andrew's and All Saints'. . . " That St. Agnes' was at a disadvantage in being a private unconsecrated Chapel (even though Canon Carter was still alive), begins to be more apparent, for from this time onwards, whenever there was a serious staff shortage, the threat of closure always loomed.

The departure from Clewer of Roland Errington was very closely followed by that of George Jones, who in January 1900 was appointed to the living of Sandford St. Martin near Oxford. While just outside living memory, all the documentary evidence of the time points to a good and earnest priest who cared deeply for the souls in his charge; a man whose musical talents enabled him to improve and beautify the worship of the Church, and who also inspired others to work for this; a man who also cared deeply for the church as the House of God, and did his utmost to continue the work of material improvement despite the chronic financial situation. One man who must have deeply regretted his departure was Oscar Fenner for he had been greatly encouraged by Jones' interest in church music. For a few years this otherwise melancholy, rather lonely little man had composed music which, without someone to encourage his talents, might never have been written.

Roland Errington had this to say of George Jones,". . . . his ministrations have been much appreciated and blessed. The music at St. Agnes' has very much improved thanks to the combined effort of the curate-in-charge and Mr. Fenner. Mrs. Jones has presided over a largely attended Mothers' meeting, while the District Visitor's work has been admirably carried out by Miss Aird, Miss Fowler and Mrs. Poynter. Indeed the organisation in that district is so complete that the new Rector should find no difficulty in carrying it on if he thinks it well to do so. Personally we have attached great value to Mr. and Mrs. Jones' work. . . . ".

In his farewell letter George Jones thanked his many helpers, " . . . I wish to thank those who have so willingly and ungrudgingly helped me . . . . week after week - sometimes at great inconvenience to themselves . . . . Mr. Shipton, my quasi-churchwarden; Mr. G. Kelsey, my verger; Mr. C. Nicholson, my sacristan and Server; W. and A. Clarke, H.

Bowcott and others whose work has forced them to retire; my servers, my Sunday School Teachers, my District Visitors, my Organist and Choir, Miss E. Beal and Miss F. Hyatt who between them have done the washing of the various sacred cloths connected with the Service of the Altar; these and many others have loyally and kindly given their willing services . . . . "

On January 30th at the St. Agnes' Supper, the Revd. and Mrs. Jones were presented with a purse of money to which some two hundred subscribers had contributed, and an illuminated address, the work of Sister Agnes. Mr. Poynter presided over the ceremony, supported by the Revd. G. D. Nicholas. The address was presented by Mr. Kelsey and the money by Mr. Shipton.

George Jones remained at Sandford St. Martin until 1903 and then went to Croydon as curate where he stayed until 1906. Nowadays it may seem odd to revert to a curacy after holding a benefice, but at the time with which we are dealing it was very common, even after reasons of ill-health have been discounted. In 1906 he became Vicar of St. John the Evangelist, Maidstone until 1912, when he moved to Shirley near Croydon as Vicar until 1926. He retired from the full time Ministry in 1926, but in 1931 became Acting Chaplain at St. Barnabas' Home, Torquay which was run by the Clewer Sisters for incurables. He died in 1932 aged seventy-five years.

## INTERLUDE: SPITAL VILLAGE IN 1900

It may be well to take a closer look at Spital in 1900, for there had been quite a few changes in the village in the intervening years since 1870.

Starting from the corner of Bolton Road (in the part belonging to Windsor Parish), and proceeding along St. Leonard's Road, as it was now being called, towards Clewer Green, the main difference is that there were many more houses. Several terraces had been built on the Park side of the road during the 1890's. They still stand with their names preserved - Devereax Terrace, York Villas, Florence Villas, Park View, Melrose Avenue, Rose Villas. In some cases older cottages had been demolished to make way for the new houses.

Marshall's Directory of Windsor for 1900 locates the kennels of the Windsor Garrison Drag Hounds next to Spital Infants' School. The cottages next to the School were known as 'Jubilee Place' and numbers 1 and 2 was a public house called the 'Foresters' Arms'. Today it is a private dwelling, but there is still a glass door with the words 'Jug and Bottle' inscribed, and the old signs are there outside, but painted over. Spital Post Office and General Stores was at 1, York Villas and was kept by J. Garlick. The site is now occupied by a launderette. The directory does not mention the old smithy which was in this immediate vicinity in 1870.

At the top of the hill was the Cemetery which had been enlarged in 1874, so that the gardens of the houses along St. Leonard's Road now backed on to it. The first building at the crown of the hill was the village bakery and grocer's shop, at this time in the hands of Mr.J.N.Hewitt. Next there was 'Rose Cottage', 'Hewitt's Cottage', and a row of houses known as 'Vine Cottages' where some familiar 'Spital' names lived - 'Bridges', 'Stevens' and 'Fowler'. Other 'named' cottages were 'Winkfield Cottage', 'Eton Cottage' and 'Myrtle Cottage'. Eton College and Myrtle Cottage still exist, and the Beal family, long-standing members of St.Agnes' lived at the latter. The terrace of houses between Eton Cottage and Myrtle Cottage was not built until the early years of this century, so this part of the road was not as built up as at the present time. Wellington Terrace and Bryn Terrace are still there (but without name plaques), the first having been built before 1870 (it was also known as Wellington Place), likewise 'Rose Cottages' next door and near to the present day traffic lights. There was still some "Green" beyond 'Rose Cottages', where there is now a garage, and from time to time a fair would come here.

Going back to Bolton Road and proceeding up St.Leonard's Road toward Clewer Green, we will look at the righthand side this time. There was an abundance of public houses - 'The Fawn', 'The Duke of York', 'The Stag and Hounds' and 'The Royal Standard', and all but the last still stand. There were quite a number of cottages between 'The Fawn' and 'The Duke of York' -'Willow Cottages', 'Abyssinia Cottage', 'Catherine Villas' and others un-named. A.T.Cockett, builder and timber merchant, was next to 'The Duke of York' and all that separated this hostelry from the 'Stag and Hounds' was a dwelling called 'Clewer Cottage'.

Next to the 'Stag and Hounds' was a row called 'Park Place', and the 'Royal Standard' consisted of numbers 6 to 8. 'The Standard' was not fully licensed (i.e. for spirits), but was simply an 'ale and wine' house. Next door was a general store kept at this time by C.Gutteridge. At right angles to the road, down an alley were Homelee Cottages. Rejoining the road, there were four cottages, also known as 'Park place', and number 1 was occupied by A.E.Bampton & Son, Ironmongers, Sanitary Plumbers, etc. Next came St.Agnes' Church and then 'St.Agnes' Cottages'. Number 1 was the caretaker's cottage, occupied in 1900 by W.R.Blythe, Mr.Moss having recently left. The other three cottages were much older and were smaller and lower than the caretaker's cottage and were also known as 'Knowle's Cottages'. They were set right back from the road with long front gardens but nothing at the back. The occupants in 1900 were; number 2 T.Rosier, number 3 Mrs.Garforth, and number 4 T.Croxford.

Clewer Lodge had recently changed hands yet again, and the new occupant was Mrs Carpenter Rowe, a wealthy widow who was to take a deep interest in St.Agnes' - truly a 'lady bountiful' in the very best sense.

A cluster of cottages known as 'Parkside Cottages' stood at an angle off the main road near where the present day junction with Imperial Road is sited. 'Lovers' Walk' still twisted along its way and eventually joined Green Lane and New Road. At Clewer Green there were 'Baldwin's Cottages' and 'Dyson's Cottages', and a grocer's shop and Post Office (this later moved round the corner into Clewer Hill Road).

## Chapter IV

### Passing Shadows

The interregnum at Clewer was a short one. The new Rector, the Revd. Arthur Thomas Carnsew Cowie, was inducted by the Vicar of Windsor on February 10th 1900. Aged about fifty years upon his appointment to Clewer, Arthur Cowie came from a clerical family, his father being Dean of Exeter until his death in 1900. Arthur Cowie was a man of wide experience in Anglo-Catholic parishes. Ordained deacon in 1872 and priest a year later, he served his first curacy at St. Paul's Oxford, after which he moved to St. Philip and St. James, Oxford from 1873-1881. He then served at the well-known London church of St. Paul, Knightsbridge until he returned to the Oxford Diocese in 1884 as Vicar of Bampton Aston with Shifford. He remained there until his appointment to Clewer.

During the interregnum at St. Agnes' many of the services were held in abeyance, particularly on weekdays. Even the services on St. Agnes' Day were somewhat curtailed and the Supper was postponed until January 30th to enable Mr. Jones' presentation to take place. Local clergy did what they could to keep things going and fortunately the interregnum was not too long. Among those who assisted at this time were - the Revd. Herbert Shepherd (Chaplain, House of Mercy); the Revd. G. D. Nicholas, the Revd. H. F. Ostrehan and the Revd. Ernest Anderson Thorne, all from Clewer St. Stephen; the Revd. J. Kinchin Smith (Dedworth); the Revd. H F Prideaux Davson (Licenced to preach in Oxford Diocese 1898-1900); the Revd. A. G. Langdon, Revd. Walter Marshall and the Revd. S. K. Tahourdin all Minor Canons of St. George's Chapel.

May 17th 1900 was a great day for the British Empire, for it saw the Relief of Mafeking. The Boer War does not seem to have had much effect on parish life in Clewer, although on March 16th 1899 there had been a "Day of Prayer in present anxiety", at St. Agnes'.

The Relief of Mafeking was described in the Parish Magazine as "one great and glorious event, which has filled every English heart with joy and thankfulness." To celebrate the event locally there was a torchlight procession to Windsor, starting from Clewer. "In our neighbourhood additional zest has been given to our public celebration by the presence of our Sovereign in our midst, in whose honour the procession was organised, and who graciously received the ovations of her people at the Castle."

The appointment of the Revd. Herbert Burges Hunt was announced in the Parish Magazine for October 1900, "we are sure that Mr. and Mrs. Hunt who have taken the house named 'Stansfield' in New Road, will receive a hearty welcome from all our parishioners, and especially from those who live in Spital district where Mr. Hunt's work will chiefly, but not exclusively, be." Herbert Hunt was forty-five years old, and had a good deal of experience in varied parishes. He served his first curacy at Tenbury in Herefordshire from 1879-1885, and then became curate at Holy Cross, Shrewsbury until 1889. He became Vicar of Wyke in the Yorkshire mining district until 1892, when he returned to Tenbury as Vicar until 1895. 1896 saw his appointment as curate of St. Peter, Bournemouth until he came to Clewer in 1900.

If the new service times were anything to go by, it would seem that Herbert Hunt made a promising but cautious start to his ministry in Spital. The pattern of worship was to be as follows:-

Sunday:- Choral Celebration on Greater Festivals and Third Sunday at 11.00 a.m. preceded by early Celebration at 7.30 a.m.

Other Sundays: Celebration at 8.00 a.m.

Sunday School - 2.15 p.m. followed at 3.15 p.m. by Children's Service.

Evensong - 6.30 p.m.

Weekdays:- Wednesdays and Holy Days, Celebration at 7.30 a.m.

Wednesdays 7.30 p.m. Evensong with Sermon.

Thursdays 7.30 p.m. Evensong.

The problem of accommodation, this time by the choir, was again keenly felt. For some time they had been singing from the gallery where the harmonium was situated, but this proved unsatisfactory as the boys were badly behaved. Mr. Hunt commented in the Parish Magazine, "It is unreasonable to expect good behaviour on the part of the youthful members of the Choir when they are out of sight of their elders and can neither see nor be seen." It was decided to place the choir boys in the front row of the nave, and the choir men on the North side of the Santuary as an experiment.

By the beginning of 1901, parish life had once again settled into the usual pattern. The Mother's Meeting had been resumed, likewise the Men's Social Club. The Sunday School thrived, and even after the 'irregular attenders had been "weeded out", there were still one hundred and thirty at the Christmas Treat and they enjoyed themselves despite the breakdown of the Magic Lantern.

St. Agnes' Day dawned with prayers at the early celebration for Queen Victoria, who lay dying at Osborne House on the Isle of Wight. The Parish Supper could hardly be cancelled, "though we felt almost ashamed of our innocent enjoyment." During the course of the supper came the news of Her Majesty's death, "needless to say, it was felt that the only thing to do was to disperse quickly and quietly." We are told that the Festal Evensong on the Monday and Tuesday (i.e. the Eve and the Festival iteself) "were not allowed to lose their brightness", and that "even under the cloud of sorrow . . . . Choir and people joined with vigour and heartiness in their hymns of praise." The preachers were the Revd. George Jones on a welcome return visit, and the Revd. G. D. Nicholas. A requiem for the late Queen was celebrated at St. Agnes' on Friday, February 1st and three people received Communion, though there may have been more present.

June 1901 saw the death of one of St. Agnes' most staunch supporters, Joseph Shipton, aged sixty-two. He had been a faithful member since the days of worshipping at the Cemetery Chapel and his death was a great loss to the church. Mr. Hunt wrote of him, "a real friend we all felt him to be - always cheery, always unselfish . . . . a true Christian and enthusiastic Churchman, he seemed the very centre of our congregation, and we feel we shall be conscious for a long time of the gap he has left . . . . But how full of thankfulness should we be for all he did and all he was, how anxious to follow the example and carry on the work with the same earnestness and simplicity, how desirous that our end may be as was his, full of humble hope and fortified by that 'Food by the way' which he received so cheerfully and thankfully in his last hours . . . . . " He was buried in Clewer Churchyard and the St. Agnes' choir and many of the congregation were present. A simple cross of lilies was laid on his grave.

July 8th was the occasion of the Mothers' Meeting Summer outing to Bisham Abbey, the home of Mr. and Mrs. Vansittart Neale. In the words of the Parish Magazine " . . . the long procession of brakes . . . . was headed by an imposing load of Spital ladies, and we received the additional honour of claiming the adventurous member, who, when starting on a voyage, couldn't make up her mind if she preferred land or water, and tried both at once and went 'topsy-turvey' in the attempt."

A Flower Service, something new in the life of the Church, was held at the end of August. It was held in the Church garden, as large numbers were anticipated! The Sunday School children and their teachers, headed by the choir, marched in procession from Clewer Lodge, home of Mrs. Carpenter Rowe, singing hymns to the accompaniment of a Cornet. Everyone was asked to bring either a bunch of flowers, or a money contribution, which would be sent to a London Hospital. This service was held regularly for a number of years.

The Harvest Festival of 1901 was well supported as usual, and it also marked the resumption of the weekly Choral Eucharist, although Mr. Hunt had been somewhat reluctant to do so - "Many have expressed their regret at its discountinance, unavoidable though it has been; but I feel bound to say that on the one Sunday in the month on which it has been held, the attendance has been anything but satisfactory . . . and I appeal to all those who value the Eucharist . . . to make every effort to be present however often or seldom the opportunity is given them."

Canon Carter died on October 28th 1901 (for details of his funeral see Introduction I: Carter of Clewer). There is no record in the service register of a Requiem although it may not have been entered as such. In a Deed of Conveyance dated June 17th 1901, Canon Carter handed over to the Rector of Clewer and his successors St. Agnes' Chapel, Mission Room and Cottage. Because his death occured less than twelve months after the date of the original Deed of Conveyance, a second Deed had to be drawn up by his daughters, re-iterating the terms of the original Deed. This was dated April 24th 1902, but I regret having been unable to trace a copy of this document. Thus the Revd. Arthur Cowie was now the legal owner of St. Agnes', and, as we shall see, he was not entirely pleased with his acquisition. He was very anxious to see St. Agnes' consecrated and adopted into the Diocesan system, and he realised that while this irregular arrangement prevailed it might act as a barrier to this end. As the action taken by him still lay a few years ahead, we will return to it in due course.

Towards the end of 1901 the Mission Rooms were thoroughly redecorated, and as a result of a Rummage Sale the work was paid for with a small balance in hand. (The sale raised £5.19.5d and the work cost £5.2.0d). During the Spring of 1902 the Church was redecorated inside, the expense of which was guaranteed by the Rector, although in fact £7.0.0d was raised by St. Agnes' congregation. The work necessitated the temporary closure of the church, during which time the congregation attended the other churches in the parish. The gallery still remained unpainted and it was hoped to complete the work by voluntary help.

The Church finances were beginning to look healthier than they had been for many years, mainly because a few wealthy people were taking a benevolent interest, chiefly Mrs. Carpenter Rowe. Several gifts are recorded at this time such as surplices and hymn books for the choir, a prayer book for the lectern and a Communicants' kneeler, the benefactors being Miss Commins, Mrs. Hunt and Miss Layton.

1902 was 'Coronation Year'. After the sobriety of the last years of Victoria's reign, the atmosphere was one of euphoria. June saw the end of the Boer War with victory for Great Britain - just in time to add to the already festive spirit. June 26th was Coronation Day, and throughout the land everyone prepared for the great occasion; treats and entertainments were planned, Church services prepared, choirs rehearsed, composers prepared new works. In Clewer Parish a Choral Eucharist was to be celebrated in all three churches at 11.00 a.m. Then on June 23rd the King was taken ill with appendicitis and at that time the operation was considered dangerous. Anxiety replaced merriment; services of intercession were held in place of Eucharists of thanksgiving. At St. Agnes' thirteen people were present at a Special Eucharist 'for the King's restoration to health.' The King recovered and the Coronation was able to go ahead six weeks later on Saturday, August 9th, although many 'official' engagements were cancelled due to His Majesty's still weak state of health. The following comments are recorded in the Parish Magazine, "The musical arrangements at St. Agnes' made with a view to the Coronation in June were sucessfully and happily carried out on August 10th (Sunday). At the Choral Celebration the Choir sang with great expression Mr. Fenner's graphic and solemn setting of 'Zadok the Priest' and at Evensong it goes without saying that the congregation took up he Coronation hymns with that vigour and heartiness which marks their singing."

By 1903 life at St. Agnes' was proceeding at a steady pace. Herbert Hunt seems to have been a good 'sound' priest who cared for his church and people, but he was not an extreme 'ritualist'. In this respect he seems to have been far more moderate than some of his predecessors. His motto seems to have been 'Proceed with caution.' By lent 1903 his work was beginning to bear fruit - the previous Christmas Day had seen seventy-seven Communicants, the highest ever, and he made plans for extra Lent services and addresses. His wife's contribution to parish life had also been deeply appreciated, and at the St. Agnes' Supper she had been presented with a leather writing case and an address from the members of the Mothers' Meeting. It, therefore, came as a deep shock when, quite suddenly at the beginning of Lent, Mr. Hunt suffered a complete breakdown and was unable to carry on with his work. This may have been a recurrence of previous trouble, for he had been Vicar of successive parishes, only to give them up for curacies at Bournemouth and the present one at Clewer. Whether or not this was so, Hunt never worked again. He retired to Richmond, Surrey and later to Torquay, where he lived until 1938 when he would have been eighty-three years old.

The Rector described the atmosphere at Spital as one of "great gloom", and he was very anxious to find a priest to take Mr. Hunt's place as quickly as possible. Services were maintained chiefly by S. K. Tahourdin. One of the chief problems concerning an appointment was accommodation, but this was again temporarily overcome, and in July 1903 the Revd. Walter Saunders Hulme was appointed and took up residence at 'Winton Cottage', Alma Road. Like Hunt he had considerable experience, this being his seventh appointment. He was aged about forty-seven, was married, and had latterly been curate at Tisbury in Wiltshire. Unlike his predecessors at St. Agnes' he was not a university graduate which was unusual for a clergyman at this time.

Sunday services were to be:-

7.30 a.m. Holy Eucharist

3.15 p.m. Children's Service

6.30 p.m. Evensong and Sermon

In addition there was to be a monthly Choral Eucharist. The only weekday services were on Wednesday, 7.30 a.m. Holy Eucharist,and 7.30 p.m. Evensong and Sermon (as in Hunt's time). As from October 1903 Mattins and Sermon was introduced every Sunday at 10.30 a.m. and the Choral Eucharist was abandoned, even on major festivals such as Christmas Day, Easter and Whitsun. It is ironical that at this time Hulme was endeavouring to start a 'Communicants' Guild' "as a means of banding us together", though it does not appear to have passed the formative stages.

Weekly Mattins did not appeal to the congregation who were used to the Choral Eucharist. Writing in the Parish Magazine for December 1903 Hulme had this to say, ". . . this service has been appreciated by a few, the congregation numbering about ten or twelve, but as the congregation includes men, women and children, we would earnestly appeal to old and young to try and attend this service, so that it may be a help to them in their preparation for the observance of Christmas Day." As to this observance, "There were forty-one Communicants on the day itself and eleven on the Sunday after, but what has become of the thirty others who made their Communion last year?" The organist and choir took great pains to get up the music for the services connected with Mattins and Evensong and in spirit of that we are very sorry to have to state that very few people came to either service; but yet we gratefully own that the services were bright and hearty."

So it seems that numbers were 'falling away' in Hulme's time, due mainly to his policy regarding worship. There were, of course, the stalwarts who kept the work going - Miss Commins and Miss Bedborough are mentioned again and again in the Parish Magazines, particularly at festivals when it seems that they did most of the work of decorating the church. The Revd. S. K. Tahourdin did much to keep up the 'spiritual temperature' - he was frequent celebrant and preacher, indeed his signature appears in the register almost as frequently as Hulme's. F. T. H. Shepherd (Chaplain, House of Mercy) and Launcelot Mitchell (Priest-in-charge of Dedworth) also assisted regularly. Tahourdin also helped keep the social life of the parish moving along. For instance, he and Oscar Fenner organised a Concert in the Mens' Club room (Upper Room) on St. Agnes' Day 1904. We are told that the room was 'quite full' and that the Rector was present as Chairman. There is no mention of a Supper as in previous years, and it will be noted that the room was only 'quite' full, not 'bursting at the seams', or a 'tight squeeze' as previously.

The Men's Club continued to meet but the Spital section of the Mothers' Meeting seems to have been in abeyance. Likewise other social activities such as penny readings, lantern shows, etc., seem to have been at a standstill.

On Good Friday 1904 four of the services were taken by a visiting preacher, the Revd. Edward Collett, and Evensong by S. K. Tahourdin, none at all by Walter Hulme, though he may have been preaching elsewhere. Both celebrations on Easter Day were taken by Tahourdin, who also conducted Evensong. Hulme officiated and preached at Mattins only.

The July issue of the Parish Magazine contained this terse note from Mr. Hulme. "It was hoped that there will be more than one person in church on Wednesdays, and in accordance with the rubric there should be three at least, otherwise there will be no Celebration."

It was obvious that things could not go on this way indefinitely. The church was emptying, the people were becoming alienated, all the work of the last thirty years or more was being undone. In the August Parish Magazine the Rector announced, "Mr. Hulme has left us for work at Wooburn Green. We shall all wish Mr. and Mrs. Hulme success and happiness in their new sphere of work . . . " That is all - no fond farewells, no presentations in crowded halls, no purses of sovereigns, no illuminated address. Whether Mr. Hulme resigned or whether the Rector dismissed him is not certain, but the latter is more than likely. Obviously he was not the 'right man' for St. Agnes', and the problem went deeper than that of imposing Mattins on a congregation who wanted Choral Eucharist. The tone of his comments in the Parish Magazine indicates that he was completely out of sympathy with the church and people of Spital. It may be said that the Rector made too hasty a decision when appointing Hulme, but it is easy to understand the Rector's haste, for it was imperative to find a priest to replace Hunt as quickly as possible in order to lift St. Agnes' out of the 'gloom' and to continue the work.

A final word about Hulme. He stayed at Wooburn as Curate until 1905 and then there was a 'gap' in his ministry until 1908 when he became Chaplain of Maidenhead Workhouse until 1910. There is a further two year break, and then in 1912 he became Vicar of Little Tew until 1915, and Rector of Plaitford 1915-1916. He then retired to Maidenhead and died roundabout 1919 aged about sixty-three years. All of his appointments (except for the curacy at Tisbury 1897-1903) seem to have lasted only two or three years which may indicate difficulties of either health or temperament. The two breaks in his ministry may indicate similar difficulties.

## Chapter V

## Edwardian Summer

By 1904 morale at St. Agnes' was very low. Herbert Hunt's ministry had come to an untimely end, and Walter Hulme was not "attuned" to the accustomed tradition of St. Agnes'. What was needed was a priest who combined missionary zeal with cheerfulness, gaiety of spirit and the ability to win people's hearts. The Rector found such a man in the Revd. Charles Farr.

Ordained deacon in 1899 and priest in 1900, Charles Farr was an Associate of King's College, London, and had trained for the Ministry at St. Stephen's House, Oxford. He served as curate, firstly at St. Paul's, Bermondsey 1899-1901, and then at St. Michael and All Angels, Bromley-by-Bow, Poplar, in the heart of London's dockland from 1901-1904. He was about twenty-seven years old when he came to St. Agnes'. Slighty built, with a boyish mop of hair, his smile was slightly crooked due to the after effects of a broken jaw, sustained in an Oxford boxing contest.

The Rector had this to say in the Parish Magazine by way of welcome, "Mr. Farr has had five years Mission work in the East of London and is strongly recommended to us as a faithful and zealous priest by the Bishop of Stepney and his late Vicar, Mr. Battiscombe, Vicar of St. Michael's, Poplar, East. Mr. and Mrs. Farr will doubtless receive a most warm and hearty welcome from us all. Let us not forget to add our prayers to our good wishes on their behalf."

Charles Farr took up office in August 1904 immediately after Mr. Hulme's departure and resided at 'Prospect Cottage', Clewer Hill. He set about the work with an enthusiasm which fast proved infectious. The people loved him - from the youngest choirboys, who affectionately dubbed him "Charlie", to the oldest members of the congregation. Whilst he was 'always the Priest', he was also 'just like one of the family'. It was this ability to mix with people and make them feel at ease with him, which made him popular with those who did not attend church as well as those who did.

Mr. Farr introduced himself in the September issue of the Parish Magazine, "a new sphere of work is generally trying and difficult at first - surroundings, however beautiful, are unfamiliar - everybody is strange - methods and uses are different to what one has been accustomed - but the very kind, hearty and sympathetic manner with which everyone has received me, makes me feel deeply thankful, and I would earnestly ask the prayers of all to whom I am called to minister, that our Heavenly Father will give me grace to serve Him faithfully and well, and that He will abundantly bless our efforts at St. Agnes' . . . "

By the end of 1904 services had been re-established in the accustomed tradition of St. Agnes':-

| | | |
|---|---|---|
| Sundays: | Holy Communion | 8.00 a. m. |
| | Mattins | 10.30 a. m. |
| | Choral Eucharist | 11.00 a. m. |
| | Catechism | 3.00 p. m. |
| | Evensong and Sermon | 6.30 p. m. |

There were also Celebrations of the Eucharist on four weekdays, including one on Saturdays, which was for the children in particular, and this was well supported with an average twenty-four present, sometimes more.

Social activities and clubs re-commenced from September onwards, starting with the Mothers' Meeting, the leadership of which was taken by Mrs. Farr. The mens' Club also re-opened and the age limit was raised from seventeen to eighteen years. A new venture was begun in the shape of a Boys' Club for Sunday School members. The Penny Readings, so sucessful during the ministry of the Revd. Henry Ley, were revived.

Early in 1905 Oscar Fenner organised a Concert in the Mission Room in aid of Church funds. It consisted of songs, duets, recitations and a piano solo and, we are told, that "the programme was all that could be desired - bright, humorous and attractive. There was not a dull moment from beginning to end. The Mission Room was crowded to its utmost capacity and everybody went away delighted." So successful did this prove that another was held later in the year. These concerts were to become an integral part of the social life of Spital right up to the time of World War II.

Alongside the concerts there were also 'Communicants' Socials'. At such a social on October 12th 1905 we are told that "Master George Kelsey presided at the piano." This is the first mention of Master Kelsey in the Parish records (his parents' record of Church attendance dated back to the days at the Cemetery Chapel, and they had been staunch supporters ever since). In years to come George Kelsey 'presided' at the piano at all the Church Socials, and I am told that he always used the same music, which with the passage of time became increasingly tattered! Anyway October 1905 saw its 'debut'! Besides glees, songs and dancing there was also a gramophone - for many people still a novelty. It seems that the happy gathering was not allowed to disband without a few words from the Rector who " . . . gave us some encouraging words and urged care and attention to religious duties."

By 1905 St. Agnes' was beginning to have more 'material' help from the wealthier residents of the district. Appeals for specific purposes were met with contributions from the local gentry. Even food for the Choir and Workers' Supper was largely donated. Among those who gave temporal assistance during Mr. Farr's ministry were H. R. H. The Princess Christian (who sent money towards a secondhand piano, for which a special appeal had been made); Lady Edward Spencer-Churchill; the Countess of Arran; Lady Dalton-Fitzgerald; Mrs. Carpenter Rowe; Sir Francis and Lady Tress Barry; Sir Theodore Brinckman; Mrs. Rhoda Maclean and Mr. Victor Biddulph. Some of these benefactors and their residences have already been mentioned, but the others seem to have begun to have taken an interest in St. Agnes' at about this time. Lady Edward Spencer-Churchill needs little introduction and many people still remember her, for she lived until 1941. Her residence was Queen's Mead, off King's Road, and is now the Brigidine Convent. Nearby was Queen Anne's Mead, the residence of the Dowager Countess of Arran. Like so many other 'desirable residences' in the King's Road/Osborne Road area, Queen Anne's Mead has been demolished. Lady Dalton-Fitzgerald lived at St. Leonard's Lodge, Winkfield Road, roughly where the modern 'Kimber Close' is now situated. All that remains today is the gate lodge, looking rather out of place against the new houses which are built alongside it.

During the years of their residence in Windsor Lady Dalton-Fitzgerald, together with Mrs. Carpenter Rowe of Clewer Lodge, and Mr. Victor Buddulph, were some of the most generous friends of the Church. Victor Myddleton Biddulph was the son of the late General Sir Thomas and the late Honourable Lady Biddulph. His father had been keeper of the Privy Purse and a Privy Councillor. Victor Biddulph was employed as a clerk in the House of Lords, but was a wealthy man in his own right, who used his money for the good of the Church and his neighbour. He was a lay reader and a stalwart of the Church in Clewer Parish. Throughout Mr. Farr's ministry he worshipped at St. Agnes' but returned to the Parish Church during the last few years of his life, when his health was failing. Born in the Henry III Tower in Windsor Castle, Victor Biddulph was educated at Eton and New College, Oxford. After the Revd. and Mrs. Hunt left Clewer he moved into 'Stansfield' in New Road and lived there for the rest of his life. He was unmarried. A familiar figure in Windsor, he was generally accompanied by a large golden retriever, even when he was riding his bicycle. He reckoned that this faithful dog once saved his life, for when walking down the lonely 'Lovers' Walk', probably on the way to Church, a ruffian attempted to waylay him, but was frightened off by the dog going to his master's rescue. He took great interest in the youth of the parish and made his home available for discussions and hospitality for the young men of Clewer, at a time when there was little in the way of Young Men's Clubs. Spital was fortunate in having a Men's Club, so too had Dedworth, but there was nothing at Clewer.

By this time there was no shortage of Church 'workers', a few of whom were Miss Commins, Miss Bedborough, Miss Beal, Miss Quarterman, Mrs. Layton and Miss Hyatt. Some younger helpers were Miss Violet Pert and Master Sydney Pert, whose father Mr. John Pert became village baker in succession to Mr. Hewitt. Also Miss Ivy Charles and the three Clarke brothers, James, William and Alfred. Doubtless there were many others, but these are just a few familiar names mentioned in the Clewer Magazine.

New caretakers were appointed in 1905 and they were to fulfil their duties for over twenty years. George and Emma Uglow had previously kept a public house in Keppel Street. Mrs. Uglow and Mrs. Charles were sisters. There were two sons, George who died in the Great War, and John (Jack) who lived until May 1979, when he was eighty-one years old.

A major change was made in Sunday worship from early October 1905 when the Sung Eucharist was transferred from 11.00 a. m. to 9.30 a. m. in the hope that more people would attend and also Communicate. The pattern of Sunday worship was thus to be:-

| | |
|---|---|
| Holy Communion | 8.00 a. m. |
| Litany and Holy Eucharist | 9.30 a. m. |
| Mattins and Sermon (Choral) | 11.15 a. m. |
| Catechism | 2.45 p. m. |
| Baptisms | 3.45 p. m. |
| Evensong and Sermon | 6.30 p. m. |

However, by the following Lent the times seen to have been altered yet again, so presumably the 'new arrangments' proved unsatisfactory.
The final times were:-

| | |
|---|---|
| Holy Communion | 8.00 a. m. |
| Mattins | 10.30 a. m. |
| Litany, Holy Eucharist and Sermon | 11.00 a. m. |
| Catechism | 2.45 p. m. |
| Evensong and Sermon | 6.30 p. m. |

A new Guild, known as the St. Agnes' Guild, had been started early in 1905 with about forty members. It had similar objectives to previous Guilds. Also there were Bible Classes for both men and women.

We cannot leave 1905 behind without recording a courageous act on the part of one of the young Church members. In the words of the Clewer Magazine . . . . ."Arthur Foreman, aged thirteen years, one of our Choirboys, proved himself a little hero on Friday, August 25th, when he pluckily rescued Dorothy Cooper from drowning in Swan Pond. Arthur swam out nearly to the middle of the pond and managed to catch hold of the girl's hair as she was sinking for the third time. Having brought her safely to the bank and done his best to restore conciousness he carried her some distance across the Park in spite of the fact that in getting out of the water he had cut his foot badly on a broken bottle. The matter has been placed in the hands of the Royal Humane Society and we hope Arthur Foreman will receive a well deserved reward." Arthur's bravery was indeed rewarded. During the interval at a Concert held in the Mission Rooms on November 9th the Rector presented him with the Royal Humane Society's Certificate. It was handed to Arthur by Dorothy Cooper, the girl whose life he saved.

Charles Farr's first full year of ministry in Spital ended on a hopeful note. Spiritual life had revived (total Communions for 1905 were one thousand two hundred and sixty-four as opposed to eight hundred and fifty-five for 1904), and social life was thriving. Money was still a problem when it came to day-to-day running costs, but at least for a time there were some wealthy friends who, when it came to 'treats' and special appeals, were very generous.

The children of St. Agnes' were given a Christmas treat which doubtless they remembered for long after December 1905. We are told that ". . . .there were one hundred and thirty children present, who did ample justice to the excellent tea provided for them, and their delight was unbounded when they saw the lovely tree a blaze of light, and hung with pretty and useful gifts. Besides the tree, Lady Dalton-Fitzgerald had most kindly and thoughtfully chosen a suitable present for each child, some of the older girls receiving warm cloaks or gloves. The prizes were given away by Lady Fitzgerald, the children showing their great appreciation of their splendid treat by continuous and ringing cheers when she left the Mission Room. At the close of the Gramophone Entertainment, Mr. Knight was also enthusiastically cheered. An orange, a bun and a bag of sweets were given to each child as they left the room . . . Sister Agnes gave all the children beautifully illuminated Christmas Cards." Such treats had been provided for the children of All Saints', Dedworth, for a number of years through the kindness of Lady Mary Currie, a wealthy widow who resided at Clewer Hill House. However, nothing of the kind had been done at Spital until 1905, but henceforth these treats were to become part of the 'St. Agnes' Year' for many years to come. Nowadays, children have an abundance of Christmas presents, and parties are so frequent as to be almost commonplace, but in the early days of the present century there was precious little extra at Christmas for the average working class family. Not without reason were these parties known as 'treats', for it was often the only treat a child had.

The gift of a Magic Lantern had enabled Mr. Farr to provide Lantern Services during Lent 1906, and these had proved very successful. The Church had been packed with children for their service, and on two occasions the door had to be closed for no more could be accommodated. A second service for adults had been equally well attended, and indeed had attracted many who would not have come to an ordinary service.

A new venture was the formation of the St. Agnes' Dramatic Society in the Spring of 1906.Two 'Comic Sketches' were performed on April 18th and the Mission Room was "crowded to its utmost capacity." The production was directed by Mr. Ernest Higgins who had recently come to work in the Parish. A further concert in December consisted of songs and two farces. Parts were taken by the Misses Bridges, Miss Charles, Messrs. Clarke, Bridges, Hughes, Vokins, and Caudell.

A social event which had become something of an institution was the Clewer Horticultural Society Show, held since 1884 in the grounds of Clewer Manor by kind permission of Mr. and Mrs. Foster. Like mighty oaks, this event had grown from very small beginnings, but by the period under review it had become of major importance locally, and was participated in by all classes. From the large mansions, whose wealthy occupants sent floral displays, and whose head gardeners vied with one another for the best exhibit, down to the cottagers who competed for prizes with their garden produce, everyone took part and thoroughly enjoyed it. However, it was not only the Flower and Produce Show which made this August Bank Holiday Monday event so popular. There were other attractions too such as sports, dancing, swings, coconut shies, sideshows and a Band. It all contributed to make a jolly day, away from the normal long day's work, and was to continue to do so until the old way of life was swept away in the aftermath of 1914-18.

January 4th and 5th 1907 saw the Sunday School treats (senior and infants). At the Senior treat the prizes, which had been donated by Lady Dalton-Fitzgerald, were distributed by Mrs. Carpenter Rowe. The entertainment took the form of a lantern show - always a favourite.

St. Agnes'-tide 1907 was a stirring time. There were several guest preachers during the Octave and the Festival, including the Rector; the Revd. W. Anderson (Curate Clewer St. Stephen); the Revd. R. P. Quilter (Chaplain, Clewer House of Mercy); and the Warden of the House of Mercy, the Revd. G. S. Cuthbert. However, the 'star attraction' was the Revd. Arthur Henry Stanton, curate of St. Alban's, Holborn. It is not an exaggeration to say that Arthur Stanton was one of the greatest priests of the Anglican Church since the start of the revival of 1833. He was already an ageing man when he came to St. Agnes', and by the time he died in 1913 he had served as curate at the same Church for half a centry. Ordained in 1862, Bishop Tait of London had warned him, "If you go to Mackonochie of St. Alban's you must never expect any Church preferment." So it was to be, but this never deterred Stanton, even though Bishop after Bishop inhibited him from preaching in their dioceses. For what reason? Simply because St. Alban's, Holborn was an Anglo-Catholic stronghold and because Mackonochie had pronounced 'ritualist' views which he would not compromise. (Alexander Heriot Mackonochie, Vicar of St. Alban's was hounded through the Courts by the Church Association for sixteen years. When he was finally persuaded, as a death-bed wish of Archbishop Tait, to exchange his benefice for that of St. Peter's London Docks, his persecutors continued the onslaught there. Having been driven to resign this benefice too, he died a broken man, wandering in a blizzard in the Scottish Highlands).

Arthur Stanton was one of the few priests at this time to be accorded the title 'Father', though it is a sign of the love his people had for him that they usually called him 'Dad'. His personality was so magnetic that he drew people to St. Alban's who might never have normally entered a church. Once inside they were riveted, for in the midst of all the ceremonial Stanton's sermons were full of Evangelical fervour. He once described himself as a "Catholic Evangelical". He never wrote his sermons in full but entered the pulpit with the basic idea and preached extempore.

Father Stanton was no stranger to the Windsor area, for his sister, Mrs. Devas, had lived at Woodside in the Windsor Forest, and he had spent many happy times there in his youth. He also seriously considered a curacy at Holy Trinity, Windsor, as he recounted in a letter to his mother, "Before I came to him (Mackonochie) I refused to serve a curacy at Windsor, which I should have liked beyond all others as the garrison would have been given to me, simply because I was told I must not boldly declare my colours . . . " There were also links with Clewer through the Sisters, who had been working in St. Alban's Parish since 1869. No doubt Charles Farr was well acquainted with Stanton through his years in dockland, and possibly the Rector would have known him from his period as curate at St. Paul's, Knightsbridge.

Anticipating a large crowd, arrangements were made for the regular St. Agnes' congregation to enter church through the vestry before 6.00 p. m. in order to secure a seat. "By this means we were enabled to accommodate some outsiders, not many, considering the smallness of our space . . . Evensong was heartily sung and Fr. Stanton chose as his text the last words of the last Book of the Bible 'Our Lord Jesus Christ' . . . A wonderful discourse, after which Te Deum was sung." This was the first of five visits to St. Agnes' by Fr. Stanton. 'The church was absolutely packed', recalls an elderly resident of Spital who still vividly remembers those visits.

The February issue of the Clewer Magazine recounts how the St. Agnes' Dramatic Society gave a performance of "Cinderella" on two nights. Indeed, the venture even gained a review in the "Windsor and Eton Express". Among those taking part were some familiar names in Spital - Miss E. Russell (The Prince), Miss Ivy Charles (Fairy Godmother), who with her attendant fairies "made an entrancing picture"; Mr. Ernest Higgins (The Baron); Mrs. Charles (The Baroness);Miss Millie Bridges (Cinderella), who "evoked much applause when drawn across the stage in her chariot by the fairy escort"; Mr. Bridges and Mr. Caudell (the two Ugly Sisters); John Uglow (Page); and Mr. Foreman. Miss Green accompanied the items in the programme, and Master George

Kelsey occupied the piano during the performance "and played well". The Mission Room was so crowded on each night that many had to be turned away. Looking at the same room nowadays, it is very difficult to imagine how anything so ambitious could have been contemplated. An elderly gentleman who used to manage the seating arrangements assures me that he could accommodate one hundred to one hundred and twenty people on wooden forms "if they pushed up together a bit"!

Sir Francis Tress Barry, baronet, died early in March 1907 and was laid to rest in Clewer Churchyard on March 5th, his body being conveyed, according to local tradition, on one of his own farm wagons through the forest, down Langley's Lane (now Wolf Lane) to All Saints', Dedworth Church and from there to Clewer Churchyard. He was eighty-one. The Rector wrote of him, "Possessed of great wealth, he seemed only to value it as a means of doing good. His gifts to public works of utility, were indeed on a princely scale, but bore no comparison with what he did in private, where his munificence knew no bounds. He has left behind him a most valuable example to men of wealth - an example inspired by deep religious convictions and one which cannot fail to leave an abiding impression for good on all who came in contact with him."

Lent came soon after the Patronal Festival and followed the pattern of former years. The Three Hours Devotion on Good Friday was preached by the Revd. S. K. Tahourdin. Services on Easter Day were well attended and there were ninety-three Communicants plus the sick and housebound. On Whit Sunday Clewer Parish Church had a visit from Revd. Cyril Bickersteth, C. R., who had been the Missioner in the 1896 Parish Mission. The following day he came to St. Agnes' where he presided at the Sung Eucharist at 8.00 a. m. There were twenty-two people, and nine received Holy Communion.

## Chapter VI

### Without let or hindrance

For many years accommodation had been a major problem at St. Agnes'. It had been temporarily resolved by the addition of the gallery, but now, with ever increasing numbers, it had to be faced fairly and squarely. The only solution lay in an extension to the church. With this in mind the Rector wrote in the May and July Magazines, "Mr. Farr's earnest and devoted work at Spital has brought us face to face with the fact that St. Agnes' Chapel is altogether inadequate to the needs of that large district. The greater part of Spital, no doubt, belongs to Windsor Parish, but there the needs are even more apparent than in our own portion. We have to provide for nine hundred souls, and as St. Agnes' Chapel is only capable at the utmost stretch of accommodating eighty worshippers the result is that many have to be turned away for want of room. St. Agnes' has a Communicant Roll of one hundred and forty of whom one hundred and nine Communcated last Easter; there are in the Sunday School one hundred and forty-five children. A scheme is now being considered for the enlargement of the present building and plans have been laid before us which, if carried out, would more than double the present accommodation. No doubt eventually a Church will have to be built for the whole of Spital district, but in the meanwhile, the need is pressing. The present site . . is sufficient for the proposed enlargement. It is true that St. Agnes' Chapel, through the generous gift of the late Canon Carter, subsequently confirmed by his family, is my own private property; but it is my intention, as soon as the Enlargement is carried out, to resign all proprietary rights and, by having the Chapel dedicated by the Bishop of the Diocese, to place it on a sound parochial footing. The total cost of the Enlargement will not exceed £500 towards which sum upwards of £200 has already been guaranteed. I now appeal therefore for the remaining £200."

The contributions already received were from the Rector (£100) and Mr. Victor Biddulph (£100). Within a week of the launching of the appeal £76 was received, including donations from Lady Barry (2 guineas); Lord Edward Spencer-Churchill (£5); the Revd. S. K. Tahourdin (£5); the Revd. G. D. Nicholas (5 guineas); the Revd. the Marquis of Normanby (5 guineas); the Revd. G. S. Cuthbert (£10). A donation of £2 was later received from the Revd. Roland Errington. In addition to donations from wealthy benefactors, many of the Spital people had collecting cards and gathered weekly subscriptions for the Building Fund. People were encouraged to "buy a brick", and in this way, brick by brick, penny by penny, a substantial proportion of the money was raised.

Fund raising events were also held including a Sale of Work at the Rectory, and another at "White Lilies", in Clewer Village, the home of Mr. and Mrs. Vanderbyl. This latter sale was opened by the Dowager Countess of Arran and raised £21.15.9d. A fund raising event of a slightly different nature took the form of a show of Marionettes in the Mission Room. This was given by Mr. Curling, a professional entertainer, who always worshipped at St. Agnes' on his visits to Windsor. On this occasion he gave two-thirds of his profits to the Enlargement Fund.

With all the hard work associated with fund raising, it must not be thought that St. Agnes' people were too busy to enjoy their annual summer outings Sixty-nineMothers from the whole parish enjoyed a visit to All Saints' Home, Hawley, near Blackwater, on June 25th. This was an orphanage run by the Clewer Sisters. (St. Andrew's, Clewer, recently acquired 'new' Lady Chapel furnishings from the now redundant Chapel at Hawley). Notwithstanding the inclement weather, the Mothers enjoyed themselves greatly.

On July 15th the men from St. Agnes' Choir joined the men and boys of Clewer and Dedworth Choirs for a day at Weston-super-Mare. Seventy men left Windsor at 6.00 a.m. and did not return home again until past midnight. "No-one, not even the smallest boys, seemed a penny the worse." Finally, on August 12th the St. Agnes' choirboys enjoyed a visit to Portsmouth where, after watching the King's yacht pass by, they were taken on a conducted tour of H. M. S. Goliath. They also saw battleships, cruisers, destroyers, torpedo boats, submarines and the famous 'Dreadnought'.

By October the builders had moved in and work had begun. Fortunately, for posterity's sake, the exterior of the Church was photographed before the builders took over. Not only the Church but also the Mission Rooms and Cottage were clad in ivy, so that in some cases the windows were almost completely obscured. At the East end of the Church the growth had been allowed to ascend even to the apex of the roof. An interested little group of children in pinafores and wide-brimmed summer hats cluster around a perambulator in the foreground, and a bit further back Mrs. Rosier stands in her garden holding one of her infants. (See Plate 2).

The builders anticipated taking about ten weeks, and it was Mr. Farr's hope that the work would be completed free of debt. The cost, including architect's fees and furnishings, would be in the region of £500 and there was still £172 to raise.

The builders, William Green & Sons, were a local firm who as well as general building work, undertook work for the Diocese. Mr. Green's grandson, Mr Arthur Green, lives in retirement in Spital and is a member of St. Agnes' congregation. It was Mr Arthur Green's father who was actually in charge of the Church enlargement.

Building operations did not interfere with the Harvest celebrations on October 6th and 7th when we are told, "The church looked at its best. Mr. Pert gave us some splendid loaves which were placed on the altar steps, and Mr. Clarke decorated the Altar Cross with wheat." At Evensong the Church was filled to overflowing. During Mr. Farr's ministry the Harvest services were always repeated on the Monday, and these too were well attended with the Rector preaching at Evensong.

It was 'business as usual' during the building operations, as this extract from the December magazine shows, "Evicted. This is literally the case! On Monday, the 11th instant, the Church was abandoned to the builders, who have broken through the South wall to go on with the enlargement, and on the following Saturday we were told that we could not have the Church the next day. There was nothing for it but to fit up the Mission Room as a Church for the time being. Accordingly the platform was fitted up as a Chancel, an Altar was set up with the proper fittings, and on each side Choir stalls were extemporised. The whole of the Services thus went on as usual, without let or hindrance, the piano supplying the place of the organ. We shall probably be in the same condition next Sunday, and should be rather grateful if a violinist would volunteer assistance for the 11.00 a. m. Choral Eucharist. It would be a good addition to the piano."

By St. Agnes' Eve 1908 the Church extension was complete, but alas, the debt was still not cleared, there being well nigh £200 still to raise. By April the margin had narrowed, but the last elusive £100 was still needed and subscriptions had almost ceased to come in. Mr. Victor Biddulph once more rallied to the cause and cleared off the remaining debt, so that by Easter the work was paid for. The total cost was £534:4:11d. The Rector paid great tribute to the great effort made by all. "This excellent result is due, in no small measure, to the generosity of one benefactor,but the splendid way in which all, even the poorest, did their part in both giving and getting together the sum required, is the best proof that the work was needed, and that the blessing of God will rest upon it."

However, we are anticipating events and must go back to St. Agnes'-tide 1908. The first Evensong of the Festival afforded the first opportunity for the use of the enlarged Church and everyone was most favourably impressed with the 'new and very handsome interior.' The preacher was the Revd. H. O. Shore of Farnham Common and, we are told, that "for the first time in our history" the Procession took its proper place at the conclusion of Evensong. On the Festal Day itself there were fifty-eight Communicants at four celebrations, the last being the Choral Eucharist and Procession at 11.00 a. m. Just before the Choral Eucharist began a telegram addressed to Mr. Farr arrived, "from one of our best and truest friends, the revered Bishop of Lincoln, who is known to many of us, and who has always manifested a deep and sincere interest in our work." Before preaching his sermon, the Rector read the telegram from the pulpit: "May God guide and bless you and all with you." He then preached on the text from II Kings, Ch.6.v.1. "And the sons of the prophets said unto Elisha, 'Behold now the place where we dwell with thee is too strait for us.'" In the evening, despite heavy fog, the church was crowded for a visit from Father Stanton, who preached at Evensong. His text was Phillipians Ch.4.v.4: "Rejoice in the Lord alway, and again I say, Rejoice." Some indication of the numbers who came may be gained from the fact that over £6 was taken in the collection - a colossal sum for one service at a village Church over seventy years ago.

On Monday, January 27th, the Bishop of Reading, the Right Revd. James Leslie Randall, Dedicated the Church. We are told that, "with appropriate Psalms, the Bishop was escorted from the porch to his seat in the Sanctuary. Here he performed the Service of Dedication . . . After this, followed a shortened form of Evensong and the Bishop gave a most helpful address, dwelling upon the unique structure which has been given to our Church, the Altar being visible to all within it . . . At the conclusion of the service was sung the hymn 'Round the Sacred City gather Egypt, Edom, Babylon'". Among the clergy present were the Revd. G. Foster (Sub-Warden, House of Mercy); the Revd. G. D. Nicholas and the Revd. E. A. Thorne (Clewer. St. Stephen); the Revd. J. M. C. Crum and the Revd, Everett (Windsor Parish). The days services were concluded by the regular Evensong which was sung at 7.30 p. m., the Bishop again taking his place in the Sanctuary. The preacher was Revd. W. La Trobe Bateman, Rector of Ascot Heath, and the Church was quite full.

The narrative of the Parish Magazine indicates that the Bishop Dedicated the whole Church, not just the extension. Maybe the Rector had doubts as to whether Canon Carter had ever Dedicated the original building for, as we have already seen in Chapter I, the original Dedication date is uncertain. Alternatively, the Rector may have felt that the Bishop should Dedicate the whole Church as an initial step towards St. Agnes' formal incorporation into the Diocesan system as a daughter Church of St.Andrew's.

It has already been noted that the Rector was unhappy about the legal status of St. Agnes' and had determined to do something about it when the idea of extending the Church was first mooted. He, therefore, took Counsel's opinion to ascertain whether the legal status of the Church could be altered. It was the opinion of Mr. W. R. Sheldon of Lincoln's Inn that the second Deed of Conveyance (Miss J. F. M. Carter to the Revd. A. T. C. Cowie, April 24th 1902) was a good conveyance and that its effect was to make the property part of the endowment of the benefice in the same way that glebe lands are held. This is why a later Rector, the Revd.William Elwell, wrote in his 'History of Clewer Parish Church' that St. Agnes' Spital is part of Clewer Glebe. There have been later attempts to 'regularise' St. Agnes' position but so far to no avail - it would seem that nothing can alter it.

St. Agnes' Spital in 1908 looked exactly as it does today - from the outside at least. Two of the original four lancet windows from the old South wall were retained and set into the extended West wall. The stained glass from these has recently been renovated. A large window incorporating five clear glazed lancets graced the new South wall, and must have made a dramatic difference to the lighting of the Church. It was claimed that the altar was visible from all parts of the Church, a claim I would consider debatable. The new aisle not only gave extra seating for the congregation but also provided a haven for the Choir, who sat in the part which is now the Lady Chapel Sanctuary, but which in 1908 was not furnished as a chapel. Their benches faced sideways to the altar as in a conventional 'Choir', and a long-standing problem was thus solved.

Incidentally, Mrs. Carpenter Rowe gave some coconut matting for the aisle of the Church. No doubt she would have been somewhat surprised to know that they were replaced seventy years later, when a generous present-day benefactress gave new carpets!

The opening of the enlarged church seems to overshadow all other events of 1908 but one or two items must be noted before moving on.

An anonymous gift was given in the form of a Statue of the Good Shepherd. It later became known, after his death, that the donor was none other than Father Stanton. Later in the year Mr. Lawrence Brooks, a member of the congregation, gave an oak pedestal and canopy for the statue.

Social events such as outings, treats, concerts, proceeded as usual. Two choirboys, George Uglow Jnr. and Cecil Cooper, arranged a Concert on April 30th. In the words of Mr. Farr, "It is cheering to feel that even the boys are anxious to help on the work of our Church. They are full of mischief though. Don't think they are very tame. We thank and congratulate them on their successful entertainment."

The fourth Sunday in Advent saw Ernest Higgins' ordination as deacon at Bristol Cathedral. The St. Agnes' congregation presented him with a silver Communion Set and an album containing the names of the subscribers. He returned to St. Agnes' fairly frequently as a visiting preacher, although he was serving as Curate at St. Jude's, Bristol. In 1913 he moved 'nearer home' to St. Luke's, Kingston-upon-Thames and was there until 1917. He seems to have been in delicate health and was seriously ill during his time at Bristol. His name does not appear in "Crockford" after 1918.

So 1908 passed on - an eventful year and a fruitful one. 1909 dawned in the spirit of joyful 'working together', which was so typical of those years during Charles Farr's ministry and which was epitomised by the celebration of the Patronal Festival.

The Revd. Ernest Higgins, recently ordained, preached at the first Evensong of the Festival. On the day itself the Revd. S. K. Tahourdin was Celebrant and the Rector preached at the Choral Eucharist. Mr Fenner's 'Missa de Sancta Agnete' was sung as usual,and we are told that the service was very solemn and devout. Before the service commenced a telegram from Dr. King, Bishop of Lincoln, was read: "May God guide you all and bless you, and refresh you with His presence and His love - E. Lincoln." The high point of the Festival was undoubtedly the visit of Father Stanton, who preached at Evensong. "It was delightful to see how he remembered us all - boys and men in the Choir, and all connected with the Church, and, needless to say, all were glad to see him." The service concluded with the Processional hymn "Bride of Christ". Father Stanton's biographer, G. W. E. Russell, recounts a curious incident which doubtless took place at St. Agnes', but there is no mention of it in the parish records:- "Early in 1909, Stanton was preaching in a Church not far from Windsor, and said in his sermon that, after preaching, he sometimes sat over the fire and wondered whether what he had said was true, or whether he meant all he had said. This excited a clerical brother in the congregation, who entered the pulpit after a hymn had been sung, and said that, for his own part, he never said what he did not know was true, and what he did not mean. The action was unwise and gave offence. The offender wrote to Stanton and expressed his regret, and received the following characteristic reply . . . . .

> "My dear Fellow, UPFIELD.
>
> I know you acted conscientiously and in good faith, and I wasn't the least hurt, and only said I wanted my supper. But the preaching is a great burden now I am in my seventieth year, and I have to preach here tonight and tomorrow in London.
>
> Always yours very truly,
>
> A. H. STANTON.
>
> If your words were a help to others, so much the better after all."

A new red cope, the gift of Mr. Arthur R. Thomas who was Sacristan as well as being a server, was worn for the first time on St. Agnes' Eve. The hood was embroidered with the figure of St. Agnes' and the Lamb, the symbol of purity, with which she is usually portrayed. During the following year the cope was further enriched with embroidered orphreys, i. e. borders, which included the figure of St. George and St. Andrew. This cope has recently been completely restored by the Clewer Sisters, and was used for the first time since its restoration on St. Agnes' Day 1980.

Another generous gift in 1909 was that of a white cope, given by Mr. Lawrence E. Brooks and first used in the procession on the Sunday evening after Ascension Day, having been previously blessed at the altar. The lengthy description in the Parish Magazine is reproduced here for the vestment must indeed have been beautiful. "The festal cope is made of cream coloured silk damask, with hood and orphrey of wallflower - red silk velvet. It is lined throughout with azure blue silk. The hood is Gothic in shape and design,and in its centre is a quatrefoil of cloth of gold. On this is embroidered a very beautiful figure of St. Agnes from a design by the late C. E. Kempe . . . .Mr. Kempe has been a master in English ecclesiastical art . . . .has designed may beautiful vestments, the work of which, under his guidance, has been mainly executed by the Clewer Sisters in London. In the present cope the figure of St. Agnes on the hood is embroidered in coloured silks and gold thread, and is considered perfect of its kind. The further details are worked out in golden fleurs-de-lys and leaf ornamentation. Around the figure runs, in gold letters, the title "Sancta Agnes Virgo et Martyr." In the details of the orphrey are seen canopied angles worked in blue, white and gold, holding scrolls bearing the word "Alleluia", and also ornamented crosses, roses and fleur-de-lys, the whole being worked out in the old English Style. In the centre of the orphrey (above the hood) is the sacred monogram worked in gold on a blue ground, and set in a gold-rayed sun. The cope is fastened with a morse, on which is a golden star bearing the sacred monogram in its centre. The whole work of the cope is done to stand the test of time and we hope it will be in use for many generations to come at St. Agnes' Church'" Further embellishments were made later in the year by the addition of four figures to the orphrey - "St. George, as patron Saint of Windsor; St. Andrew, Patron Saint of the Parish; and St. Leonard and St. Richard for personal reasons."

Upon recent examination, with a view to possible restoration, the cope was found to be beyond repair. The cope had already undergone extensive restoration with the unfortuate loss of the orphreys. Only the morse and hood survive to testify to the beauty of the original vestment. At some stage the hood was inset with semi-precious stones given by Mrs. Carpenter Rowe. The Clewer Sisters have recently altered and repaired a newer white cope for St. Agnes' and the morse and hood from the old vestment have been incorporated in this work.

Following the departure of Ernest Higgins, the St. Agnes' Dramatic Society was shepherded by Victor Biddulph and continued to go from strength to strength. "Sleeping Beauty" delighted crowded audiences for three nights in the Mission Room and again at Clewer Hall. On this latter occasion the pantomime was performed by the Sunday School, and the Dramatic Society performed the Eighteenth Century farce, "Cross Purposes". On Shrove Tuesday and on two nights after Easter there was a performance of "Robin Hood". Amoung the cast were Mr. H. Price as Robin Hood; Victor Biddulph as Little John; Philip Foreman as Friar Tuck; Cecil Cooper and Sydney Pert as outlaws; George Uglow as Richard I; Miss Muriel Garner, Miss M. Cooper and Miss Dorothy Cooper as Rustic Maidens; and Miss J. Harmsworth as Maid Marion.

Possibly one of the most ambitious social events held in the Mission Room was that of April 14th 1909, of which there is a vivid description in the Parish Magazine: "A most successful Fancy Dress Ball was held in St. Agnes' Rooms . . . The numbers were limited to fifty, and dancing was kept up until 2.30 a.m. Everyone expressed themselves delighted with the arrangement made for their comfort, and a large room was temporarily built for the occasion and used by some of the dancers, thus relieving the other room of the crush. The dresses were all exceedingly pretty and effective and great care had been taken by the ladies in their choice of characters, the gentlemen also being most picturesque. The scene at times was very brilliant . . . . The rooms were charmingly decorated by Mr. Skerrett and Mr. Sydney Pert. The musical arrangements were under the direction of Mr. George Kelsey. We are much indebted to Mr. J. Pert for his great interest and kindness in arranging the dances."

With the coming of Summer came also the annual excursions. A favourite outing with the Mothers Meeting was a trip on the river. Once more the description in the Parish Magazine is so vivid and conjures up the atmosphere of a happy day out, so long ago

that it is worth quoting. "A wet June so far, and yet on the 21st . . . it was. . . .a Summer's day from start to finish. The steam launch, 'Belle of Windsor', took us off at 9.30 a. m. and brought us home at 9.30 p. m. singing 'God Save the King'. A piano on board was well played and the singing exceedingly soft and sweet. Some dancing too . .
A few laughable mishaps occurred. The tea urns were forgotten, but at Henley others were hired. At Henley a dairy cart was applied to for milk; plenty of it there, but not enough cans to carry it away. The boy promised faithfully to fetch cans and deliver milk to the steamer waiting by the shore in a quarter of an hour; but, oh! Faithless urchin! He never turned up! Everyone had returned on board, ready to return to Temple Island, where permission to land had been given, and where a sumptuous repast was waiting, so the Rector and Mr. Farr went off to the dairy and came back each carrying a great can of milk. The Mothers and ladies clapped them with gratitude. From all the genial mothers most gratifying remarks were made. "Beautiful Milk." "My tea is so hot and good." "Well I have enjoyed it all." "No more, thank you; I have done nicely."

"The homeward cruise was simply delicious. At Temple Lock, the man hearing singing, said; 'Very pretty, ladies, but give us something for the Navy.' 'Rule Britannia' was struck up and he held his hat in his hand. Mrs. Cowie asked him if he had been in the Navy. 'Thirty-four years and six months,' was his answer.

"At Boulters Lock, on our outward way we were photographed, and on our return a rough proof was shown us. Orders for postcards were given, many of us recognizing good likenesses of ourselves. Thus passed our enjoyable, cheery and restful outing. Most of us must have slept like tops after so much fresh air. Babies and all; they were very cheerful and amusing, and wide awake in the cool of the evening."

A copy of the photograph has survived as a lasting record of a happy day in a now vanished world. A striking thing about the photograph is the uniformity of dress, which was obviously 'Sunday best', and consisted of either dark costumes or highnecked white blouses with long sleeves, and dark skirts. But when it comes to hats then individuality emerges in the grand manner. Flowers, fruit, bows, ribbons and feathers abound -indeed Mrs. Uglow's hat looks good enough to eat! The babies are bedecked in frills and petticoats, and the older children wear the then fashionable sailor suits. One or two of the women are not looking, 'camera shy' perhaps, whilst the majority look on rather demurely - it was after all an age when one didn't smile for the camera, even on a pleasure cruise. There is however, one exception in the company - the Revd. Charles Farr who smiles broadly. (See Plate 3)

The congregation at St. Agnes' continued to flourish in numbers although the average number of Sunday Communicants was only ten to twenty, which seems surprisingly low. However, as we have previously noted, the main Communicating Eucharist was at 8.00 a. m. The Choral Eucharist would have been attended by those who had already received their Communion early, plus a fair number who only received Communion monthly or even less frequently. More frequent Communion was often urged by the clergy but a good many people still kept to their old ways. Far more people attended Church on festivals, particularly Christmas, St. Agnes'-tide, Easter and Harvest. Visiting preachers were always sure to 'draw a crowd', especially when it was someone famous like Father Stanton. Evensong was well attended and so too were the special Mission Services held in Lent and Advent.

Visiting preachers at St. Agnes' during this period included the Revd. Lewis H. Tiarks (Chaplain, St. Andrew's Hospital, Clewer); the Revd. Rowland P. Quilter (Chaplain, House of Mercy); the Revd. Cuthbert Trower (Private Chaplain to the Countess of Craven); the Revd. Thomas Calvert Brown (Curate, Clewer St. Stephen); and the Revd. Ernest Higgins.

The preacher at the Harvest Festival Evensong was the Revd. George C. Battiscombe, formerly Mr. Farr's Vicar at Bromley-by-Bow, and from 1904-1915 Vicar of Uxbridge. In his sermon he urged people to believe more in the actual blessing of God, and not in luck or chance. The preacher at the second Festival Evensong was the Revd.Roland Errington, on a welcome return visit. This service concluded with a Procession and Te Deum.

All Saints and All Souls (November 1st and 2nd) had always been observed at St. Agnes', but in 1909 the latter Commemoration was kept with extra solemnity. Vespers of the Dead was sung on the Eve of All Souls and a sermon preached by the Revd. Calvert Brown. On All Souls' day itself there was a Choral Eucharist at 11.00 a. m., the Rector being the Celebrant and the preacher being the Revd. Edward F. Russell of St. Alban's, Holborn. The singing included 'Dies Irae' and a special solo, 'The Souls of the Righteous."

Father Russell, along with Mackonochie and Stanton, formed the 'famous three' of St. Alban's, Holborn. He was the eldest son of an Admiral and the nephew of Lord John Russell, sometime Whig Prime Minister. He joined the Staff of St. Alban's as a deacon in 1867 and stayed there throughout his ministry. He was never an extreme 'Ritualist' like Mackonochie. Russell was interested in medicine, and for a time walked the wards of St. Bartholomew's Hospital as a medical student (in conjunction with his priestly ministry), until his health forced him to give up. Amongst his Chaplaincies he numbered that of St. John's Home for Girls in Clewer. He was an impressive looking man - tall and lean, with a Van Dyke beard, inclined to looking solemn but with a bright sense of humour. He lived until 1925 well into his eighties. His two visits to St. Agnes' (All Souls' Day 1909 and 1910) are still remembered by some of the older residents of Spital.

## Chapter VII

### A few farewells.

St. Agnes'-tide 1910 was celebrated in the customary manner. The Festival began with First Evensong at which the preacher was the Revd. A. F. Bliss of Dedworth. On St. Agnes' Day the Rector celebrated and preached at the Choral Eucharist, and the 'Missa de Sancta Agnete' was used. Once again there was a telegram from Dr. King - "God bless you and keep you and all your dear people, and refresh you each Epiphany with an increasing consciousness of His presence and His love - E. Lincoln." On the Sunday within the Octave of the Festival the congregation was fortunate enough to have three guest preachers. At the Choral Eucharist the Sub-Warden of the House of Mercy, the Revd. G. J. Foster, preached on Eucharistic Worship. In the afternoon there was a Corporate Service for the local branches of the Church of England Men's Society, at which about eighty men were present. They listened to an address by the Revd. G. C. Battiscombe, Vicar of Uxbridge. However, the highlight of the day was Evensong, at which the preacher was Father Stanton, and the Church was crowded as usual. This service was concluded by a Procession at which the red cope was worn, and the Te Deum was sung. The Patronal Festival was brought to a conclusion on January 27th which was observed as the Dedication Festival.

Lent began early in 1910 and there were the usual extra services, namely Mission Services on Friday afternoons and on Wednesday and Sunday evenings. In addition a Quiet Day was held at the church on Saturday, March 5th. The conductor was Mr. Farr and the programme consisted of:

| | |
|---|---|
| Holy Communion | 8.00 a. m. |
| Matins | 8.30 a. m. |
| Litany and First Address | 2.15 p. m. |
| Veni Creator and Second Address | 3.30 p. m. |
| Tea | 4.00 p. m. |
| Evensong and Third Address | 5.00 p. m. |

The Holy Week services were very well attended and on the first three days the Revd. T. Calvert Brown led a Meditation after Evensong. Services on Good Friday were as follows:-

| | |
|---|---|
| Matins, Meditation and Ante-Communion | 8.00 a. m. |
| Children's Service (led by Victor Biddulph) | 11.00 a. m. |
| Three Hours Devotion | 12.00 to 3.00 p. m. |
| Children's Service (led by A. R. Thomas) | 5.00 p. m. |
| Evensong and Sermon | 6.30 p. m. |

There were one hundred and thirty four Easter Communicants - but many of these represented people who did not attend Church regularly throughout the year.

A new set of Eucharistic vestments were blessed and used for the first time on Easter Day. These were the generous gift of Mr. Lawrence Brooks and they are described in the Clewer Magazine. "The material.....is of cloth of gold, with pillar and cross of red velvet, stamped with St. Andrew's Cross and embroidered. A pelican feeding her young is represented on the pillar, and on the cross Our Lord in glory." The Chasuble is still at St. Agnes' but unfortunately the cloth of gold has tarnished and, therefore, the vestments are no longer used. The embroidery is still in a very good condition.

The St. Agnes' Dramatic Society reached the high point of its successes so far, when on Shrove Tuesday, they performed "A Midsummer Night's Dream." at Clewer Hall. The 'Windsor and Eton Express' reviewed the performance with unbridled enthusiasm, describing it as: "An excellent performance". "In the more important characters Mr. Victor Biddulph was an imposing 'Theseus', who was ably supported by Miss Emily Beal, in the complementary part of 'Hippolyta.' Miss Ivy Charles ('Hermia'); Miss Daisy Fuller ('Helena'); and Miss Millie Bridges ('Titania') were also attractive and engaging personalities, played with grace and animation. Messrs. Arthur Foreman ('Lysander') and Alfred Caudell ('Demetrius') evoked great interest by their declamatory energy. As 'Bottom the Weaver', Mr.Philip Foreman was very entertaining....Mr. Frank Brown acquitted himself very creditably as 'Oberon', while Messrs. G. Uglow and Edward Herberd were equally successful as 'Ageus' and 'Philostrate'. Messrs. Alfred Bridges, Fred Copas, William Knight, John Whiteman and George Bridges were good as 'Quince', 'Snug', 'Flute', 'Snout' and 'Starveling'.....From among the juveniles we must single out Master Ernest Caudell as 'Puck', whose evident enjoyment of the role, and entire self-possession, made a decided impression. The dresses and make-up were very effective....Mr. G. A. Kelsey kindly presided at the piano." There were, of course, other concerts and entertainments at this time, but this particular production was the most ambitious undertaken by the Dramatic Society.

1910 was a year tinged with sadness, for there occurred the deaths of several friends of St.Agnes'. However, before we think about these, there was one death which affected not only the whole Country but the British Empire too - that of King Edward VII on May 6th. He was still in his sixties and had endeavoured to "make light" of his failing health. However, his increasing tendency towards bronchial troubles was putting a strain on his heart. It was not until May 5th that news broke of his grave condition and of the anxiety which was felt by those around him. By the following day anxious crowds had gathered outside Buckingham Palace. He died at 11.45 that night. The stunned reaction of the late King's subjects was summed up by the Rector of Clewer:- "The death of King Edward VII is the great event which overshadows everything else. It has come upon the whole Nation - we may say without exaggeration the whole world - with such tragic suddenness, that we can hardly yet estimate our sense of loss and bereavement. Probably not even the death of Queen Victoria produced such a widespread feeling of consternation as that which filled us all when we heard on May 6th that the King was dying.....". Following the Lying-in-State in Westminster Hall from May 17th to 19th, the King's body was brought to Windsor for burial on Friday, May 20th. On the Funeral Day, Memorial Services were held throughout the Country. In Clewer Parish there were Choral Requiems in all three churches. At St.Agnes' forty people were present, of whom twelve received Holy Communion. The 'Missa de Sancta Agnete' was sung, and the 'Dies Irae' was said by the congregation between the Epistle and Gospel readings.

The April issue of the Clewer Magazine records the death on March 8th of Edward King, Bishop of Lincoln. "At St.Agnes' we always felt that in him we had a true friend, who was deeply interested in the welfare of our little Church. For the past three years the Bishop has kindly wired a blessing on our Patronal Festival, as well as on one or two other occasions. The writer was struck with the fact that in his farewell letter to the Diocese of Lincoln the Bishop concluded with the same words of blessing that he gave us at St. Agnes' on January 21st last. May God grant to his soul, refreshment, light and peace." A Requiem was offered at St. Agnes' for Bishop King on March 16th and there were twenty-two people present, of whom eight received Holy Communion.

On August 12th 1910 the Revd. Stephen King Tahourdin passed to his eternal rest, aged fifty-nine years. The funeral took place in Clewer Church on August 16th. He had been a Minor Canon of St. Georges' Chapel since 1881 and had also served as an honorary curate of Clewer. He was, as we have seen, a frequent visitor to St. Agnes', especially during periods of interregnum, when it was largely due to his efforts that the Church was kept open. He had been seriously ill during 1909 but had seemed to have made a good recovery. The Revd. Roland Errington wrote of him: "Mr. Tahourdin was a man whom to know was to respect and love. He was a most sincere friend, and could not make an enemy. He had a great sense of humour: he could tell a story well, and his readings at an entertainment......were inimitable...His Sermons were thoughtful, carefully prepared and beautifully delivered, for he had... a most melodious voice. It was a great treat when he took a Choral Celebration.... The influence of one so deeply spiritual and so great a lover of souls could not be otherwise than great...."

A young Communicant, Herbert Vokins, died aged twenty-six years and was buried on May 4th, following a short but severe illness. He was the Assistant Secretary of the flourishing Men's Club and had been very keen in his work for it.

Finally, a member of the Sunday School, Percy Simmonds, died aged nine years and was buried on April 12th. We are told that he was a bright little fellow who had always been rather delicate. One of his friends, Bertie Ives, wrote the following verse:-

"Farewell, little Schoolmate, your lessons are done;

You have climbed the golden ladder, your golden crown is won.

Jesus loves little children, and I shall come some day,

When my lessons here are finished, and I am called away."

R. I. P.

By the Summer of 1910 the idea of a further extension to the Church was mooted but on a more modest scale than previously - "Our present Vestry is much too small, and it is proposed that a Vestry and Sacristy be added on the South side of the Church. The present Vestry....will be thrown into the Church....it is only a case of pulling down the dividing wall, and resting the roof on arches similar to those on the South side." By October plans had been drawn up and the appeal for subscriptions was launched. The estimated cost was about £500 and already £122:1:4d had been collected, of which £100 was the gift of Mr.Victor Biddulph. Despite constant appeals, the money was very slow coming in, and, as we shall see, this attempt at a further extension of St.Agnes' was destined to come to nought.

Preachers at St.Agnes'-tide 1911 included the Rector; the Revd T. Calvert Brown; the Revd. W. La Trobe Bateman, and the Revd. G. C. Battiscombe. Father Stanton came for his fifth, and what was to be his final, visit on Sunday, January 22nd, and as usual the church was crowded to the point of overflowing.

St. Agnes' was once again fortunate in being the recipient of a set of Eucharistic Vestments. On this occasion the donor was Mr. A. R. Thomas, and the new red vestments matched the red cope, which he had given in 1909. They were worn for the first time on St. Agnes' Day 1911 and are still used on all major feast days when red is the appropriate liturgical colour.

1911 was Coronation Year, and the mounting excitement must have pervaded through all the social activities of the Church. The annual St. Agnes'-tide Supper for Choir and Workers was the usual happy gathering, and there was a special word of thanks in the Clewer Magazine for, "Mr. Pert for his endless trouble in cooking and Mr. King and his friends for their entertainment which was much appreciated." No doubt Mr. Pert's bakers oven was a boon in cooking the meat for the supper, for most of the cottages would have had only the limited cooking facilities afforded by the kitchen range.

From February 1911 onwards, a new name appears periodically in the St. Agnes' Service Register, that of the Revd. George Bryan Budibent, newly appointed Curate of Clewer. He stayed in the Parish until 1920.

During 1911 a full sized font was acquired for St. Agnes' (previously a small receptacle the size of a holy water stoup had been used). The font had a curious history - at least according to the information given in the Clewer Magazine, but I have not been able to substantiate it from any other sources. At some time or other, the font came into the possession of a Miss Hibberd of Dedworth, who presented it to All Saints' Church in 1904. It was late Norman c.1135, 'barrel' shaped and with a regular pattern resembling oak leaves. It was said to have originated from a Church at Glastonbury, and was dug up in a garden about the year 1850. At the time of its presentation to All Saints', Dedworth, it was hardly fit for use, having been in the open air for many years. It was subsequently placed on a tree stump outside Dedworth Church. We must assume that the font was dug up at Glastonbury, for there is no other evidence that it actually came from there. A possible reason for burial was so that it should not be desecrated or defaced either at the Reformation or later by Puritan iconoclasts. It was common practice to bury stone altar slabs for this reason. In 1911 the decision was made to present the font to St. Agnes' and it was accordingly restored and placed on a base and step of Portland stone. On March 27th it was blessed and Dedicated by Bishop Corfe,* acting for the Bishop of Oxford. Evensong was said at 3.00 p. m. at the end of which the Dedication ceremony took place. Thus this ancient font was restored to its original purpose.

* (Charles Corfe was Bishop of Corea 1889-1904, and, although retired, frequently assisted in the Oxford Diocese. He died in 1921 aged seventy-eight years.)

A distinguished visitor came to preach at St. Agnes' on Trinity Sunday, the Revd. Walter Julius Carey, Librarian of Pusey House, Oxford (1908-1917). He preached at a service of the Church of England Men's Society and at Evensong. In 1921 he became Bishop of Bloemfontein until his resignation in 1934. During the late 1940's he helped Brother Edward (the Revd. Edward Gordon Bulstrode) with the organisation of the work which became known as the Village Evangelists, and from 1948 Bishop Carey became the Co-Warden. He died in the 1950's.

The Coronation of King George V and Queen Mary took place on June 22nd. At St. Agnes' there was a Eucharist at 6. 30 a. m. at which sixty people were present and forty received Holy Communion. It is with hindsight that we see the irony in the words written by the Revd. A. F. Bliss of Dedworth in the Clewer Magazine, words which were so full of hope for the new Monarch and his reign - "Never in the Nation's history has a king ascended the throne in more auspicious circumstances, blessed by peace in all parts of the world, blessed by the good-will of all the nations of the earth. It is true that there are clouds on the horizon both at home and abroad. Still one feels that he stands at the threshold of an enormous advance in civilisation and social improvement, and that we may hail with enthusiasm the new regime that is beginning....These are magnificent days in which we live....". Likewise, the Rector wrote, "....The loyalty of the whole nation has been demonstrated in the most satisfactory manner and, not least, in Ireland. Certainly our King and Queen possess the hearts of their subjects, and have every prospect of a happy and prosperous reign....". Hopeful words written in August 1911 just three years before the first major European war since that of Napoleon broke out, and with it a generation of young men were to die, Monarchies were to fall and the map of Europe was to be re-drawn.

However, in June 1911 the 'clouds on the horizon' were forgotten in the festivities. It was a glorious Summer and everyone took advantage of the sun to forget the problems of the moment such as unemployment, strikes, the Irish Home Rule Question, Suffragettes, and the recent controversial attempt to curb the powers of the House of Lords. On July 3rd and 4th there was a 'Review' of the Officers' Training Corps, and the Boy Scouts in Windsor Park. "On the two days 52,000 youngsters from all parts of the kingdom testified their willingness to serve their King and Country." The older school-children attended the Windsor Fete at which 6,000 children greeted the King and Queen and received Coronation medals. On July 8th the Infants had their Tea and Treat in the Rectory garden and also received Medals. Two days later there was a similar Tea Party at the Rectory for the Mothers' Meeting.

Two signs that times were changing are evident from the Parish Magazine of this period. The first was the increasing problem of unemployment - "There is quite a large company of men and women in our district who are longing for work. The revd. C. Farr will gladly supply the names and addresses of reliable people - decorators, painter, plumber, gardeners, coachmen, clerk, labourers and other workmen; a few boys, a girl just leaving school; a Mother's help, housekeeper and several women." By November the situation was so chronic that prayers were being offered at Sunday Evensong that those who could afford it would give the necessary help.

The second was the fate of the Mothers' and Choirboys' Excursion. "We were proposing to journey to Brighton, but alas, at the eleventh hour came the Strike, and the excursion was cancelled." Not to be outdone they went by brake to the White City and thoroughly enjoyed themselves.

Two deaths occurred in 1911 which must be mentioned. Firstly, Lord Edward Spencer-Churchill died in May, and a Requiem was offered at St.Agnes' on Tuesday May 9th at which sixteen people attended. During August, the death occurred of the Right Revd. Francis Paget, Bishop of Oxford. Seven people were present at the Requiem on August 9th.

In the midst of the Coronation festivities came sorrow, for in the July magazine the Rector announced the forthcoming departure from the Parish of the Revd. and Mrs. Farr. "It has caused great regret throughout the Parish, and something like consternation in the Spital District," wrote the Rector. The reason for their leaving was Mrs. Farr's ill-health and the consequent need to get away from the climate of the Thames Valley. (In fact Mrs. Farr outlived her husband). The news was a deep blow to everyone, not least to the Farrs themselves, who, it would be seen, had no prior intention of leaving Spital. It was, therefore, with great sorrow that Charles Farr wrote his farewell letter which was published in the October parish magazine:-".....We must all pray for God's blessing on your new Priest. Mrs. Farr and myself are exceedingly sorry to be compelled to relinquish our work, which we have truly learned to love. All of you dear people have been so kind to us, and the little we have been enabled to do, under the blessing of God, is due to your loving and loyal co-operation. We have pulled together. Were names written, the list would be too long for this magazine. I want to thank everyone for their kind and generous gifts... If I have been the means of helping any soul sometimes offer a prayer for me. God bless you, and keep you all true to the Holy Faith. Your sincere friend in Christ, Charles Farr."

Elsewhere in the magazine, Mr. Farr urged the people to keep on with the effort to raise enough money for the Church extension. The sum of £250 had been raised, including £35 promised by the Church Building Society; also the Rector had promised a substantial sum.

The following statement also appeared in the October magazine. "Certain vestments have been given to the Church of St. Agnes' Spital, Clewer, and have been accepted by the Priest-in-charge (Revd. C. Farr), between the years 1908 and 1911 inclusive, on the express condition that they shall not be alienated in any way from the Church above named. The donors expressly stipulated that in the event of the vestments ceasing to be used at St. Agnes' Church, at any time, they are to be handed over to the before-mentioned Revd. C. Farr, to be disposed of as he may think fit. The vestments referred to are the following:-

1. A White jewelled Cope, Morse and Hood, embroidered.
2. A Red embroidered Cope, Morse and Hood.
3. A complete set of Cloth of Gold vestments, comprising a Chasuble, Stole, Maniple, Burse and Veil.

4. A complete set of embroidered Red Vestments, comprising a Chasuble, Stole, Maniple, Burse and Veil.

(Signed) CHARLES FARR
LAWRENCE EDWIN BROOKS (Donor)
ARTHUR R. THOMAS (Donor)."

It is a sign of the great esteem in which the Farr's were held that there were no fewer than four farewell presentations. On Sunday, September 10th, Mr. Victor Biddulph, on behalf of the young men, presented Mr. Farr with a tobacco pouch which had a gold plate with the name 'Tobies' engraved upon it. (The gatherings of parish youths at Mr. Biddulph's house were known as 'the Tobies'). Saturday, September 16th, saw the presentation by the Sunday School children of two silver table napkin rings, together with a book containing the signatures of the "kind little donors". On Sunday, September 24th, Mr. Bampton presented on their behalf a framed photograph of the Choir (See Plate 4) and an illuminated address. Immediately afterwards Mr. A. R. Thomas presented, on behalf of the congregation and friends of St. Agnes', an illuminated address and a purse containing £43. Finally the Mothers' Meeting gave Mrs. Farr two silver toast racks and a pair of sugar tongs.

Charles Farr's last Sunday at St. Agnes' was on September 24th 1911. There were fifty-eight Communicants at three Celebrations. He left the Parish on September 29th, the feast of St. Michael and All Angels, after celebrating the Eucharist at 7.00 a. m. There were twenty-six people present at this final Celebration.

Charles Farr did not move a very great distance, but went to Uxbridge, where he again became Curate to George Battiscombe, his former Vicar at St. Michael's, Bromley-by-Bow. He remained at Uxbridge until 1913 when he moved to St. John's, Potter's Bar, as Curate to the Revd. G. R. P. Preston, who had also been at Bromley-by-Bow (he had succeeded Battiscombe as Vicar from 1904-1913). In 1916 Charles Farr returned to the Oxford Diocese as Vicar of Minster Lovell, and stayed until 1924. He then moved to the Diocese of Peterborough to be Vicar of Little Houghton with Bradfield on the Green, where he remained until his early death in 1930, when he would have been about fifty-three years old.

So passed one of the most thriving periods in the history of St. Agnes', and it is significant that out of all the priests who have ministered to the people of Spital, only two, Charles Farr and William Brook, have had permanent memorials placed in the Church. The pulpit is Charles Farr's 'official' memorial, and of this there will be more later, but surely his most abiding memorial is the extended Church of 1908, which serves Spital, though a much changed Spital from the one which he knew. However, if he were to walk along St. Leonard's Road today he might recognise in some of the now elderly faces some of his Choirboys, servers and Sunday School pupils, who still remember "Charlie" with warm affection.

## Chapter VIII

## Cloud Capped Towers.

There was no interregnum at St. Agnes', the Revd. Marsh Kirkby having been appointed as soon as Mr. Farr's proposed departure was known. Marsh Kirkby was a man of wide and varied experience both at home and abroad. He was ordained deacon in 1883 and priest in 1884, and must have been at least fifty when he came to Spital. He had served two curacies in Oxford, St. Barnabas (1883-1887) and St. Paul (1889-1892). Also he had served at St. Agatha's, Landport, Portsmouth (1901-1906), a church synonomous with the name of Father Robert Dolling, a well known Anglo-Catholic priest, although Kirkby was there after Dolling's time. Kirkby had also served curacies in several other parishes including a period as Chaplain at Singapore, 1908-1910. Immediately before coming to Clewer he was senior curate at Witney. He was married with a family of three little girls and took up residence at 'Prospect Cottage', Clewer Hill. He used a goat-cart as transport, which must have been a little unusual.

When he took up his work at St. Agnes', Mr. Kirkby found a flourishing foundation upon which to continue building up the Christian community. Of the various clubs and societies in operation at St. Agnes' in September 1911 we may mention, the Mothers' Meeting and Penny Bank; Dramatic Society; Men's club; Boy Scouts; Girls' Club. There were also the monthly meetings of the Confraternity of the Blessed Sacrament and occasional corporate meetings of the Church of England Men's Society. By the time Charles Farr left there were celebrations of the Eucharist on about four weekdays with a Choral Eucharist on major Saints' days. There was also a monthly Requiem and Vespers of the Dead. As we have seen, vestments were worn and processions were a common adjunct to the services.

Financial matters were still a problem and, although Charles Farr's ministry had been a fruitful time, yet despite the presence of a number of generous benefactors, money was still an abiding worry. Indeed when Charles Farr left there was still a deficit of about £9 a year on day to day Church expenses. Mr. Kirkby decided to tackle the problem by forming a Finance Committee. It was composed of Mr. Arthur Thomas (who was a Chartered Accountant) acting as secretary, assisted by Messrs. Biddulph, Weston and Clarke. The Committee managed to pay off the deficit fairly quickly assisted by a donation of £5 from the Rector. The problem of inflation was even then, as now, acute and people were being urged to give more and to give regularly. Three funds were established - the Church Fund, which received all the alms and dealt with all expenses connected with the running of the Church; the Sick and Needy Fund, which dealt with all cases of Sick and Poor relief; and the General Purposes Fund, which dealt with Summer outings, Christmas treats, etc., the money for which came from special donations given for that purpose. By this means the Church alms were relieved of objects which were not strictly 'Church Expenses'. The Sick and Needy Fund was an indispensable means of relief to the poor in those days before the emergence of the Welfare State. For example, in 1912 two children were sent to Bournemouth to convalesce after serious illness, and a mother who was 'run down' was also sent to Bournemouth for a break. In those days much emphasis was put on a 'change of air' as an integral part of treatment, and it was often the Church who paid the bill.

Miss Maclean and Miss Wilkinson, assisted by Mrs. Uglow, were at this time running the Girls' Club and it flourished under their guidance. In Mr. Kirkby's words -"The Girls' Club is doing splendidly. It was really astonishing to see Miss Wilkinson sitting quietly in the midst of some twenty-five girls actually '<u>quietly sewing</u>' the other night. How she managed to keep them quiet is as great a mystery as how Miss Quarterman can interest the boys' in the wonders of parlour games called 'Post' and 'Friends'. The general impressions of Spital with regard to our boys and girls is noise, riot and tomboyism. However they are a splendid lot, generous and open-hearted, with plenty of pluck and endurance." The Boys' Club referred to was run for the Choir Boys by Miss Quarterman. The Mothers' Meeting continued to flourish and Mrs. Kirkby was assisted in the running of it by Mrs. Rhoda Maclean and Miss Yeats. The Men's Club was affiliated with the Church of England Men's Society.

Spital Village lost a generous benefactress early in 1912 when Mrs. Carpenter-Rowe announced that she would be leaving Windsor to live on the Continent in the hope of regaining both her own and her daughter's health. "So many will miss her, her hand has been everywhere where there has been some kind act to do, some poverty to lessen . ." Her residence, Clewer Lodge, stood empty for a number of years. She had kept a number of horses and rather than sell them to owners who might ill-use them, she had them all destroyed. I have tried unsuccessfully to find out what became of this good lady, for in 1912 the Continent was a melting pot, and in less than two years it had boiled over.

Victor Biddulph's health was failing too, and in the February 1912 Parish Magazine we learn he was in Church on St. Agnes' Day after an absence "owing to a slight breakdown". This may account for the lack of activity by the Dramatic Society, and also for the reason why, by the end of the year, he had returned to Clewer Church, which was nearer his home in New Road.

St. Agnes'-tide 1912 must have seemed like something of an anticlimax when compared with former years, for on this occasion there was no visit from Father Stanton. The Rector celebrated and preached at the main Eucharist, and the Warden, the Revd. G. S. Cuthbert, preached at Evensong. Mr. Kirkby commented that the number of Communicants was "just above average, but not sufficient".

Lenten observance was similar to previous years although there was an absence of the popular Mission Services. Evensong and Sermon was held on Wednesday evenings with guest preachers and also there was a Sunday evening Sermon Course. Stations of the Cross were held on Friday evenings, and the Rector also held a Bible Class for women. Mr. Kirkby, as a rule, only held two weekday Eucharists unless there was a major Feast day.

Holy Week and Easter were well observed, especially the Three Hours Devotion on Good Friday. There were one hundred and seventy-two Easter Communions and the alms were above average.

An added attraction of Easter 1912 was the presence of a new organ in the place of the "American Organ". This was gained through the kindness of Sir Frederick Dyson "who has taken our old Organ off our hands, and we have to pay him £19 for the new organ. . . This is much less than we should have to give for any ordinary harmonium." This sum was met by July, partly through a donation of £5 by Arthur Thomas, and partly through holding a Rummage Sale. This organ is still in use at St. Agnes' and is to be rebuilt during 1983.

Springtime saw the completion of a good deal of work to the fabric of the Church and Mission Rooms. "The Rector has kindly spent some £8:15:0d in doing some very necessary repairs and making improvements to our Mission Buildings as well as gravelling the path . . . The whole of the gas piping has been overhauled and two great leaks found out and repaired. The floor near the porch was repaired as the wood had perished through dry rot . . . "

July brought the usual spate of Summer outings. The Spital Mothers stayed nearer home this year and accepted the invitation of Lady Edward Spencer-Churchill to visit Queensmead on July 15th. "All the Mothers enjoyed the beauty of the garden and the goodness of the tea, and beyond this the real and thoughtful kindness of their generous and gracious hostess. With great thoughtfulness, Lady Edward sent her motor and pony cart for those who would have felt the walk to Queensmead. It was nice to see Lady Dalton Fitzgerald there. She remembered all the old faces, and asked after several not there, showing that her interest in us is very great. She kindly gave £5 towards the Sick and Needy Fund to help us . . . "

The Choir and Girls' Club, seventy-one in all, had a day at Weymouth, most of the time being spent on the sands and donkey riding. They arrived home just after midnight. Miss Wilkinson was in charge of the girls, assisted by Mrs. Uglow, Mrs. Stevens and Mrs. Oxley; Mr. Thomas had charge of the boys.

The St. Agnes' Scouts went to camp in Hayling Island during August and Mr. Kirkby accompanied them as Chaplain . . . "The weather was too awful for words. However, the merry little Scouts, capital little fellows, made the best of it. . . . On Saturday, August 17th, some of them visited H. M. S. Victory and were much amused by the gallant Marine guide, who first pointed out on the main deck where Nelson was killed, and then took them below to the cockpit to show where he died . . . Afterwards we went back to camp to wet blankets, tent and soaked ground. We had plenty of company in camp in the shape of earwigs, blackbeetles, ants and a black lizard. On Sunday the poor priest was hauled out to preach at Hayling Parish Church . . . The Church was crowded . . . The preacher's brown rubber shoes, light trousers and cycling shirt were carefully hidden under his cassock, surplice and false collar, so he seemed alright . . . In the afternoon the priest (Mr. Kirkby) cycled off home . . . He got back in just under six hours which was excellent riding for an old man . . . . "

Clerical changes were being made in Clewer Parish. At Dedworth, the Revd. A. F. Bliss was compelled to resign through ill-health after a ministry of four and a half years. He was succeeded by the Revd. Ernest Clement Eddrup, curate of St. Martin, Portsmouth. At the House of Mercy it was a case of "all change", for the Warden, the Revd. G. S. Cuthbert, had announced his resignation, and under the terms of the Constitution of the Community this also involved the resignation of the Sub-Warden (the Revd. G. J. Foster) and the Chaplain (the Revd. R. P. Quilter). The new Warden, the Revd. Bernard Moultrie, former Vicar of Christ Church, St. Leonard's, was Instituted to the office by the Bishop of Oxford (the Right Revd. Charles Gore, C. R.) on April 24th. Mr. Moultrie remained in office until 1915 when he left the Anglican Church for the Church of Rome, an action which would no doubt have scandalised Canon Carter. The new Sub-Warden was the Revd. Arthur East who in turn succeeded Mr. Moultrie as Warden in 1915. The new Chaplain was the Revd. Francis Murray Downton who stayed until 1916.

A Parochial Mission was being planned for the Parishes of Clewer and Windsor along the lines of the 1896 Mission. It was to begin on St. Andrew's Day (November 30th) and to last for ten days. At Clewer the Revd. Cyril Bickersteth, C. R., was again to be Missioner, and at St. Agnes' the Missioner was to be Fr. Andrew, of the Society of the Divine Compassion.

(The Society of the Divine Compassion was founded in 1894, one of the founder members being a theological student named Ernest Hardy. He took the name Andrew and was ordained to the priesthood in 1895. The work of the infant community was centered around St. Philip's Plaistow in London's East End, and here they endeavoured to help the poor and suffering. The brothers adopted the black habit as worn by the Friars Minor Conventual and they drew up a Rule based on the Franciscan ideal. The Community undertook much needed pastoral and social work, and they soon won people's affection as being poor men amongst the poor. During the London Smallpox epidemic of 1901-1902 the Bishop of London appointed them to minister among the victims. It was at this time that the Revd. William Sirr joined the Society and began a special ministry among the dockers, and even joined with them in a vast procession of the unemployed through the streets of London to Hyde Park in May 1906. From 1906 to 1912 Fr. William was Superior of the Community and these were years of great activity and expansion, with the Brothers in demand all over the Country for missions, retreats and sermons. In 1912 Fr. Andrew became Superior and remained in office for four years. From about 1911 Fr. William began to feel drawn towards a solitary life of prayer rather than the active work of the Society, but it was not until 1918 that the long-sought permission was granted by the Chapter and he withdrew to Glasshampton in Worcestershire. Here he established the Monastery of St. Mary at the Cross, but the discipline by which he lived and expected the Brethren to live was so austere that no-one reached the stage of Profession, and so the new Community never became properly established. The health of this saintly man finally gave way in 1936 and he died a year later. The Monastery buildings later became the noviciate of the Society of St. Francis whose Mother House is at Hillfield near Cerne Abbas, Dorset. As to the Society of the Divine Compassion, it had died out. It was never a large Community even in the most flourishing years, and by 1918 there were only five priest members, although there were others who where not ordained. In 1941, St. Philip's, Plaistow, was destroyed by a land mine - after having previously been bombed and restored. Fr. Andrew died in 1946 and by the early 1960's the last member had also died. A further reason for the decline was the growth of other Communities embracing the Franciscan ideal, notably the Society of St. Francis founded in 1921, which flourishes.)

The Parish Mission was accompanied by a period of intensive preparation. On June 23rd Fr. Bickersteth came to the Parish to address all those who would be taking part in the visiting, distribution of pamphlets, etc. Among those who had prepared to help with preparatory visiting were Mr. Squelch, Mr. Rosier, Mr. Simmons, Miss Cummins, Miss Quarterman, Miss Bridges, Miss Charles and Mr. Edgar Bartholomew. Fr. Dunstan, S.D.C., one of the Mission team, came to St. Agnes' in September. "Father Dunstan's visit," wrote Mr. Kirkby, will not readily be forgotten. His kindly, simple manner, together with his earnest words, which still ring in our ears, has opened our hearts." On September 29th Fr. Andrew, S. D. C., made his introductory visit and preached at the Harvest Festival. This was described as "simply splendid. We rarely have a Thanksgiving service such as this." The harvest produce was sent to Fr. Dunstan's congregation of poor in London's City Road.

Between coming to preach at the Harvest and the start of the Mission, Fr. Andrew was elected Superior of the Society of the Divine Compassion and found himself unable to conduct the St. Agnes' Mission. Instead Fr. William took his place as Missioner and came to meet the people on Sunday, November 3rd. (See Plate 5) He preached at the Solemn Eucharist and Evensong as well as addressing the children in the afternoon.

The Mission itself had a rigorous timetable:-

| | | |
|---|---|---|
| SUNDAYS: | Holy Communion | 6.0, 7.0, 8.0, and 11.0 a. m. (The latter being Missa Cantata) |
| | Street Procession | 3.0 p. m. |
| | Men's Service | 4.0 p. m. |
| | Mission Service | 6.30 p. m. |
| WEEKDAYS: | Holy Communion | 6.0, 7.0, and 9.30 a. m. (The latter with hymns, Intercession and Address.) |
| | Mothers' Service | 2.30 p. m. |
| | Mission Service | 7.30 p. m. |

Preparation for Holy Communion Saturdays - 7.30 p. m.

The street processions were something new in the life of St. Agnes' but were to become a familiar part of spiritual life and witness during the next few years. Mr. Kirkby wrote in the Parish Magazine: "Fr. William is anxious that the processions on Sunday December 1st and December 8th may be inspiring, and has asked everyone who can to attend, and help to sing the hymns and to keep order. The order will be, Cross-Bearer, Choir and Priests, children of the Catechism, men of the C. E. M. S., and others who will help, then the Parish in general. There will be a band of four or five instruments to lead the hymns. Also banners, etc. If possible there will be other processions during the week nights in connection with Clewer and Dedworth, and also street preaching." These torchlit evening processions through the main part of Clewer "made a deep impression on the bystanders, many of whom followed on and stayed to the service at St. Andrew's". The very fact that a procession with Cross-Bearers, robed Choir and Clergy, together with banners, was able to make its way through the streets of Spital, Clewer and Dedworth without disruption, and even managed to attract bystanders to its ranks, is an indication of how much ground the Anglo-Catholic Movement had gained since the persecuted days of Canon Carter. It is also an indication of the popularity which the Movement had won, particularly amongst the poor whose lives were enriched by the colour and flamboyance of this mode of worship. Had it not been for the willingness of such priests as Canon Carter to stand up for the Faith, even if it meant going to prison, the Church of England would have remained firmly shackled to the State. While it is true that she is the "Established Church", she has won a degree of liberty in the matter of worship which she did not have a century ago. That liberty was won by men like Carter and Mackonochie who withstood Lord Penzance and the Public Worship Regulation Act in order to win true freedom of worship for future generations.

In summing up the Mission, Mr. Kirkby noted that, "A very large number have made resolutions and solemn promises to God before the Missioners. We are sure these promises will be observed by most, and that there will be a far more regular band of Communicants."

It will be remembered that during the ministry of the Revd. George Jones (1894 to 1900) a benefactor gave a donation towards a tabernacle, and although there is no direct evidence that there was permanent reservation of the Blessed Sacrament at that time, it is quite likely that the Sacrament was reserved. During Charles Farr's ministry there are many register entries for "Private Holy Communion", but it is not clear whether these were full Celebrations in the homes of the sick or Holy Communion from the Tabernacle. Marsh Kirkby used the same phrase in the register but after the 1912 Mission "Communion from the Reserved Sacrament" is entered. There is, therefore, no doubt that the Blessed Sacrament has been continually reserved since December 1912, but it is uncertain about the period before. If George Jones had Reservation, it is quite likely that Herbert Hunt, who was more "moderate", ceased it, and I cannot imagine Walter Hulme either continuing or restoring the practice. Alternatively, it may have ceased in the interregnum following Jones' departure. Charles Farr is likely to have re-instated the Reserved Sacrament but his Register entries are ambiguous to say the least.

1912 ended with one hundred and seventy-one Christmas Communions. There were no services after the 11.00 a. m., which was "Missa Cantata". Mr. Kirkby, who had three young children, gave his reason for not having any service after 11.00 a. m. - "Everybody ought to spend Evensong as well as the afternoon at his own fireside, and do his best to give the children a snug and comfortable evening to be long remembered." A nice human touch!

Throughout 1912 Mr. Kirkby had been feeling more and more discontented with the lack of progress on the Church extension. Looking around at the still small Church and the increasing demands being made upon it, he decided that what was needed was not simply another small extension but a new church. This conviction increased throughout the rest of his ministry at St. Agnes' and, as we shall see, was the final cause of his departure. Mr Kirkby first gave detailed expression to his plans in the Clewer Magazine of August 1912. "Before this Magazine is published, we hope that we shall have in trust, the land near St. Anges' to build a larger church suited to the needs of the district. Ours is too small, too stuffy, too inconvenient, and not the best we can have for the honour and glory of God and for the greatest help to worship. In the new Church (which will come in time) it is hoped there will be no pulling down of the Altar and central part of the present Church, which is very dear to our hearts. We would like it to be retained almost as it is, to serve as the Lady Chapel. It would be grand to have it half panelled in oak, and the upper part decorated after the style of the little Chapel in the House of Mercy. It was Canon Carter's Mission and as the large Church will be in memory of his work it seems the right thing to preserve the Chapel he set apart as a Mission Church for Spital. Let us thank our gracious Lord in answering our weekly public prayer. He has removed the difficulties so far that the land is put into our hands. Now we must use it . . . " By November little response had been made to these plans and Mr. Kirkby wrote rather impatiently, "There has been hardly any response to the call for help in the many wants of St. Agnes', so there will have to be the usual begging. So much money has been needed during the year for repairs and improvements, and there is a great fear of there being a heavy outlay during the Winter. It is false economy to patch up buildings which were built only to serve a time, and the time passed. It would be much better it seems, to go straight ahead with a new Church . . . . Our Mission Rooms are too small for our clubs, our Church too small for our people.

What is to be done? The work of the Master is cramped." This was perhaps a little unfair, for the Spital people were already "stretched to the limit" financially. The men earned poor wages, and many were out of work. The villagers had already given all they could spare towards the present extension fund and to the previous one in 1907.

The coming of Spring did nothing to lighten Mr. Kirkby's sense of frustration, -"Lent is just upon us, and arrangements are being made for Special Preachers although it is a hard matter. Our Church is small, draughty, damp and none too warm. It does not seem kind to ask strange priests to come to us at present with our many drawbacks, although, of course, in the face of the great work for our Lord these things are minor difficulties. Our stoke-hole is a disgrace, our drains not in good order, our Mission Room poor and almost disreputable and unsuited for the growing work. The repairs are constant and annoying. Last Sunday the clapper of our bell came rolling down the tiles just before the service. Oil stove and a gas fire are substitutes for firing and are "make believes". However, our poor old "dears" endure it and come to Church and the congregation keeps up. The men of the Choir seem to feel it the most!"

However, we are moving ahead too fast and must go back to the beginning of 1913. St. Anges' Day dawned with pouring rain and as a result there were only twenty-eight Communicants at the two early Celebrations. The celebrant at the Solemn Mass (note the word "Mass" was being used) was the Revd. T. Calvert Brown and the Rector preached on the life of St. Agnes', "It was a good service in spite of 'Organic' troubles." The guest preacher at Solemn Evensong was the Revd. Fr. Dunstan, S. D. C.

"Our Entertainments are over," wrote Mr. Kirkby of the Annual Christmas Treats. "What a relief! We do not grudge the labour when we see the happiness that is given, yet the labour and anxiety attatched to these things are like an extra load on an already over-laden camel."

For their treat the Infants had a Christmas Tree which was decorated by the girls of the Catechism. The Choirboys sang Carols, and then with Mrs. Rosier's assistance the toys were given out. One hundred and ten children were present and upon their departure each received a bag containing sweets, oranges, buns and a cracker. No doubt the buns came from Mr. Pert and the sweets and oranges from Mr. Bridges.

The children of ten years and over were taken to the pantomime, "Babes in the Wood". "Nearly one hundred went, and as they went down they called in to Mr. Bridges' shop* and received a large bag of most excellent sweets and two oranges. They had to get to the Theatre Royal at 7 o'clock, and by arrangement they were admitted to the Upper Circle . . . Certainly our children had a lovely time. They were comfortable, warm and happy, and enjoyed their sweets and made the theatre smell sweetly of oranges . . . Miss Wilkinson, Miss Quarterman, Miss Layton, Mr. Rosier and Mr. Alf Clarke kindly came to assist if necessary in keeping order, but our children were excellent and absolutely good. We came home quite a happy crowd, and good Mr. Knight brought his cab and drove some who lived far away right home. We have to thank Lady Dalton Fitzgerald for giving us this pleasure."

(*Mr. Herbert Bridges' shop in St. Leonard's Road is now occupied by Mr. and Mrs. George Knowles.)

During Mr. Kirkby's ministry the 'Guild of St. Agnes' was again re-formed, but this time with a new emphasis. "Only those who earnestly desire to join are wanted. It should be the one great, ruling force in the parish, taking in the fullest sense the place of a Church Council. All matters concerning the District in connection with the Church of St. Agnes' will be referred to it. The members will be consulted in all matters and their advice asked and acted upon."

As this was before the days of Parochial Church Councils, the idea must have seemed something of an innovation - I wonder what the Rector thought about it! Of course, the Guild members had to be regular Communicants but the Parish Magazines convey the impression that the Guild was a rather 'exclusive' gathering. Entry to the Guild was not automatically granted to all who sought it; the members themselves elected new candidates. There was also a junior section known as the Guild of the Catechism. The members were 'selected' by the adults for their constant attendance at the Solemn Eucharist.

March 27th 1913 saw the death of a great priest and a faithful friend of St. Agnes' - Arthur Henry Stanton, aged seventy-four years. He died at his sister's home at Upfield, near Stroud, and his body was taken back to St. Alban's, Holborn. There the coffin lay for twenty hours and during that time the Church was never empty. People queued to pay their last respects and many kissed the coffin. After the Solemn Requiem on April 1st the first part of the Burial Service was said and then the procession set out for Waterloo Station. Traffic came to a halt to make way for the cortege which was led by servers bearing Crucifix, candles and incense, then the Choir of St. Alban's and over a hundred surpliced priests. Next came the bier followed by members of St. Alban's congregation, Post Office workers (to whom Stanton had a special ministry in the St. Martin's Guild), Boy Scouts with staves reversed and Sisters of Mercy. All the way was densely lined with crowds of people many of whom were visibly moved by the specticle - and not just by the Solemn pageantry, for to many it was farewell to "Dad". About a thousand people had assembled at the St. Alban's burial ground at Brookwood Cemetery, Woking. The coffin was laid in a grave lined with flowers next to his former Vicar, Alexander Mackonochie. The pall bearers were the Revd. R. J. Suckling, Vicar of St. Alban's, Holborn (who had been pall bearer at Canon Carter's funeral) and the Revd. E. F. Russell, the Revd. G. R. Hogg and the Revd. W. A. Pearkes, all curates of St. Alban's. At St. Agnes' a Requiem was offered on April 2nd for Fr. Stanton at which eighteen people were present and six received Holy Communion.

As we have seen, Mr. Kirkby was becoming increasingly disheartened at the state of the fabric of the Church and was very eager to begin building a new Church in its place. The seemingly insurmountable financial problem which this project would have generated does not seem to have made any great impression upon him, or if it did, it only quickened his impatience with the local people for not producing the requisite funds. Also, there was the problem of the legal status of St. Agnes', which the Rector had already unsuccessfully attempted to regularise. This was another factor against building a larger Church, but Mr. Kirkby does not seem to have grasped the legal implications. There is, of course, the possibility that he had been appointed without realising the limitations of the situation. However, in April 1913 Marsh Kirkby was offered the living of Wardington, near Banbury, and he accepted it. In the words of the Rector, - "Mr. Kirkby has ably maintained with great success the work of Mr. Farr . . . It will be a difficult matter to find a suitable successor, as the work at Spital requires much energy and self-sacrifice . . . . Many regrets mingle with our congratulations on his preferment. He has worked with us but for a short time, but his zeal and self-sacrificing energy have left, we trust, a permanent mark for good on the district of St. Agnes'. The excellent work of Mr. Farr, whose departure we have never ceased to regret, has been well maintained . . . . ."

Mr. Kirkby's farewell letter sums up his reason for leaving. It is a poignant testimony of a good, zealous priest who, feeling that his efforts to do God's work were being thwarted, left the parish in disillusionment.

> "My dear People of St. Agnes',
> . . . . The Bishop has done me the honour to give me the Living of Wardington, near Banbury, which I am told by a friend who knows the Parish (and has advised me to take it) comes in the shape of a 'call'. Of course, there are many reasons even besides this, that would make me think the offer of a Living as something to be considered. I am older than most curates to begin with, and have developed . . . . certain characteristics that prevent me from being always so amenable to the ordinary directions from an Incumbent as I should be. Possibly because my experience of life has made me see things in a different way from what traditional Vicars or Incumbents usually look. This is trying both to myself and the ordinary Incumbent. Now, do not go and say to your neighbour, 'Ah, there is the difficulty.' Because I am not speaking in anything else but a general way,

and I am happy to say that apart from any policy that should or might be used with regard to our own dear district, there never has been the slightest friction, nor even the smallest misunderstanding between the Rector or myself . . . Now, my dear people . . . . I shall leave this district with far greater sorrow - personal sorrow -than I have left any other. I have learnt to love you, and I believe there has grown up some sort of genuine sympathy between us . . . Again few Churches have such faithful Church workers as Miss Agatha Cummins, Miss Layton, Miss Beal, Miss Quarterman, Mr. Thomas, the three Mr. Clarkes, Mr. Tom Rosier, Mr. Weston and our little boy servers, Hugh Garner, Charles Wilkins, Merryfield and others. I am waited on hand and foot and when any extra help is wanted Mr. and Mrs. Uglow are always ready and anxious to serve me. I tell you all, it is with the utmost sorrow I leave. You may say, then why do you go? Well, dear friends, to speak plainly I should not do so (1) if I could manage on my stipend, and (2) if the Rector of Clewer and the Vicar of Windsor could give me a guarantee that I should be allowed to do the work that I feel personally MUST be done so that the work of Christ may go forward in the district of Spital in a more efficient way. This guarantee would give me fixity of tenure and also the power to build a Church in accordance with the needs of the district. It would mean independance as far as Spital are concerned, and freedom of any outside restraint; but, as I look upon it, with the hearty co-operation of the members of the Guild of St. Agnes' in building up a suitable MISSION Church to extend the work already begun and being carried on. I am quite convinced that I should never get this guarantee and I quite recognise the difficulties of the two authorities in giving it, and I know they have even more right to their opinion than I to mine

Every your affectionate friend,

MARSH KIRKBY"

Marsh Kirkby's last service was Solemn Evensong on Wednesday, May 14th, after which he was presented with an oak triptych containing a Crucifix from Oberammergau on behalf of the Guild of St. Agnes'. There was a further presentation on July 23rd.

So ended a dream, for the new church was never built. Mr. Kirkby must have been bitterly disappointed when he left St. Agnes'; let us hope he found fulfilment at Wardington. He stayed there for the rest of his ministry and died in office in 1928 or 1929, when he would have been about sixty-eight years old. Perhaps he would have been gratified to know that the building which he regarded as being so unworthy to serve as God's House has passed its Centenary and is still 'going strong'. In all probability the large church which he dreamed of building would have been closed years ago, for the rising costs of running a church building - heating, lighting, maintenance, etc., and the 'falling off' in post-war congregations, together with the resultant lack of finance, have all but closed St. Agnes' on a number of occasions. Years of neglect have rendered the present-day fabric far worse than Marsh Kirkby ever saw it; repair bills for formidable sums seem endless, but the saving factor has been that St. Agnes' is a small church and, therefore, even the largest bills have not proved insurmountable.

## Chapter IX

## The last of the Old World.

St. Anges' was closed for a short time following Marsh Kirkby's departure, for the new priest, the Revd. William Brook, was not due to arrive until early July. The Rector already had staff problems due to the ill-health and subsequent absence from the Parish of his curate, the Revd. G. B. Budibent. Services were fully restored at St. Agnes' as soon as the new priest arrived.

The Revd. William Brook was ordained deacon in 1892 and priest in 1893. His first curacy was at Christ Church, St. Leonard's (1892-1896) where he served with the Revd. J. Frank Buxton who had been Missioner at St. Agnes' in the 1896 Parochial Mission. Curacies followed at Etchingham, Benenden and Bexhill between 1896 and 1907. A frail man, his health eventually gave way and from 1908 to 1912 he held licences to preach in the Dioceses of Canterbury, Chichester and Winchester, but was not attached to any parish. From 1912 to 1913 he was Rector of Felton, but the weight of responsibility again proved too arduous and he resigned the benefice. The appointment as Curate of Clewer, in charge of St. Agnes', proved to be just right, for he had charge of the Spital district without the overall responsibility of a parish. He stayed at St. Agnes' for the rest of his ministry, resigning in 1935. William Brook was in his mid forties when he first came to Spital and was sixty eight years old when he died in 1936.

William Brook was married, his wife being the sister of the Revd. Ernest Clement Eddrup, priest in charge of Dedworth 1912 to 1916. A second brother, the Revd. Theodore Basil Eddrup, became curate of Clewer St. Stephen from 1915 to 1917. The Eddrups were fairly 'well off' and throughout Fr. Brook's ministry St. Agnes' had no serious financial troubles - for the first and last time in its history.

Because of the length of his ministry in Spital many people still remember William Brook, although many only recall his declining years, when failing health gradually overtook him. All who knew him speak with deep affection and respect of his kindness, his pastoral care and his gentlemanly and dignified manner. He was always known as "Father Brook" whilst his predecessors had been "Mr.".

The ministry of William Brook, spanning twenty-two years, was a bridge between two worlds. When he came to Clewer in 1913 England was still a year away from the Great War. By the time William Brook retired from the ministry in 1935 there were again storm clouds over Europe, but blacker ones than ever before.

The abiding problem of clergy accommodation again reared its head and for a time the Brooks resided in Sheet Street, Windsor, at a house called "Hatfield". Soon, however, a house in Bolton Crescent, known as "Rednal", was rented and this became the residence of the Spital priest until about 1940. "Rednal" was an Edwardian house (it still stands, although the name has gone), in a 'desirable area'. Mrs. Brook had staff to assist in the running of it - I am told that Miss Beal, a staunch St. Agnes' supporter for many years, worked there as housekeeper. Mrs. Brook, in common with most parsons' wives of the period, took a benevolent interest in the Parish, visited the sick and needy and entertained guests. Those tea parties are recalled by one who would have been a small girl at the time, "Tea was always laid out beautifully, and I remember being impressed with the spirit kettle which was always on the tea table and from which Mrs. Brook filled the teapot. It all seemed extremely ladylike to my childish eyes." Doubtless, this spirit of Edwardian graciousness, so typical of both Father and Mrs. Brook, is still recalled by many people long after the period has passed into history.

Father Brook soon established a pattern of worship which was in the same tradition as his predecessors. His first Eucharist at St. Agnes' was on Friday, 4th July 1913 at 7.00 a. m. at which fifteen people were present. Sunday services were as follows:-

Holy Communion 8.00 a. m.

Matins and Litany 10.30 a. m.

| | |
|---|---|
| Sung Eucharist | 11.00 a. m. |
| Children's Service | 2.45 p. m. |
| Evensong and Sermon | 6.30 p. m. |

At first there were three weekday Celebrations plus special feast days. The daily Eucharist was introduced at the beginning of 1915.

In 1913 the first edition of the English Missal was published and many Anglo-Catholic Churches, St. Agnes' included, adopted it. This was a translation into English of the Roman Missal, adapted for Anglican use and including the Eucharistic Prayer of Consecration from the Book of Common Prayer. It was used by Anglicans as a supplement to the Prayer Book. Formerly Anglo-Catholics had used various "home-grown" Missals, and although the English Missal was never officially sanctioned by the Church of England, its appearance helped to give a hitherto unknown uniformity to Anglo-Catholic worship.

Father Brook kept the Service Register in meticulous detail and often signed for visiting clergy himself. He also made notes in the Register, which at times are of great interest both concerning religious observance in Spital and current events in the World. On one or two occasions his attention to detail led to conflict with the Treasurer, and the final written declaration that only the priest-in-charge should write comments in the Register! In addition to the celebration of the Eucharist, there was the monthly Vespers of the Blessed Sacrament, for the Confraternity of the Blessed Sacrament.

In 1912, shortly before Marsh Kirkby's departure, the St. Agnes' altar servers had joined the Guild of Servants of the Sanctuary. This Guild had been established within the Church of England to foster greater devotion to the Blessed Sacrament, and a deeper life of prayer and dedication amongst Altar Servers. It still exists for these ends. Fr. Brook maintained his predecessor's interest in the Guild and later in his ministry St. Agnes' became a centre for Guild meetings.

October 12th saw the welcome return for Evensong of the Revd. Charles Farr. "It was a joy to have Mr. Farr with us at Evensong and to see so many of his old friends giving him such a hearty welcome. I know how very glad he was to be at St. Agnes' once more, and we all hope it will not be long before he comes here again."

Mr. Fenner was in failing health and it is probably for this reason that the congregation was requested to join in the weekly choir practices. In any case we are told that there was a good response and that "soon we should have the happy result of helping the Choir and making our services more congregational."

The latter part of 1913 saw the deaths of several people connected with Clewer Parish. The September Parish Magazine records the death in Italy of Miss Mary Macbean aged sixty-three years, a great benefactress of St. Andrew's. She had been living in Italy for two years and was about to return to Clewer.

On November 18th Samuel Poynter passed to eternal rest. He had lived in the Spital district and had been a prominent member of Clewer Church and its Choir for over fifty years. For twenty-six years he had been Head Master of Clewer Green School under Canon Carter. The Rector described him as "a faithful and loyal Churchman, a devout Christian, and a trusted friend and servant of the Parish of Clewer."

At Spital, two members of the congregation died within a few weeks of each other. Thomas Rosier, of 2, St. Agnes' Cottages, died aged fifty-five years and was buried on September 20th. Mrs. Mary Best, of 4, Vine Cottages, died on October 23rd aged eighty-five years. She was affectionately known to all as "Aunt Mary".

Miss Rose Layton was thinking of moving away from Spital at the end of 1913. "It will be a great loss to us if Miss Layton carries out her intention of moving away from this neighbourhood after her seven years indefatigable work at St. Agnes'. She has so long thought of moving that we all hoped she would continue only thinking of it . . . . We must now be prepared to face the worst by losing her at an early date, and we sincerely wish her every happiness for the future . . . . " Miss Layton did in fact leave the district but not until July 1914 when she was presented with a purse containing £3:0:0d. In a letter of thanks she said, "I feel very touched by your kind thoughts of me . . . .my work with you has been my happiness, and I very much regret I am obliged to give it up."

There were special preachers during Advent, mostly from local churches, but including Fr. Dunstan, S. D. C., who came on December 14th (Advent III). It was customary at this time to regard Advent as a minor form of Lent, with Sermon Courses and special preachers. The second Sunday in Advent was kept as a day of special prayer for foreign missions, with the alms being sent to the Universities Mission to Central Africa.

So 1913 passed into history - a typical year in many ways, with few people dreaming that before the New Year was out the country would be embroiled in a full-scale War with no sign of an end.

1914 was ushered in by the customary round of Treats and Tea Parties. Lady Barry donated the Infants' Christmas Tree on this occasion and Father Christmas arrived in time to "shower presents upon all". The Rector and Mrs. Cowie were also present and the former presented the prizes. The children of the Catechism went to the Windsor Pantomime "Dick Whittington" thanks to the generosity of Lady Dalton Fitzgerald who also gave a Tea for the whole Sunday School a few days later. The members of the Girls' Club went to the Pantomime a few days later, having delayed in the hope that Miss Wilkinson would be well enough to accompany them. Alas she was not, but instead the girls had the company of Mrs. Uglow who was described as "always ready to do anything for others, however busy she may be."

The Mothers from the three Churches had their Treat in the shape of a "sumptuous Tea" given by Mrs. Mosscockle at the Clewer Hall. About ninety ladies were present, and in addition to the tea party there was a play, plus music and songs. "The excellent acting was highly appreciated by the assembled Mothers, who were thus enabled to enjoy the rare privilege of a good laugh. Between the tea and the acting Mrs. Mosscockle, who had come down from Town on purpose to be present with her guests, addressed a few words of greeting to them wishing them all "A Happy New Year". Mrs Mosscockle had resided at Clewer Park since the departure of the Gooch's in 1906. She was a very wealthy, eccentric widow who, for nearly forty years, modelled her appearance on that of Queen Alexandra. (See Angus MacNaghten: "Windsor in Victorian Times")

January 20th, the Eve of St. Agnes', was observed as a day of perpetual prayer and thanksgiving. This vigil of prayer was introduced by Fr. Brook and was to become a regular observance throughout his ministry. It was offered for twelve hours from the morning Eucharist until the Solemn First Evensong of the Festival. Guest preachers and celebrants during the Octave of the Patronal Festival included the Revd. E. E. B. Grant (Chavey Down); the Revd. Francis Murray Downton (Chaplain, House of Mercy); the Revd. H. J. Adams (Curate, Clewer St. Stephen); the Revd. H. W. Harcourt (Curate, All Saints, Ascot); and the Revd. James Frampton (Chaplain, Ascot Priory). Fr. Frampton had been Chaplain at Ascot Priory since 1881 and retired in 1916. He continued to live in the vicinity and was a frequent visitor to St. Agnes' until his death in 1929. Elderly residents of Spital recall his visits and his arrival by pony and trap.

Fr. Brooks' summing up of his first St. Agnes'-tide was that "there was a spirit of reverence and devotion that could be felt, but the number of Communicants leaves much to be desired."

The evening of St. Agnes' Day was given over to a social event called a "Smoker", which seemed highly successful. The following night there was a concert organised by Miss Fennemore and the Clewer St. Stephen's Girls School, who performed, amongst other sketches, "Mechanical Jane".

Lent rapidly followed the Festival, the pattern of the services being very much the same as in previous years and seem to have been well supported. For instance, there was an average twenty-five to thirty-three people present at Stations of the Cross on Wednesday evenings. Similarly, the Friday evening Mission Services had about forty people present - there were visiting preachers at these services. It must be remembered that this was still the 'age of sermons' when people expected the sermon to last for at least thirty minutes. They were not usually disappointed! About one hundred people took part in a Quiet Day at St. Andrew's on February 26th. It lasted from the Eucharist at 7.30 a. m. until Evensong at 6.30 p. m. and the conductor was the Revd. E. W. Field, Chaplain of St. Peter's Home, Woking.

Services on Good Friday were as follows:-

| | |
|---|---|
| Matins and Litany | 8.00 a. m. |
| Children's Service | 10.30 a. m. |
| Devotions | 12.00 to 3.00 p. m. |
| Evensong | 6.30 p. m. |

Of the Devotional Service, Fr. Brook wrote: "The whole congregation can take a more active part than is usually the case, as there will be more united prayer and Litanies of Intercession, and less lengthy Meditations from the Pulpit. The first part of this Service will consist of Ante-Communion and the Reproaches." A new banner of St. Agnes was dedicated before the First Evensong of Easter. There were one hundred and thirty Easter Communicants in 1914.

The last Summer of peacetime arrived and with it the Summer treats - the Mothers went to Bisham, the Clewer and Dedworth Choirs to Portsmouth. Alas for the St. Agnes' Choir - their outing was postponed "owing to the outbreak of War."

May and June in Spital was marked by Fr. Brook's absence due to illness. He did not resume duties until June 21st. A week later, on June 28th, in far off Serbia, a grammar-school boy lit the fuse to the European powder barrel. As the Archduke Franz Ferdinand, heir to the vast Hapsburg Empire, accompanied by his wife, drove through Sarajevo, the boy, Gavrilo Princip, stepped onto the running board and shot them both. Thus a schoolboy fired the first shot of the Great War.

There were still a few weeks of peace left. Indeed back in England very few people, except at the highest government level perhaps, would have attached any importance to Sarajevo. Life went on as usual. There had been clouds on the horizon before; few thought the storm would actually break.

There were wedding bells at Spital, though not in St. Agnes' for the Church was not licenced for Marriages until 1957. Mr. William George Clarke, sidesman at St. Agnes' for more than fifteen years, married Miss Susey Ann Webb at St. Andrew's on July 11th, preceded by a special celebration of the Eucharist early in the morning at St. Agnes'. The happy couple were given a clock by Mr. Clarke's fellow servers, Choir members and other friends from the congregation. A few weeks later, on September 24th Mr. Alfred Howells and Miss Violet Constance Pert were married at St. Andrew's.

By the end of July the international situation was causing some concern, although the majority of English people still did not think the Country would become embroiled in what many thought was simply a further development of the Balkan troubles, which had been a vexed problem for many years. Throughout the coming weeks the situation worsened until on August 2nd Germany demanded a free passage through neutral Belgium. Throughout the last week of July Britain had dithered on the brink unsure which way to jump. Public opinion was divided, so was Parliament, even the Cabinet itself. However, as soon as Belgium neutrality was threatened Britain stood as one man. Even the Irish shelved their problems and threw in their lot with the Government. On August 4th Britain sent Germany an ultimatum demanding that Belgian neutrality be respected. The ultimatum was ignored: Britain was at War.

The Rector wrote of the outbreak of war in the September Parish Magazine, "This War, foreseen for several years past, has at last broken out . . . . All the resources of our Country are being strained to the utmost in order to prevent the military despotism of Germany from gaining the upper hand in Europe. If we had stood aside and allowed Germany a free hand with regard to Belgium and France, we should have broken our treaty obligations to the former, and been false to our friendship with France. England's honour was at stake, and she was, therefore, forced by dire necessity to enter into the terrible conflict. With a clear conscience we can pray the prayer 'God defend the right'. Our duty is plain. If we cannot actually wield the sword, we can all use the weapons of the spirit and unite in fervent ceaseless prayer to God that His cause, the cause of Truth, Justice and Liberty, may be vindicated."

The Rector's words more or less summed up the Church's attitude to the outbreak of war - it was a war of Honour, a war in which Truth, Justice and Liberty, as epitomised in the plight of Belgium, was at stake. The crucial issue for Britain was Belgium. For the average English "Tommy", who found his way into the trenches, the war had little to do with the assassination of an Austrian Archduke, but it had everything to do with Belgium. The great foe was Germany, a Germany epitomised by Kaiser Wilhelm II, who in common with King George V was Queen Victoria's grandson. One wonders what thoughts passed through the Crowned Heads of Europe, so many of whom were blood relations, as their respective Countries prepared to go to War.

The August Bank Holiday in that fatal year was taken up with the usual pursuits though most people's enjoyment was marred by anxiety. In Clewer there was the usual Horticultural Society Show at Clewer Manor. In fact it was the thirtieth consecutive year that it had been held. The shadow of War loomed however, and attendance was 'down' slightly.

The reality of War became immediately apparent in the Service Registers. Friday, August 21st, was observed as a Day of National Intercession. At St. Agnes' it was kept as follows:-

| | |
|---|---|
| 7.00 a. m. | Holy Mass - 13 present. Seven received Communion. |
| 12.15 p. m. | Litany |
| 7.30 p. m. | Prayer Meeting. Forty-nine present. |

From this time onwards a weekly Prayer Meeting was held to pray for those involved in the War. Attendance varied but never fell below thirty-five and at times reached as many as fifty-five.

Thousands of Belgians had been made homeless by the invading German Army and had sought refuge in Great Britain. In the October issue of the Clewer Magazine the Rector wrote, "We are anxious to do something for the poor homeless Belgian refugees who are coming over to this Country . . . . .We propose to take in a few orphan children for three or four months till a new home has been found for them in their own Country. No doubt many of our local mothers would be willing to receive two little children to board and lodge between the ages of five and eight till after Christmas. The payment would be at the rate of 7/- per child." In the event there were at that time no orphans needing homes. The interesting thing about the statement is the assumption that lodgings would only be required until "after Christmas", and that the refugees would then be able to return home. When the War broke out the popular belief was that "it will all be over by Christmas." In fact it was only just the beginning, for in September at the Battle of the Marne the long drawn out horror of trench warfare began.

On the practical side of the "War Effort", a "Bandage Society" was formed in Clewer to supply sick and wounded soldiers from the 4th Dragoon Guards with clothes and dressings. Mrs. Cowie started a "Work Party for the War" at the Rectory for similar ends. Members of the St. Agnes' congregation made twenty-four shirts for the soldiers, and the Mothers' Meeting made garments for the Belgian refugees, during the first few weeks of the War.

By December the Clewer Bandage Society had sent the following to the Front:-three hundred and forty-nine shirts, five hundred and one pairs of socks, three hundred and seventy-four flannel day shirts, over one thousand bandages, one hundred safety pins, three small pillows, one sweater, one pyjama suit, cigarettes, a parcel of old linen, two hundred flannel belts, one hundred pairs of muffatees, blankets, and plum puddings for Christmas. In addition the Clewer Bandage Society "has supplied two thousand bandages to the 4th Dragoon Guards and a box of bandages, old linen and lint to the London Hospital, St. Bartholomew's, the Lonsdale Hospital, Barrow-in-Furness which receives accident cases from Vickers Shipbuilding yard amounting to fifty daily . . . and also the Connaught Hospital, Aldershot." The Matron of the latter wrote ". . . . the most useful gifts are so acceptable as we are using a tremendous amount of dressings."

A margin note in the Service Register on Wednesday, December 16th states, "Scarborough, etc., bombarded this morning." Late in 1914 the British Grand Fleet perturbed by the presence of German submarines in the North Sea, sailed North to Scapa Flow leaving a temporary gap in Naval defences. The Germans seized the opportunity and bombarded the Yorkshire coast with shells. A number of people died, some damage was done to boarding houses at Scarborough, and the fine monastic remains of Whitby Abbey standing high on the cliffs were reduced to the ruin which can be seen to-day.

"We are to have five hundred soldiers as our guests for a considerable period," wrote the Rector in the December Parish Magazine, "And nearly every home has been requisitioned to afford them hospitality. No doubt we shall give them a very cordial welcome, and be very glad to do what we can to help the Country to bear its many burdens at this critical time." St. Agnes' was also involved in this as Fr. Brook's words testify, "Our Mission Room and the Room above it have been, and still are, much valued by the soldiers. It is thanks to the generosity of many subscribers, and to the personal service of a strong committee of local men, that we have been able to set these rooms apart - one as a Reading and Writing Room, and the other as a Recreation Room. The liberal gifts of books, magazines and papers have indeed been welcome."

On New Year's Eve the Misses Clowes and Miss Temple gave a Variety Entertainment for the soldiers at 7.30 p. m. and for all at 3.00 p. m. It was "an unqualified success", there being a balance of £4:11:0d, and full houses at both performances. A lamp for the lower room was bought from the proceeds, Mr. Bampton fitting it free of charge.

James Merrifield of 4, Vine Cottages, Spital brought a note of pride to St. Agnes' when he won the President's Shield for the best all round Scout in the 5th Windsor (Clewer St. Andrew) Boy Scouts, a distinction he was to repeat the following year. The Shield was presented by Mr. Henderson, the President.

So 1914 passed with no end to the War in sight. Fervent patriotism mingled with fervent hatred of all things German. Men were still flocking to "join up". The Cabinet was against conscription and for the time being there was no need for it. Kitchener, aided by his now legendary poster, set out to raise an army of volunteers. However, it wasn't just Kitchener. There was something "heroic" about fighting for one's Country and the "media", such as it was in those days, was quick to seize the opportunity to appeal to men's sense of duty and conscience. Music Hall artistes such as Edna Thornton sang, for example:-

> "We don't want to lose you,
> But we think you ought to go,
> For your King and your Country, both need you so . . . ."

So they went; young men from every town and village in the Country, including Clewer, Spital and Dedworth. A good many from Clewer Parish had probably never been abroad before. Now they saw foreign place names in plenty - Mons, Arras, St. Quentin, Ypres, Loos, Amiens, Cambrai, Messines, Passchendaele, Kut-el-Amara, Gallipoli. Rivers so different from the peaceful Thames with its pleasure boats - the Marne, the Aisne, and the Somme. So passed 1914 and with it the Old World.

## Chapter X

### A time for war . . . .

1915 came in on a solemn note as befitted solemn times. Sunday, January 3rd was officially designated a National Day of Humiliation and Intercession. It had the full support of the Roman Catholic authorities and of the Free Churches. The Bishop of Oxford authorised Saturday, January 2nd to be observed as a day of fasting in preparation for the following day. At St. Agnes' the observance of January 3rd took the following form:

| | |
|---|---|
| 7.00 a. m. | Holy Eucharist. Seven received Communion. |
| 8.00 a. m. | Holy Eucharist. Twenty-two received Communion. |
| 10.30 a. m. | Matins. |
| 11.00 a. m. | Sung Mass. |
| 2.45 p. m. | Children's Vespers. |
| 3.30 p. m. | Evensong. |
| 5.45 p. m. | Outdoor Procession. |
| 6.30 p. m. | Service of Solemn Intercession. |

Alms throughout the day were sent to the Sick and Wounded Fund of the British Red Cross. The outdoor procession was well supported and the Church was crowded for the service of intercession, there being many men present.

Miss Beal, Fr. Brook's housekeeper, suffered a double bereavement in February 1915 when both her parents died within a few hours of each other. They were both seventy-eight years old, were long-standing supporters of St. Agnes' and had lived at Myrtle Cottage, St. Leonard's Road.

The children of Clewer Green School were busily engaged in the "War Effort" by making night shirts during school hours. Also they had, in their own time, made socks, sleeping socks, scarves, mittens and gloves, which along with letters from them were sent to the Front. Some of the soldiers replied and here are a few extracts:-"I am glad you are so cheerful and not expecting the Germans over there. They will never pass our troops . . . . . The enemy in the trenches are trying to learn our song, their trenches being less than one hundred yards away in some places. They have a gramophone, and our fellows like this and join in the chorus."

We notice how you hope we shall get through to Berlin, and I must tell you that we all hope the same thing, and when a lot of English 'Tommies' set out to go to a place, they usually get there."

"I have just received a parcel and found inside a letter from you, and I think about the finest pair of gloves I have ever had the pleasure to wear . . . .We were one and all pleased to know that the boys and girls in England were doing their best for us all and helping to keep the old flag flying."

"Bovril for the Soldiers" was another attempt by those at home to care for the soldiers in the trenches. This particular scheme was co-ordinated by a Miss Storey of Broadhurst Gardens, London N. W., and Clewer Parish sent £12:0:0d for the cause. An extract from a letter received by Miss Storey reveals both the ghastly conditions in the trenches, which was only just being realised by those at home, and also the unquenchable optimism of the British Soldier: "When coming off sentry, something hot to drink is A. l. Our trenches are pretty comfortable, especially where situated just in the edge of a wood. Although the enemy are only one hundred and twenty to one hundred and fifty yards away from where I am writing, we are able to pass the time away by a little dart throwing with perfect safety. To reach us the Germans would have to splash across plenty of water, so our listening patrol would have plenty of warning and might dive, and I trust enable us to give them a 'Hearty' welcome."

Spital people made an extra effort to keep St. George's Day in 1915, there being Solemn Evensong, Prayers for the Country and Procession on the Eve, and a Solemn Eucharist at 6.00 a. m. on the Day. There were fifty-two people present at the Eucharist, thirty-two of whom received Holy Communion. Ascension Day was also well supported, for thirty-five people attended the Procession and Sung Eucharist at 4.45 a. m., and a margin note in the Register states that it was a very wet morning!

On May 7th 1915 a German submarine sank the ocean liner "Lusitania" with the loss of one thousand one hundred lives. Among those who died was a Mr. Edgar Gorer of Sutherland Grange. Although he was Jewish he was a great benefactor to Dedworth Church. Since the outbreak of War he had undertaken to pay the rents of married men so that they could enlist in the expeditionary forces.

Instead of the customary Empire Day celebrations on May 24th children throughout the Kingdom were requested by an organisation called the "Overseas Club" to each take one penny to school so that parcels could be sent to soldiers and sailors on active service. The children of Clewer Green School together collected twenty shillings which was sufficient to forward twenty parcels, each containing a card with the name of the School on it.

Summer outings were somewhat curtailed due to the War. The combined Choirs went to London as there were no excursion trains to the Coast. The Mothers had separate tea parties instead of an outing, that at Spital being provided by Mrs. Rhoda Maclean. At Dedworth the Mothers were entertained at Bishop's Farm by Mr. and Miss Wright and we are told that "A great feature of the entertainment were the motor rides to and from Bishop's Farm kindly arranged by the Priest-in-Charge (Mr. Eddrup), the only drawback being that, once in the car, the distance to be traversed suddenly became most disappointingly short!"

By June the soldiers billeted in Clewer had moved away and so the St. Agnes' Mission Rooms were again free for social activities. The Boy Scouts also resumed their weekly parades which had been temporarily discontinued while the soldiers were using the Rooms.

A break with tradition was made in August when the Clewer Horticultural Society decided not to hold its annual show at Clewer Manor because a Military Gymkhana was being held at the Imperial Service College. It was felt that everyone ought to support the latter event.

The Imperial Service College was an amalgam of several schools and had its origins in this way. On April 25th 1862 (St. Mark's Day) the Revd. Stephen Hawtrey (Vicar, Holy Trinity, Windsor) opened a boys' school in Alma Road, which he called St. Marks. Although at first a day school, it was run on public school lines, and in 1870 became a boarding school. In 1894 the Revd. C. N. Nagel became Headmaster. He had been Head of a small school at Bath called the "Hermitage" and upon coming to St. Marks brought one hundred boys with him. (The Chapel by the side of the 'Link Road' originally was the Chapel of St. Marks School.) Another public school, the United Services College, had been founded at Westward Ho in 1874 to allow boys to take entrance examinations for Woolwich and Sandhurst. This was not altogether successful. In 1912 the Imperial Service College was formed from an amalgamation of St. Marks, the United Services College, and a third school known as the Army School which was run at Holyport by Mr. E. G. A. Beckwith. Mr. Beckwith became the first Headmaster of the new Imperial Service College in 1912 and brought with him twenty-five boys from the Army School. The senior school occupied buildings off Alma Road most of which have since been demolished. In 1922 the Junior School transferred to Clewer Manor. In 1942 the Imperial Service College amalgamated with Haileybury College (Hertford) and vacated all the Windsor buildings except for the Junior School.

October 1st saw the arrival at St. Agnes' of "our Mission Worker, Miss Lack, who will be living with a friend of hers at 4, Bolton Road." Quite a number of people remember Miss Lack. I am told that she had worked with Fr. Brook in a previous parish and I imagine she was a licensed 'lady worker.' She dressed very soberly in black, with a black cloak and bonnet and preferred to be known as 'Nurse' Lack. One of her responsibilities was the Sunday School over which she ruled very firmly. She kept order by blowing a whistle, long and shrill, so that it could be heard in Church too! She also undertook the running of a Girls' Bible Class, and Christian Instruction for Boys and Girls during the week.

Several Spital families lost sons and brothers during 1915. Among them was Cecil Arthur Stevens of the Royal Engineers aged twenty. His mother, Alice Stevens, of Vine Cottages, Spital was a lifelong member of St. Agnes'. Others who died included Frederick James Dunn killed at Gallipoli, Frank Giles and John Henry Digby all of whom still have relatives living in Spital.

1915 ended on as solemn a note as it had opened with a Week of Prayer for Foreign Missions at the beginning of December. The whole Deanery was observing the week and individual Churches were taking a specific day. Thursday, December 2nd, was St. Agnes' Day of Prayer and it was fairly well supported. The services were:-

| | |
|---|---|
| 7.00 a. m. | Holy Eucharist. Twenty present. |
| 12.00 noon | Intercessions for Missions. Seven present. |
| 6.15 p. m. | Prayer Meeting. Thirty-three present. |

There was also continuous prayer in Church between the services.

Christmas was well observed with one hundred and three Communions. December 31st was kept as a National Day of Penitence in preparation for the Day of National Intercession on Sunday, January 2nd. In addition to all this there was the usual day of Prayer on St. Agnes' Eve.

A welcome visitor amongst the congregation at St. Agnes'-tide was Mr. Victor Biddulph who still took a friendly interest despite being prevented from regular attendance by his declining health.

One of St. Agnes' altar servers, Herbert Bowcott was killed in action at the Front on New Year's Day. A Requiem was offered for him on January 17th at which eleven people were present.

Both of Mrs. Brook's clerical brothers were working in Windsor by 1916. The Revd. T. Basil Eddrup was a curate at St. Stephen's, and was among the Lenten preachers at St. Agnes'. He stayed at St. Stephen's until the retirement of Fr. Nicholas in 1917, when he became Vicar of Thorpe, near Egham. The Revd. E. Clement Eddrup presently at Dedworth, announced his forthcoming departure, soon after Easter, for the living of Corfe Mullen, near Wimborne in Dorset. He remained at Corfe Mullen for the rest of his active ministry and retired in 1959. He then went to live in Tunbridge Wells and died about 1966 when he would have been ninety-three years old. Basil died round about 1960 aged ninety-two years.

Oscar Fenner died on March 9th 1916 after a long illness. Fr. Brook wrote of him, "The passing of Oscar Thomas Fenner . . . was a painful shock, with such unexpected suddenness did his long illness came to its close. A lonely man, who longed to be with those at rest, those words of the Psalmist seemed latterly to be stamped on his expression - 'I went heavily as one that mourneth for his mother.' A quarter of a century is a long time; but for more than that, for twenty-nine years he has been our Organist. Many of us gathered together . . . . when his body was brought to the Church, to plead for him in the Holy Eucharist . . . . Committing his body to the ground and his soul to God. The Solemn Requiem and the Burial were marked with quiet simplicity and dignity such as he himself would have desired: and a cross of flowers was placed on his coffin with the following inscription: 'From St. Agnes' Choir and other Friends in affectionate memory of Oscar Thomas Fenner. May he rest in Peace.' A little man with a great soul, we who miss him most are truly thankful that God has delivered him out of the miseries of this sinful world." Fr. Brook concluded with a note of thanks to Miss Green and Mr. George Kelsey for their help at the organ. After a short time George Kelsey became organist and held the post for fifty-one years. So in eighty years St. Agnes' had just two regular organists.

Fr. Brook's words probably sum up Oscar Fenner fairly well bearing in mind the short time they had known each other. Increasingly bad health had kept Mr. Fenner off the organ stool for considerable periods during his last few years. During those last years his playing had become increasingly erratic. Never a cheerful man, he became even more melancholy as illness overtook him. A little man, he had much to contend with at Choir Practice, for the Choirboys were merciless in their pranks. However, they were sometimes repaid when his Scots temper rose and the offender would find himself rapidly transported from the bench to the floor! He did, however, have real musical talent which flowered to the full during the ministry of the Revd. George Jones, and which was nurtured by that priest's own deep love of music. The 'Missa de Sancta Agnete' may sound out-moded to modern ears, and it may be un-usable with the modern Liturgy, but the achievement lies in its lowly origins. The fact that it was written by the organist of a small village church with nothing better than a harmonium is a testimony to his talent and ambition.

Two members of St. Agnes' congregation had a Spring Wedding at St. Andrew's. Sergeant Arthur Foreman married Miss Ivy Mary Louise Charles on May 6th. It must have brought a ray of sunshine to those cheerless wartime days.

Social life in the Parish went on albeit in a more restrained manner. Treats and outings were still enjoyed by the Choir and also the Mothers' Meetings, although generally they didn't go so far afield. Money, always in short supply, was in even shorter supply because the War had sent prices soaring. The Choir, numbering seventeen in all, went by the 9.20 a. m. boat to Boulters Lock, and walked to Maidenhead where they stopped and had dinner. Then to Cookham by motor 'bus where they had tea, and finally by ferry to Cookham Lock and home by the evening boat. The Sunday School treat took place even nearer home, thanks to Mr. Powell who lent his field (roughly where Bulkeley Avenue is now.)

The Church of England authorities decided to hold a National Mission of Repentance and Hope during the Autumn of 1916, "to arouse the conscience of England and especially the Church of England, with regard to the grave evils which exist amongst us, and are threatening the well-being of the Nation." It was not to be confused with Parochial Missions which aimed to convert the individual, but was rather a Corporate Act of Repentance on the part of the Church as a whole, in the hope of bringing about a religious revival.

The 'content' of the Mission varied from parish to parish throughout October and November. In Clewer Parish, two conferences and prayer meetings were held at Clewer Hall. About one hundred and fifty people were present at the first of these. Among the speakers were Colonel Clowes (Chairman, who was a sidesman at St. Agnes'), Mr. Shorter (Headmaster Clewer Green School), Mr. Poynter, Fr. G. D. Nicholas and Miss Lack. In his address Colonel Clowes pointed out the need for unity, not only in the Nation, but in the Parish, and spoke of Clewer Parish being in greater need of unity. In his summing up of the discussion the Rector denied that there was any 'disunion' in Clewer except geographically. "There were," he pointed out, "present at the Meeting representatives of both Spital and Dedworth."

Besides participating in these Conferences the Spital congregation had their own observance connected with the Mission. On Wednesday, October 4th, the usual Prayer Meeting was held at which forty-eight attended, followed by a "Communicants' Office" attended by forty-one. The subject of the address was the National Mission.

Outdoor processions of witness were a feature of Fr. Brook's. ministry. (Earlier in 1916 he had introduced the Rogation Procession through Spital and it became an annual observance for many years). On Sunday, October 15th at 3.00 p. m. an Open Air Mission Service and Procession was held, the preacher being Fr. Frampton. £1:1:0d was collected for Soldiers and Sailors blinded in the War, which later became known as St. Dunstan's).

In September 1916 George Henry Uglow, eldest son of George and Emma Uglow, caretakers at St. Agnes', died of wounds. He had been an altar server for several years. Amongst the many others from the Parish who died in 1916 were William Ives, killed at Gallipoli, and George Frederick Shurley whose parents lived at 4, St. Agnes' Cottages.

"A strong desire has been expressed to erect War Shrines in different parts of the Parish," wrote the Rector. "We hope very shortly to organise the carrying out of this work." Fr. Brook wrote in more detail, "Before this magazine is out the first of our War Shrines will probably be up, but as one alone can take only a comparitively few names, you will no doubt wish for several Shrines. The first column on the Roll of Honour is for names of those serving, and the second column for those fallen. Names only from this district, as it is the system which is being adopted throughout the Country. One advantage of our Shrines is that they are weatherproof, and can therefore be left out day and night."

The Spital War Shrine was Dedicated at 3.00 p. m. on Sunday, December 10th (Advent II), in the presence of a large congregation. The hymn, "Onward, Christian Soldiers", was sung. To again quote Fr. Brook's words, "It must have been evident to every passer-by that the word of the hymns were used as real prayer, so heartily were they sung - prayer that went up straight to God as surely, and was answered by Him as speedily, as the incense without ceasing floated up in front of the Procession, with Christ on the Cross between it and us." The Shrines were later painted by Mr. Charles.

Christmas came and went, Communicant numbers being one hundred and ten, much the same as in the previous year. The Sunday after Christmas was again observed as a National Day of Prayer. The special intercessions at 6.30 p. m. were conducted by the Revd. T. Basil Eddrup. As 1917 dawned the War seemed interminable. Once people had visualised it being over in weeks, now they speculated in years. As wounded soldiers came home, people began to gain an insight to the horror of this seemingly endless conflict. The national morale dropped as many thought again about those high ideals of August 1914. Britain was in fact the nearest she had ever been to defeat.

"Christmas Entertainments must necessarily be on a small scale, during this time of War," wrote the Rector. "The increased price of provisions and of all commodities, as well as the urgent need of economy, renders this imperative. We hope to have a Tea for the Mothers in the different Districts; and also a Tea for the Sunday School Children who have made the required number of attendances."

The St. Agnes' Sunday School was flourishing under the firm guidance of Miss Lack. In Fr. Brook's words, "Not only have the numbers and attendances increased vastly, but also throughout the year from Advent 1915 to Advent 1916 there has been a steady improvement in the whole tone of the School . . . . . There is very little difference in the numbers between the attendance of boys and girls: both are excellent . . . Three members have an unblemished record for using their religious opportunities on Holy Days, and once a week in Advent and Lent at the early hour of seven o'clock - Ivy Carron wins distinction for the girls; Cecil Upton and William Wilkins for the boys, and Rowland Garner adds to the record of the boys, as he has used most of his opportunities." In addition to the Sunday School, the Boys' Bible Class met on Sunday evenings at 5.45 p. m. "Members of the Choir are in the majority at present because it is they who are always to the front in the good work of the Church. These have been the heart and soul of the Sunday School . . . . "

The "War Effort" continued in one way or another, either to raise funds for those injured and maimed, or their dependents, or to send comforts to those on active service. The weekly "Penny Readings" were revived in the Mission Room and a small tax was levied on the tickets, which was "a help to the Country" as well as being a source of enjoyment to those present. For the women left behind without their menfolk, life became even harder with no-one to do heavy manual work. Despite his frail health, Fr. Brook wrote, "I will most gladly dig up some more gardens if any of you whose husbands or sons have joined up, are in difficulties about getting it done. So please let no-one hesitate to ask."

The number of Easter Communions were 'down' in 1917, there being only ninety-two. The reason, however, was somewhat novel; a note in the Register states, "Summer Time began to-day, and therefore many overslept themselves."

The Rogationtide Procession through Spital was well supported and was blessed with perfect weather. "We were a large gathering throughout, and good numbers awaited us outside their houses to join in Prayer when we halted on our outward and return journeys. Thanks to the kindness of the Second Life Guards, we had a good Band and a big drum."

Two St. Agnes' Choirboys, Rowland Garner and Austin Caudell, made a wooden Cross which was erected at the head of Oscar Fenner's grave. It bore the inscription, "Sacred to the Memory of Oscar Fenner who died on March 9th 1916. R. I. P." A similar smaller Cross was also made for the foot of the grave with the inscription, "For thirty years Organist at St. Agnes' Spital."

For sometime efforts had been made to obtain a Memorial for the fallen of St. Agnes' Church and district. The original plan was for a large figure of Our Lord on the Cross, flanked by statues of Our Lady and St. John, but in the event only the Crucifix was erected. The Memorial was Dedicated on Wednesday July 4th 1917 at 7.00 p. m. by the Rector of Slough, Canon P. H. Eliot. The Church was full despite it being one of the wettest days of what was so far a wet Summer. Fortunately the rain held off for the Service but came on again immediately afterwards. Other Clergy present were the Revd. Arthur East (Warden, House of Mercy); the Revd. G. H. Warlow (Chaplain, House of Mercy); the Rector of Clewer, and Fr. Brook. The figure of Our Lord on the Cross was originally not painted, being of terra-cotta. In later years it was painted over to combat the effects of frost, with disastrous results, for no matter how carefully, or frequently, the work is done the paint peels within a few months. The Cross was surmounted by a slate roof on the front of which was an inscription from the Book of Revelation, "There shall be no more Death, neither sorrow, nor crying."

On July 26th the Sunday School had a Sports Day on Mr. Powell's field instead of an outing or tea party. The judges were Mr. Doe and Mr. Keir. The course was prepared by Jim Merrifield, Rowland Garner, Donald Keir and William Wilkins who, we are told, "worked as hard as niggers". The programme was drawn up by Fr. Brook and Miss Lack, and the prizes were presented by Mrs. Rhoda Maclean.

George Kelsey was married at the end of October 1917. He and his wife, Rosa, remained "pillars" of St. Agnes' until old age and infirmity prevented them taking an active part in Church life, but this lay far ahead in the late 1960's.

In common with many Churches at this time St. Agnes' had its own "War Corner" in which photographs of men on active service were displayed. "Any photo that you have," wrote Fr. Brook, "has a place of honour waiting for it with all the rest among the Flags of the Allies around the Symbol of the Great Sacrifice." All trace of this has, of course, disappeared from St. Agnes', but a few years ago whilst looking round a remote East Anglian Church I came across a similar War Corner dating from the Great War.

November 1st 1917 saw the passing of Mr. E. B. Foster of Clewer Manor at the great age of ninety-three. "His death," wrote the Rector, "has left a blank in our midst which will be felt for many years to come. The Squire, as he was always called, was not only the oldest resident in Clewer, but had lived continuously in the Parish ever since he inherited his property, and indeed all his life. He identified himself with its interests to the very last . . . As Correspondent for many years of Clewer Green School, he witnessed its successive developments from a very small beginning till it attained its present stately proportions. It was the pride of his heart and it was greatly owing to his business-like and artistic perceptions that the additions to the School were so satisfactorily carried out. He has left behind him the memory of a simple and consistent life which will long be treasured amongst us. He was buried on November 4th after a solemn service in Church which was largely attended by many private friends and officials representative of the Country and neighbourhood. R. I. P."

The passing of Squire Foster saw the virtual end of Clewer Manor, there being no son to carry on the line.* Mrs. Foster remained at the Manor, but after her death in 1921 it was bought by the Imperial Service College to accommodate the Junior School. The house thus remains to-day (though the school is now Haileybury Junior), unlike other onetime "desirable residence," St. Leonards, St. Leonards Lodge, Clewer Lodge, Clewer Park, which have fallen prey to modern housing estates.

*Squire Foster's only daughter, Florence Baroness van Heemstra, died in 1982 aged 105 years. She married in 1906, and was widowed in the 1940's.

## Chapter XI

## ... And a Time for Peace

The War was calling to prayer many who had not seriously considered it before. It was also instilling doubts into the minds of many others, some of whom had never previously questioned their faith. It became increasingly difficult for many people, especially servicemen, to reconcile the horrors of this conflict with the Christian Gospel of Love. The "National Mission of Repentance and Hope" of 1916 had not been as successful as many people had expected, and indeed many deemed it a failure. Many clergymen had joined the Forces as Chaplains and were staggered by the ignorance of spiritual matters shown by their uniformed brethren. The Great War cannot be wholly blamed for the downward trend in Church attendance during the next twenty years, but there can be little doubt that it was a contributory factor.

The first few months of 1918 were crucial to the Allies. Two factors helped turn the tide in their favour - the arrival of the Americans, whose fresh troops did much to boost the morale of the war-weary Allies; and the spread of an unseen enemy which swept the World from June to December, killing twenty million people - Spanish 'Flu'. Historians have suggested that this epidemic helped tip the scales against the German army.

In Clewer Parish influenza took its toll as it did everywhere. Fr. Brook was ill during Holy Week and services had to be greatly curtailed. By June the illness was rife and Fr. Brook was again struck down. Fr. Frampton officiated at the Sunday services for two weeks and daily services were cancelled. Services were again disrupted by illness at the end of October and did not get back to normal until 19th November.

The 'Windsor and Eton Express' of July 6th, 1918 had this to say about the 'Influenza Demon', as they called it: "The influenza epidemic has claimed a number of victims in this district and reports from all parts of the country indicate a considerable extension of the epidemic..... The present visitation is chiefly remarkable for the suddenness of the attack. A few persons have died from pneumonia following on. On one day alone there were one hundred boys away from the Royal Free School."

The tide finally turned against Germany on 8th August, when Britain attacked, and although the German line was not broken, it was beaten back and continued to be. The Allied 'Big Push' began on 26th September, and on 4th October the Germans formally asked for an Armistice. The Armistice was not signed until 11th November, for in the intervening weeks there had been domestic upheavals within the Central Powers themselves. In August 1914 there had been four vast Empires covering the map of Europe - the Russian, the German, the Austro-Hungarian and the Turkish (Ottoman). By the time the Versailles Settlement was concluded they had passed from reality into the archives of a vanished World.

News of the Armistice was greeted in England by the greatest public rejoicing since the Relief of Mafeking. In London all work ceased, public houses were broken open and the streets were filled with cheering, singing and dancing crowds. This continued for another two days until finally the police were called in to check what was fast becoming a destructive free for all. In Windsor the streets on November 11th were filled with cheering crowds. A procession of Guardsmen and Firemen was organised, headed by the Band of the Second Life Guards and the drums and fifes of the Coldstream Guards. A Thanksgiving Service was held at Windsor Parish Church and was attended by Princess Alice, Countess of Athlone. A service was also held at Holy Trinity Church. A similar torchlit procession was held in the evening.

The 'Windsor Express' does not record details of services in the parishes of Clewer and Clewer St. Stephen, and the Clewer Parish Magazines for the whole of 1918 are missing from the Parish records. Fr. Brook was still recovering from influenza and the 'Victory Thanksgiving' Service at St. Agnes' was not held until Wednesday, November 13th. According to the Service Register, the Church was full and 11/0d was sent to the King's Fund for the Disabled. Sunday, November 17th was designated 'Victory Sunday', and in addition to the usual services there was a 'Procession through Spital for Thanksgiving' followed by an address at 3.0 p.m by the Revd. Bernard Hardy (Sub-Warden, House of Mercy and temporary Chaplain to the Forces). At Evensong the Choir sang a Solemn Te Deum and the services throughout the day were well supported. A total of £4/0/6d was collected throughout the day for the King's Fund for the Disabled.

"Influenza rampant", was Fr. Brook's comment in the St. Agnes' Register from November 27th to December 4th and indeed the congregation was to lose one of its stalwarts. On December 2nd William George Clarke died as a result of falling from the back bedroom window of his house, 57 Gardner Cottages, Clewer. He and his wife together with their small daughter were all suffering from influenza and on the night before his death he had been suffering from severe head pains and delirium. His mother-in-law was nursing the family and found him lying in the backyard early in the morning. The Coroner concluded that he had gone to the window for air while delirious and had accidentally fallen out. William George Clark was thirty seven years old and was employed at the Royal Gardens. He was an altar server at St. Agnes' and for many years carried the Crucifix in processions. Fr. Brook wrote of him: "The unfailing regularity of his presence at the Services, together with all that he did in every way for the welfare of the village, is one of those good examples of his which we may profitably follow." A Solemn Requiem was offered at 7.0 a.m. on December 6th at which thirty nine people were present. He was buried later the same day in Clewer Churchyard.

On December 14th 1918 there occurred at Lynton, North Devon, the death of the Revd. George Seignelay Cuthbert. The Rector wrote of him: "He began his work at Clewer as Curate under Canon Carter in the early 1870's. He was then for ten years Rector of Market Drayton, Salop, but returned to Clewer in 1884 to succeed Archdeacon Hutchings as Sub-Warden of the Community, and on the death of Canon Carter in 1901 became Warden in the following year, retiring in 1912. His saintly character, scholarly mind and unfailing kindness and courtesy endeared him to all who knew him." He had a long connection with St. Agnes' coming there in the very earliest days, indeed his signature is frequently to be found in the Cemetery Chapel Register.

The Rector heralded the New Year with a note of hope,"The Great Victory which Almighty God vouchsafed to us in 1918, has opened out to us such glorious prospects of better things to come if only we prove ourselves worthy of them, that we realise that the present year is the most critical period in the history of mankind........" The first Sunday in the New Year was kept in all Churches as day of special prayer and thanksgiving.

The people of Clewer were saddened by the sudden death on February 13th 1919 of Victor Myddleton Biddulph, aged fifty-eight years. He had been in declining health for several years and had retired from his work at the House of Lords a year previously. For a few days immediately before his death he had been suffering from a chill and was found dead in bed by his housekeeper, Miss Louisa Nurse. (Was he yet another victim of the dreaded Spanish 'flu which was still playing havoc throughout the Country?) The Rector wrote, "The unexpected death of our dear friend, Mr. Biddulph, has caused widespread sympathy amongst all classes in Clewer.... His enthusiasm for the Service of God, and artistic sense of the beautiful led him to bestow many valuable gifts on the Parish Church, and on St. Agnes' Spital, which will remain as abiding tokens of his devotion. He had many friends among the young men of the Parish. During the War he kept up a correspondence with several of them and supplied them with many comforts while abroad, and was always ready to open his house to them when at home on their periodical furloughs. While we mourn our loss we commend him thankfully into the all-merciful keeping of Him Whose service he loved so well. R.I.P." He was laid to rest in the family grave in Clewer Churchyard on Tuesday, February 18th in the presence of a large number of relatives and friends. Earlier in the day a Requiem had been offered at St. Agnes' at which twenty-seven were present. The funeral service was conducted at Clewer by Canon Edgar Sheppard (Canon and Precentor of St. George's Chapel), assisted by the Rector and Fr. Brook. Other clergy present were the Revd. Arthur East (Warden, House of Mercy); the Revd. G.B. Budibent and Mr. Biddulph's old friend the Revd. Cyril Bickersteth, C.R. The Spital Choirboys joined Clewer Choir and there were several young soldiers present. The hymns "Let Saints on Earth" and "O God, our help in Ages Past" were sung. The inscription 'The peace of God which passeth all understanding", was chosen by Miss F. Biddulph, sister of the deceased, for the coffin.

Without the generous financial assistance of Victor Biddulph St. Agnes' would probably not have been extended in 1907, for the sum required was too great for the meagre finances of the village people. His untimely death took away one of the "characters" of Clewer - a wealthy man who loved God and his neighbour. Born the son of a trusted Courtier, Victor Biddulph was himself in the confidence of Royalty including Queen Victoria. He loved the colourful flamboyance of Anglo-Catholicism, and perhaps that is why he had a particular love for St. Agnes', which during the years he knew it was to the forefront of the local Anglo-Catholic Movement. His name is on the memorial pulpit at St. Agnes' where he is described as, "Another of God's good men." Perhaps that sums him up best of all.

Just before his death Victor Biddulph again gave a generous donation to St. Agnes' in the sum of £25 for the repair of the heating apparatus. He had hoped that the sum would be sufficient, but in fact it cost a total of £37:15:9d, the balance being raised by subscriptions. The debt was cleared by July.

The various activities which had constituted the 'War Effort' were gradually 'wound up' during the early part of 1919. Not a small part of this work had been organised and carried out by women. The women of Spital were no exception and had carried out munitions work in the outhouses behind the 'Stag and Hounds'. Filling shells with explosives must have been both unpleasant and unhealthy, and I am told that the work gave a yellowish pallor to the skin of those engaged in it.

The Clewer Parish Magazine for April 1919 contains the following extraordinary letter concerning the 'War Effort": "Now that the need for collecting eggs for the Wounded Soldiers in the hospitals in England and France has come to and end, I should like to express my thanks to all those in Clewer who have so kindly assisted in the good work by giving eggs and money. Since I commenced collecting in March 1915, Clewer has contributed seven thousand eight hundred and ninety eggs and £56:11:0d in cash, and I especially wish to thank the children of Clewer Green Schools who have collected four hundred and sixty-two eggs and £49:1:9d towards the result." M. Dorothy Durrant, Collector for Clewer.

Miss Beal, faithful member of St. Agnes' for many years, and housekeeper to Fr. and Mrs. Brook during their time in Spital, was planning to move away in June 1919, and was presented with a watch from her fellow members of the congregation. However, her departure turned out to be a 'false alarm' and in the November Magazine Fr. Brook wrote: "She is very glad to say the watch is not a parting gift after all, having returned to a more interesting work, which enables her still to continue some work for the church." The Uglow's had also planned to move away but decided against it, and so their 'parting gift' was presented as a thankoffering instead.

The Versailles Settlement was concluded in June and there was again great public rejoicing. On June 28th, five years to the very day of the Archduke's assassination, Germany signed the Treaty of Versailles. It is generally agreed by historians that within those terms, particularly those relating to the German payments of war reparations, lay the seeds of 1939. The reaction of Marshal Foch, Allied Commander-in-Chief, was prophetic, "This is not Peace, it is an Armistice for twenty years".

For the time being, however, Britain basked in the glory of Victory. On Sunday, July 6th, the theme at St. Agnes' was "Thanksgiving for Peace", and the Choir sang a Solemn Te Deum at Evensong. Saturday, July 19th, was declared a National Public Holiday and the people of Windsor celebrated in style. There was a combined march of demobolised soldiers and those of the garrison, numbering about two thousand in all, plus lady workers, Boy Scouts and Girl Guides and other war workers. There were also river fetes, aquatic sports, a torchlight procession, a bonfire and illuminations. "Notwithstanding the slight rain which set in about midday, nothing daunted the enthusiasm of the sightseers, who paraded the streets till the late hours of the night," wrote the Rector. All the preceding week had been 'Peace Week' and in Clewer Parish it had been devoted to treats and excursions, which in their gaiety evoked the spirit of pre-1914 days. On Monday, July 14th, ninety Mothers and helpers (about a hundred and one in all) had a trip to Henley aboard the 'Windsor Belle'. Tea was served on Temple Island and the remains consumed on the way home. On Thursday, July 17th, about four hundred children attending the Day and Sunday Schools were entertained by Mrs. Mosscockle at Clewer Park. Races and games were organised by Mr. Shorter and his staff from Clewer Green School. Mrs. Mosscockle was prevented from being present as her car had broken down in London. "This was a disappointment to us all and we had to content ourselves with giving her three hearty cheers in her absence," wrote theRector. The Clewer Choir and Servers had a river trip to Marlow on Friday, July 18th. Mr. Rupert East played the piano on board, as indeed he had for the Mothers' trip. The St. Agnes' Choir had already enjoyed their trip to Marlow on July 1st.

The Revd. Roland Errington, former Rector of Clewer, suffered a double bereavement when he lost first his brother and then his wife. On February 22nd Arnold John Errington was buried in Clewer Churchyard, aged seventy-eight years. Mrs. Errington died at a nursing home in Bournemouth on October 4th 1919. She was buried at Ranmore near Dorking where she had relatives.

It took some time for all the armed forces to be demobilised, but by the end of 1919 a good many men were home and looking for work. With election promises of 'a land fit for heroes' still ringing in their ears, many of these men were to return not to jobs but to dole queues and disillusionment.

## Chapter XII

### Stability, Station Days, and the Golden Jubilee

Despite the upheaval and uncertainty of the post-war period, the Twenties represent a time of stability at St. Agnes'. The pattern of worship remained very much as in former years. A new observance, which thence became annual, was first held in 1920 - a Requiem on November 11th for the Unknown Warrior and all who fell in the War. Communicant numbers again again increased as men returned home. During 1921 there were one thousand eight hundred and four acts of Communion, the most for several years. Visiting preachers were not so much in evidence during the early twenties, but among those who did come were the Revd. E. Clement Eddrup; Fr. Boys (Clewer St. Stephen); the Revd. Henry Tower (Vicar, Holy Trinity, Windsor) and Fr. Menin (Chaplain, House of Mercy).

Early in 1920 the Revd. G.B. Budibent finally left Clewer after a curacy lasting nine years. Beset by ill-health throughout his ministry, he had resigned once before and then changed his mind. A considerable part of his time at Clewer had been spent away in convalescence. After leaving Clewer he spent two years in a parish near Ilminster, Somerset in an honorary capacity, after which he became curate at St. Clement's Bournemouth until his death in 1928. Assuming he was not a 'late' ordinand, he was only in his late forties when he died.

By 1921 the Revd. A.J. Clarke had been appointed to Dedworth; and to replace Mr. Budibent, the Revd. Walter Richard Flex, a Master at the Imperial Service College. He acted as Curate at Clewer in conjunction with his duties at Imperial Service College until 1926 when he became Curate at Holy Trinity. He left Windsor in 1937. During his Curacy at Clewer, Mr. Flex spent a great deal of time at Dedworth during the interregnum caused by the Revd. Clarke's subsequent departure from the district and the appointment of his successor.

St. Agnes' Scouts continued to thrive under the guidance of Scoutmaster R. Cooke. Many people still remember him, particularly when there was a concert, for he was a 'star turn' with his repertoire of songs and recitations. He was disabled, having lost an arm during the War, I am told.

St. Agnes' lost two generous benefactresses during the early 1920's - Winifred, Dowager Countess of Arran and Lady Dalton Fitzgerald. Lady Arran was the second wife of the Fifth Earl of Arran whom she married in 1889 and who died in 1901. She too had been previously widowed. By her second marriage she had a daughter, Lady Winifred Gore. Lady Arran had resided for many years at Queen Anne's Mead and did much good work for charity in the Windsor area. Her death occurred on November 13th 1921 at 50 Eaton Square, London. The first part of the funeral service was held at St. Peter's, Eaton Square, and was conducted by Bishop Gore, a relative, assisted by the Vicar of St. Peter's. The internment took place in the family vault at Windsor Cemetery when Bishop Gore again officiated.

Lady Agnes Georgiana Dalton Fitzgerald was the widow of Sir Gerald Richard Dalton Fitzgerald, 10th Baronet, whom she married in 1861, and who died in 1894. During her husband's lifetime the 'ancestral seat' was Castle Ishen, County Cork. There was also a London house and two Country houses. There was no heir to the title. Following her husband's death Lady Dalton Fitzgerald resided at Henley-on-Thames and also retained the London house. She moved to St. Leonard's Lodge, Winkfield Road, soon after the turn of the century and as we have seen took a benevolent interest in St. Agnes'. She left the district during the early 1920's, possibly 1922. Ironically I have not been able to trace the exact date of her death and, therefore, have not found any obituary notice.

The file of Parish Magazines is incomplete for this period.

Dramatic productions in the Mission Rooms seem to have ceased by the early 'twenties', due partly to the War, and also to the death of Victor Biddulph whose flamboyance and love of amateur dramatics had given the impetus to many 'St. Agnes' Dramatic Society' productions. However, there was still a thriving social life attached to the Church. Foremost were the Scouts who frequently performed entertainments for the enjoyment of the congregation. During May 1920 they went 'on tour' to Dedworth where they performed in aid of All Saints' Church Funds which were at a very low ebb. They must have been a talented group for we are told that "they sustained the audience for two hours and Mr. Cooke's own songs and recitations were especially appreciated." Another favourite form of social activity were the Parish dances which were usually organised by Sydney Pert. During 1921 he raised Ł4:10:0d for the General Purposes Fund in this way.

January 1922 saw the first of many visits to St. Agnes' of the Revd. Frederic J. Evans, formerly Archdeacon of Zanzibar and at that time Organising Secretary for the Universities Mission to Central Africa. Collections on that day, amounting to over Ł6:0:0d, were given to the U.M.C.A. From this time F.J. Evans came to St. Agnes' at regular intervals until 1944.

St. Agnes' people were stunned by the death early in June 1922 of Arthur William Weston, aged sixty-nine years. He lived in Vine Cottages, opposite the Church and had been a sidesman for many years. Fr. Brook wrote of him "....a decent Christian man whose place in Church was never vacant without real reason, a good neighbour, and a true friend, he has set an example for us all to follow. For many years a sidesman, he has always done his duty thoroughly, giving a real welcome to all who come to Church: and for many more years a fellow worshipper with us, his loyalty to Jesus Christ and the unfailing regularity of his Communions have above all been a great power for good as well as a sure comfort for his own soul....The highest honour we can do to Arthur William Weston, in Church and home and neighbourhood, is to bear such faithful witness as his own to Our Lord and Master." It is a measure of the high regard in which Arthur Weston was held that sixty-one people were present at the Solemn Requiem on June 8th. This was later followed by burial in Clewer Churchyard. At a meeting of the Parochial Church Council on July 6th a vote of condolence with Mrs. Weston and Family was passed by the Council, standing. Along with Mrs. Uglow, Arthur Weston had been Spital's representative on the Parochial Church Council. A brass memorial tablet was placed on the West wall inside St. Agnes' and was dedicated at Evensong on Sunday, December 10th. The inscription reads as follows: To the Glory of God. In loving memory of Arthur William Weston for many years Sidesman of this Church who died June 3rd 1922. God rest his soul."

(The "Church of England Assembly (Powers) Act" of 1919, otherwise known as the 'Enabling Act' led to the establishment of the Church Assembly. The Assembly's most important function was the preparation of ecclesiastical measures for transmission to Parliament. An early measure was that which established Parochial Church Councils.)

Clewer Manor had changed hands, Mrs. Foster having died in December 1921. In September 1921 Mr. E.G.A. Beckwith, Headmaster of the Imperial Service College moved into Clewer Lodge (formerly the home of Mrs. Carpenter Rowe). This had been empty for some years. Soon after Mrs. Foster's death the Imperial Service College purchased Clewer Manor and its grounds for use as a Junior School. In September 1922 the Junior School duly moved from Alma Road and was installed at Clewer Manor under the Headship of Mr. Harold Wood, M.A. In 1934 Mr. Wood resigned and the Headship passed to Mr. Sidney Beckwith.

The grounds of Clewer Manor and Clewer Lodge, which thus passed into the ownership of the Imperial Service College, were extensive, covering in all about two hundred and twenty-five acres, and extending virtually from Hatch Lane to St. Agnes' Church.

The August Bank Holiday Fete, such a popular feature of Clewer's social life before 1914, was resumed during the Twenties by kind permission of Mr. Beckwith. There were two special attractions in 1923. Mr. Try had offered to take a party of twenty for a ten mile drive in his motor char-a-banc for 2/0d each, the proceeds from which would go to the fete. In addition, Mr. Fenemore was (in the Rector's words), "arranging for Broadcasting with a 'loudspeaker'; this novelty should be very interesting to many of us." Alas, the Rector missed both attractions due to illness which kept him away. Besides these novelties there were the usual stalls and sideshows, that of St. Agnes' raising £11:12:9d, which was a very good sum indeed. The event raised the grand total of £316:0:0d, which was divided among the three Churches - half to Clewer and a quarter each to Spital and Dedworth.

'Thanksgiving for the Anglo-Catholic Congress' was the margin note for July 10th to 15th in the 1923 Service Register. The Congress Movement had begun in 1920 with the joint aim of teaching the Faith and clarifying the position of Anglo-Catholicism within the Church of England. The Movement reflected the change which had come about since the War. Before that time Anglo-Catholics had been content to be regarded as a minority in the Church of England; a minority who were frequently misunderstood, misrepresented and persecuted. The Congress Movement was a show of strength, a time of thanksgiving for conflicts won, a time not only to stand up and be counted but also to loudly proclaim the Faith. It was an age of bells, banners and processions, when the Movement adopted a 'Triumphalist' stance. The leader (by popular acclaim) of the Movement was Frank Weston, Bishop of Zanzibar, and a severe setback was dealt when in November 1925 he died from the effects of a carbuncle at the early age of fifty-three.

The 1920 Anglo-Catholic Congress had surpassed all expectations. One hall after another had been engaged until finally the Royal Albert Hall was packed to capacity twice daily for a week. This was followed by provincial Congresses during the next year, but the second Anglo-Catholic Congress proper was held in London in 1923, and it is this to which the St. Agnes' Register refers.

Other notes in the Register indicate that on June 19th the Eucharist had been offered for God's blessing on the English Church Union, and on July 1st for the Society of the Faith. In 1934 the Anglo-Catholic Congress and the English Church Union merged to become the present day Church Union. The Society of the Faith is perhaps less well known to-day. It was founded about the turn of the century by the Revd. C.E. Douglas with the object of popularising the Catholic Faith. Its chief instrument was the Faith Press, and much later the Faith-Craft Works was added.

One good result of the establishment of the Parochial Church Council was that it made the laity more aware of the financial problems involved in the running of the Church. Many people came to realise, perhaps for the first time, that rising costs affected the Church every bit as hard as the Home. The economic problems which beset post-1919 Britain touched the Church too. So it was that in November 1923 Fr. Brook wrote in the Clewer Magazine, "At a meeting of all our Church Councillors and Sidesmen on October 15th <u>we unanimously agreed</u> -

i. That our Sunday Collections for Church Expenses ought to meet those expenses, which at present they do not:

ii. That more ought to join the "Happy Band of Benefactors" who give a weekly Free Will Offering:

iii. That contributions should be asked for towards necessary repairs to the Boiler and Furnace costing altogether £16:11:3d.

We, therefore, appeal to you all:

i. To make our Sunday Collections better:

ii. To give a weekly Free Will Offering if you do not already;

iii. We ask all those who can to donate towards the Furnace."

As a result of this appeal two donations of £1 were given towards the Furnace, there was an increase in the regularity of the Free Will Offerings, and some new members joined the scheme.

Clewer also had problems with finance, indeed during the post-War period they were considerable. It is fortunate that Fr. Brook had a private income for at a Finance Committee meeting on October 30th 1923 the Rector presented a quarterly statement of the accounts which were £20:0:0d. 'in the red', and this included £50:0:0d for Fr. Brook's quarterly stipend!

1924 had a cheerful start, at least Fr. Brook's letter in the February Parish Magazine has a note of optimism in it. "Our Day of Prayer did indeed bring the Blessing of God on our Patronal Festival, and our Social Festivities throughout the month of January were a succession of thoroughly cheerful meetings. Our thanks are due to all who helped in any way especially those who almost at the last moment provided a first-class Entertainment for the Mothers and the Happy Band of Benefactors."

During the Octave of the Festival the local Chapter of the Guild of Servants of the Sanctuary came to St. Agnes' to sing Vespers. A former priest of St. Agnes', the Revd. Marsh Kirkby had encouraged the servers to join the Guild as far back as 1912. The present local Chapter of the Guild (Chapter of St. Frideswide) was formed in October 1921, and they first visited St. Agnes' in 1923. This became an annual custom for several years, a custom which has been revived in recent times. To return to the Guild's visit in 1924, the weather was very bad but nevertheless servers from Clewer St. Stephen, Dedworth, Chalvey, Slough and Stoke Poges were present.

The season of Lent brought the accustomed extra prayer meetings and visiting preachers. A distinguished visitor was the Revd. C.A. William Aylen, Vicar of Shiplake and Diocesan Preacher. In 1925 he went to a missionary parish in Zululand and in 1930 was consecrated Bishop of Zululand. In 1935 he was translated to the Diocese of St. Helena, and upon his resignation in 1939 returned to the Oxford Diocese as Rector of Aston Tirrold. While home on furlough in 1936 he again preached at St. Agnes'. His last appointment was as Assistant Bishop of Peterborough from 1952 to 1963.

1924 was the year of what became known as the 'Fiery Cross Pilgrimage'. It had its origins in the 1923 Anglo-Catholic Congress when it was decided to have a 'Year of Prayer with Fasting and Almsgiving for the Conversion of our Country,' beginning on January 1st 1924. In conjunction with this a 'Fiery Cross' was passed from one Church to another, staying twenty-four hours in each Church, thus establishing an unbroken chain of prayer throughout the year. St. Agnes' kept two 'Station Days' as they were called, on April 15th and October 17th. On the first of these the time-table was as follows:

| | |
|---|---|
| 7.00 a.m. | Holy Eucharist - Seventeen present |
| 7.30 a.m. - 7.30 p.m. | Continuous Vigil of Prayer. |
| 4.30 p.m. | Children's Service of Prayer. |
| 7.30 p.m. | Devotional Service. Forty-one present. |

The October 'Station Day' was observed throughout the Parish. The ceremonies began with a torchlit procession on the evening of October 16th when the 'Fiery Cross' was brought from St. Paul's, Maidenhead. It was handed over at 'The Willows', Surly Hall Road, by the Revd. S.S. Mahoney of St. Paul's, and was received by the Rector of Clewer. The procession consisted of the surpliced choirs of all three Churches headed by the Cross-bearer (Mr. Cripps), and the Rector, together with two acolytes in scarlet cassocks and cottas. The hymns 'Onward Christian Soldiers', 'The Church's One Foundation' and 'O God, our help in Ages Past' were sung along the route, and upon entering St. Andrew's, 'The Royal Banners Forward Go' was sung. Many people joined in the procession, some from the start and others by the way, so that St. Andrew's was almost full. A short Service of reception followed with a few words from the Rector. The Cross was then placed on the South side of the Side Altar which had been prepared with flowers and lighted candles. The Vigil began with a midnight Eucharist preceded by the Litany, the Rector being the celebrant. There was a second Eucharist at 6.00 a.m., the celebrant being the Revd. H. Clark of Dedworth and a third at 7.30 a.m. (the Revd. W.R. Flex). The twenty-four hour Vigil was well maintained at St. Andrew's, the men taking the night hours and the women the day hours. At. St. Agnes' the day-time Vigil was well kept and there were good numbers at the morning and evening Services. At the end of the day Vigil at St. Andrew's the 'Fiery Cross' was passed on to St. Stephen's Parish.

Two other events were of importance at St. Agnes' in 1924 - the Golden Jubilee of the Dedication, and the retirement of the Rector. The problem of the date of St. Agnes' Dedication has been dealt with at length in Chapter I, and I will only re-iterate here that all the evidence weighs against September 9th as the true date, for it seems that the Church did not open until November 8th 1874. For whatever reasons, Fr. Brook kept the Golden Jubilee on September 9th 1924. The August and September issues of the Parish Magazines are missing and so we do not know what Fr.Brook had to say about the forthcoming Jubilee. The answer to the problem may lie in those missing magazines. Thirty-three people were present at 5.45 a.m on September 9th for the Solemn Eucharist. "The first Solemn Eucharist of our Jubilee in the early hours of September 9th struck the true note of heartfelt thankfulness for all God's mercies since our Church was dedicated," wrote Fr. Brook in the October Magazine. The weekday masses throughout the Octave were poorly supported, there being nine people at the most on two occasions. Fr. Brook lamented this apathy, "Empty places at the Altar day after day were by no means few, and it most surely is a sad fact that more than a few Communicants made no Communion at all either during or near our Festival; and other Church people are to be mightily pitied whose sense of Churchmanship is so feeble that their own Jubilee itself left them cold." There was however, a good attendance at Evensong on the Sunday in the Octave when the Rector preached for the last time at St. Agnes' before his retirement. (He returned to preach on St. Agnes' Day 1927). There was also a Procession and Te Deum, and the Church was, we are told, almost full.

A generous donor gave as a Jubilee gift, a complete set of new hangings for the Sanctuary to replace the old ones which had become very ragged. A photograph taken c. 1936 before the restoration of the Sanctuary during the ministry of the Revd. R.E. Beer shows these hangings. They consisted of dossal curtain (behind the Altar), riddal curtains (at either end of the Altar), and curtains along the East and North walls of the Sanctuary. They appear to have been made of a heavy dark brocade.

A new carpet was also bought for the Sanctuary at a cost of £15:6:0d. The money was raised by subscriptions from the congregation. It was a Turkish carpet, "of the very best quality", and was in use by St. Agnes' Day 1925. This carpet served for more than fifty years and was replaced in 1978 when a generous benefactor gave a new one as a thank offering.

The retirement of the Revd. Arthur Cowie marked the end of a chapter in Clewer Parish history, for there had been many changes in the Parish, both spiritual and secular, since his induction in 1900. Those far off days seemed to belong to a different world to those of 1924, and in many ways they were. Yet this is not to say that Arthur Cowie was in any way 'out-dated' or 'out of touch' with things. To the end of his ministry he took an interest in all aspects of parish life, and in the wider Church too, despite failing health. He was a particularly kind friend to St. Agnes' whose interests he always held dear. At all times he endeavoured to keep St. Agnes' open, even during severe staff shortages. Only once did St. Agnes' close and that only briefly until the arrival of Fr. Brook. Money was often short at St. Agnes' but it was never used as a threat for closure while Arthur Cowie was Rector. However, the advance of years brought increasing ill-health and Arthur Cowie retired to Oxford, where his priestly ministry had begun more than half a century previously.

At a ceremony on October 30th at the Clewer Hall the Rector and Mrs. Cowie were presented with a cheque for £200 and a book containing an illuminated address and three hundred and sixty-one names of those who had contributed. The many tributes paid to the Rector by fellow clergy and laity from all parts of the Parish are too lengthy to reproduce here, but are recorded in detail in the 'Windsor and Eton Express' of November 7th 1924, together with Mr. Cowie's reply.

We cannot leave 1924 behind without recording that on October 20th George Edward Bridges and Lillian Violet Aldous were married at St. Andrew's. Two pillars of St. Agnes' - the bride was a Sunday School teacher and the bridegroom had 'long been a valued member of the Choir'. In later years they were to become caretakers at St. Agnes', but this lay a few years ahead. The happy couple were presented with a clock by the Choir.

So we leave 1924, the year of the Golden Jubilee, a momentous year, behind and look ahead to the start of the next fifty years, a period which alas is less well documented than the preceding period.

## Chapter XIII

### Hail and some more Farewells

The event which overshadowed all others at the beginning of 1925 was the induction of the new Rector, the Revd. William Elwell on January 29th. (At a special meeting of the Parochial Church Council held during the previous July a decision had been made to send a letter to the Provost and Fellows of Eton College, patrons of the living of Clewer, recommending the appointment of the Revd. E. Clement Eddrup as Rector. Whether the living was indeed offered to Mr. Eddrup is unknown, but in the event the Revd. William Elwell was appointed).

William Elwell was one of ten sons, three of whom were priests. He was ordained deacon in 1908 and priest a year later. His first curacy was at Wantage, and in 1915, in common with many clergymen, he left the parochial ministry to serve as an Army Chaplain. Upon his discharge in 1919 he became curate of All Saints', Boyne Hill, in charge of St. Paul, Maidenhead. He held this position until his appointment to Clewer. He was about forty years old and was unmarried.

St. Andrew's Church was filled to overflowing for the induction service at 3.00 p.m on Thursday, January 29th. Two motor char-a-bancs brought members of his former congregation to the ceremony. As well as clergy from Windsor and Clewer there were also several from the Maidenhead area. Five of the new Rector's brothers were present. (The new Rector paid his first visit to St. Agnes' on Sunday March 8th).

Anticipation of the new Rector's arrival and induction overshadowed the usual events of January at Spital - the Christmas treats and the Patronal Festival. The treats were held on various days in January together with their accompanying entertainments. The Clewer Green school children provided entertainment for the Mothers and we are told that they were very good. Mr. Liddiard, who lived in Vine Cottages opposite St. Agnes', organised a concert on January 7th in the Mission Room and gave half the proceeds to the General Purposes Fund.

The end of February saw the departure of Miss Lack for work elswhere. She had been at St. Agnes' for ten years and Fr. Brook wrote, "She will not soon be forgotten." Indeed she was not, for many people still remember her to this day. Her place as Superintendent of the Sunday School was taken by Miss Hearmon, "A teacher of much experience and one of our most constant worshippers," to quote Fr. Brook again.

On March 10th the Parochial Church Council unanimously agreed that St. Agnes' ought to be financially self-supporting. This followed changes in Church of England financial policy, for by this time all parish churches had to pay back to the Diocese a share of their income to help shoulder the cost of clergy stipends, upkeep of parsonages, etc. Most 'daughter' churches were expected to help their parish church pay (nowadays the daughter churches have their own 'quota' to pay). The St. Agnes' congregation took the challenge and by the end of the year Fr. Brook had sent £12:10:0d towards the Parish quota and an additional £50:0:0d towards Clewer's own assistant clergy fund. Mr. Elwell was full of praise for the way in which the St. Agnes' people were accepting their responsibilities. "The priest-in-charge of St. Agnes' Church, and the congregation there are to be commended on the efforts which they are making in one way and another to see that the Church work is carried on in that part of the Parish as it has been in the past. All success attend their efforts".

A 'Garden Sale' was held at "Audley Mead", Bolton Avenue, the home of Mrs. Goodhart on Saturday, May 23rd. This made a profit of £40:16:8d. for St.

Agnes' Funds as well as providing an enjoyable social occasion. A stall at the Clewer fete held on August Bank Holiday Monday brought in a further Ł10.3.4d.

Wedding bells rang out at Clewer for two couples from St. Agnes' in August. On August 15th Austin George Caudell, a member of the Choir, married Louisa May Wrixon. A fortnight previously Cecil John Upton had married Alice May Brown. The bridegroom was a sidesman and server, and was presented with a clock by Mr. Bridges. Soon after the wedding the couple moved away from Windsor, thus ending Cecil Upton's long association with St. Agnes'. "Little did we think that he would be leaving us", wrote Fr. Brook, "and neither did he himself expect it, but a good appointment is not to be rejected. In him we lose a server of unfailing reliability and of many years standing, a good Councillor and a very faithful friend."

Wednesday October 14th was observed as the 'Station Day' for the Parish in connection with the Fiery Cross Movement. At St. Agnes' a twenty-four hour vigil was kept from 7.00 a.m. on Wednesday until 7.00. a.m. Thursday, starting and finishing with a Eucharist. It was well supported especially the Children's Watch at 4.30 p.m. at which there were seventy-three present, and also the Service of Devotion at 7.30. p.m. Alms that day were sent to the Fiery Cross Ordination Fund.

Father Edward F. Russell of St. Alban's Holborn died in November 1925. He was still a curate at the Church where he began his ministry fifty-eight years previously. He died in his eighties, and Bishop Gore later described him as a 'Saint of God'. His two visits to St. Agnes' on All Saints' Day 1909 and 1910 are still remembered by a few elderly residents of Spital. At St. Agnes' a Requiem was offered on November 12th and seven people attended.

Queen Alexandra, widow of King Edward VII, died in November. The funeral took place on November 27th and was a Requiem at St. Agnes' at which five people were present. Perhaps the arctic weather conditions are the reason why so few attended. A contemporary photograph shows the guardsmen accompanying the cortege with snow on their bearskins.

There are several margin notes in the Service Registers for 1926 'Response to the World Call' and 'Prayer for the World Call'. This was a call to prayer organised by the Church Mission to Jews.

1926 was a troubled year. "General Strike from Midnight of Monday, May 3rd" was the rather matter of fact note in the Register - almost as though it were a common occurrence. The Strike continued for nine days and on Wednesday, May 12th, at the first Evensong of the Ascension a further margin note adds, "Thanksgiving for end of General Strike to-day". It is difficult to assess the effect of the Strike on Windsor and Clewer for the Parish Magazine is missing and the "Windsor and Eton Express" was 'out' along with the rest of the Press.

A glance at the Church accounts for 1926 shows St. Agnes' finances to have been in a healthy position. The General Purposes Fund showed a balance of Ł54:0:0d and the Church Expenses Fund a balance of Ł5:3:9d. A fair amount of money was given to Missionary Societies and other Institutions, often by means of special collections. The overseas Missions which St. Agnes' supported at this time were the Universities Mission to Central Africa, the Mission to Corea and Zululand Mission. Special prayers were offered at the Eucharist on May 2nd and 3rd for the Corean Mission upon the Consecration of the first Cathedral in Corea. The pioneer Bishop in Corea had been Bishop Corfe who had dedicated the font in St. Agnes'. The Zululand Mission was a favourite with Anglo-Catholics at this time on account of the popularity of Bishop Frank Weston of Zanzibar who had died during the previous November. The U.M.C.A. had long links with St. Agnes' going back to the Revd. G.H. Swinny who, after leaving Spital, had pioneered work on the shores of Lake Nyasa and died there. November 5th 1926 saw the Register note "Prayer for first time for "St Agnes' Namatutwe, Central Africa". Two guineas were sent from the Church Expenses Fund and this U.M.C.A. project was supported for a number of years. Other organisations which received financial support from St. Agnes' at this time were the Waifs and Strays, Society for the Promotion of Christian Knowledge, Rescue and Preventive Work, the English Church Union, King Edward VIIth Hospital, St. Luke's Hostel, Earl Haig's Fund for Ex-Servicemen, St. Dunstan's and the Fiery Cross for Ordinands.

November 1926 was a busy month at St. Agnes'. A 'Station Day' was observed on November 8th with the customary twenty-four hour vigil. Ł2:11:5d was collected for the Fiery Cross Ordination Fund. Also at this time the church was redecorated thanks to a windfall from the taxman! Ł37:9:4d income tax had been recovered from rents paid on the St. Agnes' Cottages, and the Parochial Church Council decided that this should be allocated to St. Agnes' for redecoration. This was duly carried out at a cost of Ł32:0:0d by Messrs. Foreman Bros.

A further windfall fell into Fr. Brook's lap at the end of 1926 although he was reluctant to accept it. The Rector proposed, and the Parochial Church Council unanimously agreed to increase Fr. Brook's stipend from Ł200:0:0d a year to Ł230:0:0d, commencing from January 1st 1927. Although grateful for the offer, Fr. Brook declined. Nevertheless the Parochial Church Council decided that the additional Ł30:0:0d should be given as an Easter offering.

St. Agnes' lost some faithful members during 1926. Robert Thomas Aldous was buried on March 22nd and in May Mrs. Elizabeth Bowcott died aged sixty-four. Both were faithful worshippers and communicants. Another member, Mrs. Mary Fuller, moved away from the district. She was a well known member of the community, being Post Mistress at Clewer Green. At this time the Post Office was in Clewer Hill Road at the end of the first terrace of houses.

About this time the Universities Mission to Central Africa initiated the 'Coral League' for children. It was run on a parish basis and the members endeavoured to help the work of the mission. A branch of the Coral League was started at St. Agnes' in 1927 and was run by Miss Thorne who, I am told, was <u>very</u> strict. She was assisted by Miss Hearmon and Miss Scott. Boys attended as well as girls, and besides making handicrafts for the annual Sale of Work, they performed plays with a missionary emphasis, e.g. in 1928 two plays were performed in aid of St. Agnes' Namatutwe. The Magazine "African Tidings" kept the members in touch with the mother Society.

A branch of the Mothers' Union was started in Clewer in 1928 and on October 4th the first of the monthly services at St. Agnes' was held. Fr. Brook officiated and the preacher was the Revd. Joseph Leighton Bailey who had been priest-in-charge at Dedworth during the previous year. He left soon afterwards to become an Anglican Benedictine monk at Nashdom Abbey, Burnham. As Dom Dunstan Bailey he remained at Nashdom until his death on August 15th 1952 in the twenty-second year of his Religious Profession.

November 17th to 26th 1928 saw a Mission with a difference in the form of a visit of the "Diocesan Women Messengers". Messengers Agnes and Christine gave addresses at the Sunday services and conducted Mission services on the weekday evenings.

By 1928 a Parish bazaar was held instead of the fete at Clewer Manor, the proceeds being divided amongst the three churches. In addition to this, St. Agnes' held its own Summer Fair in Stag Meadow. This proved to be highly successful both socially and economically, bringing in £66:0:0d profit in 1928 and £68:0:0d in 1929.

"We regret to announce the death of the Revd. A.T.C. Cowie, M.A.,son of the late Very Revd. the Dean of Exeter, which took place at Folkstone on Thursday last week," (February 14th 1929), wrote the Editor of the "Windsor and Eton Express" in the issue for February 22nd 1929. The funeral took place at Clewer on Tuesday February 19th. The celebrant at the solemn Requiem was Fr. W.E. Boys, Vicar of Clewer St. Stephen. The organist was the Rector, Fr. Elwell, and the Requiem was fully choral. The Bishop of Buckingham conducted the funeral service which followed at mid-day. Fr. Brook read the lesson and there were numerous other clergy present. There were many mourners including children from Clewer Green School, to pay their last respects to a beloved and highly respected priest. Among the wreaths was one from St. Agnes', "in affectionate remembrance of our dear friend and Rector." Burial followed in Clewer Churchyard and a large wooden cross was later erected over the grave. It is a sad irony that this memorial to a priest who gave himself so unstintingly for Clewer Parish should have been vandalised in recent years, so that the broken Calvary now lies on the neglected grave.

February 1929 was indeed a sad month at St. Agnes' for besides the death of Mr. Cowie there also occurred the deaths of George and Emma Uglow, caretakers of the church. The "Windsor and Eton Express" of February 22nd records their passing in this way. "We regret to record the deaths of Mr. George Underhay Uglow which ocurred on Friday last week at St. Agnes' Cottage, Spital, and of his wife, Emma Maria, who passed away at King Edward VII Hospital Windsor after a serious operation on Tuesday last. Mr. Uglow was sixty-seven years and his wife fifty-seven. Mr. Uglow only took to his bed two days before his death and his wife was then in hospital...." George Uglow was a native of Denbury, Devon and as a young man had served in the Coldstream Guards. In 1890 he became licensee of the 'Oddfellows Arms' which at that time stood in Love Lane. There he remained until the property was demolished when the Victoria Barracks was enlarged. In 1905 he and his wife moved to St. Agnes' Cottage as caretakers of the Church, and he also worked at Shaw Farm. During the Great War he served in the Royal Defence Corps at the Windsor Waterworks and other places of importance until he was invalided out following an attack of pneumonia. Mrs. Uglow was a native of Windsor. Her sister, Mrs. Charles, was a fellow staunch supporter of St. Agnes'. From the very start of the Parochial Church Council Mrs. Uglow was one of the Spital representatives and only gave up in 1926 because of poor health, when she was succeeded by her son, John. Her kindness was well known, and both Mrs. Uglow and her husband were ready and willing to help others even at great personal cost. For instance, during the Great War a close friend of the family, John Henry Digby, was killed leaving a widow and large family. The Uglows, who had themselves lost a son, gave a home to one of the boys. Leslie Digby remained a faithful member of the Church until his death in the 1960's. The Uglows are commemorated on the memorial pulpit at St. Agnes'

A Requiem was held for George and Emma Uglow at 7.00 a.m. on Wednesday, February 20th, at which nineteen people were present. The funeral service followed at 2.00 p.m. with the Rector and Fr. Brook officiating followed by internment in Windsor Cemetery.

During the last year of the decade the Mission Rooms (which were by now being called "St. Agnes' Halls") were renovated at a cost of £38:10:1d. In addition some repairs were carried out to both church and hall roofs and to the the hall staircase.

All the church accounts showed a healthy balance. At this time it was customary for St. Agnes' to give £150:0:0d towards the Parish Assistant Clergy Fund, no mean sum when one considers that Fr. Brook's own stipend amounted to £200:0:0d per year.

There had been some changes amongst the faithful during the decade. Not a few familiar people had either died or moved away from the district. The Uglows were succeeded as caretakers by Mr. and Mrs. Rowland Garner. Mr. Garner had been a Choirman and Server for many years and now occupied the position of caretaker until leaving Windsor in 1933. (In recent years he and his wife have returned to Spital).

## Chapter XIV

## The Old Order Changeth

A glance at the Service Registers of St. Agnes' for the early 1930's shows a marked similarity to those of ten years previously. The services continued in the same pattern and parish life was much the same. There is, however, one marked difference from the early 1920's - the period 1930 - 1935 was the final phase of Fr. Brook's long ministry at St. Agnes' and during this time ill-health overtook him.

Church ownership of property often causes problems and during 1930 and 1931 the Parochial Church Council were preoccupied with the insanitary condition of the three St. Agnes' Cottages, otherwise known as Knowles' Cottages. Clewer had been brought into the Borough of New Windsor in 1920 and the Borough Sanitary Inspector now served notices to the Parochial Church Council to bring the cottages up to standard. The Finance Committee of the Parochial Church Council felt that the property was too old to repair adequately, and that it was undesirable for the Church to own it. Fr. Brook, however, saw things differently and the Minutes record that, "It was only out of deference to the expressed wish of the Revd. W. Brook to repair the houses that the Committee did not agree to their closure. On being put to the vote two voted for the motion, two against and three did not not vote." After much deliberation Fr. Brook announced that he would advance £200:0:0d towards the cost of putting the cottages in a sanitary condition, the terms of repayment to be arranged later, and that he would not require interest on the loan. Thus the cottages were saved though whether the right decision was made was debatable. No doubt Fr. Brook felt it would be wrong to evict the tenants, Mrs. Rosier, Mrs. Brown and Mrs. Shurley, especially as they had lived there for many years.

July 1931 marked the twenty-first Anniversary of the 5th Windsor Scout Troop. To mark the event Evensong on July 26th was followed by the Dedication of the "King's Colour."

There were dark clouds over Clewer in 1931 and, although it is not my intention to drag old skeletons from forgotten cupboards, nevertheless some mention must be made, if only to set the record straight. Amidst great controversy the Rector, the Revd. William Elwell, was prosecuted on charges of immorality. The Court case was heard "in camera" so that the full facts never emerged. However, this in turn gave rise to gossip and rumour, sometimes conflicting and mostly inaccurate. As a result many people had, and still have to this day, the wrong impression about Elwell's later ministry. The facts are these. As a result of the Court proceedings, from which he was acquitted, Elwell resigned the benefice of Clewer. The 'official' reason given for his resignation was on grounds of ill-health, and indeed the controversy had taken its toll of him. He then travelled abroad for a time and did not exercise his priestly ministry in any official capacity until 1934 when he was granted permission to officiate within the Diocese of Chester, and then from 1935 to 1937 in the Diocese of Truro. However, he did not leave the Church's ministry, neither was he unfrocked as many people seem to think. In 1937 he was instituted as Vicar of Luxulyan in Cornwall, a living which he held until his death c. 1957. From 1950 he was also Rural Dean of Bodmin.

At the Parochial Church Council Meeting on October 5th 1931 the Secretary moved the following resolution, "That the Clewer Parochial Church Council places on record its high appreciation of the Revd. William Elwell's devotion to duty while Rector of Clewer and expresses its sincere sympathy with him in his illness and trusts that with rest and change he will be completely restored to health". The resolution was seconded by Mr. Cross, endorsed by Miss Porcher and supported by Fr. Brook. It was carried unanimously.

Few people have been able to give me an unprejudiced assesment of Elwell's ministry in Clewer. I have been repeatedly told of the controversy which brought about his untimely resignation from the Parish, often with little compassion and even less accuracy. This is regrettable particularly as there is so little documentary evidence available about the day to day business of the Parish during this period. (Except for one or two odd copies the file of the Parish Magazine was not kept up after June 1926, and the Parochial Church Council Minutes of the period have little of permanent interest).

It seems that William Elwell left Fr. Brook to run St. Agnes' in the customary manner, confident no doubt that the Spital district had a devoted priest who cared deeply for his church and people. The relationship between the Rector and St. Agnes' seems to have been a happy one, certainly Mr. Elwell was full of praise for the way in which the congregation attempted to pay their way financially, and there is no evidence of any friction at any time. However, this was a stable time at Spital and for once St. Agnes' had few troubles - perhaps it would have been a different story otherwise. Certainly relations between the Rector and Dedworth were not always so cordial for a number of reasons, finance being one of them. The 1920's and early 1930's were as unstable for Dedworth as they were stable for Spital.

However highly William Elwell might have praised the people of St. Agnes' his visits to the Church were rare; in six years he came to officiate or preach on only three occasions.

Elwell had an interest in Parish history and in 1928 wrote a pamphlet entitled "The History of Clewer Parish and Parish Church". It is now out of print but may be consulted in the local history section of Windsor Reference Library.

"Memorial Pulpit Dedicated" is the heading in the "Windsor and Eton Express" for November 27th 1931. The Church was crowded for the dedication ceremony which was performed by the Right Revd. Philip Herbert Eliot, Bishop of Buckingham at 7.30 p.m. on Thursday, November 19th. Bishop Eliot was no stranger to St. Agnes' having dedicated the Wayside Calvary in 1917 when he was Rector of Slough. The pulpit was in memory of several 'friends' of St. Agnes' and bore the following inscription on a bronze plate, "To the Glory of God and in memory of our dear Friends, Arthur Cowie, Rector 1900-24; George and Emma Uglow, Caretakers 1905-29; Charles Farr, Priest-in-charge 1904-11; and Victor Biddulph, another of God's good men. God rest their souls". The pulpit was designed by Mr. A.L.N. Russell, F.R.I.B.A. and built by Mr. W. Butcher of Spital. The cost (£50:0:0d) was met by subscriptions from the congregation. Other clergy present at the ceremony included Fr. Brook and the Revd. Frank Odell- Cheshire, priest-in-charge of Dedworth. The service took place by candlelight plus a few oil lamps as the supply of gas had been temporarily cut off due to the Windsor Gas Company working in the road! Scoutmaster Cooke read the lesson and Fr. Brook led the prayers. The hymns were, "We love the place O God" and "Alleluia, Alleluia, Hearts to Heaven and Voices Raise". Psalm 100 was also sung and Mr. George Kelsey played the organ as usual. The Bishop's address followed in which he paid tribute to those servants of God in whose memory the pulpit was dedicated.

1932 began with widespread illness. Fr. Brook noted in the Service Register for Saturday, January 2nd that "all the usual members of our congregation are ill", and on January 7th, "More illness still". One hopes they had recovered by January 19th for the customary Day of Prayer in preparation for St. Agnes'-tide. The preacher at the first Evensong of the Festival was the Rector-designate, the Rev. G.G. Payne-Cook.

Thursday, February 9th (Shrove Tuesday) saw the new Rector's induction and institution. The ceremony was performed by the Bishop of Buckingham in the presence of a large congregation, St. Andrew's being filled to capacity.

The Revd. Gerald Payne-Cook was no stranger to Windsor. Following his ordination to the priesthood in 1907 he served curacies at Southport and Leeds before becoming a Minor Canon of St. George's Chapel from 1911 to 1916. He then became Vicar of Northam, Devon until his appointment as Rector of Clewer.

In appointing Gerald Payne-Cook to Clewer Rectory the Eton College authorities were making what might be called a 'safe' appointment. He was approaching fifty, married with a grown family of four, and was more in line with the 'Central' churchmanship of the Established Church, than with the 'Triumphalist' Anglo-Catholicism of the period under review. His first reaction to St. Agnes' Church decked out for her Patronal Festival is unrecorded, but it later became apparent that the new Rector had little affection for his two daughter Churches, seeing them as additional burdens to the machinery of parochial administration.

Lent proceeded as all other Lenten seasons with extra services and special preachers culminating in the Three Hours Devotion on Good Friday. In 1932 it was conducted by Fr. Wyber, Chaplain of Frensham Monastery. This Religious Community for men moved to Frensham in 1929, and the members were known as the "Servants of Christ the King". In 1928 some Anglican laymen had established a Brotherhood dedicated to the Kingship of Christ in a small cottage at Staithes near Whitby. Soon afterwards they moved to Abbey House, Pershore which had been vacated by the Anglican Benedictines upon their move to Nashdom Abbey. The Servants of Christ the King wore a grey Benedictine style habit, and their special work was with mentally defective boys. In August 1931 they moved to a large modern house, which they called 'Mount Olivet',at Frensham in Surrey. Their Chapel was very baroque and their spirituality had an extremely 'Romeward' slant. At Easter 1936 the Community made its corporate submission to Rome and became Oblates of the Benedictine order with a monk of Ramsgate Abbey acting as Novice Master and Chaplain. Their mode of life remained unchanged but they eventually disbanded due to lack of vocations.

In April 1932 the Revd. George Davenport Nicholas died in his ninety-sixth year. This remarkable man had been in Holy Orders for seventy-two years having been ordained deacon in 1860. He had served in Clewer for almost the whole of his active ministry. He first came to Windsor in 1860 as curate at Holy Trinity and left in 1862 to become Vice Principal of the Theological College at St. John's Newfoundland. In 1865 he became curate of Clewer under T.T. Carter, and was a regular visitor to Spital both to the Cemetery Chapel and to St. Agnes'. He became first of all priest-in-charge and then the first Vicar of Clewer St. Stephen until his retirement in 1917. Following his retirement he moved to Maidenhead where he ministered in an 'honorary' capacity. However, he was still a familiar figure in Windsor during the 1920's and was usually seen wearing a 'Father Brown' clerical hat and riding a tricycle. Small boys with customary irreverence called him 'Old Nick'. He was however a great priest and a great 'character' who could draw a lesson, even make a sermon, out of the commonplace. For instance, one Sunday at St. Stephen's he preached about 'wastefulness, and as an example urged those present not to waste paper when writing letters. One who was present took the point, tore off the 'spare' paper from his letters, bundled them together and sent them to the priest. The following Sunday Fr. Nicholas followed up his previous oration with a sermon on 'tidiness'. He would probably have been amused and certainly surprised to know that the "Windsor and Eton Express" devoted almost a whole page of its issue of April 8th 1932 to tributes and an obituary. It is yet another reminder of how times had changed from the early days of his ministry and the dark days of Canon Carter's persecution. A Requiem was celebrated at St. Agnes' on April 6th at which six people were present.

By the 1930's Spital was well represented on the Parochial Church Council. Members of St. Agnes' elected for 1932 were Mrs. Charles, Mr. Clarke, Mr. Foreman, Mr. and Mrs. Grutchfield, Mrs. Merrifield, Mr. Pert, Mr. Prowse, Miss. Thorne and Mrs. Brook. Sidesman at St. Agnes' were Messrs. Blake, Cooke, Cooper, Foreman, Grutchfield, Howells and Prowse.

By the end of 1932 Fr. Brook was becoming very frail. His once very neat and distinctive handwriting began to deteriorate from this time, so that by 1935 it was almost illegible. The once immaculate Service Register began to resemble an untidy jumble. From the beginning of 1933 Fr. Brook's absences from duty became more frequent, and whilst the services carried on as usual there was more 'outside' help notably from the Revd. W.R. Flex; Fr. Rokeby (Curate, St. Stephen's); the Revd. R.I. Beckett (All Saints', Windsor); Canon T.H. Dans and Canon Sheffield Grace Betham Exham (Minor Canons of St. George's).

July 14th 1933 marked the Centenary of John Keble's sermon preached to the Assize Judges in the Church of St. Mary the Virgin, Oxford. This sermon had opened the floodgates of the Catholic Revival in the Church of England.* The Centenary was a time of great thanksgiving amongst Anglo-Catholics everywhere. The religious publishing houses suddenly became flooded with histories of the Oxford Movement, biographies of its leaders, plus dozens of devotional and liturgical publications. There was much rejoicing at parish level throughout the Anglican Church and a good many clergy and parishes became caught up in the rejoicing who were not particularly 'extreme' in their Churchmanship. The reason for this was that the effects of the Tractarians had rippled out so widely that there were few churches which were not affected in some way by the Revival. Practically all aspects of liturgy, worship and ceremonial had been touched by the Revival. Even Church Music had been affected, for the Hymnals which we now take so much for granted were compiled in response to the newfound need to enliven the liturgy with congregational singing.

The chief thanksgiving to mark the Oxford Movement Centenary in Clewer Parish was centred on those parts most associated with Canon Carter - St. Andrew's and the House of Mercy. There was a solemn Eucharist at the House of Mercy at 11.00 a.m on the Saturday at which the Bishop of Buckingham presided. Lunch followed and there was a pilgrimage to Canon Carter's grave in the churchyard. The preacher at Evensong was the Revd. K.H. McMaster (Sub-Warden, House of Mercy). The "Windsor Express" noted that Miss Mary Carter, Canon Carter's daughter was then still living at the House of Mercy aged ninety-seven years.

On July 11th there was a Requiem at St. Agnes' for the leaders of the Catholic Revival. The celebrant was the Revd. R.I. Beckett and there were seven people present. At St. George's Chapel the Centenary was observed with a Sung Eucharist and Choral Evensong. The Bishop of Gloucester preached at the latter.

That perennial headache 'the hot water system' was causing trouble again, this time in the Hall, and repairs cost St. Agnes' £10:12:4d, a large sum in those days. The exteriors of the Church and Hall were repainted at this time at a cost of £10:5:0d. On the income side of the Balance Sheet, St. Agnes' Fair raised £56:15:9d, a Sale of Work raised £17:15:2d and the Whist Drives organised by Sydney Pert brought in a further £30:14:6d. The Coral League Sale raised £16:0:0d for St. Agnes' Namatutwe, and in fact that Church received £22:0:0d from Spital in 1933. The usual £150:0:0d was raised towards the Clewer Assistant Clergy Fund. The General Purposes Fund showed a balance of £57:5:5d.

The Harvest Festival continued to draw in large numbers for there were fifty-five Communicants on that day whereas a normal Sunday would produce about twelve to twenty Communicants. There was a Eucharist at 7.00 a.m. on

Harvest Sunday in addition to the 8.00 a.m. Eucharist. The Solemn Eucharist at 11.00 a.m. was still a 'non-Communicating' Celebration.

"We are most grateful to Fr. Heald and the Clewer St. Stephen's Church Council for their gift to St. Agnes' of a particularly beautiful statue of Our Lady. It is just what we often wished we had," wrote Fr. Brook in the Clewer Magazine for October 1933.

1934 was an uneventful year until September when the Diamond Jubilee of the Church's Dedication was celebrated. Regrettably there is little documentation, there being no Parish Magazines for 1934 in the Parish records, and the event passed unnoticed by the "Windsor and Eton Express". September 9th fell on a Sunday and there were fifty-one Communicants on that day. Fr. Brook celebrated at 7.00 and 8.00 and preached at 11.00, Fr. Exham being the Celebrant. The Revd. Henry Tower, Rector of Holy Trinity, Windsor preached at Solemn Evensong. It was decided to mark the Diamond Jubilee by the installation of electric lighting. This cost £26:3:3d, the money being raised by subscriptions from the congregation. The work was carried out by the Electric Light Company and a Mr. Odell. The new lighting must indeed have been a tremendous improvement on the old gas lamps.

St. Agnes' received some very favourable comments in the"Windsor and Eton Express" of September 21st 1934, not concerning the Diamond Jubilee but the Autumn Sale in St. Agnes' Hall! "In the earlier part of every year a big fete is held at Stag Meadow and last Wednesday's sale was another example of how people at St. Agnes' co-operate and make their little Church entirely self-supporting. The Church stands in a district where the people are none too well off, many, in fact, being in straightened circumstances, and that they do so well is a tribute to them and to the Revd. William Brook, who is in charge of the Church, and Mrs. Brook, who never spares herself. While everyone is a useful cog in the wheel of parochial organisation, a special tribute is due to the Honorary Secretary (Miss E. Thorne) than whom there is no more enthusiastic worker for the good of the cause". A list of stall-holders was included which gives an insight as to whom the workers were at this time -
Provisions: Miss Beal, Mrs.Kelsey and Mrs. Hughes; Flower Stall: Mrs. Fisher and Mrs. Cooper; Rummage: Mrs. Charles, Mrs. Howells, Mrs. A. Foreman, Mrs. Copas and Mrs. Liddiard; Needlework Stall: Miss Morris and Miss Exham; Sunday School Stall: Miss Hearmon; Bowls: Mr. S. Pert. The proceeds amounted to £18:5:2d.

By the beginning of 1935 Canon Exham's signature appears in the Service Register almost as frequently as Fr. Brook's. Major festivals were presided over by local clergy, for instance on St. Agnes' Day, the Rector celebrated and Fr. Heald, Vicar of Clewer St. Stephen, preached at the Solemn Eucharist. Holy Week was covered by Canon Exham, Fr. Sefton (Chaplain, House of Mercy), the Revd. John Simpson (Dedworth), and Fr. Miller (Chaplain, Ascot Priory). From Easter onwards Fr. Brook only celebrated about twice a week and this with the utmost difficulty. Other clergy officiated the rest of the time. Walking was a great effort and it must be remembered that he lived some distance away from St. Agnes', in Bolton Crescent. During these last months he required assistance from Mr. Bridges in putting on and taking off his vestments. There were problems too with speech, and even though towards the end he left preaching to others, yet for some time his sermons had become "a few words" delivered with difficulty. It was, therefore, no surprise when Fr. Brook resigned after twenty-two years devoted service. His last Eucharist at St. Agnes' was on Wednesday, July 31st, at 7.00 a.m. when twelve people were present. There was a presentation ceremony as a mark of gratitude for so many years service, but, as with so many events during this period there is no record; the only evidence which we have being a leather bound book of subscribers to the gift. It does not record details of the gift itself. Fr. and Mrs. Brook retired to Bournemouth. However his retirement was to be short for in

November 1936 he was knocked down by a car, ironically on his way to church. He died shortly afterwards without regaining consciousness. Canon Exham wrote the following tribute to him, '.....In all his work he showed himself the ideal...priest, infecting all those to whom he ministered with his own zeal and concern for the things of God and His Church. Above all things the outstanding quality of his life was love...As he himself loved Christ and his Church so he ever taught his people by word and example. He had an unfailing love and care for the souls of his people, and the regular visiting of them in their homes were all born of his sense of the great value of their souls in the heart of God. To him all human souls were precious....Living himself a highly disciplined and self-controlled life, he was indulgent, almost to a fault, to the shortcomings of others. Though choirboys may at times have been unruly and thoughtless in the vestry they never thought of going away after Evensong without shaking hands with him and their "Goodnight, Father" was a genuine expression of the affection and respect they felt for him...Having no great personal gifts as scholar or preacher, he found his power through a life of deep religious devotion. The daily Eucharist...was the fountain from which he drew his strength...and gave him his zeal and serenity, his devotion to God and his people, and the love with which he embraced the world... Mrs Brook relieved him of many worries of the ordinary parochial round, and supplied the sociability and organising powers that were perhaps his weakest points as a parish priest. His work lives on and he himself will ever live in the hearts of his friends, and our sense of personal loss makes our sympathy with his widow all the deeper and more genuine".

So passed a great priest who is indeed still loved and remembered by many people to this day. A Requiem was celebrated at St. Agnes' by the Rector on November 14th. Twenty-two people received Holy Communion. This was followed by a Memorial Service on the following Sunday evening. Mrs Brook continued to live in Bournemouth until her death in 1953.

As a postscript to the ministry of William Brook I here reproduce by kind permission of Mrs. Rosemary Young, her poem 'Village Church in the 20s', which recalls her own childhood memories of St. Agnes' and its priest and people.

### "VILLAGE CHURCH IN THE 20s"

The bell rang out at eight for morning prayer,
From the little village church upon the hill,
And every Sunday morning at eleven,
We children went to sing the hymns of praise,
The choir assembled, and I can recall
Reg's booming voice above them all,
Whilst the gentle, frail, tottering old priest,
Shaking and nodding, climbed the Chancel steps,
Uttering unintelligible prayers in quaking voice,
His long, thin, trembling hands pressed palm to palm,
Kyrie Eleison, incense burner swinging,
Holy Smoke ascending, the Angelus' solemn ringing,
Two strong lads would lift the candlesticks
High above their heads at Eucharist,
Wobbling slightly as they stood the strain,
Sea of suspense among the congregation,
Until they brought them safely down again:
My wandering gaze would light upon the sprays
Of bright Lent Lillies wet with April showers,
Palm, Narcissus, carefully displayed, by those
Elusive artists who arrange the flowers;
A little energetic nervous man
Was Mr. Kelsey, faithful organist,
Bobbing up and down upon his seat

Excitedly, whilst pounding at the keys,
A young boy pumping madly by his side,
Then priest and choir would slowly glide
Out of sight into forbidden spheres,
The vestry, sacred place of mystery,
Into which I longed to have a peep,
And those same pious choir boys, cherub-like,
Would all explode outside the church's walls,
Like evening primroses in gathering dusk,
And skip and run into the morning air:
Ladies in their Sunday best, would stand
In groups along the paths to chat and smile,
And in their plaited straw hats fruit was fixed,
And from the brims glistening cherries hung,
Looking so real as if they were just picked,
Appearing just as fresh at evensong;
The church at eventide was dimly lit,
Old people filled the pews where children sat
At morning prayer: Simeon's 'Nunc Dimittis' I loved,
Waited in awe, with bated breath, for that
To be sung after St. Luke's 'Magnificat,'
Scout-Master Mr. Cooke, who'd lost one arm
Read the lesson, his voice strong and calm,
I sat with Gran and thought of old Miss Lack,
Who taught at Sunday School and wore a cloak,
When she retired there was this sense of loss,
That we children felt in the procession
Following the priest in Holy Week,
To sing beneath each picture on the wall
The sad compassionate 'Stations of the Cross.'

## Chapter XV

## All Things New

The interregnum following Fr. Brook's resignation was fortunately short. It had been hoped that the Revd. N. Hudson would take over St. Agnes', as indeed he did from August 1st to September 13th, but he left on health grounds and does not appear to have exercised any ministry after this time. After Hudson's departure Canon Exham bore the brunt of the work, with help from Windsor and Clewer Parish clergy. Assistance was also given at this time by the Revd. Arundell Blount Whatton, a retired priest, whose last incumbency had been at East Tisted, Hants, in succession to the Revd. Roland Errington. He frequently came out of his retirement at Winchester to assist in parishes where there were staff shortages.

As was inevitable during the interregnum, the services had to be somewhat curtailed and as a result Communicant numbers fell. The Eucharist was celebrated on Sundays, Tuesdays and Thursdays and on important Saints' days. Christmas Communions for 1935 numbered a mere thirty-one.

The chief problem concerning a replacement for Fr. Brook was financial. 'Rednal' was a large house for a priest to run and without private means it was well-nigh impossible. The annual stipend of the Spital priest at this time was £225, and in October 1935 the Parochial Church Council agreed to raise it to £250.

It must have been an immense relief to the people of Spital when it was announced that the Revd. Richard Evelyn Beer had been appointed as priest--in-charge of St. Agnes', and would begin his work on Sunday, January 12th 1936. Richard Beer was about thirty-four years old, and married with a young family. He moved into 'Rednal' with his wife, Patricia, who was expecting a baby, and their adopted twin daughters, Jocelyn and Priscilla, aged two and a half years.

Richard Beer bagan his ministry in the mission field. In 1924 he was ordained deacon by the Bishop of St. Albans for work in the Diocese of Grahamstown. During the following year he became a Chaplain of the South African Church Railway Mission, a position he held until 1928. In 1930 he returned to England as Curate of St. John the Evangelist, Waterloo Road, and in 1931 became Curate of Ashford, Kent. While at Ashford he had charge of a daughter church, Christ Church, South Ashford, until coming to Clewer.

(Founded in 1890 the South African Church Railway Mission ministered to scattered railway workers over thousands of miles of country. It built churches in townships and provided priests until the churches were taken over by the diocese. The Founders were Douglas and Harry Ellison, whose nephew, Gerald, retired as Bishop of London in 1981. In recent years the Mission became known as the Railway Mission of Rhodesia and Botswana. In 1980 it was felt that it had done its work and the Mission was closed.)

Richard Beer was slightly built, with balding hair and a shy smile. He had a slight stutter of which he was painfully aware, and Mrs. L.V. Bridges recalled that he often asked her husband to hear him practise the readings in church. The Spital people at once made their new priest feel "at home", and he in time began to inject some much needed "life" into the church. Fr. Brook had worked unstintingly and had remained at the altar to the last, but during his declining years it was inevitable that his ministry lacked the vitality of a younger priest.

The Eucharist continued to be the central act of worship at St. Agnes' as it had always been. There were, of course, a few changes. For instance, the Vigils of Prayer, so frequent in Fr. Brook's time, were discontinued, and also the Servers' Guild no longer came to St. Agnes'. There were at this time plenty of servers at St. Agnes' and 1936 saw the 'debut' of a new 'boat-boy', Alan Bridges, whose job it was to carry the boat-shaped incense container. Alan and his brother, Bob, lived with their parents in the Caretaker's Cottage adjoining the hall. There have been a good many priests at St. Agnes' since 1936 but Alan Bridges is still there - but promoted now to senior server.

A great asset which Fr. Beer could rely on at St. Agnes', and which is no longer available at the present time, was a faithful team of caretakers. Mr. & Mrs. George Bridges had succeeded Mr. & Mrs. Rowland Garner in 1933. Both were long-standing members of St. Agnes', having been born and brought up in Spital. Mrs. Bridges was the actual caretaker although her husband did a good deal. At least twice a week Mr. Bridges would rise at 4.00 a.m. and scrub half the church floor. He would then go to Old Windsor and do a day's work. Upon returning home he would clean the church brass (although the altar brass was looked after by Miss Rodwell, the sacristan). They were responsible for scrubbing and cleaning the Mission Rooms, stoking and maintaining the boiler, and keeping the church garden and lawn in good order. All this for a princely salary of £10. per annum, plus £3. for lighting; after which they had to pay back almost a quarter to the Rector in rent.

1936 was a sad year both for the Nation and, as it turned out, for Spital. St. Agnes'-tide was overshadowed by the illness of King George V. On January 20th, St. Agnes' Eve, the Rector, the Revd. G.G. Payne-Cook, preached at Evensong, but the thoughts of most people on that rain-sodden night were at Sandringham where the King lay dying. "The condition of His Majesty, the King, shows diminishing strength," stated the bulletin issued at 5.30 p.m. At 9.25 p.m. came the now famous statement, "The King's life is moving peacefully towards its close." Later came the final announcement, "Death came peacefully to the King at 1.55 p.m. tonight in the presence of Her Majesty The Queen, the Prince of Wales, the Duke of York, the Princess Royal and the Duke and Duchess of Kent." So for the second time this century St. Agnes'-tide had witnessed the death of a reigning Sovereign. January 21st 1901 saw the death of Queen Victoria. King George died five minutes before the thirty fifth anniversary of his grandmother's death.

In Spital, St. Agnes' Day was observed with the celebration of the Eucharist at which twenty-one people received Holy Communion. There was a Memorial Service for the late King at 6.30 p.m. on Sunday, January 26th, and a Requiem at 7.00 a.m. on the day of the funeral, Tuesday, January 28th.

Just a few months previously, in May 1935, the Nation and Empire had given thanks for twenty-five years' reign. "It was not so much that the King had reigned for so long; it was rather that he had reigned so well," to quote from a book entitled "Hail and Farewell: the Passing of King George V." Together, Sovereign and Nation, indeed Empire, had weathered a good many storms since the Coronation in 1910 - War, Depression, Strikes and all manner of political and social unrest, and the Silver Jubilee gave the King's subjects an opportunity to show their loyalty and their gratitude. That they did so with such enthusiasm left the King deeply moved. At that time the people of Spital had joined their own prayers to those of the Nation on Sunday, May 12th, with a special Service of Thanksgiving. Now seven months later they prayed for the repose of the King's soul.

The King's body was removed from Sandringham to Westminster Hall for the Nation's last homage. At 9.45 a.m. on January 28th the funeral procession left Westminster Hall at the start of the late Sovereign's last journey to Windsor. The Royal train left Paddington half an hour late and did not arrive at the purple draped Windsor Great Western Railway station until nine minutes past one. Prior to this a succession of special trains had brought political leaders and foreign dignitaries. As the funeral procession passed into the High Street the crowds of thousands caught their long awaited glimpse of the coffin covered by the Royal Standard, and surmounted by the Crown, Regalia, Insignia of the Order of the Garter and the Queen's wreath. The procession made its solemn progress down the High Street, Park Street, through the gateway into the Home Park, through the Grand Quadrangle of the Castle, down the Upper and Lower Wards, and so to St. George's Chapel.

One major breakthrough made the funeral of King George V different from that of any other preceding Monarch: sound broadcasting. By this means people not only in England, but as far away as America, and many other countries were able to hear the funeral service. In Windsor itself the service was relayed by loudspeakers installed at the Guildhall. After the procession had entered the Great Park the troops lining the route were marched away and the crowds, estimated at 100,000, surged across the High Street. Suddenly the loudspeakers were switched on as the procession approached St. George's and everyone instinctively stopped pushing and jostling and turned in complete silence towards the Guildhall. Just as the loudspeakers commenced broadcasting, an officer with a double file of soldiers attempted to march them down the High Street towards the station. Unable to get through the crowd they were forced to halt and were completely hemmed in for three quarters of an hour until the end of the broadcast.

Two members of St. Agnes' died within a week of each other in February 1936: Mr. Arthur Foreman and Mrs. Alice Stevens. In his youth Arthur Foreman had been a chorister and a keen member of the St. Agnes' Dramatic Society. He had been a master at St. Stephen's School for over twenty years before accepting a teaching post at Ealing two years before his death. He was a keen sportsman. His death took place at his home, 'Myrtle Cottage', St. Leonard's Road. He was forty-three years old and was survived by a widow and daughter. A detachment of the Royal Berkshire Regiment, with whom he had served, provided a bearer party for the funeral which took place at Windsor Cemetery. The Rector and Fr. Beer officiated. A Requiem was celebrated at St. Agnes' on February 21st at which twelve people received Holy Communion.

Alice Stevens had worshipped at St. Agnes' for many years. She was noted for her generosity and hospitality at her home, 4 Vine Cottages, St. Leonard's Road. She had borne nine children, five of whom had died, including Cecil a victim of the Great War. Her grand-daughter, Rosemary Swatton, now Mrs. Rosemary Young, was brought up by her. Rosemary Young is known to many people by her poems. Alice Stevens was buried on February 28th 1936, her seventy-fourth birthday, following a Requiem at St. Agnes', at which fourteen people received Holy Communion.

Lent 1936 was observed with a weekly service of Compline and an Address. On Tuesday, March 31st, there was a Mission Service which was conducted by the Right Revd. C.A. William Aylen, Bishop of Zululand. This was his second visit to St. Agnes', having previously preached here in 1923 when he was Vicar of Shiplake-on-Thames.

The whole Parish was stunned by the death on Monday, April 27th, of Mrs. Patricia Beer. "There is deep sympathy with the Revd. R.E. Beer, priest--in-charge of St. Agnes', Spital in the loss of his wife, Mrs. Patricia Nooila Beer, aged thirty-two years, who died in King Edward VII Hospital on Monday.....Mrs. Beer was in good health until Saturday when she was suddenly taken ill and removed to the Hospital where she died." In this discreet manner the "Windsor and Eton Express" recorded the tragedy. In fact Mrs. Beer died in childbirth and the baby boy, who was delivered by Caesarian section, also died.

Patricia Beer came from an Irish family. Her father was the late Canon W.H. Parker of St. Peter's, Birmingham. She was educated at King Edward's School, Birmingham, and took a degree at the Royal Holloway College, London University. In 1931 she married Richard Beer at St. Jude's, Birmingham, where her brother-in-law, the Revd. E.D. Tyndall, was Vicar.

Patricia Beer's body was placed in St. Agnes' Church on the evening of Wednesday, April 29th. The following morning at 7.00 a.m. a Requiem was offered by the Revd. E.D. Tyndall, assisted by the Revd. M. Parker (brother). There was a large congregation present and thirty-five people received Holy Communion. The funeral service took place at 1.15 p.m. in the presence of a large congregation and was conducted by the Revd. E.D. Tyndall, assisted by the Rector of Clewer and Revd. J.R. Simpson (Dedworth). Before the service George Kelsey played 'I know that my Redeemer liveth'. During the service the following hymns were sung, 'King of Glory, King of Peace', 'Immortal Love for ever full', and 'Love divine, all loves excelling'. Psalm 130 and the 'Nunc Dimittis' were chanted.At the end of the service the organist played "Blest are the Departed". The service was followed by cremation at Woking. The many wreaths were placed around the War Memorial in front of St. Agnes' church, and included tributes from members of the congregation, the Mothers' Union and many from Church organizations at Ashford, Kent.

There was a Gift Day on June 20th, commencing with Mass at 7.00 a.m. and concluding with a Thanksgiving Service at 8.00 p.m. A total of £34:15:3d was raised for Church Funds. This was not the first Gift Day at St. Agnes', for during 1935 in the last few weeks of Fr. Brook's ministry a similar event had raised £40:10:0d. A photograph taken about this time shows Mrs. Louisa Charles, Mrs. Violet Howells and Miss Esme Pert standing at a table outside the church awaiting 'gifts'.

A glance through the Service Register for this time shows that the average number of Sunday Communicants was between fifteen and twenty at 8.00 a.m. No indication is given of numbers still attending the Solemn Mass at 11.00 a.m. which was still non-Communicating. Generally, people still made an extra effort to attend the Eucharist on Festivals even though the service was usually very early in the morning. For instance, on Ascension Day twenty-six people received Holy Communion at 5.45. a.m., and fifteen at the same time on the Feast of Corpus Christi. Harvest was as popular as ever, and in 1936 thirty-seven people received Holy Communion on that day. There was still a tendency at this time to regard the season of Advent as a 'mini' Lent with special services and addresses. During Advent 1936 either Compline and an Address, or Litany and Compline, was held on Wednesday evenings.

November, the month of Holy Souls, was marked in 1936 by the death of Fr. Brook. It marked the climax of a year when the Parish had bade farewell to several friends both old and young.

'Monarchy' was uppermost once more in the mind of the Nation at the end of 1936, a year which saw three Kings reign. Throughout the course of 1936 the subjects of King Edward VIII had been eagerly anticipating his Coronation. However instead of Coronation there was Abdication and long years of self--imposed exile. The Editor of the "Windsor and Eton Express" had this to say in the issue of December 11th. "End of a Reign: In a momentous message read by the Speaker to a silent House of Commons yesterday King Edward VIII announced his irrevocable decision to renounce the throne. To-night he ceases to be Sovereign. Tomorrow morning his brother, the Duke of York, will be proclaimed King. The decision of the King to abdicate was taken only after long and anxious consideration.....Thus a reign which eleven months ago seemed destined to be glorious ends in tragedy. It is not for us to judge the King's decision: only to accept it. Let us never forget now or hereafter the great services he has rendered to the peoples of the Empire both as Prince of Wales and in the brief months as Sovereign......"

During his ministry Fr. Brook had occupied the office of Church Treasurer himself for most of the time, refusing to delegate until about a month before he retired. The task was then undertaken by Miss Emily Thorne who held the 'purse strings' of the church from 1935 to 1940 and 1945-1950 when she left the district. Emily Thorne was employed in a bank at Egham and was a most able and efficient Treasurer. She was also, together with her friend, Edith Hearmon, one of the chief benefactresses of the Church at this time.

Miss Thorne and Miss Hearmon were old friends and shared a home together in Devereux Road, Windsor, not far from George and Rosa Kelsey. Edith Hearmon was very small and thin, almost frail looking. Her life's work was in the General Post Office, which she joined in Windsor in 1900, but she will always be associated with Eton Post Office of which she was Sub-Post Mistress from 1919 until her eventual retirement in 1945. During her quarter century at Eton she had contact with many "notables" both contemporary and future. But if the Post Office was her life-work, then certainly St. Agnes' was the centre of her life-long devotion to Christ and His Church. Her special interest lay in the Sunday School which she superintended after Miss Lack's departure in 1925, until ill-health made her give up in 1948. She also ran the Coral League, together with Miss Thorne and Miss Scott from the time of its inception in 1927.

Emily Thorne was taller and larger-built than Edith Hearmon, indeed somewhat formidable by comparison. However, they both dressed in similar style - grey or navy costumes, silk in the Summer, and they were never seen hatless. She made the daily journey to Egham by bicycle, sometimes along flooded roads. Those high, large-framed bicycles with baskets at the front and skirt-guards at the back became something of a 'trademark'. Emily Thorne was both Secretary to the St. Agnes' Committee of the Parochial Church Council and Treasurer, until it was decided in 1940 to separate the two 'offices', but she resumed them both again from 1945 to 1950. The Accounts and Minutes which she kept are written in a business-like and masterly hand, and there can be no doubt that while she held office everything was under a firm but devoted control.

During the inter-War years most of the wealthy 'gentry', who had supported St. Agnes', died, and particularly after Fr. Brook's retirement St. Agnes' had once more to struggle to make ends meet. It was a struggle which has never quite been overcome, but it was assistedin no small way by these two faithful friends of the Church. No-one will ever know the full extent of their generosity but it is notable that after Edith Hearmon's death in 1950, and Emily Thorne's subsequent departure from the district that the church finances took a headlong plunge - although there were other contributory factors.

The church funds continued in a healthy state for a while after Fr. Brook left, and at the Annual Parochial Church Meeting of 1936 the Rector thanked Miss Thorne for her untiring work for Spital. Even the debt on the St. Agnes' Cottages, which had been incurred in 1931, had been reduced to £30:0:0d, and it was reported that after the current year, all the income on the Cottages would be available for the Church funds. It, therefore, came as rather a blow when at a Parochial Church Council Meeting held on February 1st 1937, St. Agnes' finances were held up as an example of bad housekeeping. The incident is recorded in the Minutes thus: "Mr. Cross gave some rough figures as to the financial position (at Clewer) at the end of the year and estimated there would be a deficit of about £25:0:0d - Free Will Offering Fund, Collections and Donations all being less than the previous years, and with increased expenditure on the Assistant Clergy and Churchyard Funds. The Rector enlarged on Mr. Cross's statement and strongly criticised St. Agnes' for their failure to disclose to the full Parochial Church Council the state of their finances. He pointed out, that now Dedworth were receiving the grant from the Ecclesiastical Commissioners, it was St. Agnes' who were the burden on the Parish. Miss Thorne much resented the way the Rector compared the two Churches and said that St. Agnes' were doing everything they could under very difficult circumstances to raise all the money they could. The Rector called for a statement from all three Churches once a quarter". During the financial year 1936 St. Agnes' made contributions to the Parish Assistant Clergy Fund amounting to £150:0:0d, and £170:0:0d during 1937. A month later, at the Annual Parochial Church Meeting in March 1937 the accounts of St. Agnes' were presented and showed a balance in all funds. "The Rector commented on the work being done by the Revd. R.E. Beer and the satisfactory condition of the finances," state the Minutes. Perhaps it is only fair to add as a footnote to this incident that soon afterwards Gerald Payne-Cook was taken ill with a serious heart condition and that for sometime his return to work seemed unlikely.

The main event at St Agnes' during 1937 was the dedication of the Memorial to Rhoda Maclean and the re-opening of the re-decorated Church on Thursday, April 15th. Rhoda Maclean had been a worshipper at St. Agnes' and generous benefactor from about 1905 until her death in November 1934. The "Windsor and Eton Express" carried a lengthy report of the dedication in its issue of April 23rd - "Behind the somewhat drab exterior of St. Agnes' Church, Spital, there is a beautiful interior, which no stranger passing the building would realize was behind its much weathered brickwork. Within the past few weeks a transformation has taken place, the whole of the inside having been decorated and a new altar reredos erected in memory of the late Mrs. Rhoda Maclean of Winkfield Road, the gift of her daughter, Lady Murrough Wilson.....On the evening of April 15th the Bishop of Buckingham, the Right Revd. P.H. Eliot, dedicated the altar reredos and blessed the re-decorated Church in the presence of a crowded congregation, and among those present were Lady Murrough Wilson and members of the family. The oak panelling in memory of Mrs. Maclean is beautiful. The centre panel which forms the reredos is coloured and incorporates in its design the emblems associated with the Patron Saint, Saint Agnes. Flanking the centre panel are the arms of the Province of Canterbury and the Diocese of Oxford. The new decoration of the Church shows a modern tendency in its use of bright colours, red and gold predominating. In the east window plain amber glass has been substituted for diapher glass thus letting in more light, and the lowering of the altar has revealed the whole design of the three lancet windows. The design of the panelling and its making, as well as the direction of the re-decoration, was done by Faith Craft Ltd., under the supervision of Mr. Baden Beadle. The work of re-decoration was done by Mr. W. Butcher of St. Leonard's Road, and the alterations to the lighting by Messrs. A.G. Butler & Son of Windsor. The priest-in-charge writing in the Magazine says: 'The Church of God, though its truth remains the same, must express them in the modern way for the modern generation and we at St. Agnes' Church have tried to make the setting of our worship in keeping with what is best in the modern age'.

(In 1934 Gladys, only child of Major and Mrs. Maclean, and widow of the late Hon. Alec Henderson (d.1931) married Lt.-Colonel Sir Murrough John Wilson, K.B.E. as his second wife. His seat was Windlesham Park.

The beautification of the church has been made possible by the gifts of money of many parishioners and presents of needlework and craftsmanship. Other clergy present were the Rector; the Priest-in-charge; the Revd. Canon Audley J. Browne (Sub-Warden Convent of St. John the Baptist); the Revd. G.S. Bignold (Chavey Down); and the Revd. T.R. Parsons (Dedworth) who acted as Bishop's Chaplain. Solemn Evensong was sung by the Revd. R.E. Beer and the lessons were read by the Rector. The Organist was Mr. George Kelsey. After dedicating the panelling the Bishop blessed the newly decorated Church. The Bishop then preached the Sermon".

The inscription on the panelling ran thus: "To the Glory of God and in Loving memory of Rhoda Maclean who died November 15th, 1934 this panelling was erected by her daughter, Gladys Wilson."

We are fortunate enough to have two photographs of the interior of St. Agnes' - one taken in c. 1935 before the re-decoration of the church and the other taken during the early 1940's. (See Plates 10 and 11) The earlier photograph is very dark, the effect being emphasized by the 1924 Jubilee altar hangings and the diapher glass in the east window. In the 1937 restoration this Victorian patterned glass was replaced except for a small figure of St. Agnes' in the central lancet, which was given by the Sunday School in 1884. Also at this time the top two altar steps were removed so that the altar now stood on one larger step, and the ledge (or gradine) behind the altar, upon which the candles stood, was also lowered. The effect of substituting the red and gold memorial reredos in place of the altar hangings was both aesthetically pleasing and also gave the Sanctuary much less of a 'Sarum' appearance. The other major change executed at this time was that the light fittings installed as a Diamond Jubilee gift in 1934 were altered so that long candle-shaped bulbs could be used. This type of lighting, which was most inefficient, continued to be used until the Church was re-wired in 1978. Some of the decorative work was carried out by Miss Ann Payne-Cook, now Mrs. William Mervyn.

Fr. Beer's margin note in the Service Register, "Dedication of Memorial to Mrs. Maclean and re-opening of redecorated Church", pre-supposes that the Church was closed for the duration of the work. As Register entries are continuous for the period up to this time it must have been 'business as usual', presumably in the hall.

Tuesday, May 12th 1937, marked the Coronation of their Majesties, King George VI and Queen Elizabeth. At St. Agnes' there was a Sung Mass at 8.00 a.m. at which twenty-eight people received Holy Communion. There had also been a 'Form of Prayer and Dedication for the Coronation' at 6.30 p.m. on the previous Sunday. For those wealthy enough to own primitive television sets there was the unprecedented novelty of watching the Coronation procession make its way from Buckingham Palace to Westminster Abbey: one of the earliest attempts at outside broadcasting. (It is doubtful whether any of the Spital residents were fortunate enough to see the spectacle.) In Windsor the Coronation celebrations were held on a modest scale because there was to be a 'State Entry' into the town on June 12th, when their Majesties were to reside at the Castle for Ascot week. That day and those following were kept as Carnival Days.

The remainder of 1937 passed uneventfully. The usual socials, '6d hops' and whist drives continued to be held. Similarly the fund-raising events continued - the Gift Day in June raised £35:12:0d; also there was the usual Rummage Sale, Autumn Sale, and stall and sideshows at Clewer Fete. Since 1936 St. Agnes' had again joined in the Parish fete instead of having their own in Stag Meadow.

1938, the year of the Munich agreement which Chamberlain believed would bring 'Peace for our time' dawned uneventfully in Spital. The first Sunday after Epiphany was marked by another visit from the Revd. Frederic J. Evans of the Universities Mission to Central Africa. St. Agnes'- tide was kept in the customary manner with guest preachers, including the Revd. Charles Dunn, who had recently come to Clewer as honorary curate, and Canon Audley J. Browne, Sub-Warden, Convent of St. John the Baptist.

On Friday, May 6th, two Requiems were offered for the soul of Edward Grutchfield and altogether forty-three people received Holy Communion. Edward Grutchfield and his wife had been members of St. Agnes' for some years, and he had been a member of the Parochial Church Council since 1931.

At 6.30 p.m. on Sunday July 3rd 1938 an oak Sanctuary chair was dedicated in memory of Fr. Brook. This memorial, which was given by members of the congregation, bore the inscription, "To the greater glory of God, and in memory of William Brook beloved priest of this Church 1913-35 given by his grateful people." The Revd. C.E.M. Fry, Vicar of St. Luke's Maidenhead and Rural Dean, preached at the service of Solemn Evensong and dedicated the chair.

Socials in the hall were a regular feature of Spital life in Fr. Beer's time and indeed he took an active part in them, being a talented performer. George Kelsey played the piano, as he had been doing for the past thirty years or so, and doubtless the music was the same!

If the adults looked forward to the socials and dances, or '6d hops' as they were called, then certainly the children looked forward to the Sunday School treats. In those years just before World War 11, they were very similar to the treats of the years just prior to World War 1 - only the faces were different, but in one essential part they were exactly the same, namely that they were called 'treats' because that is precisely what they were. They were held on two evenings during the course of which between eighty and one hundred children were catered for. Every child left with a present, and there is little doubt that whilst donations were received from members of the congregation for these treats, the bulk of the expense was carried by Miss Thorne and Miss Hearmon - but anonymously.

A Nativity Play was performed in the Church by members of the congregation on December 21st and 22nd. The first night was hampered by lights fusing in the Church, and also snow which kept some people away. However, the play was favourably reviewed by the 'Windsor Express' and those who saw it found it very moving.

1939, the fatal year for peace, brought fresh problems for Spital. At the Parochial Church Meeting in March the Rector mentioned with regret the pending departure of both Fr. Beer from Spital and Fr. Knight from Dedworth. The Rector enlarged on this in the April Parish Magazine, "We are busily engaged in interviewing applicants for the work at St. Agnes', Spital.... Only one in a hundred could take 'Rednal' and live in it on the stipend we pay, without private means.....Some good men have already been to see St. Agnes' and expressed a desire to serve God in that splendid little Mission." Fr. Beer wrote in the same issue, "My own feelings are mixed. I am very sorry to say goodbye to so many good friends.....No priest could have been shown more personal kindness than you have shown me, and I shall never forget how you helped me to bear my bereavement, at a time when we were new friends. I am however happy to be going to a benefice. I have been in Orders for sixteen years and priest-in-charge of a district Church for eight years so it looks as if the time had come for me to undertake a bigger responsibility.

Richard Beer left St. Agnes' in June 1939 and was instituted as Vicar of Charlestown in the Diocese of Truro on July 1st. He remained at Charlestown until 1966 when he became Rector of St. Mabyn in the same diocese, until his death from a heart attack c. 1969 when he was in his late sixties. From 1955 to 1961 he was also Rural Dean of St. Austell and was an Honarary Canon of Truro Cathedral from 1961. Soon after going to Charlestown he re-married. He maintained friendly contact with several members of St. Agnes' until his death. His ministry can be seen as a bridge between William Brook and his own successor, Hubert Thornton Trapp, whose ideas had a far more 'Western' slant than any previous priest at St. Agnes'. Richard Beer was well-liked and is still fondly remembered, and there was genuine sorrow when his relatively short ministry at Spital came to an end.

## Interlude: Spital on the brink of War.

Spital in 1939 had changed little from the Spital of 1900, and yet within the next ten or fifteen years it was to grow so much that only those who knew it of old would ever believe it had once been a small village. It might, therefore, be worth taking a look at Spital as it was just before the last War. It is ironical that the post-War developers succeeded in tolling the village's death knell where all the German Lufftwaffe failed!

In 1939 St. Agnes' was still bordered by fields on the North side. The caretaker's cottage was sandwiched between the Hall and three small cottages which belonged to the Church. Alan Bridges, whose parents lived in the caretaker's cottage, has recalled those three cottages and their tenants, Mrs. Rosier, Mrs. Brown and Mrs. Shurley. The cottages known at various times as "Knowles' Cottages" and "St. Agnes' Cottages", were very small, much smaller than the caretaker's cottage, which itself left much to be desired. They each consisted of one low-ceilinged room all the way through with a lean-to scullery built on at the back, and two small bedrooms upstairs. Conditions must have been extremely cramped, particularly for Mrs. Brown who had six children. We have already seen how much concern these conditions had caused the Church in the early 1930's (see Chapter XIV) and the cottages were finally demolished to make way for the new Presbytery in 1955.

Turning right from St. Agnes', there were no more houses before reaching the gate lodge to Clewer Lodge, which at this time was still in use by the Imperial Service College. The boundary wall of the estate ran along St. Leonard's Road between the main gates and St. Agnes' Church. Further down St. Leonard's Road on a turning off to the right, there was still a small row of houses called "Lovers' Walk", but the tree-lined lane with its profusion of wild flowers was no more. Instead a new highway called Imperial Road linked St. Leonard's Road and Clarence Road and sliced through the estates of Clewer Manor and Clewer Lodge which were both owned by the Imperial Service College. The new road had been built in the 1920's to give work to the local unemployed, and at first was only a shadow of the present noisy thoroughfare. At the junction with St. Leonard's Road, there was a garage, "Imperial Motors" - a sign of the new age which the cheap motor cars of the inter-war years were causing to spring up everywhere. It was built on one of the last remaining patches of Clewer Green where Mr. Beech had periodically brought his fun fair. All that was in the past, and Mr. Beech himself had died in 1938.

Returning towards St. Agnes', but on the opposite side of the road, Rose Cottages, Bryn Terrace and Wellington Terrace were all as in 1900. Then there were some private houses, a few of which had been built since 1900, and then Bude Terrace, built in 1904. Near Wellington Terrace was St. Leonard's Dairy owned by Mr. A. Penicud.

The shop premises almost opposite St. Agnes' Church was owned by Mr. and Mrs. Butcher. Mr. Butcher was a carpenter and builder whose 'yard' was behind the shop bounded by the Cemetery wall. A dour, melancholy man, his workshop was in part of the double-fronted shop. Mrs. Butcher ran the other half of the business, which was a typical village general stores with all manner of confectionery and patent medicines. A large woman, she was, by contrast with her husband, of a very sweet nature and was always kind and welcoming to the children who flocked to buy her wares.

Between Mr. & Mrs. Butcher's and the village bakery were a number of cottages formerly known as "Vine Cottages", most of which had been there at least since 1900. The names of their occupants were well established locally - Copas, Weston, Fowler, Belcher, Stevens, Merrifield, Ives, Cooper - and in several cases the families still reside there. At the time of writing most of these houses are still standing except for the bakehouse.

Built onto the bakehouse, but nothing to do with it, was a small cottage where Mr. & Mrs. Cooper lived. Mr. Cooper was a familiar figure sitting outside in the porch in the better weather. Next door was the bakehouse, and next to that the shop. Sydney Pert had long since taken over from his father as village baker, a gruelling task at the best of times, but particularly at Christmas and Easter, as Mrs. Pert recalled to me shortly before her death in 1980. The shop began as a bread and cake shop but later became more general. The Perts lived next to the shop.

Just past the bakery was the property of G.W. Bishop & Sons, monumental masons. The house has recently been demolished. In 1939 the business flourished and examples of the stonemason's craft were carved and exhibited on the ground outside the house which was all conveniently near to the Cemetery.

The double fronted shop occupied at the time of writing by Mr. George Knowles, traded in 1939 under names of George and Herbert Bridges, and had done so since the Great War. Mrs. L.V. Bridges recalled that before her brother-in-law took over it had been used by Bishop's as a showroom for wreaths, etc. George Bridges in fact had nothing to do with the actual running of the shop. In the early days his sister, Millie, and their mother served in the shop, which sold tobacco and confectionery on one side and greengrocery on the other. Herbert Bridges also ran a fruit and vegetable cart around Windsor until the outbreak of World War II. A shoe repairing business was started in the late 1930's by another member of the family, Reg Bridges, in the loft over the yard behind the main shop. When the War broke out Reg was called up for service and Herbert took over the cobbling business which he moved into the greengrocery shop and managed to combine the two.

Turning back towards St. Agnes' and crossing the road, practically everything was as in 1900, but much of it was to change soon. The 'Stag and Hounds' looked as it had for many years. Between the 'Stag and Hounds' and the 'Royal Standard' was a row of six cottages all of which have since been demolished, and a detached bungalow with a long front garden now stands in their place. The 'Royal Standard' ale house was still trading at this time in what was really three cottages knocked into one. The site is now occupied by a modern block of flats called 'Talbot Court'. Next door lived Mrs. Austin and in the end house was a small general store run by Mr. Oxley. A pathway at a right angles to the road led to 'Homelee Cottages'; the pathway still exists but the cottages do not. The four cottages nearest the Church are still there at the time of writing. In 1939 the residents were Mr. Hayward, who at one time kept a greengrocery shop there; Mr. and Mrs. Warner, whose son served at St. Agnes'; the Harley family, some members of which still come to St. Agnes'; and Mr. and Mrs. Warner senior.

So we come back to St. Agnes', the exterior of which was different in 1939 from that of 1900 due to the 1908 extension, and the Calvary which dates from 1917.

Over the years the memory grows dim and acquires a rose-coloured hue, so that it is very easy to remember the old cottages which are no more, and to think only of the roses round their doors and forget the squalid, insanitary conditions which really existed. Yet there can be little doubt that pre-War Spital with its flower filled cottage gardens, its open fields and its amenities (a Church, two pubs, several grocery and greengrocery shops, a bakery and a dairy, not to speak of two Post Offices fairly near and several other public houses) was a good deal more attractive and peaceful than the post-War sprawl of tastelessly designed pre-fabricated housing by which means the local Council have engulfed a once closely-knit community.

## Chapter XVI

## Winds of Change

Hubert Thornton Trapp began his ministry at St. Agnes' on Sunday, July 2nd 1939, about one month after the departure of Richard Beer. Aged twenty-nine years he was unmarried and cheerfully good looking: qualities which were to set not a few female hearts aflutter. He trained for the priesthood at Kelham and served his first curacy at Whitstable, Kent from 1934 to 1936, and from there he moved to St. Edmund's, Forest Gate, where he stayed until coming to Spital.

Fr. Trapp moved into 'Rednal', Bolton Crescent, but was soon joined by his parents who bought their own house, 146 Clewer Hill Road. He made his home with them in what, no doubt, were more comfortable surroundings, and so 'Rednal' was given up. (This meant, of course, that after Fr. Trapp left there was nowhere for the Spital priest to live.) Many people remember Fr. Trapp's parents, although it is his mother who readily comes to mind. A forceful, aggressive personality, Amy Trapp's one pride and joy was her priest-son whom she dominated, and whose ministry suffered as a consequence.

It was at St. Edmund's, Forest Gate, under the guidance of Fr. Alfred Cordell that Thornton Trapp was trained in that flambuoyant, triumphalist brand of Anglo-Catholicism which the East End had long made its own. East End Anglo-Catholicism was always more 'Western' (i.e. more inclined to use the English Missal in its entirety and to adopt such 'extra-liturgical' practices as Benediction of the Blessed Sacrament), than its provincial counterpart. Thornton Trapp's view of Anglo-Catholicism was far more 'Western' than anything hitherto practised in Clewer Parish, and some people were to find it too 'extreme' for their liking.

Sunday services followed the same pattern as in former years except for a brief experiment from mid-September when the Sung Mass was changed to 10.30 a.m. This soon reverted back to 11.00 a.m. Fr. Trapp made an unusual comment in the Service Register on Sunday, July 30th about a month after his arrival - "Reservation on Sundays discontinued about this time on account of irreverence - after twenty to thirty years!" How long this penalty was imposed is not known, or the exact nature of the congregation's irreverence!

Constance Rodwell died on Sunday, August 6th 1939. Few remember her now, though in her day she was one of those 'pillars' who do a great deal in a quiet way. She was sacristan for many years and carried out her duties to perfection. A little lady, who always dressed in black, she lived in St. Andrew's Cottages on Dedworth Road. In September her friends gave a hanging lamp for the statue of Our Lady as a memorial. Later in the year another friend gave a set of purple vestments and an altar frontal, also in her memory.

At the beginning of August 1939 an Eton Master addressed Slough Rotary Club and prophesied that there would be war within two years unless all the democracies of the World organised themselves into a Federal Union similar to the United States of America. However, the dice had been cast long before and within a month (September 1st) the "Windsor and Eton Express" were printing the headlines - "Windsor's preparations for an Emergency"; "Thousands of children from London arriving today"; "A.R.P. H.Q. now manned day and night"; "Cellars set aside as Refuges in an Air Raid." The "Express" went on to remind readers that, "the moment war becomes inevitable, lighting restrictions would be rigidly imposed."

The Service Register at St. Agnes' for Sunday, September 3rd bears the simple comment, "War declared". All over the weekend evacuees had been pouring out of London, for it was the general belief that once war was declared Britain would immediately be subjected to intensive bombing. Between eight and nine thousand women and children arrived in about twenty-five trains at the Windsor Southern Station between Friday and Sunday and were billeted around the district. In fact the numbers were considerably fewer than was originally expected, as many refused to leave their homes at the last minute. In many cases whole schools were evacuated en-bloc so that during the course of the War, Clewer Parish found itself teeming with small Jewish boys from Stepney Jewish Boys' School which used Clewer Green School as its base and also made use of St. Agnes' Hall. St. Stephen's Parish found its population considerably increased by pupils from St. Saviour's School, Poplar.

In this time of national crisis people turned to the Churches, and this was reflected at St. Agnes' by the increase in Sunday Communicants which at this time swelled to between twenty and thirty-five people at the 8.00 a.m. Mass. Extra services were also held, for instance on the day after War was declared a note in the Service Register states, "Daily night prayers begun". These were discontinued at the end of October, but from late November, night prayers were held every Saturday at 6.00 p.m. The weekly observance of Holy Hour was kept on Thursday afternoons, consisting of silent prayer before the Blessed Sacrament.

On All Saints' Day (November 1st) there were two Masses, the Celebrant at 9.30 being Fr. Harry Stanbrook, Curate of St. Hilda, South Shields. This was the first time Fr. Stanbrook had celebrated Mass at St. Agnes' but he was no stranger to the Church having been born and brought up in Windsor. His mother was still living at Springfield Road and doubtless he was home on holiday. Later he returned to Windsor as priest-in-charge of All Saints', Frances Road. He now lives in retirement in his boyhood home and worships at St. Agnes'.

The death occurred on December 12th 1939 at his home, 31, Albert Street, of Alfred Henry Cooke, sometime Scoutmaster of the fifth Windsor (Clewer) Boy Scouts, aged fifty years. A Requiem was offered at St. Agnes' and he was buried in Clewer Churchyard on Saturday, December 16th.

The weather in late December 1939 and early January 1940 was the most severe the country had suffered since the winter of 1894 to 1895. The frost set in on the night of December 17th but the snow held off, and Christmas Day was bright and crisp, following a foggy Christmas Eve. Christmas Eve fell on a Sunday and the usual Sunday services were held, there being twenty-one Communicants. The Christmas Day services were:-

| | | |
|---|---|---|
| 12.00 Midnight | Sung Mass | Forty-four Communicants |
| 9.00 a.m. | Low Mass | Twenty-five Communicants |
| 11.00 a.m. | Sung Mass | |

This was the first time that the Midnight Mass of Christmas was celebrated at St. Agnes'. The snow managed to hold off until December 28th. New Year's Day 1940 brought the Register note: "Fog, ice and snow", but despite this twenty people turned up for Sung Mass at 6.30 a.m. A further fifteen people braved the weather for Low Mass at 9.30 a.m.

For the first time since 1895 the Thames was frozen right across during January. Even the swans were frozen in and had to be released. When even more snow fell at the end of the month, traffic ground to a halt. The skaters may have been delighted but they were alone in their pleasure. In the streets of Windsor, the blackout added to the difficulties of both drivers and pedestrians and there were many casualties. The lowest temperature recorded was at "St. Leonard's" Windsor where 24 degrees of frost were shown on the thermometer. Flooding added a further peril when the thaw finally set in during February, and many people in the low-lying areas of Windsor found themselves in real trouble.

St. Agnes' Day (January 21st) fell on a Sunday in 1940, and so the congregation were spared an early Sung Mass in the freezing weather. There were two guest preachers, both local - Canon Dunn, who preached at Evensong on the Eve, and Fr. Heald who preached on the Festival. In both cases Evensong was held at 3.30.p.m. in order to 'beat the blackout'. On February 25th, 'British Summer Time', a device first introduced during the Great War, was re-introduced.

There were plenty of extra services in Lent during the first year of the War. A typical week had the following, in addition to the regular daily services:-

| | | |
|---|---|---|
| Sunday | Mission Service | 7.00 p.m. |
| Monday | Women's Service | 3.15 p.m. |
| Wednesday | Compline and Address | 8.00 p.m. |
| Thursday | Holy Hour | 3.00 to 4.00 p.m. |
| Friday | Stations of the Cross | 6.00 p.m. |
| Saturday | Night Prayers | 6.00 p.m. |

Holy Week 1940 was significant in the history of St. Agnes' because for the first time the full Liturgy was celebrated from Maundy Thursday to Holy Saturday. The Book of Common Prayer made no provision for anything other than Mattins, Litany and Ante-Communion during this time, and for many years Anglo-Catholics had been mindful of the inadequacies of these devotions. It was for this reason that it became customary to observe the Three Hours Devotion on Good Friday. When the English Missal was first published in 1912 it reproduced the full Holy Week rites of the Western Church and a few very "advanced" Anglo-Catholic Churches, chiefly in London, began to use them. The Oxford Movement Centenary in 1933 brought a measure of "respectability" to Anglo-Catholicism, and thereafter the English Missal was adopted by many churches which might have regarded it as "ultra-Roman" a decade or two before. Except in times of interregnum the full Holy Week rites have been observed at St. Agnes' since Fr. Trapp introduced them, although in their present form they are considerably different from the long complicated ceremonies of the days before the modern liturgical reforms. One of the chief differences is that the old style liturgy was celebrated early in the morning, instead of the modern and much more logical practice, of celebrating in the evening. The timetable for the last part of Holy Week 1940 was somewhat different to that of Fr. Trapp's predecessers, Charles Farr and William Brook, both of whom represented the older generation of Anglo-Catholic. It read thus:-

| | | |
|---|---|---|
| Maundy Thursday | 6.30 a.m. | Sung Mass and Watch at the Altar of Repose. |
| | 8.00 p.m. | Tenebrae (an ancient office for Holy Week used instead of Compline). |
| Good Friday | 10.00 a.m. | Liturgy of Good Friday |
| | 12.00 - 3.00 p.m. | Three Hours Devotion |
| | 6.00 p.m. | Procession |
| | 8.00 p.m. | Tenebrae |
| Holy Saturday | 10.00 a.m. | Easter Vigil and First Mass of Easter (Congregation did not Communicate). |
| Easter Day | 7.00 a.m. | Low Mass Twenty-two Communicants |
| | 8.00 a.m. | Low Mass Fifty-seven Communicants |
| | 11.00 a.m. | Sung Mass |
| | 6.30 p.m. | Evening Prayer |

Fr. Trapp's own comment in the Service Register is that the Good Friday Liturgy was devoutly attended and greatly appreciated.

The King had requested that May 26th be observed throughout the British Empire as a Day of Prayer for Victory and Peace. The people of Windsor responded well to the summons and the local Churches, including St. Agnes', were full. The following Sunday St. Agnes' was almost full again at

Evening Prayer, and on June 16th there were "prayers for France" at all services. These were anxious days culminating in the fall of France and the evacuation from Dunkirk. At the end of May the 'Windsor Express' had warned, "The climax of the War is approaching. In two weeks the tide of battle has swept across the Low Countries and Northern France with tremendous rapidity. It is now within a few miles of our shores. At anytime we may be attacked by airborne troops or by the air bombardment so long expected..." On June 25th Fr. Trapp noted in the Service Register: "12.35 a.m. French betrayal: 1.10 a.m. First warning since September: 11.30 p.m. second warning." The so-called 'phoney war' was over.

Throughout 1940 the people of Windsor had been urged to "Dig for Victory", to "Plough the fields, increase their yields", and now they were being urged to surrender all aluminium pots and pans, kettles, hat pegs, coat hangers and shoetrees in order to help turn out more Spitfires, Hurricanes, Blenheims and Wellingtons. The popular slogan was, "Turn this raw material into War Material." On a more realistic level the Boroughs of Windsor and Slough decided in August to raise funds to buy Hurricane fighters. The Hurricane's designer was Mr. (later Sir) Sydney Camm, a local man who had been educated at the Royal Free Schools.

The latter half of August was fraught with air raid warnings as the Battle of Britain commenced and on August 25th there were seven warnings culminating in the dropping of fifty incendiary bombs locally, and a few high explosives, but no damage. September dawned even worse: Fr. Trapp noted on September 1st: "Wakeful nights during last week from anti- aircraft fire, planes and bombs", and on September 6th:- "The past week quieter: some warnings." It was the lull before the storm for Fr. Trapp's next comment reads: "During Saturday night, September 7th, intense air attacks begun on London. Many refugees henceforth." It was the start of the London Blitz.

Many evacuees had returned home during the 'phoney war' period and now that the reality of the War had finally reached them, many were unable to escape in time. For some, however, there was a second chance, and Windsor took its share of the homeless Londoners. Towards the end of September Queen Elizabeth visited some of the homeless who were being sheltered at the Thames Hotel and the Congregational Hall. Her Majesty spent two hours among them and made a point of speaking to everyone. Homeless sick children were also visited at the Sanatorium in Alma Road. Everybody was enormously encouraged by the Queen's visit, and there can be little doubt that the homeless Londoners felt an affinity with the Queen whose London residence had already taken three bombings.

The War was having a detrimental effect on weekday Church attendance as Fr. Trapp commented: "Attendance at early Mass suffers on account of sleepless nights and the numbers of Londoners here mostly Jews." No doubt the War was an unsettling factor in the life of St. Agnes', not only because the air-raids made it difficult to get up for early Mass, but because it heralded "winds of change". Spital was still very much a closely-knit village community where everybody knew everyone else and the Church reflected that spirit. No doubt the influx of "strangers" into both Church and local communities took some getting used to - by both parties. The War was not solely responsible for the changes; for Fr. Trapp had introduced several into the worship of the Church. His brand of religion was not one to accept compromise. Christianity for him meant attendance at Mass on Sundays and Holy Days of Obligation and the regular use of the Sacrament of Penance by those who wished to receive Holy Communion. A few people found this standard too exacting and duly left St. Agnes' to worship elsewhere.

On September 30th 1940 the War came to Spital! "ME 109 down behind Stag Meadow", noted Fr. Trapp in the Service Register which was fast becoming a War Diary. This was a 'scoop' for the "Windsor Express" who devoted a good deal of the front page of October 4th to it, plus a photograph of the wreckage. The report ran as follows: "The first German aircraft to be brought down in this area crashed in Windsor Great Park shortly after 5.00 p.m. on Monday. It was a Messerschmidt ME 109 fighter plane and had come over on escort duty with a formation of Nazi Bombers. When the formation was broken up this machine apparently became separated from the rest. High over Windsor Forest the ME made an unsuccessful attack on two Anson aircraft and was itself caught in the fire of a British fighter. Suddenly it dived out of the clouds and began to lose height rapidly. It crossed Winkfield Road and Stag Meadow at a low altitude and, in attempting to land in the Great Park on the Royal Agricultural Showground, it crashed into the stout posts which have been placed there to prevent aircraft landing. The tips of both wings were torn off and the machine did a somersault, the pilot being thrown clear..... The Royal Lodge-keeper at Queen Anne's Gate was the first to reach the Nazi Airman who was uninjured and appeared very cool and collected after his miraculous escape. He spoke good English and asked for a cigarette. At the time of the crash an officer of the New Zealand Air Force happened to be motoring through the Park. He disarmed the German and arrested him. Later, using his own car, he drove the Nazi to the nearest R.A.F. Depot where the man was handed over to the authorities. An armed guard was quickly placed round the machine, but the public were allowed within twenty yards of it..... Crowds of sightseers came from all parts. On Tuesday afternoon an R.A.F. "crash" squad arrived and with the aid of a mobile crane the machine was righted and towed to a spot near Queen Anne's Gate. Soon afterwards the Princesses came to see it and both seemed surprised to find it so small..... The fuselage of the machine was punctured by bullets beneath and behind the cockpit and how the pilot escaped injury is a mystery..... On Wednesday afternoon it was brought back from the Park into the town and placed on show at the entrance to Park Street". (A young boy, Victor Newport witnessed this incident. Mr. Newport recently recalled what happened, "The pilot had fuel problems. He made two circles and landed. No action had taken place.")

October 1940 saw the beginning of concerted air attacks on the provinces, and although there are accounts in the local press it is difficult, more than forty years later, to know where the attacks were, because Government censorship insisted that no places should be named. Also reports were often held over for sometime after the attack had taken place. It has been possible, however, with the aid of Fr. Trapp's Register notes, to identify one such report from the "Windsor Express". On October 11th Fr. Trapp noted: "c.2.00 a.m. two high explosives on "Lovejoy's Farm". Two cottages and farm buildings devastated. No casualties apart from shock. One choirboy in hospital for two days." This was St. Leonard's Farm at the top of St. Leonard's Hill, farmed by Mr. Charles Lovejoy. The "Windsor Express" reported this incident on October 18th: "During the early hours of Friday, two high explosive bombs were dropped on the outskirts of another place in the district. The first fell in the garden of two semi-detached houses of which the backs were blown out and the roofs partially ripped off. The eleven occupants had remarkable escapes. Children in bed were thrown among the debris and rescued by their parents, and only one boy, Leslie Radburn, aged twelve, was taken to hospital and detained suffering from a fractured shoulder. The second bomb fell in a field of swedes immediately adjoining a farm fifty yards from the houses. The farm buildings were damaged together with the model dairy but none of the animals were injured, half a dozen calves having remarkable escapes. The building in which they were had its roof blown off and both doors were blown across the farmyard. None of the cows in nearby fields were hurt. The crater made by the bomb was a big one and the blast took the tops off all the swedes. The tenant of the farm said the damage to the property was considerable as hardly one building had not suffered some damage."

There were air raid warnings throughout October and on the 23rd seven bombs fell in the middle of Windsor but there was little damage. Four days later a bomb fell in Dedworth. Bad weather on November 3rd and 11th brought a respite from the sirens but November 14th was particularly noisy with planes passing overhead all night. The next day everyone knew why - "Bad night - Coventry raided", wrote Fr. Trapp. November 15th brought a steady rain of incendiary bombs throughout the night, more than four hundred falling in the local district, two hundred and fifty of which fell in Windsor itself. The "Windsor Express" later commented, "It was shortly before midnight when the first bombs fell and they dropped in dozens causing fires in streets, gardens and fields, while a few fell through the roofs of houses and did some damage..... With so many fires raging at the same time the Fire Brigade and Auxuliary Fire Service were fully employed. Firemen were assisted by police, wardens, A.R.P. workers and many members of the public, and all fires were out within half an hour of the first bomb falling. Damage was not extensive. Quite a number of bombs fell in a river." On this occasion a fair amount of damage was sustained by Eton College.

This air of optimism which pervaded the local press reports all helped to keep up the morale of the people. It must however, have been far from cheering to live with the constant sound of the siren. A former member of St. Agnes' congregation, Mrs. Audrey Tyrell, has recalled an incident when her husband was cycling home from his office at Old Windsor and narrowly escaped being hit by bombs which dropped on either side of the road! Mr. Tyrell was an A.R.P. warden and his post was in a dilapidated stable on the corner of Clewer Hill Road. No doubt this had been one of the stables belonging to Clewer Manor in the days of Squire Foster. Mr. and Mrs. Tyrell were evacuated from London and lived for a time in St. Leonard's Road, during which period they were active members of St. Agnes'. In 1945 they moved to Harrow and at the time of writing live in Essex.

1940 gave way to 1941 with no end to the War in sight. Christmas services were fairly well attended especially the Midnight Mass. A "Nativity Tableaux" was presented on January 1st and 5th, but the local press did not report it.

It was another long, cold Winter, not quite as severe as in the previous year, but still long enough and cold enough to keep Spring at bay and hamper the earnest efforts of the gardeners who were endeavouring to "Dig for Victory". There was snow on January 1st which persisted right through to February and brought appalling conditions for St. Agnes' Day and a resultant low attendance.

On January 26th the preacher at Evensong was the Right Revd. Rocksborough Remington Smith, formerley Bishop of Algoma in the Province of Canada. He returned to St. Agnes' at the beginning of Lent when he presided at Sung Mass, and on Mothering Sunday when he preached at a special Family Service and at Evensong. There was a full Church each time. Rocksborough Remington Smith was Bishop of Algoma from 1926 until 1940 when he returned to England and served as Secretary of the Church Union 1940 to 1943. He became Rector of Lapford 1943 to 1952 and Assistant Bishop of Exeter 1947 to 1952. He died in 1955 aged eighty-three years.

On February 16th 1941 the death occurred of Miss Patience Payne-Cook, aged nineteen years. She was the youngest of the Rector's daughters and had been ill for about a month. Her condition deteriorated following an operation and she died of thrombosis just before midnight on the Saturday night. She had hoped to follow in her elder sister's footsteps and take up art as a career. Towards this end she had been assistant scenic artist at the Theatre Royal where her sister, Ann, had formerly been scenic artist. The coffin rested in the King Edward VII Hospital Chapel until its removal to the Chapel of the Clewer Sisters. On Tuesday evening it was taken to Clewer Church and on Wednesday at 8.00 a.m. the Requiem was said by Fr. Heald. The funeral followed in the afternoon.

Windsor took yet another hammering from the Lufftwaffe early in 1941 as the

"Windsor Express" revealed at a later date. "When the year opened the great night air raids were in progress. Some nights the sky in the East and North seemed aglow with searchlights and perhaps flames, and for hours on end we heard the sound of gunfire, sometimes near, sometimes in the far distance. Other nights there was only darkness and a little firing, but hour after hour we heard the drone of enemy planes and heard the next morning that some town or towns in the Midlands had suffered disaster. On one of those dark evenings..... We heard the sound of bombs in our midst. They were by no means the first bombs to fall on the town, but the only ones which up to then or since then have done any substantial damage or taken their toll of life. Five people were killed and four times that number were injured. A few houses were wrecked and many more severely damaged.... Since that February day we have had no bombs which have wrought destruction. The Civil Defence of the Borough on that night had their first real test. It revealed some weaknesses but on the whole they stood up remarkably well...."

Church attendances during Lent were good, although there do not appear to have been quite so many services. For instance the weekly Holy Hour seems to have been set aside, but instead there was Evensong on Thursdays conducted by the Revd. C.R. Meade-King (Chaplain, Community of St. John the Baptist, Clewer), and the average attendance was twenty-five. A "quiet afternoon" was held from 2.00 to 6.00 p.m. on the Eve of Passion Sunday and there was a good attendance. The Church was full on Palm Sunday for the Sung Mass and Blessing of Palms and also at 6.30 p.m. when Evensong was followed by the St. Agnes' Passion Play. This was written by Fr. Trapp and performed by members of the congregation. Other performances were held on Wednesday (for children when there was a very good attendance), Maundy Thursday (also for children, but attendance was only "fair"), and Good Friday when the Church was full.

Services during the latter part of Holy Week 1941 seem somewhat curtailed when compared with the full liturgy of the previous year. The Parish Magazine might have offered some explanation but except for one or two issues, they were not kept during Gerald Payne-Cook's incumbency. Services for the last part of Holy Week were:-

| | | |
|---|---|---|
| Maundy Thursday | 7.00 a.m. | Sung Mass (Thirty present) |
| Good Friday | 11.30 a.m. | Morning Prayer, Liturgy and Ante-Communion (No-one present) |
| | 12.00 - 3.00 p.m. | Three Hours Devotion |
| | 6.00 p.m. | Station of the Cross from Hatch Lane (Very good attendance) |
| Holy Saturday | | Nothing at all. |

On Easter Day the Church was full at 11.00 a.m. and almost full at 6.30 p.m. Ninety-three people received Holy Communion on that day.

By the early Summer of 1941 the worst of the bombing raids on Britain were over, as Hitler was concentrating the German war machine on the Soviet Union. Many towns, Windsor included, took advantage of the respite to hold a "War Weapon's week". This was not a new idea, for similar "weeks" had been held in the Great War, for example Windor's "Gun Week" of 1918. However it gave a fresh impetus to the "War Effort" by means of encouraging the public to invest in War Savings Bonds which would help the Country cover the terrific cost of providing weapons and munitions. Windsor's War Weapon's Week opened on Empire Day, May 24th, with a parade of all the Services, both military and civilian. A giant indicator board on Castle Hill recorded the daily amount invested towards the Borough's target of £125,000. Whilst the chief objective was to raise money there was inevitably a carnival spirit too, plus some friendly competition with neighbouring Slough. In the event Windsor came out on top with a grand final total of £715,794. The King sent a message to the Borough residents, "Heartiest congratulations to all". On Whit Sunday His Majesty took the salute at the final march-past in the Grand Quadrangle of the Castle. The procession was a mile long.

Windsor's residents must have been shocked to read in the September 5th issue of the "Windsor Express" of the death in a car accident of Lady Edward Spencer-Churchill. She came to Windsor some years after her marriage in 1874, and had resided at Queensmead for most of that time. Her husband, Lord Edward Spencer-Churchill, was an uncle of Lord Randolph Churchill and great-uncle of the then Prime Minister. Lady Edward, as she was always known, had been a widow since 1911. Both in London and in Windsor, Lady Edward was one of the great English hostesses, particularly during the Edwardian period. She was an honoured friend of the Royal Family from Queen Victoria to King George VI. Although a great age when she died, Lady Edward maintained to the last a youthful vigour which inspired those around her. During the Great War Queensmead was largely given over for use as a Hospital, and she was instrumental in forming the Berkshire 66 Detachment of the British Red Cross, the members of which served as nurses there. Lady Edward also started a Hospital Supply Depot at Queensmead, and she maintained her interest in the Red Cross until her death. During the inter-War years she concerned herself with the welfare of injured ex-servicemen, widows and orphans. Within a week or two of the outbreak of War in 1939, Queensmead had again been surrendered to various activities concerned with the "War Effort" including a Hospital Supply Depot. In 1920 Lady Edward was awarded the O.B.E., and in 1935 the C.B.E. Also in 1935 she became a Chevalier of the Legion d'Honneur.

Immediately before her death Lady Edward had been staying at Petworth with her younger daughter, Agnes, Viscountess Cowdray. They left Petworth in Lady Cowdray's car intending to meet other members of the family for lunch at the Ritz, after which Lady Edward was to have returned to Windsor. The accident occurred at Ripley in Surrey, no other car being involved. Lady Edward died soon after being taken to a nursing home at Cobham. Both Lady Cowdray and the chauffeur were seriously injured but later recovered. There was much uncertainty about what exactly happened but it was concluded that the brakes suddenly developed a fault. The chauffeur was exonerated from all blame.

Lady Edward was buried at Blockley in Gloucestershire and at the same time a memorial service was held in St. George's Chapel at which eight hundred people were present. Among her written requests was that a Requiem should be held at Clewer St. Stephen. This took place on the Tuesday before the funeral, Fr. Heald being the celebrant.

1942 arrived with yet another "white" St. Agnes'- tide, there being rain or snow on sixteen days in January, the heaviest snow falling on Janury 19th and 31st. The guest preacher at Sung Mass on St. Agnes' Day was the Revd. Ralph Shakespeare Eves, Vicar of St. Alban's, Holborn. This famous Church, which had past links with St. Agnes' through the late Fr. Stanton, had been destroyed a few months previously by incendiary bombs. Fr. Eves and some of his congregation had risked life and limb to save all the pictures, sacred vessels and vestments from the burning Church. He gained a reputation for courage and warm-heartedness in helping his people throughout the blitz. Fr. Eves stayed in London throughout the War and died in 1948. It was under his successor, Fr. Startup, that the new Church was completed.

It was announced in January 1942 that the Imperial Service College would cease to exist as a separate school as from the end of the present term, and that it was to be amalgamated with Haileybury College, Hertford. The Junior School housed at Clewer Manor would remain at Windsor as Haileybury and Imperial Service College Junior School. The main school buildings in Alma Road were to be taken over by the War Department for the duration, and were later acquired by the Borough Council who were then at a loss to know what to do with them! Clewer Lodge, which from 1921 had been the Headmaster's house, now became vacant, and superfluous to the needs of the Junior School. Later in 1942 and for the rest of the War, it was taken over by the Victoria Home for Invalid Children from Margate.

"Warship Week" was held from March 7th to the 14th 1942 on similar lines and with similar aims to the previous year's "War Weapon's Week". The target of £300,000 was exceeded by £50,000. For the people of St. Agnes' this week was memorable for a different reason, namely that Fr. Trapp left Spital to become an R.A.F. chaplain. His last service as priest-in-charge of St. Agnes' was Sung Mass at 7.00 p.m. on Monday, March 9th 1942. Thirty people were present. On the Sunday evening following Evensong Mr. Pert had presented Fr. Trapp with Treasury notes to the value of £30, together with an album containing the names of the subscribers. He also received other gifts from individual members of the congregation and friends in the Parish. Throughout his time in the R.A.F. Fr. Trapp's parents continued to reside in Clewer Hill Road and, therefore, he was a frequent visitor to Spital and often celebrated Mass at St. Agnes' on these occasions. His father died in 1946, and after Fr. Trapp left the R.A.F. his mother went to live with him until her death in 1948.

Thornton Trapp was in the R.A.F.V.R. until 1947 when he was appointed Vicar of St. Peter Stantonbury with St. James, New Bradwell near Wolverton in North Bucks. From there he moved to the Anglo-Catholic stronghold of St. Mary Magdalene, Paddington in 1951. At this time the Anglican Church was going through one of those periodical crises which rear up every few years and seem to threaten her Catholicity. This time the crisis hinged upon the Church of South India, which had been inaugurated in 1947 as a result of a union between four Anglican dioceses, the South India Province of the Methodist Church and the South India United Church, which itself comprised Presbyterian, Congregationalist and Dutch Reformed bodies. In 1955 partial inter-Communion was allowed between the Church of England and the Church of South India. The union was seen by many to compromise principles as hitherto upheld by the Anglican Church particularly with regard to Apostolic Succession and the Ordination Service. As a result some people were forced to re-consider their position in the Anglican Church. For a number of reasons, South India among them, Thornton Trapp decided that he could no longer remain an Anglican and so he was received into the Roman Catholic Church at this time. He then went to the Beda College in Rome to study for the Roman Catholic priesthood but found the pressure too great and was forced to give up. This must have been a tremendous blow for I am sure he never envisaged spending the rest of his life as a layman. There is a sad irony in that he was ordained to a priesthood which he presumably no longer held to be valid, only to be denied any priestly ministry in his new Church. (For a full account of the South India scheme see Anselm Hughes' "The Rivers of the Flood").

Thornton Trapp spent the rest of his life still in the service of others, still to the same high standards, but surely deprived of the sense of fulfilment of former years. For some years he worked as a courier for an American travel firm, and then worked for Eugene Istomin, the American concert pianist. By the early 1970's his health had begun to deteriorate and "disseminated schlerosis of the brain" was diagnosed. It was Eugene Istomin who took him out to Bequia in the Windward Isles to stay with Canon Alec Adams an old friend from Paddington days. Thornton Trapp knew that his illness was terminal and Canon Adams persuaded him to stay until his death.
He was at Bequia for about two months and during this time the local people came to love and respect him. Death came quickly and peacefully at 4.05 a.m. on Tuesday, August 21st 1973; he was sixty-three years old. He was buried in the churchyard at Bequia and the Church was full of people for the funeral.

## Chapter XVII

### Hornets nests and Doodle-bugs

Following Fr. Trapp's departure for the R.A.F. there was a brief interregnum from March 10th until May 13th 1942 during which time St. Agnes' was served by local clergy. Holy Week and Easter were poorly served, there being nothing after Maundy Thursday until Easter Day, when there were sixty-six Communicants.

At the Annual Parochial Meeting in March the Rector had spoken of the difficulty of finding a priest for St. Agnes' owing to the seemingly insoluble accommodation problem. However, it seemed as if a solution had indeed been found when the Revd. Basil C. Norris took office on May 13th, the Eve of Ascension. His stay only lasted until August 10th though, and very few people remember him at the time of writing. The appointment may have been a temporary one, or he may have left upon learning of the Rector's impending retirement. Whatever the reason for his leaving, St. Agnes' was back at "square one" as far as a priest was concerned, and was to remain so for the rest Gerald Payne-Cook's incumbency.

On August 20th 1942 the death occurred at her home in Oxford of Mrs. Edith Cowie, widow of the late Revd. A.T.C. Cowie. She was ninety years old. Requiems were held at St. Margaret's Church, Oxford, and at Clewer. Burial followed at Clewer Churchyard.

The second interregnum within a year at St. Agnes' was to last until July 1943. Services were taken by a number of local clergy and there was an inevitable falling away in numbers and a consequent drop in income. Services were held on Sundays and about two weekdays.
On September 9th 1942 at a special meeting of the Parochial Church Council the Rector stated that, "Owing to the housing difficulty in St. Agnes' district it was found impossible to provide a priest for St. Agnes' as well as for All Saints' (which had become vacant at the same time), so he had been reluctantly compelled, for the duration of the War at least, to arrange that both the districts would be served by one priest, who would reside at 'Hursley' in the All Saints' District. He realised that this course would necessitate some curtailment in the number of services possible, especially at St. Agnes' but he pointed out that there was at least one daily Mass somewhere in the Parish, and hoped that St. Agnes' would make the best of the arrangement. He also hoped that St. Agnes' congregation would continue to support their Church as whole-heartedly as they had done in the past".

A week later the "Windsor Express" gave notice of the Rector's resignation as from December 31st. The Rector had been in increasingly poor health since his serious illness in 1937, and he was now following his doctor's advice in giving up full-time work. The Payne-Cooks left Clewer Rectory just before Christmas and moved to Ottershaw between Woking and Chertsey. Gerald Payne-Cook lived for another five years after leaving Clewer and, during this period, did some part-time work in an honorary capacity. Before leaving Clewer he was presented with a wireless set and a cheque from the Parish, and with gifts from the Staff and children of Clewer Green School.

In his farewell letter in the February 1943 Clewer Magazine, Gerald Payne-Cook wrote," I hope all friends of mine at St. Agnes' will hold together and try to recover the joy and unity which marked the work of Fr. Brook and Fr. Beer. The Catholic Faith was always most wonderfully taught by these good men and there must be many who remember them with affection. The falling off there may in some degree be due to the absence of a whole-time priest among them but the circumstances were such that there was no other course open and the Church Council entirely agreed with the course of action which was taken".

It is difficult to sum up the ministry of Gerald Payne-Cook as there are so many mixed opinions about him. He was a somewhat controversial figure, and those who remember him usually have strong feelings. The concensus of opinion is that he always endeavoured to work for the best interests of his parishioners. He came to Clewer when it was going through a difficult period following the incumbency of William Elwell. That Payne-Cook brought much needed consolidation and respectability cannot be denied, but his brand of Catholicism was of a much more restrained type than that practised by the daughter Churches, or even by some of his own predecessors at St. Andrew's. He came to Clewer at a time when the Parish was still trying to adjust to being relatively poor. Many of the old time benefactors had either died or moved away and their estates were being turned to other uses. The new housing developments which were growing up, especially at Dedworth, were built by the Borough Council and housed the poorer paid workers. In 1936 Gerald Payne-Cook gained a seat on the Town Council in order to represent the Council tenants in his Parish, whom he felt were being overcharged for rents. It provoked a good deal of controversy and he did not mince his words in answering his critics who held that religion and politics did not mix. There can be no doubt that Gerald Payne-Cook held the interests of his poorer parishioners as dear as any, and yet many who remember him recall that they did not feel at ease with him, nor he with them. Certainly there was little love lost between himself and the daughter Churches, particularly when it came to finance, and this often led to open conflict at Parochial Church Council meetings. Perhaps the "Windsor Express" sums him up best of all in the obituary notice of 1947: "Quick to oppose, and even to resent, he was equally quick to forgive and forget. He loved people and their interests and never forgot them." Perhaps this tendency towards outspokeness might have deemed him less lovable than some of his predecessors who were content simply to mount the altar steps and leave the political platform to the politicians.

1943 dawned with a wedding, though not wedding bells, for they were banned for the duration of the War. The bride, Joan Atkins, was a member of St. Agnes', and the bridegroom, Ernest Paternoster, came from Clewer. George Kelsey played the organ for the wedding at St. Andrew's on January 16th and Fr. Donald Southeard officiated. Both 'bride and groom' are regular worshippers at St. Agnes' at the time of writing.

Weddings were not the only functions to be deprived of bells, for when the new Rector of Clewer was instituted and inducted on Saturday, February 6th 1943, the ringing of a handbell was substituted for the tolling of the church bell. The Bishop of Reading, the Rt. Revd. Arthur Groom Parham, presided over the ceremony in the presence of a large congregation which included the former Rector.

The new Rector was the Revd. Cyprian Dymoke-Marr. Young and handsome, with a wife and two sons, Peter aged nine and a half years and Simon one and a half years, Father Cyprian, as he soon became known, had been ordained priest in 1930. He was still in his twenties when, in 1935, he was appointed Vicar of St. Francis, South Shields, and was at the time the youngest incumbent in the Diocese of Durham. St. Francis, South Shields was a tough dockside parish which had its share in the wartime raids, and Father Cyprian had been with his people in the thick of it as an A.R.P. warden.

Fr. Cyprian lost no time in visiting St. Agnes', his first visit being on Sunday, February 14th, when he celebrated at 8.00 a.m. and officiated at Evensong. He took most of the Services himself during the interregnum, the rest being taken by Fr. Southeard of Dedworth. Donald Southeard did much sterling work during the two years (1943-45) he served at All Saints', Dedworth, and did much to stabilise the spiritual life of a Church which had had a rough passage for close on twenty years.

The new Rector soon began to make his mark on the spiritual life of Clewer, particularly in the Parish Church where he emulated the example of his famous predecessor, Canon Carter. Appeals were launched in the Parish Magazine and as a result St. Andrew's gained six new altar candlesticks, a set of Stations of the Cross, and a canopy for the statue of Our Lady. The full Holy Week rites were introduced at St. Andrew's, possibly for the first time.

In the meantime attempts were being made to find a priest for St. Agnes' and by June Fr. Cyprian was able to shed a ray of hope, if someone could provide lodgings. "I know it has been a difficult time for you all," Fr. Cyprian wrote in the Clewer Magazine, "And those who have remained faithful have been tried and tested. Some, of course, have fallen by the wayside; but I rejoice that so many have remained firm, and those of you who have stuck it so well will be a tremendous help to your new priest when he comes. I am looking forward to great things from St. Agnes' in the future....."

Fr. Alban Caldicott Morton Howard began his ministry at St. Agnes' on Saturday, July 31st 1943. Nine people received Holy Communion at 7.00 a.m. on that day. Aged twenty-nine years, Fr. Howard had been curate of St. Saviour, Scarborough since his ordination in 1937. For the last six months he had been in charge of the Parish following the death of the Vicar. Upon moving to Spital he took up residence with Mr. & Mrs. A.E. Howells of 315 St. Leonard's Road. (Mrs. Howells was the sister of Mr. Pert, the Baker).

In his first letter in the September Parish Magazine Fr. Howard spoke of the need for reconstruction, "....for we are all well aware that, in the long period during which you have had no resident priest, much of the work of the Church has inevitably suffered. Some have lost contact with the things of God and have fallen away, and both they and the Church alike have lost in consequence. My first appeal therefore is that those who have so loyally carried on......will undertake a piece of work for God and His Church, first by encouraging the wanderers to return to the fold, and second by praying earnestly and fervently for the conversion of the people of this district......"

The pattern of Sunday services remained the same as in Fr. Trapp's time and Fr. Howard restored the daily Mass which had been given up during the interregnum although there was often no congregation. Sunday, August 15th, was observed as the Feast of the Assumption of Our Lady and the preacher both at the Sung Mass and Solemn Evensong was the Revd. James Ridley Trotter, Vicar of All Saints', Scarborough. Fr. Trotter was well-known in Anglo-Catholic circles and his untimely death in 1960 deprived the Church of a great priest.

September was a busy month at St. Agnes'. Thursday, September 2nd, saw the start of a weekly service of War Intercessions and Devotions; September 3rd was observed as a National Day of Prayer, it being the fourth anniversary of the outbreak of the War; and September 9th was kept as the Feast of Dedication. The Sunday School was resumed after the Summer holiday break on Sunday, September 5th, at 3.00 p.m. with a Service in Church, and numbers soon swelled. Soon afterwards the children were divided into four teams and this competitive element greatly added to their enthusiasm.

On the social side of Church life, the Whist Drives continued fortnightly in the Hall and were much appreciated in those dark Wartime days. Mr. Pert's efforts as organiser were much appreciated both by the players and by the Church Treasurer whose funds were boosted by these events. Fr. Howard, who was interested in youth work, organised a weekly club for young boys who were Church members. The Coral League also continued to flourish and their annual sale at the end of 1943 realised £23:0:0d for the U.M.C.A. - their best effort so far.

The War Savings Movement received a further boost at the end of May 1943 when "Wings for Victory" Week was held. Windsor's target was £300,000 and as before this was far exceeded - by £90,800 in fact. The climax of the week was on the Sunday afternoon when His Majesty the King, together with H.M. King Haakon of Norway, took the salute in the Grand Quadrangle of the Castle.

Mrs. Rita Frances Mosscockle died in August 1943. She had lived at Clewer Park, formerly the residence of the Gooch family, since soon after its vacancy in 1906, and had been a benefactress of Clewer Parish, providing hospitality for treats and tea parties. Her late husband was formerly a solicitor and Commissioner for Queensland. Upon his death in 1904 Mrs. Mosscockle inherited a fortune amounting to £652,000. In later years she became a convert to Roman Catholicism and was a regular worshipper at St. Edward's Church. No doubt her change of religious allegiance accounts for the disappearance of her name from the Parish Magazines as a benefactress after the Great War. Her eccentricities have already been noted, particularly her obsessive efforts to look like Queen Alexandra. Mrs. Mosscockle had a great love for the Arts and wrote poetry of some distinction, some of which was published. In her youth she had been fond of outdoor sports and was a keen horsewoman. Dogs were another love and the kennels (and the cemetery) at Clewer Park were well-known in canine circles. During World War II Clewer Park was partly occupied by the Navy and a few months before Mrs. Mosscockle's death a fire broke out in the house which was brought under control by Naval Personnel. The Requiem and funeral took place at St. Edward's Church and burial followed in the ancestral plot at Himley, near Dudley. Mrs. Mosscockle left £200,311. most of which was left to institutions which included the Salvation Army, Battersea Dogs' Home, the P.D.S.A. Dr. Barnado's Homes. She also left a sum of money to endow a bed at King Edward VII Hospital, Windsor. After the War, Clewer Park fell into disuse and was demolished soon afterwards. A modern housing development was built on the site in the late 1950's and bears the name Clewer Park. There are still traces of the main drive and gateway off the Maidenhead Road, beside which is the Lodge, though modernised almost out of all recognition. The only existing photograph of Clewer Park can be seen in "The Diary of Sir Daniel Gooch" and was taken during World War II when the once elegant Mansion was fast going to rack and ruin. (a copy of the photograph is in the Clewer History Museum).

"The great event for us, as a Parish, during the month of January will be the celebrations in connection with the centenary of Canon Carter's institution as Rector of our Parish", wrote Fr. Cyprian in the January 1944 Parish Magazine. The "Windsor Express" gave some welcome publicity to the forthcoming celebrations in their issue of Janury 14th and noted that the "Lord Bishop of Reading will pontificate at High Mass," information which they had gleaned from the Parish Magazine. However, this seemingly innocent remark was enough to stir up a hornet's nest of bigotry equal to the best efforts of the Church Association sixty years previously. I quote in full from the "Windsor Express" of January 21st 1944. "We have received the following letter on the subject (of Canon Carter's Centenary) from Major Bourne-May of The Hermitage, Clewer Green:

> "Sir, I have been reading the proposed programme of services, etc., in connection with the Canon Carter Centenary. I note that the Bishop of Reading will 'Pontificate at High Mass'. This ia a so-called Church of England and a Parish Church at that! The officiating clergy, apart from the Bishops, are described as the Reverend Father so-and-so.
>
> "Why all this aping of the Roman Church by a certain section of our clergy? However I suppose that so long as our Bishops condone this kind of thing, our ecclesiastical 'Mock Turtles' will continue to flourish.
>
> "I register my protest, not only as a parishioner of Clewer, but also

as a staunch supporter of the Church of England."

"Yours faithfully,
J.B.S. Bourne-May
(Major)"

The 'Express' gave the hornet's nest another prod in the same issue by commenting on the letter in the Editorial - after all it was all 'good copy', and, as all journalists know, there is nothing like a spot of religious controversy to get people's blood boiling! This is what the Editor had to say: "We publish....with reluctance, because it is likely to arouse theological controversy. But it cannot be denied that Major Bourne-May expresses the view of the majority....We know well that many people - Major Bourne-May probably among them - think that Fr. Cyprian's teachings are contrary to those of his Church. That is a question on which nothing whatever would induce us to express an opinion. But we hope and trust that the widest possible tolerance will be shown on the one side and that on the other it will be remembered that the Church is established; therefore there cannot be that disregard for public opinion that is legitimate in any Church which is entirely separate from the State."

There was a good deal more hot air blown across the correspondence columns during the next few weeks, and anyone who wishes to read it in full should consult the "Windsor Express" files for January 21st to February 11th 1944 inclusive.

Although the attack was really aimed at Fr. Cyprian, whose teachings and religious practices were far more definitely Anglo-Catholic than his predecessor, yet it is ironical that it came in connection with the Centenary of Canon Carter's institution as Rector. Ironical because Canon Carter's ministry in Clewer was beset by just the sort of bigotry as now threatened his Centenary celebrations. Indeed Major Bourne-May's letter of January 1944 and the letter from 'a rate-payer of Clewer' which appeared in the "Windsor Express" of February 1st 1873, are two of a kind. (See Chapter 1)

On this occasion however there were strong voices to rally to the cause, not only of Canon Carter but to the ministry of Fr. Cyprian. Two respected and loyal parishioners who worshipped at St. Andrew's week by week wrote to the "Express" to set the record straight. The first was Jack Reavell of 52, Clarence Road:-

"Sir, I am at a loss to understand the object of your note on Clewer Services unless it was intended to provide theological dissension. If you published Major Bourne-May's letter with reluctance because you thought it likely to arouse theological controversy, why did you encourage this possiblity by adding, what appears to me to be merely idle gossip.
"As one who has gone to some trouble to study the teachings of the Rector of Clewer I should like to deny that they are in any way incompatible with the best traditions of the Church of England...... The establishment of the Church of England may be its strength but it is also its weakness, if it means that public opinion is to be allowed to influence her teaching. For unless we are careful it will influence her to such an extent that she will cease to teach Christianity at all.

"I am sure that the majority of your readers must regret your unusual indescretion in raising such controversial issues in connection with the Centenary Celebrations of Canon Carter,a man who was held in such high esteem, that we still honour his memory one hundred years after he commenced his long association with Clewer."

Yours faithfully,
Jack W. Reavell."

The second letter was from Miss G.M. Boycott of 'Castle View', Clewer, who with her usual charity and perception put the whole question back into the right perspective - so let her have the last word:

> "The one thing that matters is that the work of God should be done in this Parish, and it seems a great pity to hinder it by irresponsible criticism. As an old member of the congregation I am very thankful to be quite convinced that the present Rector of Clewer regards the salvation of souls as his primary object, and ceremonial, though desirable, of lesser importance. For myself I cannot understand the use or non-use of ceremonial excusing any Christian from the duty of public worship".
>
> Yours faithfully,
> G.M. Boycott."

After all the theological bantering the Centenary Celebration itself passed off as planned. High Mass was celebrated on January 24th, the Centenary itself, in the presence of the Bishop of Reading. On the following Saturday many people made a pilgrimage to the grave of Canon Carter in Clewer Churchyard. A lengthy procession led by thurifer, acolytes and processional crucifix made its way from the Chapel of the Community of St. John the Baptist to St. Andrew's Church. The pilgrims set forth reciting the Litany from the Book of Common Prayer and were greeted at St. Andrew's by a quarter peal of bells. At the graveside the assembled pilgrims were led in Prayer by the Bishop of Buckingham. They then made their way into St. Andrew's Church, where many people were already assembled, singing "For all the Saints". Solemn Evensong was sung and the Bishop of Oxford, the Right Revd. Kenneth Kirk preached. Opponents of Canon Carter's Centenary might have done well to have heard the Bishop's address in which he paid tribute to Canon Carter's work; ".....He turned his Church into a Sanctuary of the ancient symbolic and ceremonial worship of the Church of England. He fought for the truth of the Gospel against those who were trying to whittle it away until it became something very like ordinary everyday respectability and nothing more..." The celebrations were brought to a close at 6.00 p.m. when the Oxford Diocesan Guild of Bellringers rang a full peal.

January 21st 1944 saw the first of a new series of heavy raids mostly on London. They lasted until the end of March and were soon called the "Little Blitz". The week of February 18th to 24th was particularly bad with much destruction in London. "The last few nights have been rowdy nights." commented the "Windsor Express" of February 25th 1944. "There is no real comparison, however between the raids which the British and American Air Forces are carrying out on enemy territory and the raids that the Germans are carrying out here, nor, indeed, between their present raids and those of 1940." By mid-April enemy activity had again died down over Britain.

Back at St. Agnes',Lent followed similar lines to former years with extra devotional services and sermon courses. The full Holy Week rites which Fr. Trapp had introduced in his first year were again observed and there were seventy-five Easter Communicants.

The fabric was giving cause for concern at St. Agnes' in the early part of 1944, there having been heavy expenditure for roof repairs. When it became necessary to replace the boiler the Rector appealed to the rest of the Parish for help. "They are doing marvels themselves, but I do not think the rest of the Parish can stand by and expect them to find the lot." When the question of the new boiler was raised at St. Agnes' own Annual Meeting a number of people came forward with offers of help and in this way a quarter of the estimated cost was promised. "A further proof, if proof were needed," wrote Fr. Howard in the May Magazine, "of the enthusiasm and care which St. Agnes' people have for their Church."

"Salute the Soldier" Week was held in Windsor at the end of May with a target of £300,000. As in previous efforts the target was exceeded and the final total was £428,947:14:11d. There was a special treat for the local children on Empire Day in connection with the fund-raising Week when 3,000 of them attended a great Rally in the Home Park at which the Queen and the two Princesses were also present. In addition to entertainments there was also an address from Derek McCullough ('Uncle Mac') in which he urged the children not to cash their Savings Certificates nor to sell their savings stamps.

By the summer of 1944 there was a change in the air. Despite the recent "Little Blitz", people were beginning to talk about the end of the War. In spite of rationing on food and clothing, the blackout, and Churchill's warning that new forms of enemy attack might be in store, people began to make plans for when peace came. At the beginning of June came the D-Day landings and the long awaited 'Second Front' in Europe. It seemed as though victory was within the Allied Armies' grasp. Then on June 15th Hitler unleashed his secret weapon - the V.I. flying bomb. The reign of the 'doodle-bug' as it became known was short, lasting only from mid-June until August, but while it lasted it was a reign of terror and during those few weeks untold damage was done.

Windsor, Slough and district had two hundred and two 'doodle-bug' warnings although only three actually fell in the Windsor area. Because of wartime censorship the "Windsor Express" was unable to report the flying bombs until the end of September. Two people were killed when a flying bomb hit the "Bells of Ouseley" at Old Windsor, and a day or two later two more people were killed at Wraysbury. Neither of these bombs did much damage to surrounding property.

The flying bomb which caused most damage in the Windsor area fell at Dedworth a week or two after the Old Windsor and Wraysbury bombs. It was a Saturday afternoon in early July and many of the men were out, either gardening or at sporting activities, which is borne out by the fact that of the sixty-eight casualties, only eight were men. Several people connected with St. Agnes' remember this fateful afternoon. Fr. Howard has recalled the engine cutting out over St. Agnes' followed by the explosion about thirty seconds later. Mrs. Rosemary Young was helping her aunt put up curtains at 329 St. Leonard's Road when the bomb fell with a resounding crash so loud that many people thought it had fallen just behind the Church. Mrs. Joan Kidby (nee Foreman) was arranging flowers inside St. Agnes' when the flying bomb cut out overhead. She must have received a nasty shock because the 'blast' shattered the glass in the round West window. In fact the bomb struck the chimney of the dust destructor at Dedworth and exploded with a tremendous bang! A considerable number of houses were damaged, some so severely that emergency centres had to be opened for the occupants. About one hundred people had to be accomodated in this way. It was estimated that one thousand houses were damaged in some way. Many places had their windows blasted out over a wide area. All Saints' Church, Dedworth sustained extensive damage to the roof and Haileybury Junior School lost some windows. Surprisingly, no-one was trapped in the wreckage, and the work of reconstruction was begun within an hour or two. Another flying bomb fell in Windsor Park a few days later but no-one was injured.

By August the V.I. launching pads were over-run by the Allies but in September London suffered its first V.2. attack. Fortunately the inhabitants of Windsor did not suffer any V.2. attacks, and by March 1945 the Allied advance brought the V-weapon menace to an end. The people of St. Agnes' had been very industrious during the Summer of 1944. Firstly they had met the target for the new boiler, with some help from Clewer and Dedworth. Secondly extensive work had been carried out to convert the Eastern end of the South aisle into a Lady Chapel. This had formerly been used by the choir, and a photograph of Our Lady's Statue taken in Fr. Trapp's time shows the choir stalls facing inwards towards the High Altar. The choir was no longer so numerous as in peace-time and, therefore, part of this area was set aside for the altar which had recently been acquired from All Saints', Highgate. The work of erecting the altar and reredos was undertaken by Mr. Bartram.

A few months later some altar frontals, a pair of branch candlesticks and a processional cross were acquired from the same Church. Fr. Howard recalls the bewilderment of fellow passengers on the London Underground when he brought his somewhat unusual luggage back to Windsor! On Thursday, July 20th, at 7.00 p.m. the Bishop of Reading consecrated the Lady Chapel altar and also preached.

The death occurred on July 26th 1944 at King Edward VII Hospital of Mr. Alfred Edwin Kelsey. He was sixty-seven years old and had been a chorister at St. Agnes' for sixty years. Six people were present at the Requiem on Monday, July 31st which was celebrated by the Rector. The choral funeral service, followed by burial in Windsor Cemetery, took place in the afternoon and was conducted by Fr. Howard assisted by the Rector. The organist was George Kelsey, nephew of the deceased.

Two days after Alfred Kelsey's death, Miss Georgina Maria Boycott died at her home 'Castle View', Maidenhead Road, aged seventy-four years. She was the daughter of the late Revd. William Boycott, Rector of Burgh St. Peter, Norfolk, and had lived in Windsor for more than half a century. It was after a relative of hers that the phrase 'to boycott' was coined. She inherited the patronage of the living of Burgh St. Peter, and at the time of writing it is still in the Boycott family, though now part of a group of parishes. A friend wrote of her, "For fifty years or more she has served Clewer in many ways as a faithful, loyal, and devoted servant. Her business acumen, her ready wit, her cheerful laugh, and her intelligent grasp of the Faith which was in her, are a combination which are not found altogether in one person; but above all we shall miss her for her Altar flowers." Georgina Boycott rendered her service to St. Andew's, Clewer, in a quiet way and poured oil over many troubled waters of parish life. Her Christian love and practical commonsense were of especial value at the time of the Elwell crisis, when her mediation helped to quell the storm in the Clewer and Dedworth districts and saved an innocent party from becoming enmeshed in the forces of circumstance.

Georgina Boycott was one of the original members of Clewer Parochial Church Council and latterly Honorary Treasurer and secretary of the Free Will Offering Scheme. She was also the first woman member of the Windsor Town Council.

The body was taken into Clewer Church on the evening of Sunday, July 30th and Vespers of the Dead were recited. The following morning the Requiem Mass and Absolutions of the Dead took place followed by the choral funeral in the afternoon. Burial took place in Clewer Churchyard in the same grave as her life-long maid, Miss Emma Bailey, who died nine years previously, and who had been maid to Miss Boycott's father and grandfather.

"Clewer Parish has held many successful fetes in the past to raise funds for the three Churches, but the first Wartime venture beat all previous records," enthused the "Windsor Express" of August 11th 1944. Certainly everyone had rallied to the cause on August 7th and helped raise £330, which exceeded all peacetime efforts by £150. "Two thousand people besieged the Rectory gardens and spilled over into the meadow at the back where stalls had been placed on ground from which hay and clover had been cut and taken away. It was an ideal country setting and everyone spent a jolly time," continued the report. Her Majesty, the Queen sent a case of six dessert knives which were duly auctioned, the highest bidder being Mrs. Leslie Barker of Vale Road, who secured the much coveted prize for £5:10:0d. The King sent gifts of vegetables and fruit from the Royal Gardens and these were very soon snapped up. St. Agnes' had a stall of fancy goods and vegetables which was run by Miss Thorne, Miss Hearman, Mrs. Williams, Mrs. Trapp, Mrs. Spencer, Mrs. Kelsey and Miss Raine. Mr. Pert ran the sideshow 'Spinning the Fish'. Besides stalls, the children gave dancing displays and there was a show of ventriloquism and magic, not to speak of a Fancy dress parade. The day came to an end with a whist drive in the Rectory, organised by Mr. Jack Reavall.

the Rectory, organised by Mr. Jack Reavall.

Early September was a particularly busy time both at St. Agnes' and at Dedworth. Friday, September 8th, was observed at St. Agnes' as the Nativity of Our Lady, and Fr. Trotter assisted both at Mass and at Solemn Evensong. Saturday, September 9th, was kept as the seventieth Feast of Dedication. Low Masses were celebrated at 7.00 and 8.00 a.m. and High Mass at 11.00 a.m., Fr. Trotter preaching at the latter. On the following day the Bishop of Oxford, the Right Revd. Kenneth Kirk, came to preach at High Mass. This was the first time that a Bishop of Oxford had been to St. Agnes'. The festivities brought out a rash of parties - a children's party on the 9th, and a Seventieth Birthday Party on the 13th. The annual Gift Day was held on September 16th and raised £50.

A week-long teaching Convention was held at All Saints', Dedworth, beginning on Sunday, September 10th. The first Service of the Convention was the Sung Eucharist at 9.30 a.m. during which the Bishop of Oxford preached and commissioned Fr. Trotter as Conductor. Both the Bishop and Fr. Trotter almost accomplished the feat of being in two places at once on that morning as they darted between Spital and Dedworth! Indeed Fr. Trotter started at Spital by celebrating at 8.00, then to Dedworth for 9.30 and back to Spital for High Mass at 11.00.

September 3rd being the fifth anniversary of the outbreak of the War, was observed as a National Day of Prayer. However, few people had any illusions that the European War would go on much longer. Rather ironically, just as the V.2. attacks were beginning, the black-out regulations were partially lifted. On September 15th the "Windsor Express" reported that Windsor,Slough and Eton were to "light up this weekend." It was the first time in five years that the streets had been illuminated - but the public were warned "not to expect too much."

Post-War development now occupied the minds of planners, even though the War was still on. Some local speculators had been thinking on these lines for some time. As far back as December 1943 the "Windsor Express" had carried a feature, together with plans, on Mr. W. Varney's ideas for developing the old Imperial Service College site. The area lay behind the College property purchased by the Corporation and extended behind Clarence Road to Imperial Road on the North side, then down Imperial Road from Green Lane to St. Leonards Road. Over four hundred houses were envisaged with the cheaper ones at the St. Leonards Road end. The plan came to nought though most of the ground covered was eventually built upon by the Council. The Editorial Comment, however, was prophetic, "The designers.... visualise the time when Imperial Road will become a far more important thoroughfare than it is now. The idea in the minds of the Council when it was built was, we believe, that it should eventually link up with the Eton by-pass and form a new motor road to enable traffic to avoid the bottlenecks of Eton High Street and the centre of Windsor..." By November 1944 the Council had drawn up its own housing programme for the first two years after the War. In the first year it hoped to build twenty-eight houses on the 'coal dump' site in St. Leonards Road and eighty-six houses on the 'Clewer Manor' site between 'The Wolf' and 'The Sebastopol'. In the second year it was hoping to build four hundred and fifty houses - one hundred on ten acres of land purchased from Mr. W. Varney in the vicinity of St. Leonards Road, and another three hundred and fifty on about forty acres between Vale Road and Smith's Lane, and Dedworth Road and Dedworth Manor, to be called the 'Dedworth Manor' site. All in all it rang the death knell for the villages of Spital and Dedworth.

The "Windsor Express" of November 10th 1944 estimated that since the beginning of the War two thousand three hundred and three bombs had fallen in the Windsor A.R.P. area. Nine people had been killed. The breakdown was as follows:

193 High Explosives
12 Oil bombs

5 Phospherous bombs
3 Flying bombs
2,090 Incendaries

Approximately one thousand six hundred and forty-three houses, three Churches and six public buildings were damaged.

1944 had been a year of ecclesiastical comings and goings in the local area. In April Canon Henry Tower, Rector of Holy Trinity, Windsor, announced his forthcoming retirement. Canon Tower first came to Windsor a few months before Queen Victoria's death. A month later, another octogenarian, the Right Rev. Philip Eliot, Bishop of Buckingham, announced his resignation as from September 1st. The son of a late Dean of Windsor, he was ordained priest in 1887 and became Rector of Slough in 1896. In 1921 he became the second Bishop of Buckingham and continued to reside in Slough and use St. Mary's Church. Dr. Eliot was succeeded as Bishop of Buckingham by Canon Robert Milton Hay, Rector of Taplow. In June Fr. Geoffrey Heald left Clewer St. Stephen to become Vicar of St. Stephen's Bournemouth. He was succeeded at Clewer by the Revd. Arthur Digby Sheffield who stayed until 1956.

1944 gave way to the New Year on a note of hope borne of expectation of Victory and Peace. The Wartime economy had made Church finances difficult to keep up but somehow ends had been met. The Service Registers show the comment 'No congregation' quite frequently on weekdays - a sign no doubt of the future post-war apathy towards the Church attendance. Communicant numbers were still low, being an average thirteen to sixteen at 8.00 a.m. on Sundays and anything from two to five on the weekdays. No doubt the War was partly to blame for the low numbers on Sundays at least, but there is little doubt that the later trend towards giving Communion at the Sung Mass did much to boost statistics everywhere - but this innovation still lay some years ahead.

The 'lighter' feeling which the prospect of peace had engendered was manifest in April 1945 when a play called "Three Half Crowns" was produced in the Hall by members of the Congregation. Fr. Howard took part and shocked some of the ladies present by appearing wrapped in a blanket with bare legs protruding and making a rather undignified exit by diving through a window at the side of the stage! I am told that Miss Thorne and Miss Hearman never forgave him! Fr. Howard made the following comments in the June Parish Magazine, "The play appears to have caused a minor sensation. I must apologise to those who came expecting a religous play, and trust they were not too surprised at finding St. Agnes' in holiday mood." It would seem that a good time was had by nearly all, and certainly the acting was done with great enthusiasm. Many of the actors were younger members of the congregation. However, it was not all fun and games. There was a good deal of work to be done to the fabric of the Church and Hall now that the rigours of War were almost done with. In April, a start was made on painting and decorating both outside and inside the Church and Hall. The Sacristy was earmarked for similar treatment after Easter. Also at this time the last of the heavy black-out curtains, and also the shutters for the East window were removed, though the large hooks were left for another thirty-five years before being removed in the 1980 redecoration!

A margin note in the Service Register on May 8th 1945 declares, "End of European War". At 7.30 p.m. there was a special thanksgiving service for Victory. The following Sunday was observed as 'Thanksgiving Sunday' for Victory'. As soon as it was announced on the Monday evening that the following day would be 'VE Day' flags had begun to appear in the house of Windsor. The Day itself was festive, although the first official celebration in Windsor was not until 6.00 p.m. when the 'Drumhead' Service took place within the Castle grounds near St. George's Gate. This was attended by the Mayor and Corporation.

A procession of Service men and women formed up at Victoria Barracks and made its way to the Castle via Victoria Street and High Street, both of which were crowded. A religious service was held at the Castle and then the procession returned to the Barracks by way of Peascod Street and William Street. At 10.00 p.m. the Mayor lit a large bonfire on Bachelors' Acre when the Nazi flag was burned. The streets of Windsor were crowded until well past midnight. Victory street parties for the children took place on the Tuesday and Wednesday.

On Sunday, June 17th George Kelsey kept his twenty-ninth anniversary as organist of St. Agnes'. The Rector wrote of him, "During that time, except for an occasional holiday, (and he has not had one for fourteen years), he has only missed two services during the whole of those twenty-nine years." By now the Choir was not as numerous as in th days before the Great War when it was a robed Choir of men and boys. It now consisted of Mrs. Kelsey, Mrs Newport, Mrs Pritchard, Mrs Paternoster, Miss Stella Harley, Mr. Pritchard and Mr. Bill Parfoot.

August 15th was kept as the Feast of the Assumption of Our Lady and a note in the Service Register adds that it was also the end of the Japanese War. An additional service at 7.30 p.m. was held in thanksgiving for Victory and Peace. This final end to the War was welcomed by the sound of bells at the Curfew Tower and at the Parish Churches of Windsor and Clewer. V.J. Day was celebrated in the same way as V.E. Day - there was a Thanksgiving Service in the Castle grounds together with all the pomp of a civic and military procession, and in the evening torchlit processions, bonfires at Clewer and on the Acre, fireworks, and dancing in the streets.

The funeral of Isabella Cooper took place on August 30th. Aged seventy-nine years, Mrs. Cooper had been ill for some time but had maintained her interests in St. Agnes' until the last.

Whilst away on holiday Fr. Howard was offered the living of Clifford, near York, and accepted. His last month at St. Agnes' was very busy with the Dedication Festival on September 9th at which Fr. Trapp assisted; Harvest Festival on September 23rd, at which Fr. Trotter preached; and on September 27th a Confirmation at St. Agnes' by Bishop Eric Hamilton, Dean of Windsor. Fr. Howard's last Mass as priest-in-charge of St. Agnes' was on Monday, October 1st at 6.30 a.m., a Sung Votive Mass at which fourteen people were present.

Fr. Howard was Vicar of Clifford in the West Riding from 1945 to 1954 and then moved to Barley, where he stayed until 1960. Since then he has been Vicar of St. Mary Bishophill Junior with All Saints North Street in the City of York. He has recently written to me of his time at St. Agnes' which, though but a brief interval in a long priestly ministry, he recalls as a happy, rewarding time and a good training ground.

So St. Agnes' was faced with yet another interregnum which must have seemed rather daunting when so much else seemed uncertain. Though the War was over yet War-time living conditions such as rationing were to remain in force for some time. Also there was the prospect of the changing face of what had hitherto been familiar surroundings. Post-War development was no longer merely a plan - it would soon be a stark reality.

## Chapter XVIII

### Plough shares into Pre-fabs

Accommodation once more proved to be the stumbling block in the appointment of a priest for Spital. Mr. and Mrs. Howells were no longer able to make their room available and all Fr. Cyprian's efforts came to nought. As a desperate measure in February 1946 Fr. Cyprian decided to take on Spital himself for visiting. In order to be present at the principle Mass he would have to alter the time to 9.00 or 9.30. The Communicants were invited to state their views, in writing, to him. Feelings were mixed, but in deference to older members, no change was made. In the meantime the Rector urged St. Agnes' people to "stick in and do your very best." As a final gesture, accommodation was offered at Clewer Rectory.

The services at this difficult time were taken by a number of local clergy, notably the Rector, Fr. Baynes, Fr. C.D. Mead-Briggs (formerly Curate of Clewer St. Stephen and at this time Assistant Master of Haileybury School) Fr. Nawton Hall (newly appointed to Dedworth), and Mr. H.G. Brightwell, Diocean Lay Reader.

In February Fr. Cyprian announced in the Clewer Magazine that £100 had been put towards the building of a priest's house for Spital, so perhaps there was a little light at the end of the long dark tunnel. "I hope that when the moment arrives when we shall be allowed to build, we shall have enough to start straightaway," he continued.

By May the Revd. Edward Dixon had been appointed, although he was unable to take up his duties until July. Edward Ashby Dixon was thirty-one years old and was unmarried when he came to Clewer and had served as Curate of St. Benedict, Bordesley in Birmingham from the time of his ordination in 1940. His first Sunday at St. Agnes' was on July 14th 1946 when the Rector preached at Sung Mass. One of Fr. Dixon's first actions was to restore the daily Mass which had been a casualty of the interregnum.

Fr. Dixon has recalled his first months at St. Agnes' when he made the daily journey to Spital from Clewer Rectory. "I lived for about ten months at the Rectory, inhabiting a small slit of a room next to the front door. I learned that it had been Canon Carter's oratory! Anyhow it was warmer than the rest of the house as there was no central heating in those days!" The journey from Clewer to Spital was not always easy for it was an exceedingly wet Autumn. Fr. Dixon would cycle down Imperial Road which still had no houses. There was a high hedge and footpath down one side and during November the seats along the footpath were standing in twelve inches of water. By March 1947 Fr. Dixon had moved to lodgings in Alma Road. His landlady, Miss Hackamore, was a familiar figure around Windsor transporting her dogs in a basket on wheels. Fr. Dixon has recalled the "warm communal spirit amongst the little family of worshippers" at St. Agnes'. He is not alone in this, many people have spoken of the family atmosphere which prevailed and of the spirit of "pulling together". Fr. Dixon points out that the wartime privations such as rationing of food, clothing and fuel, and restrictions on travelling were still in force and that there was still the sense of "all being in it together".

There was, however, the lighter side. "The MINISTER OF ENTERTAINMENT is pleased to announce that there will be DOUBLE RATIONS for Clewer this Summer - CLEWER FETE: MONDAY 5th and SATURDAY 10th AUGUST," ran an advertisement in the Parish Magazine for July 1946! The great event was opened on Bank Holiday Monday by Lady Wilson, daughter of the late Mrs. Rhoda Maclean, and on the following Saturday by Miss Windsor! The Rector afterwards declared that it was the best fete since he had come to the Parish, and in fact the best he had ever attended!

St. Agnes' was on the brink of change. There were still some of the older generation who had been at St. Agnes' in some cases all their lives, most of whom have gone to their rest by now. The younger members who were then in their 'teens and twenties represent to-day's longest serving members, although in many cases marriage was followed by their leaving the district. The real change, however, lay just round the corner in the shape of post-war housing developments which were to change Spital from village to suburb of Windsor and, ultimately, to bring in new families. The older generation will be known to those who have read this far - Mr. and Mrs. George Bridges, Miss Thorne, Miss Hearmon, Mr. Pert, Mr. and Mrs. Kelsey to name but a few.

George Kelsey taught music but although it was his livelihood St. Agnes' was George's life - and Rosa's too. He was a little man and she wore the trousers! Someone described them to me as a 'quaint couple'; not having known them I'm unsure how accurate that description is, but their loyalty to St. Agnes' was unquestionable.. Rosa was an indefatigable baker of cakes, buns and saleable commodities for Church stalls, entertainments, etc., though she always said she "shouldn't have been doing it." Nevertheless she always did, and everybody heard about it into the bargain! It is said that George had two hats, a trilby for Winter and a boater for Summer. The congregation always knew when Winter had come to an end when George changed his hat! Fr. Dixon recalls an episode when George scored one over his spouse. They were all out carol-singing and reached the 'Prince Albert'. George when in with the collecting box while the others sang outside. "He's rather a long time", said Rosa, so they sang again. After a while George came out smacking his lips after having been treated to a drink!

The Perts were lifelong worshippers and were as well known as the bread and cakes which they baked. Sydney Pert was a regular Communicant at 8.0 a.m. on Sundays and at other times was a familiar figure cycling round Spital with an enormous basket laden with loaves.

The younger members of the congregation at this time included Bob and Alan Bridges, Barbara Giles, John Spencer, Avril Goodwin, Stella Harley and Joan Paternoster. The young men were all servers except when National Service called them away. Alan Bridges and Barbara Giles were married in 1955 and still worship at St. Agnes', as does Joan Paternoster. Bob Bridges now lives in Cambridge. John Spencer and Avril Goodwin were married in 1949 and subsequently moved away. Sometime during the 1950's Stella Harley became a Roman Catholic and later joined a Contemplative Religious Order, but her two sisters still worship at St. Agnes'.

Other regular worshippers at this time included Mr. & Mrs. Jim Cramer, Mrs. Williams, Mr. & Mrs. Keeler and Mr. Hall. Jim Cramer was Dutch and during World War II he and his wife suffered imprisonment and much hardship in the Dutch East Indies. After the War they came back to Windsor, where Mrs. Cramer had been brought up, and their two sons became altar servers at St. Agnes'. Mr. Cramer died in 1978, but his widow is still a regular member of St. Agnes' although the rest of the family live away. Mrs. Williams lived in Clewer Hill Road and was a tireless worker who supported everything until she and her husband moved nearer to Reading in 1949. Mr. Hall still lives in St. Leonard's Road. He was "Warden" and a server and also a leading light in the dramatic productions and entertainments. Mr. and Mrs. Keeler came to live at 'Sefton Lawn', Winkfield Road in 1936 and had been worshippers at St. Agnes' ever since. They were generous benefactors though usually anonymously. During the War, Mrs. Keeler, assisted Mr. & Mrs. Ham, organised sewing parties at 'Sefton Lawn' in 'Make do and Mend' spirit. The garments thus produced were sold for Church Funds. 'Sefton Lawn' was often the venue for Sunday School tea parties. At this time Mr. Keeler used to arrange dances for the parish under the name of 'Clewer Crusaders'.

"St. Agnes' makes martyrs of us all," was a familiar saying in Fr. Dixon's time when the main Communicating Mass for the Patronal Festival was at 6.45 a.m. and people had to turn out in the frost and snow. However, St. Agnes' Day 1947 was a little more merciful and the sun even shone later. But by January 28th there was the familiar note in the Service Register, "Snow and severe cold." It had been a very wet Autumn and now the Spring of 1947 was to see the worst floods in Windsor since 1894. Being on a hill meant that St. Agnes' was not affected except that it was cut off from St. Andrew's. The houses in Clewer Village were high and dry but the water came almost to the Maidenhead Road. A good many of Fr. Cyprian's parishioners were cut off and he would wade through for papers and shopping for the elderly. On March 23rd (Passion Sunday) many people from St. Andrew's and St. Stephen's attended St. Agnes' being unable to reach their own Churches. On March 26th Bishop Hamilton (the Dean of Windsor) confirmed three candidates from Spital and one from Dedworth at St. Agnes' instead of St. Stephen's.

Fr. Cyprian was very anxious that all three Churches should join together on special occasions, for instance Patronal Festivals. Rogation Processions at St. Agnes' seem to have ceased round about 1940, and in 1947 a Rogation Procession and Evensong was held at Clewer with all three congregations participating. These joint devotions were never popular - Spital people were very reluctant to go to Clewer, feeling it was too out of the way.

Fr. Trapp had been a frequent celebrant at St. Agnes' during the early part of 1947 having been 'de-mobbed' from the R.A.F., and was temporarily living with his mother who had been widowed early in 1946. On March 22nd 1947 he was instituted to the living of New Bradwell, Buckinghamshire and a coach party went from St. Agnes' to wish him well.

The death occurred in June 1947 of the Revd. Gerald Payne-Cook, former Rector of Clewer, aged 66. He had been assisting at All Saints', Woodham, near Woking for the last four years and it was there that he collapsed and died. After celebrating Mass at 8.00 a.m. he later returned to preach at the Sung Eucharist. He preached the sermon after which he collapsed and died during the singing of a hymn. A Requiem was offered at Clewer on June 25th and a memorial service was held on Friday, July 6th at 6.00 p.m. The ashes were brought to Clewer Churchyard and placed in the grave of his daughter, Patience, who died in 1941.

Bulkeley Avenue and Princess Avenue made their appearance on the Spital map towards the end of 1947. They were the first of the Council's 'St. Leonard's Estate' and the erection of the so-called 'steel houses' was met with some controversy. Soon a whole network of Council housing of various types was to appear. Fr. Dixon began visiting as soon as the houses were occupied and St. Agnes' Committee proposed sending a letter inviting the new residents to worship. These overtures met with little response.

1947 was a drab year - a year of discomfort, floods, rationing and general post-war deprivation. It was a year when small pleasures like a Bank Holiday outing to the Park, a coach ride to Fr. Trapp's induction, a party for the Sunday School, and an outing to Burnham Beeches, made lasting memories because they were a bit different. Yet the very ordinariness of 1947 shows that the real sacramental life of the Church went on too, daily Mass, feasts and fasts, Coral League, Sunday School, together with social activities, all proceeded as usual.

Fr. Dixon wrote optimistically in the January 1948 Parish Magazine, "The number of Communicants has been maintained, if not slightly increased, our children's work is growing, and we have some new roads in the district amongst which we can try to spread the influence of the Church....... Following our District Appeal last Spring the Free-Will Offering has been greatly increased, and, what is more, the contributions have been maintained. So, despite the grim outlook of the World Situation in general, we can enter 1948 with gratitude in our blessing upon our corporate worship and work during the past year........"

The preacher at High Mass on St. Agnes' Day, January 21st, was Fr. Sidney Smith, curate of Windsor Parish. New retired, Fr. Smith has made his home in Windsor where he is an honorary assistant priest at Clewer St. Stephen. St. Agnes-tide is traditionally 'party-time' and 1948 was no exception. There was a supper and entertainment for the adults and in addition, the children's parties were enjoyed with customary gusto. We are told that the Sunday School was growing rapidly with members from the new estate and that Miss Hearmon was appealing for helpers.

Despite post-ware strictures it had been possible to make some improvements to the ancillary buildings. The Hall had been re-decorated thanks to the gift of materials from Mr. Keeler and this made a great difference. During the previous year the Caretaker's Cottage had been installed with electric lighting. Previously there had been gas lighting in the downstairs rooms and nothing at all in the scullery or upstairs.

Fr. Cyprian's desire that all three congregations should combine at certain times was indulged to an unprecedented extent during Holy Week 1948. The whole Parish combined for certain devotions which included a Quiet Afternoon conducted by Fr. Baynes at St. Agnes' on Saturday, March 20th; on the Wednesday there was a 'Simple Holy Week Play' at St. Agnes' at 8.00 p.m.; and on Good Friday Fr. Dixon conducted the Three Hours Devotion at St. Andrew's. All other services at St. Agnes' were as in other years except for Holy Saturday when, instead of the Easter Ceremonies and First Mass of Easter at 9.30 a.m., there was Evensong at 6.30 p.m. followed by the Blessing of the Easter Candle and Devotions.

The Church Committee decided to clean the stone at the foot of the outside Calvary and to add an inscription to the memory of the local men who had fallen in the recent War. A letter appealing for contributions was circulated around Spital during 1948. The stonework was done free of charge by Messrs. Bishop and Sons, and at the same time the Figure was cleaned and the roof re-slated. The completed Memorial was re-dedicated by the Rector on Sunday, January 23rd 1949.

A new Ciborium (a silver vessel for the Blessed Sacrament) was blessed before the 8.00 a.m. Mass on Sunday, August 15th 1948, the Feast of the Assumption of Our Lady. This was a parting gift from Mrs. Winifred Loring, formerly Miss Drewe, who until her marriage had been a regular worshipper at St. Agnes' along with pupils from the boarding school in St. Leonard's Road (now Upton House School) of which she had been Head Mistress.

Fr. Harry Stanbrook was the preacher at Sung Mass on the Sunday within the Octave of the Dedication Festival. The festivities were continued in a different vein on September 16th, the Octave Day, with a social evening in which members of the congregation presented a farce entitled 'Pearly Pearls'. The cast consisted of:-

| | |
|---|---|
| Sir George Newton | Bob Bridges |
| Bennet | R. W. Hall |
| Ralph Newton | Alan Bridges |
| Lady Violet Newton | Dorothy Naf |
| Mrs Pilchard | Stella Harley |
| Marjorie Pilchard | Barbara Giles |
| Good | Avril Goodwin |
| Marie | Ann Potter |
| The Revd. C. Pilchard | John Spencer |

Producers: John Spencer and Avril Goodwin.

It may have not been 'high drama' but everyone thoroughly enjoyed themselves.

The Summer of 1948 was wet and several Church activities were dampened including the Sunday School outings. Even Clewer Fete fell victim to the weather!

Sunday, September 26th, saw the start of a teaching Convention in the Parish. The conductor at St. Agnes' was Fr. Donald Patey C.R. Each day there were two Low Masses, one celebrated by Fr. Patey and the other by Fr. Dixon, and in the evening a Convention Service at 8.00.p.m. Mass attendances varied between five and ten daily and the evening service between forty and fifty. The climax of the Convention was a Solemn High Mass of Thanksgiving for the whole Parish at St. Andrew's on Monday, October 18th at 6.00 a.m.

Miss Hearman retired as Sunday School Superintendent on November 21st, and was presented with a book and a cheque in recognition of her faithful service during a quarter of a century. The fourth Sunday in Advent saw the children present a Christmas Tableau at 3.00 p.m. and again at 6.30 p.m. thanks to the hard work of Miss Durnford and Miss Beckwith.

So 1948 closed - it had been a year of humdrum hard work, fund raising and evangelising. 1949 was uneventful during the first half except for the death in February of Mary Ann Kelsey, George's mother. One of the oldest members, she had been associated with the Church life of Spital right back to the days at the Cemetery Chapel.

In June Mr. Bampton reported that considerable repairs were necessary to the Hall and Caretaker's cottage,, amounting to about £100. Little had been done during the War and now the work must be done without delay. This was rather a blow, for the finances would hardly stretch this far. Miss Thorne reported that there was enough money to meet liabilities to the end of June. It was felt that the Gift Day, together with Spital's share from Clewer Fete, supplemented by an Autumn Rummage sale ought to help with this extra financial burden.

A further blow to morale was dealt by the announcement in June of Fr. Dixon's forthcoming departure for Malvern. "We shall miss him very much at St. Agnes' for he has put in three years of solid and conscientious work there, and has built up, through the Grace of God, a healthy Church life in the district," wrote the Rector in the June Parish Magazine.

Fr. Dixon's last Mass at St. Agnes' was on the Feast of the Assumption of Our Lady, August 15th 1949. On the previous evening he had been presented with a pewter tea-set and walnut tray by Mr. Keeler on behalf of the people of St. Agnes'. Fr. Dixon stayed at Malvern until 1953 when he became Rector of St. Matthew, Coates, in Gloucestershire and in 1966 became Vicar of Frampton-on-Severn. Fr. Dixon retired in 1980 and lives at Minchinhampton a few miles from his last parish.

In his farewell letter to the Parish, Fr. Dixon said, "...The worshippers at St. Agnes' continue to be a 'happy family' devoted in friendliness and faithfulness to the service of God in his Church. The district is gradually changing in character and will become one of the more central residential areas of the town. I foresee that in a few years' time there should be great opportunities for the Church. This is already apparent in the fine crowd of younger children who come to worship week by week from the part of the new estate which has so far been erected. If they can be held together into their 'teens you should have a strong body of young folk to follow the older generations of faithful St. Agnes' folk in time to come...."

Fr. Dixon looks back on his time at St. Agnes' as a happy period during which everyone co-operated in what were still difficult times. Present day members of the congregation who remember Fr. Dixon speak of his friendliness and concern for all - but particularly of his ability to get on with the younger generation. They did much to encourage the younger people at a time when post-war apathy towards Church attendance was beginning to be a problem generally. Such pastimes as Bank Holiday outings to Burnham Beeches, Bourne End and West Wycombe are still remembered with pleasure.

It was a sad day for St. Agnes' when Edward Dixon left not only because it meant yet another interregnum, but because the Parish lost a priest with the ability to unite people of all ages to a common cause - the building up of God's Church. This was a valuable gift in a place like Spital when the village was changing so drastically and when so many new people were moving into the district. With a priest-in-charge such as Edward Dixon, St. Agnes' might have presented an image of God's Church which would have attracted many of those new people, and as a result St. Agnes', Spital would have thrived throughout the 1950's. Instead, as we shall see, the 1950's almost saw the undoing of St. Agnes.

## Chapter XIX

## Rot and Rose petals

"During the interregnum at St. Agnes' it will be necessary to make some alteration in the times of services...." was the inevitable note by Fr. Cyprian in the Parish Magazine. On Sundays there was to be a Mass at 9.00 a.m. and a children's Service at 11.00 a.m. Weekday fare consisted of Mass on Monday, Wednesday and Friday and Compline and Benediction on Thursday evenings. Fr. Dixon had introduced weekly Compline which he later coupled with Devotions to the Blessed Sacrament, but Fr. Cyprian now introduced Benediction. Sunday Communicants at this time varied from fifteen to twenty with from twenty-five to thirty-five present. From August until December 1949 services were conducted by Fr. Cyrpian and Fr. Nawton Hall of Dedworth. In December Fr. Hall accepted a post in the Diocese of Lincoln, leaving Fr. Cyprian single-handed except for Fr. Alexander Baynes, Chaplain of the Community of St. John the Baptist.

As from January 1950 the Revd. William Aubrey Pike, Minor Canon of St. George's Chapel, was appointed part-time priest-in-charge of St. Agnes'. Canon Pike was forty-five years old and was an old friend of Fr. Cyprian, having served with him in a former parish.
The pattern of Services was to be:-

SUNDAYS: Low Mass at 8.00 a.m. for two months out of three.
Sung Mass at 9.00 a.m. all year round.
(Evensong was not re-introduced until October).

WEEKDAYS:Mass on about three days, plus Thursday evening Benediction of the Blessed Sacrement.

It was something of an experiment having a part-time priest, and with hindsight it is easy to say that it was doomed to failure. There are two main reasons why it failed - distance and finance. Firstly, Canon Pike resided at Windsor Castle and was without transport. Secondly, he was only being paid a stipend of £175 per annum for his work at Spital and this was too small a sum. There was very little that a part-time priest could do in the way of visiting in Spital although it was suggested that a Sister might help with this.

1950 began with the passing to rest on January 5th of Edith Annie Hearmon. Fourteen people received Holy Communion at the Requiem and a large congregation were present for the funeral at which the Rector officiated, assisted by Canon Pike. Burial followed at Windsor Cemetery and among the wreaths were tributes from the Church Committee, Choir, Friends of St. Agnes' and Sunday School.

Not only did St. Agnes' lose Miss Hearmon from their midst but also a great friend Emily Thorne, who at this time went to live with her sister at Battle in Sussex. She died in 1975 when she must have been a great age.

So two more passed from the midst of the people and with them went, for the time being at least, the Coral League. Though attempts were made to revive it, it was never quite the same. Perhaps it was becoming rather 'dated' in any case but there are still a good many local people who recall those evenings of sewing for the Missions. Not a few of them regarded Emily Thorne with trepidation especially as her embroidery was always so good compared to their own poor efforts. The plays too, always with a Missionary 'flavour', gave pleasure especially to those who played the 'Natives' and had to 'black up'.

In June 1950 the death occurred of Edith Busteed, and her Requiem and Funeral took place on June 16th. Short and 'very round', Miss Busteed was a retired nurse who lived in Gloucester Place where she was surrounded by cats. Before coming to Windsor she had worshipped regularly at St. Alban's Holborn. On Sundays she would arrive at St. Agnes' by taxi and receive Holy Communion from the Reserved Sacrament at 10.45 a.m., after which she would breakfast at Mrs. Bridges' cottage. She would then go back to the Sung Mass, arrivingduring the Gospel and would push all the children out of her way in order to reach her seat! Miss Busteed was a great music lover and had spent a good deal of her life abroad.

Like Edward Dixon, Aubrey Pike was popular with the young people of St. Agnes' and would often hold musical evenings for them at his dwelling in the Horseshoe Cloisters. If he had been full-time the appointment would have been ideal. He maintained the Catholic tradition of St. Agnes' and gave as much attention to the demands of the job as he could, bearing in mind that he had an equally demanding job at St. George's. He soldiered valiantly on at St. Agnes' until December 1950 when a full-time priest was appointed. Canon Pike stayed at St. George's until 1954 when he moved to Wakefield. In 1956 he became Rector of Burnham Deepdale and Brancaster in the Diocese of Norwich until his retirement in 1970. He then moved to Cambridge where he still lives.

Through the generosity of Mr. Keeler the long suffered problem of accommodation was at last overcome, and a cottage, 435 St. Leonards Road, was purchased for the priest of St. Agnes'. Therefore, when the Revd. Maurice Hickin began his ministry at Spital on December 21st 1950 he was able to move into a house which was for his own exclusive use.

Maurice Whitehouse Hickin had been ordained priest in 1935 and had served in no less than six parishes, including a spell abroad, before coming to Clewer, but had never held a living. Among those parishes were St. Peter, London Docks, St. Mary Magdalene, Paddington, and St. Andrew's, Worthing, all well known in the Anglo-Catholic Movement. Except for his curacy in Paddington where he spent six years, he was never anywhere more than two or three years. Fr. Hickin was short in stature with a beard. He always wore a cassock, no-one remembers seeing him in an ordinary clerical suit. His wardrobe was completed by a' Father Brown' style clerical hat (otherwise known as a poached egg), and long cloak! His means of transport was a lady's bicycle with basket on the front. From the very start Fr. Hickin made it clear that his religious outlook was of the most extreme and uncompromising variety of Anglo-Catholicism. For the time-being though, the people of St. Agnes' were only too pleased that at last they had a full-time priest once more. "We welcome with a sigh of relief the advent of Fr. Hickin. We hope he will have many happy years at St. Agnes'," wrote Fr. Cyprian in the Parish Magazine of January 1951.

St. Agnes-tide 1951 was full of activity as usual despite the fact that both the Rector and Fr. Methuen, newly appointed to Dedworth, were ill so that the High Mass had to be abandoned. Fr. Baynes preached at the Sung Mass which was celebrated instead, and Fr. Hickin preached at 8.00 a.m. and Solemn Evensong. Also during the Octave there was a party for the Friends of St. Agnes'. The food was organised by Mrs. Kelsey and her faithful band of helpers, whilst the 'M.C.' for the games was Mr. Pert. A couple of days later it was the children's turn for a party and we are told that "Fr. Hickin seemed to have an inexhaustable store of prizes at the games, for even the helpers got a consolation prize".

It was not all parties though, for many items were still rationed and people were still feeling the post-war pinch. There was much to be done on both spiritual and material level and the congregation, spurred on by having their own priest once more, set about tackling all the challenges which came their way.

The sewing Class which had made such a contribution to the Church finances re-opened at Sefton Lawn in February and was appealing for new recruits. The Sunday School also re-opened nder the care of Fr. Hickin and Sister

Helen Elizabeth, C.S.J.B. Later in the year Fr. Hickin opened a club for all boys who attended Mass. This met every Friday in the Upper Hall. A similar organisation for older girls was to meet on Tuesdays in the Lower Hall under the leadership of Mrs. Ham and Miss Harley.

The three cottages adjoining that of the caretaker were condemmed as being unfit for human habitation and beyond repair. Demolition did not take place until 1953 owing to the problem of rehousing the tenants.

The priest's house, 435 St. Leonard's Road, was in need of repairs and extension and the work was put in hand. Meanwhile Fr. Hickin lodged with parishioners. When completed the work was found to be unsatisfactory and a long wrangle ensued over rectifying the faults. In the meantime the bills mounted up but the Church Committee refused payment until everything was completed to their satisfaction. At about this time Mrs. Keeler proposed to the Church Committee that a house be built for the Spital priest. It will be remembered that in 1946 Ł100 had been set aside for a house and this sum had been slowly added to whenever possible. At the Parochial Church Council meeting during the previous week, various suggestions had been made about a memorial to Canon Carter. Mrs. Keeler now suggested that a Priest's House would be a perpetual memorial and would also meet a special need in the District. The St. Agnes' Committee, therefore, directed the Secretary to write to the Rector asking him to put forward the proposal to the Standing Committee of Church Wardens. It was the first step towards the final solution to the accommodation problem.

As the result of various appeals Fr. Hickin was able to acknowledge a number of gifts for the Church during 1951, which included an up-to-date English Missal, an Eighteenth Century silver 'angel' thurible, lace, altar linen and an Exposition Throne for the Blessed Sacrament.

George Kelsey was still receiving the same salary that he was given on becoming organist thirty-five years previously! Fr. Hickin pointed this out to the Church Committee and they unanimously agreed to pay his National Health stamp contributions and that a bonus of Ł5 granted in May 1947 should be paid to him! The Rector further promised that a grant from the Charity Fund would be made at the end of the year.

The Church fabric was in dire need of repair by this time, there being leaks in the roof of the nave and sacristy, the Lady Chapel floor was in need of repair and the whole Church interior needed re-decorating. Mr. Ham undertook to repair and stabilise the Lady Chapel floor, but upon taking up the boards the whole floor was found to be rotten and in imminent danger of collapse. The floor had been constructed with no airway underneath thus causing a condition conducive to wet rot. Mr. Ham feared that the damage might extend to the High Altar and recommended that the whole area be examined by an expert. The Church Committee decided to ask Heelas of Reading, a firm of builders who were coming to estimate for the re-decoration, to look at the floor. Heelas' estimate amounted to Ł365:10:0d for re-decorating the whole Church and Ł120 for repairing the Lady Chapel floor. As this was considered to be too high Ireland's of Eton were approached and their estimate was accepted. This amounted to Ł105:8:0d for re-decorating the Church and gallery together with excavating the Lady Chapel floor and laying tiles to save any further trouble. It did not include any work on the Sacristy. Work commenced on the Lady Chapel floor in July and took four days. Re-decoration of the Church followed and although this led to some alterations in Mass times on weekdays and a re-arrangement of the seating it did not necessitate closure of the Church.

It had been planned to buy a statue of St. Agnes as a memorial to Miss Hearmon and subscriptions had brought in nearly Ł20 by July, but it was decided to make the restored and re-decorated Lady Chapel into her memorial instead. Accordingly a plaque with the following inscription was placed on the wall: "To the Glory of God and in honour of the most

Blessed Virgin Mary, this Chapel was restored in thankful remembrance of His faithful handmaid, Edith A. Hearmon who departed this life on January 5th 1950. Of your charity pray for the repose of her soul and the souls of all the faithful departed. Jesu, Mercy. Mary, Help.

August 1951."

At the end of 1951 Mr. & Mrs Bridges resigned from their post as caretakers due to Mr. Bridges' failing health. They were persuaded to stay on for a few more months, the hard work of stoking the boilers being done by their sons, but it was obvious that Mr. Bridges would not be able to carry on much longer. One of the problems was accommodation for their house was 'tied' to the job. In 1953 they moved to the house formerly occupied by Mr. & Mrs. Pert, next to the bakery, the latter having moved to a new home near Stag Meadow.

1952 dawned with a deficit of £123:16:1d due to the heavy expenditure on the Church fabric during the previous year and also the debt which was still outstanding on 435 St. Leonard's Road. When compared with 1949, the last full financial year during which there had been a full-time priest, the running expenses of the Church were being met and a surplus was being shown. In May Fr. Hickin was able to report to the Church Committee that Her Majesty had granted £200 to the Church from the State Apartments Fund. This was a considerable boost and enabled the Treasurer to report a balance of £238:9:1d.

In the January Parish Magazine Fr. Hickin paid tribute to the people of St. Agnes' for their hard work since his arrival. "May I here thank most sincerely all those who have helped and worked with me for the greater Glory of God in this place? Much has been done and much has been given, by the faithful Church workers, the servers, the choir, the working parties, the Committees and the congregation. Little may have been said, but nothing has been forgotten, least of all by Him, Whose House has been served and Beautified, Whose worship has been maintained. It is my earnest prayer that 1952 may see a like co-operation and an even greater advance along the way to God, as we walk together in the House of God, as friends."

Fr. Trapp preached on the Sunday evening in the Octave of St. Agnes'. The festival was busy as ever with parties for both adults and children and also a servers' outing to Nashdom Abbey early in February.

For several months the health of His Majesty King George VI had been deteriorating. In the early hours of February 6th 1952 he died peacefully in his sleep at Sandringham. At St. Agnes' Solemn Vespers of the Dead was sung on Thursday, February 14th, the eve of the funeral. The last journey to Windsor was made on February 15th and the streets were lined with people hoping to pay their last respects. Earlier a Requiem had been celebrated at St. Agnes' and fourteen people received Holy Communion.

There were twelve people present at Mass on St. George's Day, April 23rd. Roses, the National Emblem, were blessed and distributed to those present.

On Saturday, July 5th, the children of St. Agnes' held a Sale in the Hall. Stalls were run by the Boys' and Girls' Clubs and the Catechism. A great deal of effort had been put into the venture, the children having sold three hundred tickets in four days. Their work was well rewarded, for the Sale raised £49:4:3d for Church Funds and was deemed both worthwhile and happy.

It would seem that the children were setting a good example not only in fund raising but on Church attendance too. "I wish to appeal to all our people to do much more about their Sunday worship," wrote Fr. Hickin in the

July Magazine. "The children are responding so well that they are putting men and women to sham. It rarely happens that we have less than fifty children regularly at the 11.00 a.m. Mass. Grown-ups are few. This, coupled with the fact that attendance in the evenings is extremely poor, means that we are getting little instruction in the Faith, and so are not in any position to combat the widespread and deep ignorance of the Christian religion everywhere around us....."

Having improved the Church fabric, the Hall was now found to be in urgent need of repair, so much so that there was a danger that parts would collapse. The work was set in hand at once which included repair work and re-decoration of the interior at a cost of £28:14:0d. Some of the income from the children's Sale was used to pay for the work.

July 1952 saw a number of thefts of money from the Church, culminating on Sunday, July 13th, in the theft of candlesticks from the Lady Chapel and the bell from the High Altar. The thief was later caught and the articles recovered.

October 1952 saw Fr. Hickin endeavouring to form a Boys' Choir. Boys between eight and fourteen years were welcome, "but it must be clearly understood both by the parents and the boys themselves, that it will entail regular attendance at ....Solem Mass....and Evensong, and at the practice in the week." The Guild of the Sacred Heart (for boys) recommenced meetings after the Summer break, but Fr. Hickin was less enthusiastic about the Guild of Our Lady (for girls) which he said, "is at present of little spiritual benefit in the Parish, so until there is a better response to the demands of our religion it will not meet." Confirmation classes began at this time but prospective candidates were warned not to submit their names, "unless you mean business in your religion. Otherwise it is a waste of your time and mine."

Gifts received during the latter part of 1952 included a credence table for the Lady Chapel and a Tabernacle, the latter being the gift of Fr. Hickin to replace the existing one which he felt to be both unsafe and unworthy.

Towards the end of October Fr. Hickin was involved in a minor road accident and suffered a fractured rib which, whilst not keeping him away from his work, proved both painful and inconvenient and nessesitated taking things at an easier pace.

It had been hoped to hold an eight day teaching mission in Spital in October 1953 preceeded by a Children's Mission in June. The conductor was to be Fr. Ralph Bell, C.R., and on November 19th 1952 Fr. Bell paid an initial visit. Afterwards the Church Committee decided that Fr. Bell "was not likely to be the right type of Missioner for the Spital area." As the coming year was also Coronation year it was decided to postpone the Mission to a later date and ask the Society of St. Francis to conduct it. In fact these plans never materialised.

Two St. Agnes' members were laid to rest within three weeks of each other at the end of 1952. On November 26th Frances Mary Cooper was buried following an early Requiem at which thirteen people had been present. On December 16th the body of Annie Nottingham Reid was brought into Church. Twenty-three people were present at the Requiem early next morning.

As 1953 dawned Fr. Hickin looked back on the past year and painted a rosy picture. "It is good to record that to date an increase of seven hundred acts of Communion have been made over the total for 1951 - that is an overall increase of one thousand five hundred Communions since 1950....On the financial side we have paid in full for the interior decoration of the Church, our weekday and Sunday collections have increased considerably and our Grift Days and sales brought in almost £200.....On the debit side we have still to pay for the cottage bought on loan in 1950;

for necessary repairs....must be met. Our target for 1952 was the payment on the cottage and the decoration. We have achieved half, let 1953 see the completion of the task. Again, our almsgiving is still not comensurate with our dues, and we need to do more for the work of the Church Overseas."

Fr. Hickin's statistics are misleading. Communicants at daily Mass numbered between five and ten people, which was a good deal more than hitherto, but they represented a small proportion of the congregation who attended in the week and these few helped boost the annual figures. It did not mean that there was an increase in the congregation. In fact by this time several members of the congregation had left to worship elsewhere. Although Fr. Hickin had worked hard on both spiritual and material levels of Church life, the happy family atmosphere, which had always been a hallmark of St. Agnes', had been undone since his arrival. His uncompromising manner had the effect of alienating people from St. Agnes'. By 1953 a number of people, not a few who had worshipped at St. Agnes' all their lives, found themselves unable to continue and went elsewhere. By the end of Maurice Hickin's ministry St. Agnes' was bereft of many old friends and benefactors, and was at a very low ebb indeed.

Financial affairs were indeed gloomy and the end of April saw the Treasurer reporting that £581 wa still outstanding on the priest's cottage. It was then decided to pay £20 or £25 at the end of the next month, but in order to do so the payment to St. Andrew's of £59:5:0d for the previous quarter's Diocesan Quota would have to be held over! By the end of the year there was still £505 owing on the cottage.

1953 was uneventful at St. Agnes' except for the one major event which captured the interest and enthusiasm of the World - the Coronation of Her Majesty Queen Elizabeth II. At St. Andrew's there was a Vigil of Prayer from 9.00 a.m. on Monday, June 1st, the Coronation Eve, until 9.00 a.m. on the Day itself. The whole Parish joined in this event. At St. Agnes' there was a Solemn Mass of the Holy Spirit at 8.00 a.m. on Coronation morning. Thirty-six people were present and twenty-three received Holy Communion.

St. Agnes' held its own Summer fete in 1953 seperately from the Parish event and raised £74. It took place in the upper and lower Halls and on the vacant 'site' following the demolition of the three cottages. It was also decided, in addition to having a stall at the Clewer Bazaar, to have a Christmas Fair at St Agnes'.

Fr. Hickin had a shock upon returning from taking the senior boys to their annual Summer camp, for during his absence there had been a heavy fall of plaster from the Church ceiling, which involved further, unlooked for, expense. The congregation were urged to be as generous as possible at the forthcoming Gift Day. By this time the priest no longer sat outside the Church to receive gifts of money following the District Appeal. Instead, envelopes were issued with the Parish Magazine and parishioners were asked to return them to the Church during the Dedication Festival. This cannot have had as wide a circulation as a door to door appeal, and certainly in 1953 the amount raised was only £10 which was much less than in former years.

Visiting preachers during the Dedication Festival were two old friends of Fr. Hickin, the Revd. Sir Clifford Wigram, Bt., of Marston St. Lawrence, near Banbury, and the Rev. J.G. Whitehead from St. Augustine's Kilburn. Commenting on the Festival Fr. Hickin noted that, "Both our visiting priests were impressed with our little Church, but it was unfortunate that the attendance at the festival services fell so much below the past two years, though it is true that one or two of our 'regulars' were still away on holiday. May the breath of the Holy Spirit rekindle our old enthusiasm!"

On October 15th 1953 Ella Grace Elizabeth Brook, widow of the Revd. William

Brook, died at a great age. Her interest in St. Agnes' had never waned and to the time of her death her benefactions to the Church continued. In her will she left Ł5,500 upon Trust to the Bank to invest, the income thereof to be paid to the Oxford Diocesan Board of Finance, to be used by them towards the stipend of the priest-in-charge of St. Agnes', Spital. This would cease to be payable in the event of there being no priest-in-charge for a period of twelve months at any one time. In the event of St. Agnes' becoming a separate parish then the whole of the capital and income would be payable to the Board of Finance to be applied as part of the endowment of the new parish. On October 23rd 1953 a Requiem was said at St. Agnes' for the soul of Mrs. Brook at which thirteen people were present.

1953 closed with forty-three Christmas Communions, the lowest number since 1942 when there had been an interregnum which always affected attendance.

There was a slight 'glossing over' the problems in Fr. Hickin's resume' of the past year in the January and February Parish Magazines."...It is good to record that our spiritual life has been maintained at the record Acts of Communion made last year, and this despite the number of deaths and departures.... The boys' choir is now an established part of our Church life and has not failed us once....The Catechism is again stronger in numbers, and I am happy to see more girls turning up, and the daily Mass has never lacked support. On the financial side the picture is not so rosy.... Our collections have been kept up but our expenses seem to have increased. Our Summer and Christmas Sales of Work brought in more than Ł150 so that we have been able to pay off the debt for the decoration of the Hall, as well as pay the interest and part of the loan at the Bank. Owing to the generosity of the Parish Church the debt on the cottage has been settled at the Bank, but, of course, we must pay this back as soon as we can. Added to this we were Ł50 short in our payment to the general fund last year, and this year we have fallen short by Ł150. This is rather serious because it represents a defaulting in the payment of the stipend of the priest-in-charge which should in fact be the first call on our funds".

A new statue of St. Agnes' was aquired by Fr. Hickin early in 1954 and this was duly blessed and installed before the Solemn Mass on Mid-Lent Sunday, March 28th.

At Clewer there were changes afoot in clergy accommodation which were eventually to affect St. Agnes'. A former curate of Clewer, Fr. White, had sold his residence, 14 Parsonage Lane, to the Parish for Ł1,500 on the understanding that if the Parish sold it any money in excess of Ł1,500 should go to the Oxford Diocese to be used for ecclesiastical purposes at the Bishop's discretion. In 1949 Fr. Cyprian moved out of Clewer Rectory into 14, Parsonage Lane which became known as 'Parsonage House'. There now followed almost five years of negotiation after which, in 1954, the Church Commissioners bought 14, Parsonage Lane as the Rector's official residence, which henceforth became 'Clewer Rectory'. (The old Rectory was demolished in 1963). The Church Commissioners now bought 14, Parsonage Lane from the Parish out of the proceeds of the sale of the old Rectory at a valuation of Ł3,600. This, after the deduction of charges and fees left Ł2,000 within the discretion of the Bishop who decided that the whole sum should be kept in trust by the Diocese and used towards the building of a Priest's House at Spital next to St. Agnes' Church.

Morale was at a very low ebb at St. Agnes' and, while a few faithful held together, the team spirit which had seen the Church community through eighty years of worship, work and socila life, was almost lost. Something had to be done and in the early Autumn of 1953 the Rector gave Fr. Hickin three months' notice. However, because of a legal loophole, nine months passed before Fr. Hickin finally left St.Agnes'.

Fr. Hickin's last Mass at St. Agnes' was on May 6th 1954 when twenty-five people were present. Maurice Hickin went to assist at Holy Trinity, Reading for a brief time and had the Bishop's 'Permission to Officiate' in the Oxford Diocese until 1958. He then became curate of Kirkley in Suffolk until 1961 when he became Rector of Runwell in Essex. In 1975 he retired and now lives abroad.

In February 1954 Fr. Brian Elliott-Smith had joined the Clewer staff and upon Fr. Hickin's eventual departure he was appointed to St. Agnes'. Brian Elliott-Smith was, to quote Fr. Cyprian; " a most delightful person" but he came to St. Agnes' at the wrong time and it was to prove his undoing. Fr. Brian's elderly parents lived in Clewer, and he was a victim of the still recent War having been badly wounded and left on the battlefield for dead. He was in constant pain as a result of his wounds and, therefore, sought solace in alcohol which during his brief ministry at St. Agnes' became an increasing problem.

> "Fr. Brian is no stranger to the Parish and we have every confidence in him", wrote Fr. Cyprian in the May Magazine, "but the work of St. Agnes' has become an increasingly bigger and more difficult task in the past few years, and he will need the whole-hearted co-operation of the laity if he is to tackle this exacting task successfully."

Services continued as before in the accustomed tradition. The weekday Masses were maintained together with Mattins and Evensong and the weekly Compline and Benediction. Work and worship continued to 'tick over'but there was much remedial work to be done in the district - old wounds to heal, aggrieved souls to comfort, the reputation of St. Agnes' to restore to a good standing within the community, and Brian Elliott-Smith was too ill to undertake this arduous task. The Church finances were 'in the red' and there was little hope of improving the situation, which was grim with an even grimmer outlook.

As 1954 drew to a close the burden of the preceding months began to take its toll on Fr. Brian. His alcoholism became increasingly chronic and in January 1955 his health broke down completely. At first it was hoped he would be back in time for Easter; then hope faded until it became obvious that he would not come back at all. "I very much regret to anounce the resignation of Fr. Brian Elliott-Smith," wrote the Rector. "His response to treatment has not been as successful as we hoped and it will be a long time before he will be fit to do any work. Rather than leave St. Agnes' vacant for so long, he has offered his resignation, and in the interest of St. Agnes' I felt bound to accept it. I am extremely sorry, for given the time, I believe he would have done great things at St. Agnes'..... St. Agnes' have had a rough time of late and it is a matter of great credit to those who have remained faithful in spite of all the difficulties... Will you please remember Fr. Brian regularly and frequently in your prayers. He is travelling along an extremely difficult road at the moment, and he needs all the help and support your prayers can give him". Brian Elliott-Smith never exercised his priestly ministry again. When he eventually recovered he took a job with the Inland Revenue.

So it was that interregnum conditions were imposed upon St. Agnes' once more. Generally there was a Mass on Sundays and two weekdays, plus Sunday School and Evensong. Benediction was dropped for the time being. Services were taken by the Rector; Fr. Methuen; Fr. Boyles (Curate, Clewer St. Stephen); Fr. Stanbrook; Canons Bean and Vidler (St. George's Chapel); and Mr. S.T. Lewis, Headmaster of Clewer Green School.

The first glimmer of light at the end of what had proved to be a very long, dark tunnel appeared in the Parish Magazine for June 1955 with the announcement that the Revd. Arthur Wood had been appointed to St. Agnes' and would commence his duties at Michaelmass.

## Chapter XX

## Sundry and Manifold Changes

Arthur Wood came late to the priesthood, having for many years worked at Aspreys, the well-known West End jewellers. Following his ordination in 1953 he served as curate at St. Paul's Oxford until coming to Clewer in 1955.

"The most important event in the Parish this month," wrote Fr. Cyprian in October 1955, "is the arrival of Fr. Wood...St. Agnes' have had a lean time lately through no fault of their own, and it has not been easy for them to carry on unshepherded...Those who have remained faithful have done so in spite of many difficulties, but through their faithfulness they have managed to keep the flag flying, and Fr. Wood will find a nucleus, though I fear, a small one, to help him in the gigantic task which lies ahead of him... Lack of support and encouragement from the laity can always make a Priest's task more difficult, but in such circumstances as prevail at St. Agnes' at the moment such lack of support can well nigh break a Priest's heart. There is an enormous job of work to be done in the Spital district and, if it is to be successful even in a small way, it will demand a maximum effort on the part of all St. Agnes' people. May God bless the efforts of Fr. Wood and his faithful helpers."

Fr. Wood moved into 435 St. Leonard's Road as the new Presbytery was far from complete and was not ready until June 1956. The pattern of Sunday worship was maintained as before and the daily Mass was re-introduced. In addition, Compline and Benediction was held on Thursday evening. During the interregnum the Mother Superior, C.S.J.B. had permitted Sister Dorothy Ellen to take over leadership of the Sunday School. Sister Dorothy Ellen was already a sick woman when she took up this work but the Spital families grew to love her and her sudden death in 1958 deprived many of a good friend. When Fr. Wood arrived in Spital he at least found a thriving Sunday School with about a hundred members and this must have been an encouragement at the outset when there seemed to be so much else to discourage him. It was always Fr. Wood's wish to have a temporary hut or meeting place for Catechism and a second sister based in the new housing developments off Clewer Hill Road, but this never materialised.

The Coral League for girls was revived at this time thanks to the efforts of Sister Dorothy Ellen assisted by Mrs. Joan Paternoster, who was herself a former 'Coral Leaguer'. A further venture for young Church members which began at this time was a Boys' Club run by Mr. Brown who had also taken over the weekly Whist Drives.

We cannot leave 1955 behind without mentioning the wedding at St. Andrew's in August of Alan Bridges and Barbara Giles, both lifelong members of St. Agnes'.

On October 9th Margaret Elizabeth Merrifield died and eight people received Holy Communion at the Requiem three days later. Mrs. Merrifield had been a regular worshipper at St. Agnes' and an active member until ill-health made her housebound.

December 11th 1955 saw the Rector's twenty-fifth Anniversary as a Priest and the occasion was marked by a High Mass at Clewer at which the Bishop of Oxford was Celebrant. The congregations from all three Churches combined on this joyful occasion.

1956 was an important year for St. Agnes' and it dawned in a party spirit! The Catechism had their party on January 4th, and on the following Sunday afternoon they led the Festival of Carols and Nine Lessons, assisted by an augmented Choir. A note in the Service Register tells us that the "Church was entirely filled with children and parents."

Notwithstanding the traditional St. Anges'-tide weather, good numbers braved the frost and cold to participate in the festival services and social events. Visiting preachers were Canon Douglas Bean of St. George's Chapel, who preached at Solemn Evensong on the Eve, and the Revd. A.C. Boult, Priest-in-charge of St. Peter's, Chalvey who preached at the Sung Mass on Sunday, January 22nd. Over fifty people attended the service on the Eve which was followed by a social gathering.

The children of Clewer Green School came to St. Agnes' on January 24th for a Votive Mass of St. Agnes. This became a regular feature for several years. The festivities were brought to a close on January 25th with a St. Agnes-tide party.

Lent was well catered for with Sunday Sermon Courses at 11.00 a.m. and 6.30 p.m. Also there were Stations of the Cross for Children on Tuesdays, and Address, Compline and Benediction on Thursdays. Bad weather at the start of Lent prevented some from attending. Generally Fr. Wood was disappointed at the poor turnout during the forty days. There was, however, one resounding success, namely the special service on Mothering Sunday when there was a full Church.

1956 marked the beginning of liturgical changes in the Roman Catholic Church, changes which were to lead eventually to services in the vernacular language and a much shorter and simplified liturgy, particularly the Order of Mass. In updating their services the Roman Catholic Church was to establish a presedent which has since been followed by others, notably the Anglican and Methodist Churches. It has been noted that Anglo-Catholics had been in the habit of "borrowing" the Holy Week rites from the Roman Church. In 1956 the new, shortened Holy Week rites were published by the Roman Catholic Church, and Anglo-Catholic publishers were quick to snap up these improvements and bring out an English translation - albeit in Passion Week. Like many other Anglicans that year, Fr. Wood and his servers had rehearsed all the old, lengthy rites but changed to the new at the eleventh hour, and found them to be a great improvement. The new services were indeed an improvement for by reverting to the custom of the Early Church the services were put back to their logical times, thanks to the relaxation of the rules concerning fasting before Communion. Therefore, the Maundy Thursday Mass and the Easter Vigil Mass could now be celebrated at night instead of early in the morning. It is, therefore, interesting to compare the 'new look' Holy Week of 1956 with Holy Week in 1940 when Fr. Trapp first introduced the full rites. In 1956 they were as follows:-

| | | |
|---|---|---|
| PALM SUNDAY | | Blessing of Palms, Procession and Sung Mass. 10.45 a.m. Sixty-three present. |
| MAUNDY THURSDAY | | Sung Mass, Procession to Altar of Repose and Stripping of Altar. Twenty-nine present. 8.00 p.m. (Register note - "Liturgy in the evening for the first time at St. Agnes'"). |
| GOOD FRIDAY | 9.30 a.m. | Liturgy. Thirty present. |
| | 2.00 - 3.00 p.m. | One Hour before the Cross. |
| | 6.30 p.m. | Evensong and Stations. |
| HOLY SATURDAY | 6.30 p.m. | Evensong. |
| | 11.15 p.m. | Easter Vigil with First Mass of Easter. Twenty-seven present. |
| EASTER SUNDAY | 8.00 a.m. | Mass. Thirty-two Communicants. |
| | 11.00 a.m. | Sung Mass. (Sixty plus present). |
| | 2.45 p.m. | Catechism. |
| | 6.30 p.m. | Evensong and Benediction. |

Congregations were more numerous over Holy Week and Easter and this may reasonably be accredited to the shorter rites and different times.

Still on a liturgical theme, Fr. Wood gave voice to a desire which was to have a far-reaching effect on St. Agnes'. Writing in the April Parish Magazine he said, "It was my privilege to be invited to preach at the Parish Communion at St. Peter's Chalvey on Passion Sunday.

The Church was crowded and the majority of those present received Holy Communion, so that one was conscious of taking part in a real act of corporate worship....Ever since I first came to St. Agnes', I have felt that in present-day circumstances a similar service here would eventually mean that many more might be able to attend Church than is the case at the moment...." As Fr. Wood recently recalled, "There were a small nucleus of the faithful who loyally attended the 11.00 a.m. Sung Mass which was well served if not well sung! - but it was no use expecting it to appeal to the newcomers," i.e. the young families who were settling in to the fast growing estates in and around Spital. The idea of 'change' is rarely an attractive prospect so to make things easier Fr. Wood held a 'demonstration service' at 11.00 a.m. on April 29th. Writing about this in the May Magazine he explained that "the 8.00 a.m. Mass would be maintained but since Communion would be given at 9.30 a.m. the latter service would have to be simplified. The sermon would be reduced to about five minutes, incense would (normally) cease to be used, and the singing of hymns would cover much that is now said by the priest alone. Such a form of service would be in complete conformity with Catholic tradition and the Book of Common Prayer and is widely being adopted as the principal service in churches far more important than our own: above all it should enable very many more, who now live in this district to find in St. Agnes' their spiritual home." On May 3rd there was a Committee and General Meeting in the Hall at which it was unanimously decided to adopt the 9.30 service beginning on June 10th. There were over sixty present at this first 'Parish Communion', twenty-five of whom received Holy Communion.

Writing in the July Magazine Fr. Wood noted that the new service had made a good start but that "for some of us it will take a little time, as well as a certain measure of self-sacrifice for us to adjust our Sunday time table accordingly." The Rector had been present on June 10th and was beginning to hope that the area served by St. Agnes' would become a seperate "Conventional District." (This is the first step towards an area becoming a separate parish. Negotiations between the Rector and the Bishop of Oxford for Dedworth to become a Conventional District began at the same time. All Saints, Dedworth did not become a parish until 1982. St. Agnes' was not so fortunate and never even attained the status of a Conventional District.)

Two important organizations were born during 1956 - a Young Wives Group and a Scout Group. The Young Wives Group was formed in February under the leadership of Mrs. Russell. Monthly meetings were held in the Church Hall and the Group soon flourished. There had, of course, been a Scout Group in former times but in 1956 Mr. W.D. Hayward approached Fr. Wood with a view to re-forming a St. Agnes' pack. Mr. Hayward was already committed to the Third Windsor Scouts (Clewer St. Stephen) but had helped run the St. Agnes' Scouts before the Second World War. He now offered to start a Group - the Sixth Windsor - at St. Agnes' and Fr. Wood readily agreed. "The new Group is a sponsored one," wrote Fr. Wood in April, "That is to say, it is definately attached to the Church: but it is open to all boys who are eleven and over, who are baptised members of the Church of England, and who either attend St. Agnes' Church or live in the district which it serves." Cubs for boys eight to eleven were started soon afterwards.

The Scouts' 'Investiture' Service was held at 8.00 p.m. on May 11th 1956. On Sunday, June 24th, their flag was blessed at Solemn Evensong and Benediction, there being fifty people present. Mr. Hayward gave a statue of St. George for the Lady Chapel and this was blessed at 6.30 p.m. on Sunday, July 15th.

On May 26th Ernest Warner, organ blower for more than twenty years died, following a fall. Fourteen people were present at the Requiem on May 30th and a large congregation was present at the funeral the following day.

After a number of setbacks the new Presbytery was completed. It was blessed by the Rector after Evensong and Benediction on Sunday, July 1st 1956. So an eighty-two year old problem was at last solved. The priest of St. Agnes' is simply 'priest-in-charge' so his residence is designated 'Presbytery' which means 'priest's house' rather than 'Vicarage' or 'Rectory'. 435 St. Leonard's Road was sold, and the new Presbytery must have seemed palatial after that small dwelling or the succession of furnished rooms which preceded it. However, the house is much smaller than one would expect, and does not comply with present Diocesan housing standards, so that in the event of St. Agnes' becoming a separate parish the house would have to be extensively altered. During 1957 Fr. Wood attempted to obtain permission to let part of the Presbytery garden to a nurseryman. This caused some controversy locally and permission was refused despite an appeal to Whitehall.

There was a stern tone to Fr. Wood's notes in the September Magazine which probably indicates some of the problems he was facing at this stage of his ministry at St. Agnes'. "On Saturday, September 8th, the children of the Coral League are to hold a Missionary Sale in the Church Hall. Do please come and support the work which Sister and they do in order to raise money for the Universities Mission to Central Africa. It is nothing short of disgraceful that at present we are unable to do more than try to meet our own expenses at St. Agnes'; if only more of you would follow the example of the few who realise they have 'freely received' and therefore 'freely give' it would not only relieve me of what is a constant anxiety, but also greatly increase your own interst in the Church and all for which it stands since you would share the responsibility for running it. For the same reason, I wish more of you would try to use the Church more frequently, by attending some of the weekday Masses, the Thursday evening service, and by stopping to spend a few minutes in prayer sometimes when you are passing by. After all, having been a layman for most of my life, I know from experience that, with a little effort, all these things can be done, and the reality they can give to one's spiritual life." As to the Sale itself, it did very well and the Univeristies Mission to Central Africa benefitted by £14:6:6d.

Sunday, September 9th, was kept as the Dedication Festival and there were special preachers - Fr. F.C.T. Lancaster of St. Mary's Slough at 9.30 a.m., and Fr. J.T. Abell, Sub-Warden of the Community of St. John the Baptist at 6.30 p.m. At 3.00 p.m. there was a Children's Festival and the Church was 'well-filled'. However, there is again a note of disappointment in the October Magazine. "It was a great personal disappointment to me that more of you were not in Church to hear their (i.e. the guest preachers') timely messages, and to render thanks to Almighty God for the many spiritual privileges and blessings which are here at St. Agnes'. I am well aware that there were some of you, at least, who might have been present if only you would have made the effort. On the other hand the Church was well-filled for the Catechism Festival Service. It was good to welcome so many of the parents who obviously appreciated taking part in such an act of worship..."

Sunday, December 9th was a 'Red Letter Day' at St. Agnes' for it marked the visit of the Right Revd. Harry Carpenter, Bishop of Oxford. The Bishop was unable to be present at the inaugural Parish Communion on June 10th, but now presided and preached, and also Confirmed four candidates.

This was not the first Confirmation to be held at St. Agnes' because in March 1947 Bishop Hamilton had Confirmed four candidates here instead of at Clewer St. Stephen because that Church was cut off by floods. However it was the first time that a Confirmation had been specifically planned for St. Agnes' and was the begining of a regular practice. The candidates were Wallace Holloway, Emily Skinner, Catherine Miles and Eileen Nightingale. There were forty-one Communicants but the Church was full there being over one hundred present.

So a busy, eventful year drew to a close with sixty-five Christmas Communions and a total of two thousand and ninety-five acts of Communion for the year, both figures representing an increase.

The New Year, 1957, was to be a typical year in many ways and it opened with the usual hectic pace of St. Agnes'-tide. The Mayor of Windsor, Alderman Barney, was present at the Festival Evensong and the preacher was the Revd. Eric Perkins, Rector of Slough. The children of the Catechism presented a Nativity Play called 'Asleep on the Hay' during the afternoon of January 27th. This was written by Mr. Denis Grahame and produced by him with assistance from Miss June Mackrory. The Church was full for the performance and we are told that the audience was greatly impressed.

The Holy Week and Easter services followed the pattern established in 1956 it being generally agreed that the new times and ceremonies were a great improvement. Commenting in the May Magazine Fr. Wood noted that, "Lent has been on the whole better kept than it was last year: but in any case, the weather has been much kinder, which has helped very considerably. The congregations on Good Friday and Easter Day were much larger, and it is encouraging to find that more people are beginning to attend the Parish Communion..." indeed the latter service was drawing attendances of fifty to sixty on an ordinary Sunday, and more on Festivals, which was a great improvement on the 11.00 a.m. Mass, although still only fifteen to twenty people received Holy Communion. On the other hand it must be remembered that this represented an extra fifteen to twenty Communicants as the 11.00 a.m. Mass had been non-Communicating, and the introduction of the 9.30. a.m. Mass had not affected 8.00 a.m. Communicant numbers.

Changes were taking place in Clewer Parish in 1957. On February 15th Fr. Methuen was admitted and licensed by the Bishop of Reading as Priest-Missioner of the Conventional District of All Saints', Dedworth. Much to the Rector's disappointment Dedworth decided to 'bow out' of the Parish Magazine as from the end of the year and henceforth produce their own.

At the same time as this change in the status of All Saints', St. Agnes' hopes for Conventional District status were dashed. In June it was proposed at a meeting of the St. Agnes' Committee that "the Rector enquire of the Bishop of the Diocese whether there might be a reconsideration of the question of the district served by St. Agnes' Church becoming a Conventional District, with a view to improving the financial status of the Priest-in-Charge and the likelihood of there being a greater continuity of pastoral charge, now that the Church served such a large housing area." Data was collected concerning the population and number of houses in the District and this was presented to the Diocesan authorities, but to no avail. On December 19th the Rector reported to the St. Agnes' Committee that he had received official notification that the Diocese "were unable at present to recommend independent status but were prepared to increase their grant to £150 per annum on condition that the Committee would be responsible for raising £35 to guarantee the priest-in-charge a stipend of £450 per annum". This offer was accepted by the Committee.

A 'by-product' of the negotiations for Conventional District status was that St. Agnes' was licensed for marriages in April 1957. The first Wedding at St. Agnes' took place at 1.30 p.m. on August 7th 1957 between two members of the congregation, Mr. Donald Dobson, a sidesman, and Miss June Mackrory, a Sunday School teacher. Over one hundred people were present on this memorable occasion.

1957 continued on its way - a typical year of hard work and good fellowship, but one or two events stand out towards the end of the year. On Thursday, October 24th, Mr.Eric Longfield-Jones was licensed as a Lay-reader. On Sunday, November 3rd, the new altar rail in the Lady Chapel was blessed by the Rector in memory of Mrs. Brook.

The Church was closed from December 4th to 6th in order to allow repairs to be made to the Lady Chapel arch. Fr. Wood explained, "When the builders came to repair the break in the Lady Chapel arch, it was discovered that the beam above it was crumbling away on account of dry rot. The result was a much more extensive repair than had been anticipated; but it was felt the work had better be proceeded with irrespective of cost (£68:9:4d) and to have the beam replaced without further delay. But for this, we should certainly have ended the year with a balance in hand, hence my urgent appeal for funds to defray the cost in the hope that it might prove still possible: for we ought to be able to pay our way in present circumstances. So far the response to this special appeal has been very good, thanks largely to the very generous gifts of two or three friends of the Church and the donations of several members of the congregation...."

On December 18th the death occurred of Alice Jane Doe aged eighty-six years. She had long been connected with St. Agnes' though infirmity had kept her away for a considerable time of late. However, she had vivid memories of the Church half a century previously. The body was brought into Church on the evening of Sunday, December 22nd, when Vespers of the Dead was recited after Evensong. The Requiem and Absolutions followed next morning and the funeral took place in the afternoon.

St. Agnes' Day 1958 was marred by snow and ice which also kept the guest preacher away. Fr. Ware of All Saints', Boyne Hill, Maidenhead, was unable to come to St. Agnes' following a road accident earlier in the day. Lent also began badly, again due to the weather, but an influenza epidemic added to the problem by claiming many victims including Fr. Wood. A further misfortune was the illness of George Kelsey which kept him away from the organ stool for the first time in forty-two years. During his stay in hospital Mr. George Lansbury, organist at Ascot, and Miss Bess Reid stood in for him.

The bad weather continued and on Sunday, March 9th (Lent III) there was more snow. As Fr. Wood wrote in the April Magazine, "Sister Dorothy Ellen was on her way to Sunday School, when feeling very unwell, she decided to return to the Convent instead: but before she could do so, she collapsed at the bus-stop, and Mrs. Ives took her into her house and looked after her. I was sent for in time to anoint her by administering the Sacrament of Extreme Unction and the end came very peacefully a few minutes later..." There was a Solemn Requiem for Sister Dorothy Ellen at St. Agnes' on Saturday March 15th, at 9.00 a.m., when sixty-three people were present including many children. Several members of St. Agnes' had also been present in the Convent Chapel on March 12th for the Solemn Requiem followed by burial at the Convent Cemetery in Hatch Lane. A wreath of Daffodils was sent by the St. Agnes' congregation and the children sent a spray of Spring flowers. A week later St. Agnes' was full, with over one hundred parents and children for the annual Mothering Sunday Service.

1958 saw Philip Strong, Bishop of New Guinea, home on furlough - as always he was a welcome visitor to St. Agnes' on a number of occasions between May and September. On Sunday, August 3rd, he preached at the Parish Communion before going to St. Andrew's. The collection from both Churches were given to the Church in New Guinea. Bishop Strong was the celebrant at the 7.00 a.m. Sung Mass on Tuesday, September 9th, the Feast of Dedication, and thirty people were present. Fr. Ware preached on the following Sunday at 9.30 a.m., thus fulfilling his engagement deferred from St. Agnes'-tide.

The St. Agnes' Committee in 1958 consisted of Mr. Harold Russell, Treasurer; Mr. Eric Longfield-Jones, Secretary; Mr. Donald Dobson, Mrs Rosa Kelsey and Mrs. Knibbs, with Mr. Denis Grahame co-opted. It was decided at this time to run a 'no-bazaar'- effort! Approximately thirty people had promised to give a sum of money instead of making items to be sold, and this amounted to over £60 - precisely the amount raised by the previous year's bazaar. (In fact £130 was raised in this way, the original sum being supplemented by periodic 'draws'). Although this policy was adopted it did not prevent individuals from running their own 'efforts', so that Mrs. Kelsey ran a Sale for the Coral League, and the Sunday School held a Sale to finance their Summer outing.

The Bishop of Reading, the Right Revd. Eric Knell, paid his first visit to St. Agnes' on Thursday, October 2nd 1958 when he preached at the Harvest Thanksgiving. The Church was packed with an estimated one hundred and ten to one hundred and twenty people which included visitors from neighbouring Churches and a group from Oxford. There was an informal gathering in the Hall afterwards at which, despite the crush, the Bishop managed to greet most of those assembled. The choicest fruit was given to housebound Church members and the remainder of the produce was auctioned to augment the proceeds of the House to House collection for the Church funds which was made at this time.

A number of gifts had been received during the year including a new thurible as a thankoffering from two members of the congregation. Four dozen copies of the Book of Common Prayer and a set of Altar Cards were given in memory of Sister Dorothy Ellen. An unexpected gift at the end of the year came in the form of an American Organ for use when no-one was available to pump the Church organ. The condition of the Church organ was beginning to arouse concern.

Two offers of help in the St. Agnes' district came towards the end of 1958. First of all. Miss A.R. Campbell came 'home' to Windsor after many years in the service of the Church including work with the Village Evangelists. In her youth Miss Campbell had worshipped at St. Andrew's and was well acquainted with Rectors Cowie, Elwell and Payne-Cook. Fr. Wood was, therefore, very glad to accept her offer of help with parish visiting. At about the same time Sister Alice Mabel, C.S.J.B. commenced work with St. Agnes' Catechism.

It was 'Epiphany with a difference' in 1959 for the High Mass was celebrated at 8.00p.m. With the exception of the Maundy Thursday and Easter Vigil Masses, this was the first time an evening Mass had been celebrated at St. Agnes'. To-day it is common practice but in the late 1950's it was only just 'coming in'. The main reason why Fr. Wood introduced it for the Feast of Epiphany was because the Schools began their new term on January 6th, thus making it impossible for children and staff to attend in the morning. (Low Masses were celebrated at 7.00 and 9.00 a.m. to cater for those who preferred the early service). Eighteen people were present at the evening Mass, and five at each early Mass. From now onwards it became more common for the principal Mass on weekday festivals to be celebrated in the evening.

On February 21st 1959 George Edward Bridges passed to his rest aged seventy-eight years. He first joined St. Agnes' Choir in 1889 when he was eight years old and he had served St. Agnes' in a number of capacities ever since, not least as joint caretaker with his wife for nearly a quarter of a century. The body was brought into St. Agnes' on the evening of February 24th and Vespers of the Dead was recited. Next morning thirteen people were present at the Requiem. The Rector was present at the burial in Windsor Cemetery. Later in the year two memorials were given - an oak credence table by the Bridges family, and a set of white Low Mass vestments was given by a 'regular Communicant'.

Lent once more got off to a slow start due to yet another influenza epidemic. Church attendance was causing Fr. Wood some concern due to the perplexing fact that while more people were attending the Parish Communion, still the vast majority did not receive Holy Communion and many who had been confirmed fell away. Special occasions continued to draw the crowds, for instance on the afternoon of Passion Sunday the servers and children performed the 'Way of the Cross' in Tableaux. However, Fr. Wood could not hide his disappointment as he noted in the Parish Magazine that those "who should be forming the backbone of this growing congregation of faithful worshippers are conspicuous by their absence......"

The first quarter of 1959 presented a financial problem for the Church Committee. During the previous November the Church had been inspected under the Diocesan scheme and certain exterior repairs were recommended. As a result of the work being done the Church's finances were exhausted. To add to the burden the Hall chimney stack was found to be leaning dangerously and the cost of rebuilding estimated at £40. As if this was not enough, it was well known that the heating apparatus was practically worn out and beyond repair and the organ desperately in need of cleaning and overhauling.

All this added expense came suddenly and no-one can be accused of neglect. Fund-raising had been carried on all through Fr. Wood's ministry and all necessary repairs had been dealt with. It was, however, unfortunate that this arose at this juncture because Fr. Wood had just been offered the living of St. Paul's Oxford, and so it meant that his successor would begin his ministry at Spital with the Church at a financial disadvantage.

"I think we must congratulate the Bishop of Oxford upon his wisdom in appointing Fr. Wood to be Parish Priest of St. Paul's, Oxford," wrote Fr. Cyprian in the March Magazine. "Nevertheless it is a heavy blow to St. Agnes', and the Parish in general. Fr. Wood has done magnificent work at St. Agnes', sometimes under difficult circumstances - for I do not think he has always had the full co-operation of some who might have been expected to give it; he has worked hard, he has visited well, he has helped the newcomers to the district to feel a welcome, and he has laid a foundation which should be a great help to his successor....To Fr. Wood we offer our congratulations, our best wishes for his future work, our gratitude for the past three and a half years, and the assurance of our prayers."
Fr. Wood's last Mass as priest-in-charge of St. Agnes' was on Corpus Christi, May 28th 1959 at 6.30 a.m. It was a Sung Mass and thirty people were present. He was instituted to the living of St. Paul's, Oxford by the Bishop of Oxford on Saturday, May 30th at 5.30 p.m. and a number of people from St. Agnes' were present. On the previous Sunday evening a 'farewell party' was held in the Hall after Evensong. Fr. Wood was presented with an attache case, the 'luggage' consisting of a cheque!

Writing in the Parish Magazine, Fr. Wood said, "My aim has been to try to make it possible for the majority of those who live within its boundaries to feel that the Church is at least trying to know, understand and sympathise with their own particular problems, yet at the same time offering them that stability for which we all instinctively crave and which has the Faith of the Church for its sole foundation". Fr. Wood went on to express his hopes that St. Agnes' people would support Fr. Stanbrook during the interregnum. "The future of St. Agnes' depends much more than ever you can realise on your doing this, as it will enable my successor to make a far better start than was the case when I first came in October 1955."

So Fr. Wood returned to his beloved Oxford to be Vicar of the Church where he had served his first curacy and where he was to stay until that Church was declared redundant in 1964. He then became Chaplain of St Mary's

Convent with St. Joseph's Hospice, Chiswick until 1966. In that year he became Curate-in-Charge of St. Francis' Conventional District, Hammerfield, Boxmoor until 1975 when he retired from the full-time ministry. Fr. Wood still lives in Boxmoor and is actively involved in the work of the Church in that locality.

A shy, retiring man, Fr. Wood made a lasting impression on a district which had come to regard its local Church with suspicion. His quiet determination broke down many of the barriers which had grown up of late, though there were some who did not, or would not, appreciate his full worth while he was here. " I have many happy precious memories of St. Agnes'," Fr. Wood wrote to me recently, "and I always think of it as the one place where I was able to start something on which those who followed me found they were able to build." Amen to that.

## Chapter XXI

### Boilers, Blowers and Bank Balances

The vacancy at St. Agnes' was soon filled so Church life did not suffer from the ravages of a long interregnum. On July 1st, 1959 the Revd. Frederick John Prebble began his ministry at St. Agnes'. Ordained deacon in 1956 and priest a year later, Fr. Prebble served his first curacy at Bickley in the Rochester Diocese. In 1958 he moved to St. Silas, Pentonville in Islington after which he came to St. Agnes'. Fr. Prebble was the first married priest at St. Agnes' since Fr. Beer.

Fr. Prebble came to St. Agnes' at a time when the whole of the Western Church was poised for change - indeed some changes had arrived already. The effects of these changes in liturgy and worship are still being experienced to-day throughout the whole Christian Church. Fr. Prebble's ministry at St. Agnes' was marked by the maintenance of a high standard of Communicant life amongst the congregation. In Fr. Prebble's own words, "the local district was reasonably responsive to the Church, though one always found those for whom we were too High!" This may be so (there is nothing like incense to induce a coughing fit even amongst chain smokers) but many people found in Fr. Prebble's interpretation of the Faith a new depth and insight which enriched their spiritual lives. Indeed when Fr. Raymond Hayne took over from Fr. Prebble he found "an excellent core of well instructed and praying people for which I shall always be grateful." A good cross-section of the 1980's congregation began their association with St. Agnes' during the ministries of Fr. Wood and Fr. Prebble.

Sunday services continued in the same pattern as during Fr. Wood's time:-

| | |
|---|---|
| 8.00 a.m. | Low Mass. |
| 9.30 a.m. | Sung Mass and Sermon. |
| 2.45 p.m. | Catechism. |
| 6.30 p.m. | Evensong and Benediction. |

Mass was celebrated daily, and on Thursday evenings there was Compline and Benediction.

The Maintainence work which had arisen on the Church and Hall was still partly outstanding during Fr. Prebble's first few months due to the inevitable hold-up during the change-over period. Notably the work on the Hall chimney was urgent and the need for a new boiler becoming desperately so, not to speak of the organ. "The most immediate of the many tasks which face us is the raising of £230 for cleaning, overhauling and repairing our organ," wrote Fr. Prebble in the September 1959 Parish Magazine. "This sum also includes the cost of electric blowing equipment....To raise this money we are having a Talents Scheme which will run from the beginning of September until Christmas Day ... What better Christmas present could we give our lovely little Church than the cost of the organ repairs?" The Talent Scheme brought in just over £50 and it was decided to continue it indefinitely. Money continued to come in - but slowly. By October 1961 there was £111:10:5d in the fund but a revised estimate given by Walker & Co. put the cost at £561 for cleaning, repairing, reconditioning of the pedal board and the fitting of an electric blower. Mr. George Lansbury thought that the recently acquired American Organ could be made useable, and suggested selling the pipe organ and forming the nucleus of a fund for a future new instrument. This suggestion was not taken up, however, and apart from a few repairs no major work was done for the time being.
In common with the continuing climate of liturgical change in the Church, Fr. Prebble made a few alterations to the services during his ministry.

From this time onwards it became customary for the Sung Mass on Weekday festivals to be celebrated in the evening and there was no longer first Evensong on the Eve. In 1960 a weekly evening Mass was introduced and met a real need. Slight changes in the Holy Week services may be noted so that in 1960 they were:

| | | |
|---|---|---|
| MAUNDAY THURSDAY | Mass of the Last Supper | 8.00 p.m. |
| GOOD FRIDAY | Children's Service and Stations. | 9.30 a.m. |
| | Stations of the Cross | 12.00 noon |
| | Liturgy | 2.00 p.m. |
| HOLY SATURDAY | Easter Vigil and First Mass of Easter. | 8.30 p.m. |

Benediction of the Blessed Sacrament was a frequent devotional practice at this time - always on Sunday evenings and usually twice during the week sometimes coupled with Holy Hour or Compline. At this time in many Churches the English Missal was still used to supplement the Book of Common Prayer - the mixture varying according to how 'Western' each priest considered himself. Fr. Prebble recently recalled that he made the "maximum use of the English Missal with an absolute minimum use of the Book of Common Prayer."

A great deal of St. Agnes' Committee time was taken from 1961 onwards discussing the heating system. The main problem, of course, was financial but eventually it was agreed to replace the boiler with another solid fuel boiler at a cost of around £478. The work of installation was done by Mr. Arthur Bampton of Clewer Hill Road who agreed to have his payment as and when the Church could afford it. As a result of all the buck-passing between the St. Agnes' Committee and the Parochial Church Council, the congregation did not have warm feet until the Winter of 1962. Even less fortunate was Mr. Bampton who did not get the final instalment of his money until 1964.

Apart from the organ which had never been thoroughly overhauled, and the precarious heating system which was renewed at such considerable expense, the fabric of the Church was in fairly good order during Fr. Prebble's ministry. The Hall left a lot to be desired but the finances did not allow anything to be done at the moment. The finances of St. Agnes' were under a certain amount of strain at this time due to circumstances almost beyond the Treasurer's control, namely the debt of £444 which was still owed to Clewer on the Presbytery, and the expenses incurred by the 1961 Stewardship campaign. This was in addition to the heating system and expenses arising from necessary repairs to the Church cottage. It was an added blow when in the Spring of 1960 Mr. Harold Russell, Treasurer since 1955, left Windsor to be Headmaster of Ryburgh (Church of England Aided) School near Fakenham, Norfolk. The purse-strings of St. Agnes' were taken over by Mr. Denis Grahame.

In 1961 Clewer parish, in common with many others throughout the Country, embarked on a Christain Stewardship Campaign. The early Sixties saw the flowering of Stewardship and there were various organisations which specialised in advising parishes as to the best methods. 'Planned Giving Ltd.' was one such organisation and they ploughed a percentage of their profits back into the Church by means of donations to central funds. Having surveyed the parish at the invitation of the Rector, Planned Giving Ltd. informed him that the Parish was not ready for the scheme. However, the Rector was very keen to have Stewardship and so he employed the Wells Organisation instead. This firm exacted a heavy fee which inevitably caused dissent amongst some parishioners who sensed that a lot of work was being done for little return. The whole parish was canvassed with brochures between February 19th and March 25th and those who agreed to participate pledged to pay a certain sum of money each week for the following three years. The objective was to raise £11,900 throughout the whole parish in order to carry out the following work:-

| | | |
|---|---|---|
| | Repayment of loans on Priests' Houses | £2,200:0:0d |
| | Rehanging of bells (Clewer) | £1,500:0:0d |
| | New Heating (St. Agnes') | £1,000:0:0d |
| | Maintenance and Redecoration both Churches | £1,000:0:0d |
| | Maintenance of Churchyards | £500:0:0d |
| | Running Expenses and Missions | £8,000:0:0d |
| | | £14,200:0:0d |
| LESS: | Present Investment Income | £2,300:0:0d |
| | | £11,900:0:0d |

By March 1962 Mr. Grahame had to report to the St. Agnes' Committee that St. Agnes' had gained very little from the Stewardship Campaign. Indeed, for an increased income at St. Agnes' of £27 the organisers had been paid £233! The final share of the expenses payable by St. Agnes' was £371. An additional drawback of Stewardship was that there was a 'no fund-raising clause' which virtually tied the hands of the Church Committee. No special efforts were allowed because in theory everything should have been covered in the Stewardship budget. By the close of 1962 as a result of the installation of the new boiler together with the outstanding amount on Stewardship expenses, St. Agnes' had debts amounting to about £900.

The 9.30 a.m. Parish Mass on Sundays was well supported but the 8.00 a.m. Mass had fallen off so much that early in 1963 Fr. Prebble decided to have an evening Mass at 5.30 p.m. instead. This was followed by Benediction, and at 6.30 p.m. there was Evensong. There was always a faithful few, i.e. three to seven people, at daily Mass at this time. A further feature of Fr. Prebble's ministry was the introduction of Study Groups in the Christian faith. The junior group was for boys and girls aged ten to sixteen years and the senior group for seventeen years plus.

Mention must be made of the tragic death in September 1961 of Simon Dymoke-Marr. A brilliant young man, whose life had already been touched by the finger of tragedy, Simon was drowned whilst on holiday in Spain.

George Copas, a life-long resident of Spital, was laid to rest on November 20th 1961. In July 1962 the Dean of Windsor, Bishop Eric Hamilton, died. He had been in Windsor for eighteen years and had been a visitor to St. Agnes' during that time.

December 14th 1962 saw the death of St. Agnes' oldest member, Mrs. Harriet Selina Newport, aged ninety-six years. She had been a stalwart Communicant but latterly at home. Her body was brought into Church on December 17th and next morning she was laid to rest following the Requiem and Absolutions of the Dead.

A number of people associated with St. Agnes' during Fr. Prebble's ministry are still regular members, but a few have since died. Those since departed include Maude Reid, her sister Sarah Squibb, Helen Spencer, Ida and Nellie Bennett, Clare Taylor, George and Rosa Kelsey and Phyllis Richardson. Others who have since left the district included Mr. and Mrs. Harold

Russell, Denis Grahame, Joan Stilwell and Daisy Clarke. Norman Knibbs, a member of St. Agnes' who was also a server at the Convent of St. John the Baptist was accepted by Ely Theological College in 1961. He was ordained deacon in 1963 and priest in 1964 and became curate of St. Giles', Reading. In 1967 he became Vicar of St. David's, Northampton.

The 'good old days' when St. Agnes' had a resident caretaker had long since passed and for most of Fr. Prebble's time the Church cleaning was done by Mrs. Prebble and members of the congregation. Fr. and Mrs. Prebble also had the task of maintaining the boiler throughout the Winter season and on many occasions they had to bale out the boiler house, which was below ground level, before they could light and stoke the boiler! It sounds a gruelling task especially when done before Mass early on a cold Winter morning on an empty stomach! Despite this Fr. Prebble maintains that he actually enjoyed the chore.

By Fr. Prebble's time social life had more or less succumbed to the T.V. set although a number of organisations existed, attached to the Church. The Scouts and Cubs had a Church Parade periodically on Friday evenings. The Coral League continued to meet under the leadership of Sister Alice Mabel, C.S.J.B. and Joan Paternoster. The young Wives also continued to meet but in May 1963 thay changed their name to the St. Agnes' Young Wives League.

On May 2nd 1962 Fr. Prebble was one of twelve Anglican priests to be received in semi-private audience by Pope John XXIII. Fr. Alban Howard, formerly of St. Agnes', was also in the group. The following January Fr. Howard returned to Spital as guest preacher on St. Agnes' Day. Despite the usual bitter weather (it was the year of the 'big freeze') a good congregation turned out to meet Fr. Howard, and in some cases to renew old friendships.

The Right Revd. Philip Strong was enthroned as Archbishop of Brisbane on March 28th 1963 and later in the Summer came back to England on furlough. He celebrated Mass at St. Agnes' on June 29th, the Feast of St. Peter and St. Paul, and on a number of occasions during the succeeding weeks.

"We congratulate Fr. Prebble upon his appointment as Vicar of St. Saviour's, Saltley, Birmingham," wrote the Rector in the August Parish Magazine. "He is taking on a difficult job as well as one of great responsibility, and our prayers will be with him and Mrs. Prebble in their new undertaking." Fr. Prebble's last Mass at St. Agnes' was on Friday, August 2nd 1963 at 6.00 a.m. and nineteen people were present. He was instituted to the living of St. Saviour's on Thursday, August 8th and a coachload went from St. Agnes'. St. Saviour's, Saltley was a tough 'down town' parish of about twelve thousand souls, many of them West Indians. Fr. Prebble stayed there until 1975 when he became Rector of Capel St. Mary with Wenham Parva, near Ipswich. After leaving Spital Fr. Prebble's ministry was beset by increasing ill-health which led to his early retirement in 1979. He and his wife now live in Norwich where he offers a regular Mass at the Cathedral and ministers to a number of Religious Communities. Fr. Prebble has looked back to his days at St. Agnes' with affection and regards them as the happiest of his ministry.

## Chapter XXII

## Stewardship and a spot of D-I-Y

Fr. Prebble's successor was soon appointed so that the interregnum was mercifully short. During this time there were no Sunday evening services and weekday Masses only on Wednesday and Friday mornings and Thursday evening, the latter followed by Benediction. These services were taken either by the Rector or his curates, Fr. Brian Brindley and Fr. Philip Nickisson.

There was a full Church including members of St. Andrew's and St. Stephen's congregation to welcome Fr. Hayne for his first Mass at St. Agnes' on Thursday, October 3rd 1963. This was followed by a reception in the Hall at which the Rector spoke words of welcome.

Raymond Guy Hayne was borne in 1932 and was ordained deacon in 1960 and priest in 1961. He served his first curacy at All Saints', Kings Heath, Birmingham, from 1960 to 1963 before coming to Clewer. Fr. Hayne was married with a small daughter, Clare.

Writing to the people of Spital in the October Parish Magazine, the Rector outlined some minor changes which he hoped to institute with the coming of a new priest-in-charge; "When Fr. Hayne takes over at St. Agnes' I am going to ask him to make two slight alterations in the order of Service used at 9.30 a.m. on Sunday mornings. First I think it would be better to have the Gloria at the end of the Service....because it is in this position in the Book of Common Prayer and people who are strangers to the district will find it less muddling than by having it all at the beginning of the service. Secondly I think everyone is entitled to hear the words of Consecration and so these should be said in a clear voice. On Sundays the service should conform as nearly as reasonably possible to the Book of Common Prayer so that those using the Prayer Book may follow it without undue difficulty. I hope you will give Fr. Hayne and his wife all the support you possibly can both by your friendship and by your prayers. There is a vast amount of missionary work to be done in the district, but no Priest can make much headway unless he has the ardent support of the faithful. If, for instance, the men of St. Agnes' could get a club going which would meet possibly once a month either for social activities and/or for talks and discussion it might fill a need, and do a power of good..."

The Rector's wishes regarding Sunday worship were complied with. One other major change was that the Sunday evening Mass, begun shortly before Fr. Prebble's departure, was discontinued and the 8.00 a.m. Low Mass restored. "I believe we should aim at making the Parish Mass the one great gathering of the Church each Sunday; this will give us greater unity in the Church and in the Parish. If I ever feel that there is genuine and considerable demand for an additional Mass on Sunday, then we will have it....." wrote Fr. Hayne in December.

The second parish Christian Stewardship Campaign was launched in February 1964. The previous Campaign had entailed pledges for a period of three years and now it was time for a Renewal Campaign. A good deal had been learned from the first Campaign and its limitations and faults as well as the successes had been noted. There were still a good many people for whom Stewardship was unacceptable but the Rector was convinced of its value. Fr. Hayne expressed his own views in the Parish Magazine of January 1964; "I am well aware that this is a controversial subject, and I suppose most people have reservations about it, at least in the beginning. But I am convinced that it embodies an utterly Christian Principle. We will be co-operating with the Parish Church in a 'Booster Campaign'in the New Year, and I have assured the Rector that this will be fully supported in this area."

The Campaign began officially with a Commissioning Service at St. Agnes' for all Visitors and Campaign Workers on Wednesday, February 5th at 8.00 p.m. This was followed next day by a Parish Dinner at the Castle Hotel to which all parishioners were invited to be guests of the Parochial Church Council, the cost being met from Parish funds. The guest of honour was the Right Revd. Eric Knell, Bishop of Reading. After being welcomed by the Rector and Mrs. Dymoke-Marr and meeting the Bishop, the guests were introduced by twenty hostesses to the Visitors who would be responsible for collecting their pledges during the next three weeks.

As with the previous Campaign, the dinner raised some eyebrows on account of the expense involved. This was especially the case with the present Campaign which was 'home-grown' and not organised by an outside body. The Rector pointed out in the Parish Magazine that, "In terms of fellowship and family friendliness which it produced it was worth much more than the money spent on it....I would venture to remind those who refused the invitation.... that Our Lord did not despise the invitation to the marriage feast at Cana, nor did He seem to think the expense unnecessary."

The emphasis in the present Campaign was on the Stewardship not only of money but also of time and talents, and this threefold offering was stressed in the attractively produced brochure which was distributed during the "canvassing" period. Mr. Arthur Pearson had overall responsibilty for the Campaign but the two Churches had their own teams of Visitors and Hostesses. The particular 'projects' aimed at by St. Agnes' during the coming three years consisted of the re-decoration of the Church, the Sacristy and the Hall; the clearing of the ground around the Church and the renewal of pavements; and the cleaning of the organ and fitting of an electric blower.

The Parochial Church Council came to the rescue of St. Agnes' precarious finances in May 1964. Day to day running costs were not in difficulties - for once there was a bank balance of £33:0:0d. However, there were some heavy debts over and above normal running costs which the congregation had been unable to clear. For instance, Mr. Bampton was still waiting for £438:0:0d due from the work done on the heating system nearly two years previously. (This sum had been included in the previous Stewardship Budget but, as we have seen, the income fell far short of the target - at St. Agnes' at least). Therefore, the Parochial Church Council offered St. Agnes' a loan of £500:0:0d to pay Mr. Bampton, and this was gladly accepted.

Miss Ida Bessie Bennett died suddenly on March 4th, 1964. She had lived in Windsor since 1923 when she joined the staff of St. Stephen's Infant School. A very quiet, gentle person she had a great sense of humour with those who knew her well. She found great joy in music and for many years accompanied the hymns at the Ward services at King Edward VII Hospital. For several years she had worshipped at St. Agnes' together with her cousin Nellie, with whom she lived. Her body was brought into St. Agnes' on March 10th at 4.15 p.m. and Vespers of the Dead was recited. This was followed at 8.00 p.m. by a Requiem Mass, Fr. Wood being the Celebrant. Next day there were Requiems at 7.00 a.m. and 7.30 a.m. followed at 11.00 a.m. by the funeral service, which was conducted by Fr. Hayne and Fr. Wood. Later in the year it was decided to renovate the six brass High Altar Candlesticks as a memorial.

"After many years - too many - we at long last have real hopes of an electric organ-blower," wrote Fr. Hayne in the May Parish Magazine. "The organ itself is in quite good condition, but there is always the uncertainty at the beginning of every service, not knowing whether we will be able to use it or not...Now that we have sufficient money in the Organ Fund I am sure we should not ask Mr. Kelsey to play at such inconvenience... Meanwhile we are indebted to those who do all the pumping." The blower was made and fitted by Walker & Co. at a cost

£102:0:0d. It must have seemed like sheer luxury!

In spite of the Stewardship pledges, the St. Agnes' finances were rather gloomy in July 1964:-

Bank Balance £17:11:0d.

Organ Fund £22:10:1d (after paying for the blower)

The income from the collections for the first six months of the year amounted to £269, which was a decrease of £80 for the same period in 1963. By the end of the year the accounts showed a deficit of £110:12:8d.

The Church roof was repaired by Mr. Bampton at this time and the pews and floor treated for woodworm. The Sacristy was re-decorated by some members of the Church who pledged their time and talents, and the materials were paid for from a parting gift of £25 from Mr. Lansbury.

In September 1964 Mrs. Hayne started a pre-school play group in the Hall, a venture which proved highly successful. Changes were made in the Sunday School at this time. Henceforth the nine to twelve year olds would meet at 10.30 a.m. on Saturdays and be known as 'Crossbearers'. Younger children continued to meet for instruction on Sundays, but at the new time of 10.45 a.m. Attendance at Sunday Mass was still obligatory. Scouts and Cubs still thrived and attended Parish Mass for Church Parade.

1965 brought changes to some familiar institutions. The St. Agnes' Young Wives League decided at their Annual General Meeting in January to 're-form' and became a Young Wives' Group affiliated to the Mothers' Union. It was hoped that this would induce more people to join.

The Universities Mission to Central Africa and the Society for the Propagation of the Gospel in Foreign Parts merged early in 1965 to become the United Society for the Propagation of the Gospel. A casualty of the merger was the Coral League which now became the "Adventurers", though in Windsor at least the new name was confusing since there was already a thriving Boys' Club called the "Young Adventurers".

There were extra services during Lent with no shortage of courses and addresses, including one run on a nationwide scale called 'No Small Change'. Holy Week and Easter services were as in Fr. Prebble's time except that the time of the Good Friday Liturgy was brought forward to 11.30 a.m. In addition to the changes laid down by the Rector, Fr. Hayne had made a few more minor changes to the services. For instance the Thursday evening Mass was brought forward from 8.00 p.m. to 6.00 p.m. although Sung Masses on festivals remained at 8.00 p.m. There was also a mid-week Intercessions and Benediction or Rosary and Benediction instead of Holy Hour. The October Devotion to Our Lady was no longer observed.

1965 saw the passing to rest of several of the faithful. A great shock to all was the untimely death in March of the Revd. John Anthony Wynne, Vicar of Clewer St. Stephen since 1957. A flambuoyant, energetic personality, Fr. Wynne was a thorough 'triumphalist' in his Christian outlook and his enthusiasm was infectious. People flocked to St. Stephen's from near and far especially on Corpus Christi and St. Stephen's Day (December 26th). During Fr. Wynne's time there was a very close fellowship and co-operation between the two Clewer Parishes.

Miss Nellie Priscilla Bennett died in May 1965 just over a year after the death of her cousin, Ida. She had been in poor health for some years. Her body was brought into St. Agnes' on May 6th and Vespers for the Dead followed. At 6.00 p.m. the Requiem Mass was celebrated. The next day there was a Requiem and Absolutions celebrated by Fr. Wood who also assisted at the funeral.

A week later Mrs. Helen Selina Spencer died. Sacristan during the 1940's, Helen Spencer was one who did much, but quietly. Latterly she had been in poor health but remained throughout a regular Communicant. Her body was brought into St. Agnes' on May 12th and Vespers of the Dead followed. The Requiem and Funeral followed next day at which the Rector officiated in the absence of Fr. Hayne.

"After four years as Treasurer Denis Grahame feels that the time has come for him to resign," wrote Fr. Hayne in the September Magazine. "During this period he has had to manage the funds that have been in an almost continuous state of poverty. More recently we have been overdrawn....I am particularly grateful to Arthur Dobson for accepting the post and hope that we will before long be able to give him more money to work with than has been the case hitherto. Certainly we ought to pay our way here. Our overheads are not that heavy; and our monthly income will have to double in the near future if we are to clear ourselves and this is a tall order; at the moment I do not see how we are to go about it. Certainly Christian Stewardship gives us the soundest possible basis to work on, and if everyone would accept their responsibilities in this direction most of our financial difficulties would be solved."

The Windsor Girls' Club had been founded in the upstairs hall and before holding their first meeting the girls and their parents scrubbed and re-decorated the upper room. This Club had foundered by the end of the year but was re-founded as a mixed youth club for fourteen to twenty year olds. Though not a Church Club it had the approval and support of Fr. Hayne and the St. Agnes' Committee.

Various sums of money were given to St. Agnes' during 1965 as memorials and a number of items were bought including altar linen, chairs for the Hall and a kneeler for the High Altar.

St. Agnes'- tide 1966 was a particularly joyful occasion. Fr. Wood returned as a guest preacher at the evening High Mass and there was a gathering in the Hall afterwards at which many people were present. On the following Sunday the Bishop of Oxford, the Right Revd. Harry Carpenter, preached at the 9.30 a.m. Sung Mass.

Maude Elizabeth Reid died after a short and sudden illness on Sunday, January 30th. After the death of her sister, Annie, Maude Reid had taken on the duties of sacristan during Fr. Wood's time. Her body was brought into Church at 9.00 p.m. on February 2nd after the Candlemass Ceremonies. Vespers and Absolutions of the Dead followed. Next morning a Requiem was offered followed by the funeral in the afternoon. Two pewter cruets were given as a memorial.

There was a general meeting of St. Agnes' members in the Hall on March 30th which was reported in the May Parish Magazine. "Sister Joan C.S.J.B. told us that work with the children was going ahead. Certainly the Adventurers are flourishing well. The Sunday School is small, but there is a large number of children at the 9.30 Mass on Sunday; these children usually come with parents, and receive their instruction in the Hall during the sermon. They are very well behaved in Church and we have all ages from one year to Confirmation age....One rather serious matter arose out of the Treasurer's Report. There are outstanding bills totalling over £100 with a single-figure balance in the Bank. This is nobody's fault in particular; it means simply that we are not paying our way as a congregation and something must be done about it. Various suggestions were made. One way to raise money is through bazaars, whist drives, etc. These, however, are time-absorbing, and I believe Church members have more valuable work to do than fund-raising. One thing is clear. Regular and sacrificial giving will solve many of our financial problems. It will not make our Church and property any cheaper to run, but at least the Church will remain open. God does not exact love from us - we offer it in terms of worship, talent and money".

June 29th, the Feast of St. Peter and St. Paul, marked the Golden Jubilee of George Kelsey as organist. To mark this achievement there was a High Mass of Thanksgiving at which Fr. F. Treadwell preached and forty-two people received Holy Communion. There was a gathering in the Hall afterwards. George's achievement was noted in the 'Around the Dioceses' columns in the "Church Times."

The 9.30 Parish Mass was ten years old in June 1966 and during that decade it had grown and flourished. "Since that time the number of Communicants has increased steadily and to-day the Parish Mass is a live and encouraging act of worship as Sunday by Sunday families come together to Mass", wrote Fr. Hayne.

St. Agnes' people were deeply shocked when on June 13th Stuart Roy Bolan was killed in a road accident. Aged nine years, Stuart was a member of St. Agnes' Sunday School. Fr. Hayne was away on holiday but returned for the funeral on June 20th. On Tuesday, June 28th, at 8.00 p.m. there was a Votive Mass of the Holy Angels at which forty people were present. Later in the year Stuart's parents gave a statue of St. Andrew as a memorial.

For the second year running Fr. Hayne assisted in the joint parish pilgrimage to the Shrine of Our Lady of Walsingham, with Fr. Brindley from Clewer and Fr. Knibbs from Reading. Members of Clewer St. Stephen also joined the group on the weekend of July 2nd/3rd.

Holidays and pilgrimages over, it was time to roll up the sleeves and start decorating the Church! The family of the late Helen Spencer had given £100 as a memorial and the bulk of this was spent on materials for re-decorating the Church which needed doing very badly. The balance was spent on four lightweight wooden Requiem candlesticks as a more tangible memorial (two more were bought later to complete the set). Builders' estimates amounted to more than could be afforded and so in true 'Stewardship' spirit it was decided to do the work by voluntary labour. About a dozen men, including Derek Mills, Alf Eagle, Alan Bridges and Tony Blackwell, took part, and after an evening of painting would finish with Compline. All except the East end, which was done by contractors, was done by the men. "Work on the decorating is progressing and has been under way for some four weeks," wrote Fr. Hayne in the September Magazine. "Some two hundred hours of work have been put in all told and we are now more than halfway through....Now at last there is something to show for it." Next month he wrote, "The decoration is now virtually completed with the walls, ceilings, gallery and woodwork repainted. The work has been long and at times precarious....It is difficult to remember what the Church looked like before we began." After something like twelve weeks the work was completed. It must have been doubly difficult as the Church continued to be used for worship and Fr. Hayne recalls that sometimes the scaffolding tower was more than a little in evidence. This was the first re-decoration since 1951 and certainly the first effort at D-I-Y on such a large scale. It produced a sense of achievement and fellowship amongst the workers and Fr. Hayne recalls that it did as much, if not more, in terms of getting people involved than the Stewardship Campaign had done.

In the midst of all the upheaval the Feast of Dedication (September 9th) was kept for the first time in several years. Thirty-four people were present at the Solemn High Mass when they heard an address from the Revd. J.N. Scott, Vicar of Clewer St. Stephen.

The custom of the two Churches joining together on special occasions was revived on Sunday, October 16th when the entire St. Agnes' congregation went to St. Andrew's for Pontifical Sung Mass at which the Bishop of Oxford presided. St. Agnes' again joined St. Andrew's on the evening of February 2nd 1967 for Sung Mass and the Candlemass Ceremonies. This was Fr.

Brindley's last Mass at Clewer before leaving to be Vicar of Holy Trinity, Reading.

The old year went out and the New Year came in with more manual work but this time it was done for the Church. "We have always been very fortunate in offers of labour," wrote Fr. Hayne in January. "Recent efforts have been on the part of the parents of the Play Group who have completely re-decorated the downstairs room in the Hall, together with repainting the Kitchen and relaying the floor with linoleum....The money required has been little but even this has been raised by the Hall users so the total work has cost the Church nothing: I am most grateful to all concerned for the hard work involved, and not least for the able leadership of Mrs. Dennis of Upcroft. The final stage of the entire work of re-decorating the Church premises is now under way - namely the painting of the stairway to the 'Upper Room' which is being undertaken by a member of the Youth Club."

Another Stewardship Renewal Campaign was launched in the early part of 1967. The Agnes' Committee decided to operate their Campaign as a seperate entity from the rest of the Parish in order to emphasize their own responsibilities and also to relieve St. Andrew's of some of the administrative work. The Budget for the next three years at St. Agnes' was estimated at £2,738. This figure included St. Agnes' share of the Diocesan Quota and contribution to the payment of the priest-in-charge.

The St. Agnes' Stewardship Dinner took place on Friday, February 17th, at Clewer Green School, and the guest speaker was Fr. F.W. Goddard, Rector of St. Nicholas', Guildford. About seventy-five people were present at the Dinner which consisted of a four course meal produced by Mrs. Fletcher and the Catering Committee. Mrs. Bessie Barrow was in charge of the team of Hostesses who were responsible for introducing the guests to the Visitors. Overall organisation of the Campaign was in the hands of John Saunders. On Sunday, February 19th, the team of seven Visitors were 'commissioned' at the Parish Mass, and on Sunday, March 26th, the Pledges were offered. John Saunders reported in the April Magazine that, "Fifteen families have decided to give regularly through the scheme for the first time...Only a few of those formerly in the scheme considered themselves able to promise to give more to God." "It is very difficult to assess the results of the Stewardship Campaign," wrote Fr. Hayne, "because only the years that follow will testify to the value of the pledges made. One thing is quite clear, the amount promised for the next three years, which is about £1,822, is quite inadequate for our needs. On the other hand, this amount is over £800 more than was received over the last three years, so it would seem that the situation has improved....The visiting team was small but in the end over eighty families were visited, which is quite a remarkable effort."

It was with great pride to the Parish, and to St. Agnes' in particular, that of the eight places allocated to the whole of Berkshire for the World Scout Camp in the U.S.A. three places went to Queen's Scouts living and worshipping in the Parish. They were Peter Knowles, Raymond Barber and David Eagle.

Holy Week was observed as in former years although Fr. Hayne later commented that the services were very poorly attended. There was a new venture on Maundy Thursday, in addition to the evening Liturgy, in the form of a Day for Young People. Held from 10.00 a.m. until 5.00 p.m. it catered for seven to fifteen year olds and included discussion, instruction and worship.

A Quiet Afternoon was held on the Vigil of Pentecost as had been done throughout the years of Fr. Hayne's ministry. There was no Walsingham Pilgrimage in 1967 but a day pilgrimage to the Roman Catholic Shrine of Our Lady of Mount Carmel, at Aylesford, was held instead with the intention for Christain Unity.

Sister Joan C.S.J.B. had been doing valuable work amongst the children of Spital but in 1967 she was recalled for work at Reading. Thereafter Mrs. K. Blackwell and Mrs. J. Paternoster took on the work with the 'Adventurers'. A senior section was formed for nine to fourteen year olds, meeting on Mondays from 5.30 to 6.30 p.m. The juniors from four to nine years continued to meet at 4.00 p.m. on Mondays.

Sydney Pert died on June 12th 1967 and was laid to rest in Windsor Cemetery. Although he had worshipped at Holy Trinity, Windsor, for the last few years of his life, St. Agnes' had been his spiritual home for the greater part. A Requiem was offered for him at St. Agnes' on June 20th, and it is a sign of the affection in which he was still held that there were eighteen Communicants.

The second Vatican Council had concluded its deliberations in 1964 and the effects of it sent shock waves throughout the Roman Catholic Church - and beyond. Writing in the Parish Magazine of January 1964 Fr. Hayne had commented: "The results will not be known for some considerable time. One thing is certain. The effect on the Christian world at large will be one calling for the most profound thanksgiving." By 1967 the effects were being felt at parish level. But the winds of change did not all begin to blow with Vatican II, for as we have seen, some considerable liturgical changes took place in the late 1950's. Neither was change confined to the Roman Catholic Church. As far back as 1955 the Church of England had established its own Liturgical Commission. Subsequently, new services were authorised for experimental use under the Prayer Book (Alternative and other Services) Measure 1965. (The culmination of all this work and revision came with the publication in November 1980 of the Alternative Service Book). In the Parish Magazine of August 1967, the Rector made the following anouncement; "By a majority of twenty-three to one your Parochial Council gave its approval to the experimental use of the Series 11 Holy Communion Service...We shall start using the service at all Masses in the Parish as from the first Sunday in October - our Dedication Festival at the Parish Church".

The first Sunday in October was to be the last Sunday at which Fr. Hayne officiated as priest-in-charge of St. Agnes'. "We shall miss Fr. and Mrs Hayne very much when they leave us for their new work in Grimsbury,"wrote the Rector. "Fr. Hayne has accomplished an outstanding job of work while he has been at St. Agnes' and it will not be easy for the man who follows him to keep up the high standard. On the other hand he will come into a community which has become a strong Christian community during the past four years. Of course, Fr. Hayne would be the first to acknowledge that he had only been able to build because of the foundations laid by his predecessors - nevertheless he has built, and he has built a very fine structure in the time he has been with us. Mrs. Hayne will also be greatly missed not only for her parish work as such but more particularly for the able way in which she has edited the Magazine...One of the greater achievements of Fr. Hayne has been to get both ends of the Parish working much more together as an integrated Christian Community."

There were fifty Communicants at Fr. Hayne's last Sunday Mass, on October 1st, which also saw the introduction of the Series 11 rite. Fr. Hayne remained at Grimsbury, near Banbury, until 1976 when he became Vicar of Brightwell-cum-Sotwell, near Wallingford. In 1981 he also became Rural Dean of Wallingford.

Apart from the financial strain, Fr. Hayne's years at St. Agnes' were years of a thriving Church life, when the congregation flourished and Communicant numbers increased. Perhaps as a family man he offered a special message to the young; certainly his ministry was marked by efforts to attract children and young people to the Church. Mrs. Hayne too was to be greatly missed for she had managed to combine a growing number of parish activities with the demands of a young family, which had increased during the time in Spital with the birth of Christopher in January 1964, and Dominic in June 1965. Fr. Hayne's ministry was also a time of 'self-help' amongst the congregation, a time when the people themselves would do manual work because the 'professionals' cost too much! Perhaps this aspect of Stewardship was the most valuable; certainly it was one of the most successful aspects. Fr. Hayne's ministry stood at the liturgical crossroads, for henceforth the Church of England was set upon the road towards the present day modern liturgy. With the coming of Series II there was a great deal of liturgical 'levelling out' so that extremes in ceremonial largely disappeared. Whilst a few Anglo-Catholic strongholds clung doggedly to their English Missals and refused to use the new rites, the majority, St. Agnes' included, bowed to the will of the Church realising that change was inevitable if God's work were to continue and prosper.

## Chapter XXIII

## Full Circle

Fr. Graham Alan Friend took office immediately after Fr. Hayne's departure. His first Sung Mass at St. Agnes' was a Votive Mass of the Holy Spirit on October 5th. Fr. Friend was twenty-eight years old when he came to St. Agnes' and was married with two children, Aidan and Felicity. After training at Chichester Theological College he was ordained deacon in 1963 and priest a year later. Fr. Friend served curacies at Syston in Leicestershire from 1963 to 1965 and Barnstaple, Devon, from 1965 to 1967 before coming to Spital.

The start of Fr. Friend's ministry at Spital may well have had a 'new broom' image coinciding as it did with the introduction of Series II, but as we have seen the Parochial Church Council had made the decision before Fr. Hayne left. In keeping with the new liturgy, at the end of October, Fr. Friend outlined his plans to the St. Agnes' Committee to give the Sunday 9.30 Mass more of a family atmosphere and to make the congregation have a deeper sense of involvement. This included the reading of the Epistle by a member of the congregation, the introduction of an offertory procession, and a gathering for coffee in the Hall after the service. These changes were implemented for the first time on Sunday, November 5th, and those who took part from the congregation were Jeremy Williams, Joan Paternoster and the Mills family.

Sunday services remained at the same times as before and the daily Mass was maintained, but midweek devotions such as Rosary and Benediction were discontinued. Towards the end of 1967 the Revd. Canon Ronald Dupre Grange-Bennett came to live in Winkfield Road and joined the staff of Clewer Parish in an honorary part-time capacity. He was a frequent celebrant at St. Agnes' until shortly before his death in June 1972.

Earlier in 1967 and shortly before Fr. Hayne's departure George Kelsey was taken ill and was forced to resign as organist after fifty-one years. On October 25th he and Rosa celebrated their Golden Wedding Anniversary. Henceforth ill health and old age were increasingly to keep them away from their beloved St. Agnes'. Miss Bess Reid now agreed to take over as organist on a temporary basis until another appointment could be made.

Church finances were in a reasonably healthy state in the last quarter of 1967 with a balance in hand of £104:9:8d, due mainly to money paid by St. Andrew's in respect of Covenants. There was, of course, always something waiting to swallow it up! That perennial problem the heating system was again giving trouble and it was finally decided to replace the solid fuel boiler with a gas one. The cost was to be £375 and the Rector offered a loan at 6% interest, repayable by quarterly instalments over five years. The new boiler was installed in time for Christmas. "This is most generous of the Parochial Church Council in view of the squeeze and the disastrous nature of some of the financial transactions between ourselves," wrote Fr. Friend in the February 1968 Magazine. "....We ought to be aiming at repayment as soon as possible for this is merely a first step in tackling the difficulties of our 'plant'."

There was great rejoicing at Clewer on January 25th to mark the Twenty-fifth Anniversary of Fr. Cyprian's institution as Rector. The Archbishop of Canterbury, the Most Revd. Michael Ramsay, preached at the High Mass and officiated at the presentation at the Princess Margaret Rose School.

Fr. Friend, meanwhile, was having doubts about the feasibility of Sunday Evensong and Benediction which had an attendance of between four and eight. A questionnaire was issued to the congregation in order to sound out their views on whether or not Sunday evening House Groups would be a better method of worship than the more traditional forms. The questionnaire aroused little response and so the status quo was maintained, for the time being.

St. Agnes' finances were healthier in May 1968 when Mr. Arthur Dobson resigned as Treasurer than when he took up the post, there being a bank balance of £155:3:4d. He was succeeded by Mr. Jeremy Williams. However, the finances at Clewer were not so rosy as John Saunders, newly elected Parish Treasurer pointed out. The suggestion was made, therefore, that St. Agnes' should at least pay her own priest's expenses.

Youth work began to take a new direction at this time. The Adventurers' Club which had succeeded the Coral League was ailing; younger children no longer came in any number and the older girls were drifting away. The greatest problem seemed to be in catering for the ten to fourteen year olds and so it was decided by the Church Committee to form a Church Youth Club for boys and girls. After a trial period a larger St. Agnes' Youth Club was formed with senior and junior sections, the juniors having the larger membership.

Autumn 1968 saw two new activities launched to deepen the spiritual lives of St. Agnes' people. Firstly, on St. Michael's Day, September 29th, a 'Chain of Prayer' was maintained from the end of Sung Mass, 10.30 a.m., until Evensong, 6.30 p.m. This was the first day of prayer to be held at St. Agnes' for many years. Secondly, the 'Five Minute Prayer League' was formed. Those who joined pledged to spend at least five minutes each week before the Blessed Sacrament. Members usually met once a month for Benediction.

Fr. Friend's first full year at St. Agnes' came to a close with a total of four thousand, eight hundred and twenty-five acts of Communion which was an increase.

1969 had a busy start. The Patronal Festival was preceded by a Chain of Prayer on January 19th from 10.30 a.m. to 6.30 p.m. with the special intention for Christian Unity and for the Confirmation candidates. There were ninety-six Communicants at the High Mass on St. Agnes' evening when the Bishop of Reading, the Right Revd. Eric Knell, confirmed eight adults. A St. Agnes'-tide party at Clewer Green Shool organised by Derek Mills and a team of helpers was joined by about one hundred and twenty people.

The Guild of Servants of the Sanctuary visited St. Agnes' on February 12th to sing their Office together with an Address and Benediction. This was their first visit for some years.

Lent and Holy Week proceeded in the usual manner but a prolonged spell of illness kept Fr. Friend away from his duties from just after Easter until the end of June. During this period services were maintained by the Rector and his assistants, Fr. Toon and Fr. Grange-Bennett.

Much structual work was done to the Hall during 1969 and 1970. Particular attention was paid to the open space between the staircase and detached toilet block at the back of the Hall, all this area being made into a covered way with a concrete floor. Mr. Philip Painter was in charge of the planning and supervision of the work, which was set out on a six month schedule worked out in fortnightly phases. The team of willing workers included Mr. George Roberts and Fred and Richard Fletcher. The whole work, including repairs to the Hall floor was completed by the Summer of 1970. Re-wiring and re-decoration was deferred for lack of funds. The upstairs Hall had already been redecorated by the Youth Club supervised by their leaders Richard Fletcher, David Williams and Raymond Barber.

During the Summer of 1969 Mr. E. Lawrence of the Windsor and District

Theatre Organ Trust undertook work on St. Agnes' organ. The Trust comprises enthusiasts who save and repair old organs of all types. Mr. Lawrence proposed carrying out extensive repairs for the cost of the materials only. Miss Bess Reid, organist of St. Agnes', preferred to approach a conventional organ builder, but the St. Agnes' Committee decided to proceed with the offer as it seemed to be the only way they could afford to have any work done. The work was completed in June 1970 at a cost of £25.

Fr. Alexander Edward Baynes, formerly Chaplain of the Clewer Sisters, died on February 10th 1970 in Old Windsor Hospital. He had also served as part-time assistant priest at Clewer and had worked with Fr. Cyprian for twenty-six years. His death at the age of eighty-three years came only five months after his retirement. A Requiem was celebrated at St. Agnes' on February 17th.

One of the major breakthroughs to come out of the 'Liturgical Movement' of the 1960's was the return to the Early Church practice of the 'Westward' position, i.e. the priest faces the people across the altar at the Eucharist. Maundy Thursday 1970 saw the beginning of the Westward experiment at St. Agnes'. The High Altar was pulled forward to the edge of the step and the priest and servers gathered behind. The experiment was well received by the congregation, so that Fr. Friend decided to adopt the Westward position at the Sung Mass on the first Sunday of each month, commencing on Low Sunday, April 5th. At other times the altar was in its usual position and the priest faced 'Eastwards.'

Stewardship came to the fore again in 1970 with the inauguration on Sunday, May 3rd, of the West Windsor Stewardship Campaign, involving the three Churches of Clewer Parish and Clewer St. Stephen. The Inaugurul Mass was held at Clewer St. Stephen., the celebrant being the Bishop of Reading.

The latter half of 1970 saw Fr. Friend lamenting the poor attendance on greater festivals. A case in point was the Dedication Festival, September 9th. The preacher at the evening High Mass was the Archdeacon of Berkshire, the Venerable Eric Wild, but there were very few St. Agnes' people present. Fortunately, there was a good sprinkling of people from St. Andrew's and St. Stephen's. The preacher on the following Sunday was the Dean of Windsor, the Very Revd. Robin Wood.

1970 ended with a death - that of the Clewer Parish Magazine which had survived since June 1882 and now succumbed to printing costs. So a valuable record of parish life ceased to exist, at least until its successor the 'Clewer Messenger' arose Pheonix-like in November 1971.

Winds of change were blowing very strongly in 1971. Easter Sunday was Fr. Cyprian's last Sunday as Rector of Clewer after an incumbency of twenty-eight years. Alas, there is no parish magazine to record tributes to such a ministry, but it may be appropriate to quote one or two correspondents to the Clewer Magazine at the time of Fr. Cyprian's Silver Jubilee in 1968. "Many things stand out over the years. There was the institution of daily Mass; his preaching which threw new light and interest on the eternal Gospel; the inevitable parish parties and fetes; the great Mission to Clewer; the tea stall which encouraged racegoers to help put the roof right. It's not really possible to describe C.D-M. as a very popular priest, nor, we suspect, would he really want to be decsribed as such. Underneath the flambuoyant exterior there is a good deal of shyness which occasionally shows itself in an apparently abrupt mannerism.

But he has been a good friend to a great many, and his priestly ministry has been marked by a great love and compassion for those in real need to the great frustration of those who sometimes like to 'try it on'." Another wrote of him, "....We have noted with sympathy and understanding his fortitude over the years, and that of his family, in the face of considerable suffering and discouragement. Tough and determined, with a dislike of being opposed, his resounding voice and tremendous sense of humour have been so to speak outstanding features of his stay with us." Many former priests of St. Agnes' have testified to the good relationship existing between Mother and Daughter Churches during Fr. Cyprian's incumbency, and to the way in which Fr. Cyprian maintained just the right balance between fatherly guidance and too deep an involvement. And so the colourful, flambuoyant Fr. Cyprian left the Clewer scene, and many people missed seeing the familiar bearded, be-monocled figure in cassock, preaching tabs and cape, around the parish. Fr. Cyprian and Mrs. Dymoke-Marr now live at Swanage where he serves the Church there in an honorary capacity. Fr. Cyprian has contributed to this book many of his memories of clergy and people connected with St. Agnes' and has spoken warmly of the Church and "its wonderful atmosphere of devotion."

There was a brief interregnum before the institution by the Bishop of Reading on Thursday, July 22nd 1971 of the Revd. Denis Shaw as Rector of Clewer. Denis Shaw was a late-comer to the priesthood having found his vocation, and indeed his Christain faith, by a long road which had included Hindu-ism, journalism, acting in provincial repertory and tea planting in India! This varied background has given Clewer Parish yet another 'colourful' personality yet totally different from his predecessor. With the theatre in his blood Fr. Shaw's ministry at Clewer has brought the media into religion, (or vice versa,) so that on a number of occasions he has written the scripts for religious plays which have been broadcast on radio and T.V. A further attribute of Fr. Shaw's is his passion for the past, for local history, which has led to the establishment of the Museum of Clewer History in St. Andrew's Church Lodge. After training for the ministry at Westcott House, Cambridge, Denis Shaw was ordained deacon in 1959 and priest in 1960. He served as curate at St. Mathew's. Bethnal Green, from 1959 to 1963 and was Rector of St. Wilfrid's, Newton Heath, Manchester from 1963 to 1971. Fr. Shaw is married with two sons.

There was not only change at Clewer. The 'Westward' experiment at St. Agnes' had given rise to the suggestion that it should be adopted every Sunday. Fr. Friend was careful to avoid acting too soon for the step once taken would be irrevocable. He had written in the Clewer Magazine for October 1970, "If we are to make such a major change, then it must be given very serious consideration indeed. We must all pray about it, talk about it, learn about it.... In the end the decision must be one that is accepted and respected by all who have a hand in making it. And if it should be that the decision is to go West then it is more than likely that at least some work will have to be done to the inside of the Church to make provision for the Blessed Sacrament as well as to ensure that the Mass is celebrated reverently." A questionaire was prepared by Fr. Friend for the congregation in April 1971 concerning the future worship of the Church and the consensus was that a permanent change should be made. It was decided, therefore, to remove the Sanctuary step during 1972. This work was not completed until the end of the year and the cost was £98:89p.

The roof was causing grave concern in the early part of 1972 following the Diocesan Surveyor's inspection and report, which revealed that the whole of the South side needed complete renewal. An estimate from H. Painter & Sons, Ltd. for £843, including £125 for any timber or lead renewals, was accepted, and a request was made to the Parochial Church Council for the loan of the money. The work which was sub-contracted to another firm did not get under way until early in 1973.

The question of Sunday evening worship was still posing a problem and from the beginning of 1972 Holy Communion with hymns and address was celebrated at 6.00 p.m. Evensong was recited at 6.45 p.m. The number of Communicants varied but averaged half a dozen. From mid-May Compline was said instead of Evensong, but this did little to attract extra people.

Fr. Hayne was the welcome visitor on St. Agnes' Day 1972 when he preached at the Evening Mass. There were fifty-three Communicants, so a good crowd is indicated.

A new venture was launched during Lent when various members of the congregation preached at 9.30 a.m. on Sundays. Their sermons were then discussed on Thursday evenings. The preachers were John Saunders, Rose Campbell, Derek Mills, Joan Paternoster and Diane Williams.

The roof was not the only part of St. Agnes' in need of attention and on November 2nd 1972 Fr. Friend informed the Church Committee that "assuming the roof goes well and that no serious work is necessary the Committee should establish, in order of priority, work to be carried out inside the Church." It was decided that Mr. Roberts should investigate the source of the damp on the Church walls, that the flooring by the font should be attended to, and that part of the Church needed re-decorating. At the same time the work on removing the Sanctuary step was about to be done. Work on the Hall had been resumed earlier in the year when it was re-decorated thanks to the efforts of George Roberts and his team of workers.

Social life around the Church had largely fallen prey to the T.V. set but there were still a number of organisations for those who were interested. The Wives Group continued to meet at this time twice a month, though later they reverted to once a month. The Youth Club for ten to fourteen year olds was revived once more early in 1973 after a break of several months, and at this time the Scouting organisations flourished.

St. Agnes' Day fell on a Sunday and the opportunity was taken to make it a real family gathering by holding Sung Mass at 11.00 a.m., following it with a buffet lunch in the Hall organised by Mrs. Sonia Mills and a team of helpers. The Revd. Austin Thorburn, a retired priest living in Slough, 'stood in' as guest preacher for the Revd. David Niblett, Fr. Friend's former Vicar at Barnstaple, who was struck down with 'flu' at the last minute. The Mayor and Mayoress of Windsor were guests of honour and they were impressed by the family atmosphere at St. Agnes'. Certainly there was a good turnout of people, there being one hundred and fourteen Communicants.

Liturgical changes were still to the fore in 1973, namely the re-ordering of the Sanctuary and the introduction of the Series III Holy Communion. Series III was published by the Liturgical Commission in its original draft in 1971. In the 'foreword' the objectives were clearly stated; "It is clear from the use of which has been made of Holy Communion Series II both at home and abroad during the past four years that the rite has served a useful purpose. It has been a valuable means of experiment.... Nevertheless, it was never intended to be a finished product; and experience has revealed its limitations. We believed that it was simply a step in the right direction. That belief has been justified: for we have been able to build Series III on the foundations of Series II; and although there are all kinds of changes in language and detail, we have found no solid reason to make any serious departure from the basic structure of our original rite....We hope that the Church of England will find in this rite a further significant step towards the creation of a new and worthy Book of Common Prayer in the not too distant future." After a good deal of liturgical wrangling the new rite was revised and authorised for use for a period of four years as from January 1973. On Monday, April 2nd 1973, Series III was used at St. Agnes' for the benefit of the Church Committee, and similarly on Tuesday, September 11th, for the Parochial Church Council. The Parochial Church Council approved the use of the new rite at St. Agnes' but decided to retain Series II at St. Andrew's. Series III was, therefore, used at St. Agnes' at all services as from October 7th 1973. As the modern language of the new rite gave rise to the need for a different musical setting, it was decided to have a 'said' Mass with hymns on Sundays at 9.30 a.m. until an organist could be appointed, Miss Reid having retired from the post.

In April 1973 the St. Agnes' Committee gave approval to a new altar, candlesticks and altar furnishings. The new free-standing altar in light oak was constructed by Mr. Donald Ashworth who had made similar altars for Clewer St. Stephen and All Saint's, Dedworth. This was followed later by matching servers' benches and celebrant's chair. The former High Altar was removed to the Lady Chapel to replace the existing one and the Blessed Sacrament was reserved there henceforth. The new altar was ready for use for the first time on Sunday, November 18th.

Friday and Saturday, December 21st and 22nd saw the production of a play, 'Christmas in the Market Place' by Henri Gheon. The cast consisted of the Revd. Tim Reader (Curate, St. Andrew's), Norman Iley, Vicki Friend, Gill Fleury, Isabel Delamere, June Boddington and Stephen Snell.

1974, the Centenary Year, came in with a special meeting of the St. Agnes' Committee to decide how to celebrate the event. It was not a particularly fruitful meeting there being a decided dearth of original ideas. Fr. Friend commented that it had not been possible to ascertain whether or not St. Agnes' was one hundred years old - but the Committee agreed that arrangements should still go ahead! The events which were finally decided upon were as follows:-

| | |
|---|---|
| September 9th | Feast of Dedication Service |
| September 15th | Lunch after 10.30 a.m. Mass (Sunday) |
| October 6th | Harvest Festival Mass at 10.00 a.m. |
| November 10th | Remembrance Sunday service to follow usual pattern. |
| November 30th | Afternoon of Prayer at St. Andrew's. |
| December 22nd | Service of Carols, Lessons and Children's Nativity Play. |
| January 4th 1975 | Children's Party. |

It was also agreed to ask the Parish Social Committee to consider arranging an 'Old time Music Hall' evening during the Centenary Year.

On March 9th 1974 a regular Communicant at early Mass, Mrs. Clara Alice Taylor, died aged eighty-eight years. A Requiem was offered on Wednesday, March 13th at 7.30 p.m. and the funeral followed next day.

On Monday and Tuesday, April 22nd and 23rd, the play 'The Devil in Antioch' was performed by a cast drawn from St. Andrew's and St. Agnes'. There were good attendances at both performances including on the first night Archbishop Strong.

Apart from the fact of it being the Centenary Year, 1974 was rather uneventful. Work continued on the fabric of the Church, and in particular four tons of debris were cleared away from the East wall in order to uncover the damp course. A rota of volunteer organists and pianists was drawn up in order to bridge the increasingly long gap in the appointment of a regular musician. The willing volunteers were Mr. George Read, Miss Bess Reid, Mrs. Vicki Friend, Mrs. Ann Roderick and Miss A.R. Campbell.

In July it was announced that Fr. Friend would be leaving St. Agnes' to become Rector of East Hendred and Vicar of West Hendred as from the end of August. His last Mass was on Tuesday, August 26th, at which fifteen people received Holy Communion. It was decided, therefore, to have a buffet supper after the Centenary Mass on September 9th, which was to be a combined Centenary Mass and Farewell for Fr. Friend who would return for the evening. The Bishop of Reading, the Right Revd. Eric Wild, presided at the Sung Mass at which eighty-four people received Holy Communion. Afterwards there was a presentation and farewell gathering in the Hall. Sometime after Fr. Friend's institution to the parishes of East and West Hendred a re-organisation of boundaries resulted in the amalgamation of six parishes to be known collectively as 'Wantage Downs' with Fr. Friend as Rector. Fr. Friend remained in the Wantage Downs group until the Summer of 1982 when he was appointed to the benefice of Syston in Leicestershire where he served his first curacy.

The Centenary celebrations should have been a time of great joy and thanksgiving, a time of looking forward to the future in thanksgiving for the past. Instead September 1974 became a time of anxiety and deprivation, for with the interregnum there was the inevitable cut-back in services, and as time went on there was the growing doubt as to whether a new priest would be appointed, or whether the Church would close. During the interregnum the services were maintained by Fr. Shaw and Fr. Reader.

The St. Agnes' Committee decided to review the question of Series II versus Series III before a new priest was appointed. In order to refresh memories Series II was used for one month and on Sunday, February 23rd, 1975, a vote was taken. The result was Series II twenty-eight votes, Series III thirty-two votes and the Committee accordingly agreed to retain the use of the Series III rite.

There was no shortage of applicants for the post at St. Agnes' but for various reasons an appointment was not made, and during this lengthy interregnum a much closer link was forged between the two Churches. It was slightly over a year since Fr. Friend left - on Sunday, September 21st 1975 - that the Revd. Frederick Thomas Bonham celebrated his first Mass as priest-in-charge of St. Agnes'.

## Chapter XXIV

### To arrive where we started

"We shall not cease from exploration
And the end of all our exploring
Will be to arrive where we started
And know the place for the first time."

T.S. ELIOT. FOUR QUARTETS: LITTLE GIDDING.

"If you don't write about your own time at St., Agnes', no-one else will," someone said to me quite recently when I stated my intention of finishing this book at the Centenary. My objection was that it would not be right to 'blow our own trumpet'. On reflection, a good deal has happened since the mystical date of 1974, and there has been much which reflects the St. Agnes' tradition of team spirit and family atmosphere. So with this in mind I will try to set down a little of what has happened in 'our time'.

Frederick Thomas Bonham was ordained deacon in September 1972 and priest in June 1973. Before training for the Church's ministry he spent five years as a Benedictine monk at Nashdom Abbey but, having realised his priestly vocation, left without making life vows and was accepted for ordination training. His first curacy was spent at St. Edmund's, Northwood Hills, Middlesex. Those three years at St. Edmund's were a tremendous though rigorous experience for us both. The Vicar, Fr. Reg Ames, had come to a dual purpose Church-cum-Hall built in the 1930's along with much of his suburban parish. The congregation had been fund-raising in a half-hearted manner for many years to build a new Church, and in the end they had given up the attempt and sent the money to build a Church in Lesotho. Reg Ames changed all that, and within two years of his arrival the new Church was built and paid for and was consecrated in 1964. The money had come in through coffee mornings, jumble sales, raffles, Saturday markets and anything else, but the force behind it was the dynamic personality of Fr. Ames, who expected everyone else to have the same zeal, energy, enthusiasm and stamina! Working with him was physically and mentally exhausting, often infuriating but immensely fulfilling, and it was not until after we had left that we came to fully appreciate the value of those three years. St. Edmund's was a valuable training ground and it gave Fr. Fred the zeal to undertake the tremendous challenge at St. Agnes'.

The desire for "a Church like St. Agnes'" had been with us both throughout the three years at St. Edmund's, and we little thought that having known it in former times we would ever return. This was particularly true as Fr. Friend left a whole year before Fr. Fred was free to leave St. Edmund's. It was therefore, with a feeling of great joy that we moved into the Presbytery on September 12th 1975.

Sunday worship follows the familiar pattern of recent years:-

| | |
|---|---|
| 8.00 a.m. | Holy Communion |
| 9.30 a.m. | Parish Mass |
| 6.00 p.m. | Holy Communion. |

At first the Sunday evening Mass was said with hymns and an address, but later the hymns were dropped owing to the poor attendance. Benediction of the Blessed Sacrament is given at 6.45 p.m. on the first Sunday in the month and on major Festivals which fall on a Sunday. The Guild of Servants of the Sanctuary meet at St. Agnes' from time to time. Other societies which meet here periodically, Fr. Fred being their Chaplain, are the Society of Mary and the Society of Our Lady of of Walsingham. Since 1976

Fr. Fred has led an annual pilgrimage to the Shrine of Our Lady of Walsingham from St. Agnes' and other local Churches.

The full Holy Week rites are used in their modern form, the chief observances in 1982 being as follows:-

| | | |
|---|---|---|
| PALM SUNDAY | 9.30 a.m. | Blessing of Palms in the Hall, Procession to Church and Parish Mass. |
| MAUNDY THURSDAY | 8.00 p.m. | Sung Mass of the Lord's Supper followed by Watch at the Altar of Repose until midnight. |
| GOOD FRIDAY | 10.30 a.m. | Children's Service |
| | 12.00 noon | One Hour's Devotion |
| | 3.00 p.m. | Liturgy of the Passion |
| | 7.30 p.m. | Stations of the Cross |
| HOLY SATURDAY | 10.30 p.m. | Easter Vigil and First Mass of Easter. |
| EASTER DAY | as usual but 9.30 a.m. Mass included the Renewal of Baptismal Promises by the congregation. | |
| | 6.45 p.m. | Benediction. |

When Fr. Fred took office, the Eucharistic rite in use was Series III which in itself was a stepping stone to the present Rite 'A' of the Alternative Service Book. One of the attractions of St. Agnes' for Fr. Fred was that it was liturgically 'up to date', and although Series III left much to be desired its successor has been very well received.

I called the work at St. Agnes' a 'tremendous challenge' because that was exactly what it seemed when we came to look round Church, Hall and Presbytery. Very little maintainance work had been done on the Church during the interregnum because the possibility of closure was so real. Although much had been done in both Fr. Hayne's and Fr. Friend's time there was still so much to do, and there had always been the money problem. That problem was still there, but at least the parish was no longer shackled by Stewardship with its 'no fund-raising clause'. It was obvious that if St. Agnes' was to stay open and be a worthy house of God then the fabric must be restored. The task of setting the fabric right was primarily a question of priorities. "Modern Man" cares enough about his own dwelling place to spend enormous sums on central heating, double glazing, building extensions, every comfort imaginable. How much greater then the necessity to spend time and money on God's dwelling. Who would want to live in a house with a leaking roof, dangerous wiring, windows with perished frames, and a rotten and worm-eaten floor? So why should we imagine such a building a worthy Tabernacle for the Most High?

Fr. Shaw had made it clear from the outset that St. Agnes' must henceforth be financially viable, and that she must pay her own way for work done. St. Andrew's was herself far less affluent than of old and was no longer in a position to keep St. Agnes' solvent.

Fr. Fred, therefore, proceeded to clear off the last £50.00 owing to St. Andrew's for the repairs to the South side of the roof. This done, it was full steam ahead with repairs to St. Agnes' and the methods used were those which Fr. Fred knew from experience. The first Saturday Market was held on October 25th 1975 just six weeks after our arrival, and the proceeds were earmarked for the Church roof, having decided it was logical to start at the top and work downwards! The fortnightly Markets have become an indispensable boost to our income. Held in the Church Hall and manned by a rota of helpers they consist of jumble, bric-a-brac, books, household goods, cakes and refreshments. The whole of the North side of the Church roof, i.e. that which was not restored in Fr. Friend's time, was restored in the Spring of 1976 at a cost of Ł443, which was raised by Saturday Markets. This was lower than the original estimate as the contractors re-used the old tiles wherever possible and did not use scaffolding. Their monkey-like agility was fascinating to behold! St. Agnes' roof with its steep pitches and deep gullies is a constant source of trouble as numerous damp patches on the ceiling testify. At least Ł700 has been spent on the entire roof since this time in numerous attempts to cure rain water leakages. Later in 1976 the Hall roof was extensively repaired, gutterings replaced and a new roof put on the covered way.

The next major project was the re-wiring of the Church which had become dangerous. On St. Agnes' Day 1977 the wiring at the back of the Church 'gave up the ghost' just before the evening Sung Mass which necessitated calling out the emergency services with only minutes to spare before the congregation began to arrive! The work of re-wiring was completed by Mr. Doe of Longmead, Windsor at a cost of around Ł700, all of which was raised by Saturday Markets. Later (during the Spring of 1980) the Hall was re-wired too.

The Church windows were in a poor condition, in particular the round West window and the two lancets by the font. The lead had perished on all three which allowed the rain to pour in and course down the walls. Thanks to an anonymous donation of Ł500 it was possible to have an attractive representation of Our Lord's Ascension in the round window. This was completed and in place by July 1979. The lancet windows were re-constructed, using the best glass from all three windows, and these were completed by March 1980. The craftsman was Mr. Michael Farrar-Bell of Haddenham, Buckinghamshire. The total cost was about Ł900, and the money was raised by various means, including coffee evenings and a sponsored knit by the Ladies Group.

By this time the Diocesan Quota payable by St. Agnes' had risen so sharply that the income from the Saturday Markets was needed to help pay this and other normal running costs such as lighting and heating. In 1982 the quota stands at Ł2,500 with a further increase expected each year.

The greatest challenge of all came early in 1980 when repairs reached floor level! It was already known that the floor was in a bad condition and that parts were rotten and would need replacement. We little expected to be told that the whole floor was so dangerous that something must be done at once. Initially sums in the region of Ł12,000 to Ł14,00 were being talked of and this raised some very fundamental questions about the future of St. Agnes'. For several weeks the axe was poised while both the St. Agnes' Committee and the full Parochial Church Council deliberated, and then after their having agreed to the work being done, Diocesan approval had to be obtained. Not everyone at St. Agnes' was in favour of the work being carried out, and this would not be a true record if I gave the impression that they were. A very small, but vocal, minority had never agreed with the efforts to beautify and restore St. Agnes' right from the start, and the thought of raising several thousand pounds to secure the future of St. Agnes' for the next generation was too much. However, the St. Agnes' Church Committee decided to meet the challenge four square. Fr. Shaw could easily have closed the Church, but instead he wrote to the Diocesan authorities praising the work of Fr. Fred and the great loyalty and determination of the congregation. As a result, permission was granted and the way lay clear. Those who opposed, finding themselves outvoiced, left St. Agnes!

Mr. D. Curtis, the Church's architect, diagnosed 'Coniophora puteana' - wet rot - together with wood worm. Except in one or two places the floor looked alright, but the trouble was underneath and was working its way outwards. The floor joists were completely infected and, in places, particularly near the font, had crumbled away completely causing the boards to sag dangerously. In the Sanctuary the upright posts, which joined onto the lower joists, crumbled away when tapped with a hammer! There was a four foot cavity under this part of the floor so an accident could have had a nasty outcome. The cavity under the rest of the Church varied from three feet on the North side of the nave to a few inches on the Lady Chapel side. Part of the trouble was caused by the lack of air circulation underneath the floor. Ironically the safest place was the gallery which was supported on brick piers down to the foundations.

The factor which more than any other made the work on the floor become possible was the realisation that the project would not be as expensive as we first thought. After considering a number of estimates the one submitted by Rentokil was accepted because they were prepared to allow four years for payment. The Restoration Fund target was set at £7,500 which included the re-decoration of the Church. At this time the full Parochial Church Council gave £1,000 to St. Agnes', which was used partly for extra work done by Rentokil on damp course injections in the Church wall, and partly for the re-surfacing of the Church paths. This extra work was not included as part of the Restoration target thanks to the help of St. Andrew's.

In order for the work to be done it was necessary to strip the Church of all furnishings and movable items, and not for the first time we gave thanks for the Church Hall. This was now made into a temporary Church with the Sunday School upstairs and, although it was a crush, everyone took the upheaval in their stride. The 'move' was made on Wednesday, July 23rd and Rentokil moved in on Friday, July 25th. Mr. Ray Crabbe of Leighton Organs moved our delicate instrument with utmost care into the Lady Chapel, where the various parts were covered with polythene to await the move back and the eventual re-assembly. Rentokil wasted no time in ripping out the old timbers, an unpleasant task which filled the air both inside and outside the Church with a nauseous smell. Within ten days the new floor was down and sprayed with preserving fluid which was equally noxious. Their task completed , they left on Tuesday, August 5th. The floor had to be left to dry out for a week or so, but as soon as was possible the re-decorating commenced. It had not been done since Fr. Hayne's time and was by now looking very bad. Economy prevented having contractors in so it had to be a 'do-it-yourself' job or nothing. A scaffold tower was hired for the ceilings, and among those who found themselves on top at one time or another were Fr. Fred, Tony Blackwell, Ernie Paternoster, Graham Field, Darren Dobson, Michael Saunders and myself. Nearer the ground was a motley collection of ages, ranging from Stephanie Field at fifteen years to William Green at eighty-plus. Between those two extremes were Elizabeth Gorsuch, Jack Roderick, Thelma Harland, Audrey Field, Rita and Frank Woodall, Michael Sumner, Olive and Kim Dobson, Barbara Saunders and Rankar Wilson. It was hard work but immensely rewarding, and it lasted for almost five weeks, Sundays included. On Sundays the work continued from the end of the Family Mass until the evening service. There was a marvellous fellowship amongst all who helped and the feeling of achievement at the end of it was worth every bit of the fatigue which all felt! When the painting was completed Fr. Fred hired an electric sander for the floor and then sealed and polished it. Mr. Crabbe re-assembled and tuned the organ and the Church furnishings were thoroughly cleaned and polished by a number of ladies from the congregation. On Sunday September 14th, we had a triumphant Dedication Festival in Church at which the Rector preached.

The whole work had been a great act of faith, because even while it was being done we had only £200.00 towards paying for it, most of which had been raised by the Ladies Group while we were still waiting for the Diocesan approval! Fund-raising continued all through the time when the work was being carried out. Using the Hall as a Church meant that it could not be used for anything else, so we availed ourselves of the good Summer weather and held the Markets in the Presbytery garden. Mr. David Roderick kindly donated a tent for the purpose and this, together with our caravan awning, provided covering for several stalls. Cakes and refreshments were served from the Presbytery kitchen. During those few weeks the Markets were held weekly to boost the income.

Local interest was soon generated in the Restoration Fund when an appeal board was placed outside with its 'thermometer' marked off in £500 divisions. Individual fund-raising efforts were many, varied and often ingenious. Several substantial bequests and donations were given, including one from Her Majesty's State Apartments Fund. Money and support was given not just by the congregation but by many local people who value the presence of the Church in their midst. The red line began to move up the thermometer by leaps and bounds so that by January 1982, just seventeen months after Rentokil began their work, the target of £7,500 was reached. It seemed like a miracle, but the miracle was really in people's hearts. Having weighed the future of St. Agnes' in the balance, we all realised it was something worth keeping.

Another miracle took place while the Church was being restored. Early in August 1980 we received the stunning news that one of our servers, David Saunders, aged fifteen years, had been taken desperately ill with a brain tumour while in France with his Venture Scout group, and was in a Paris hospital. While his family went to be at his bedside, St. Agnes' people waited and prayed. On the Sunday following the news, a day of prayer was held from the end of the Family Mass until the start of Evening Mass. All day long people came to and from the Church Hall and those who were painting in the Church painted and prayed in relays. The initial operation was followed by a second one in the National Hospital for Nervous Diseases to which David was transferred as soon as he was well enough.
David's miracle didn't happen overnight, his road to recovery has been long and tedious but nonetheless miraculous to those of us who know and love him. David once more leads a full life which includes Scouting and life-saving duties in the precarious Thames, and has achieved considerable academic success at the Windsor Boys' School.

Unfortunately the restoration of the Church did not cease with the floor. "We have now reached the £7,500 target," announced Fr. Fred at the beginning of January 1982, "but next comes Phase II!" This is the long awaited and desperately needed organ rebuild. Following George Kelsey's death in 1976 an Organ Fund had been opened in his memory with the intention of buying a new pipe organ or rebuilding the old one. An appeal had even been launched and it had reached several hundred pounds, but there were always other more vital jobs which needed doing. Once the floor was completed the way was clear to tackle the organ. The work will cost approximately £4,700 pounds, of which £3,100 had been raised by December 1982, and will consist of a complete rebuild of the present instrument. The end result will be a two manual electric-action pipe organ with pedal board. Mr. Ray Crabbe, of Leighton Organs, will begin the work in July 1983. As from Easter 1982 Mr. Tim Chapman was appointed organist of St. Agnes' and we now look forward to a promising chapter in what has been in recent years a sad musical history.

When Fr. Shaw was appointing a new priest to replace Fr. Friend, he expressed the hope that St. Agnes' would serve a special role for the children of the district. Only time will tell how much that hope has been fulfilled since 1975, but at least the effort has been made. The Sunday School had been phased out during Fr. Friend's time, as indeed it had in many parishes, in favour of encouraging children and parents to worship together at the Sung Mass. However, there was a need for some means of instruction and soon after Fr. Friend left, creche facilities were begun in the Church Hall, which later formed into a new Sunday School. This Sunday School met at 9.30 a.m. and the children came into Church for the second part of the Mass.

In July 1980 it was re-organised with Mrs. Barbara Saunders, Mrs. Elsie Crossland and myself as teaching staff, under the supervision of Fr. Fred. Numbers of children are small but consistent and already older members are offering themselves for Confirmation and are becoming integrated into the adult life of the Church. This is our aim in the Sunday School - to teach the Faith and to prepare members for the full Sacramental life of the Church; to be a stepping-stone rather than an end in itself. To emphasise that we are part of the Church and not a separate body the Sunday School service has the same structure as the first part of the Eucharist - prayer, Bible reading, teaching and intercessions. To emphasise this further, on the major Festivals we join with the congregation for the whole of the Sung Eucharist, in this way making the later transition from Sunday School to adult Christian life a natural progression. At St. Agnes'-tide 1981 the children performed a play depicting the 'Martyrdom of St. Agnes' and on Passion Sunday 1982 we produced a Passion Play. Both productions were performed during the 9.30 a.m. Sung Mass.

A wider means of extending our children's work is our annual mission wrapped up in the form of a holiday club. "Seekers' Week" caters for six to ten year olds towards the end of the long Summer holiday. Numbers vary from twenty-five to fifty depending on the weather and secular competition in the town. Each two hour session consists of a mixture of Christian teaching, activities such as painting and crafts, team games, quizzes, tuck-shop and an outing on Saturday afternoon. Though we would hope to see the children in Sunday School as a result of the week this rarely happens, but we do not deem it a failure, for the Seed of the Faith has been sown and it may be dormant for many years before being awakened.

There are no Youth Clubs at St. Agnes' at the time of writing, not for want of effort by various members of the congregation, but simply for want of support. It would seem that the youth of Spital has no need for the facilities offered and so until such time as there is a need, there is a dormant patch.

The Scouts no longer parade at St. Agnes' following their amalgamation with the group based at Holy Trinity, Windsor. The new Central Windsor group now hold their parades at Holy Trinity.

There is a faithful team of servers led by Alan Bridges who in 1981 completed forty-five years in the Sanctuary. Others in the team are Frank Woodall, who like Alan has the Bishop's permission to administer the Chalice at Holy Commmunion; Graham and Martin Field, Peter Crossland, Matthew Sumner, Richard Greenaway, Peter Tindall, Alexander Sumner and Darren Philips. Peter Tindall has recently been accepted for training for the Church's Ministry, following graduation from University.

Mention may here be made of those from the congregation who have died since September 1975. Two of the faithful were buried within two days of each other in June 1976. Sidney Hunt, a regular Communicant at home for many years, was buried on Monday, June 6th. Later the same day the body of Sarah Squibb was brought into Church. The Requiem Mass was offered next morning, followed later by the funeral at which Fr. Wood preached.

George Kelsey died on September 8th 1976 after several years of failing health which had kept him away from St. Agnes'. Soon after his arrival Fr. Fred began visiting George and taking Holy Communion to him either in hospital or at home. George Kelsey's body came to St. Agnes' for the last time on September 15th 1976, the Requiem and funeral following the next day. One person missing was his wife, Rosa, who was by now too ill to attend. One of my greatest regrets is that I never met him and I count this book the poorer for being without his reminiscences.

The whole congregation was stunned by the news of the sudden death on December 21st 1976 of Bessie Barrow. Bessie was a quiet, cheerful person whom everyone loved. Involved very much in the Stewardship Campaigns, Bessie also helped the Treasurer, Miss Strong, to count the Sunday collections and cleaned all the Church brass - jobs which she did in an unassuming way so that most people little realised how much she did. Bessie was confirmed during Fr. Hayne's time and was a faithful Communicant right up to the Sunday before her death. Her funeral took place on December 29th at Slough Crematorium and there was a Requiem in Church later in the evening.

Phyliss Richardson died on September 3rd 1977 after an illness of which few people were aware. Her simple piety was an example to us all, for she saw her Lord in everybody and nothing was ever too much trouble. The mainspring of her strength was the Blessed Sacrament and she was present at daily Mass right up to a fortnight before her death, often at great sacrifice to herself. Her body was received into Church on September 7th and Vespers of the Dead followed. The Requiem and funeral took place next day which happened to be the Nativity of Our Lady. I can well imagine her look of joy if anyone had told her that September 8th would be the day of her funeral; 'Oh, Our Lady's Birthday, how lovely," she would have said, for her devotion to Christ's Mother was very deep.

Jim Cramer died on July 5th 1978 and was buried on July 12th. His health had been very poor, following a stroke some years previously, and this had cut short his active involvement and attendance at St. Agnes'. He had received Holy Communion at home every week until his death, which came as a merciful relief from his sufferings.

Rosa Kelsey died on December 28th 1978 after a long period in hospital and was brought back to St. Agnes' for the Funeral Requiem on January 9th 1979. 1978 also saw the passing of a number of other former members of the congregation. Ivy Simpson was buried on May 17th; Harry (Jack) Merrifield, one-time server, was buried on June 19th; and Eric Longfield-Jones' funeral was on September 15th.

One of St. Agnes' longest serving Communicants, Daisy Wilkins, died on February 21st 1980. Confirmed in 1912, Daisy had faithfully served her Lord ever since, and many of her memories are contained in this book. Domestic service took Daisy away from Windsor for much of her working life but following her retirement she returned to the Church of her youth, and home to care for the elderly members of her large family. Daisy was a truly humble soul and always sat at the back of the Church by the font. I could never persuade her to call me anything but 'Madam', a habit no doubt derived from her years in domestic service. Her other great interest was the St. John's Ambulance Brigade of which she was a proud and loyal member until shortly before her death.

Mrs. Susan Hunt, another faithful Communicant at home, was laid to her rest in Windsor Cemetery on August 11th 1980. The funeral service took place in the Cemetery Chapel owing to the closure of the Church for restoration. Two more elderly people, forced by ill-health to receive Holy Communion at home, were Edward Hounslow, whose Requiem and funeral was on March 2nd 1981; and Maud Holloway whose Requiem and funeral was on September 7th 1981. George Simpson, a friend and benefactor, died in December and his funeral took place on December 14th 1981.

George Read, former Headmaster of the Royal Free Boys' School on Bachelors' Acre, died on January 29th 1982. For several years George had been an 'honorary part-time' organist at St. Agnes', and before that had been organist at All Saints', North Ascot. A graduate in music, George had written especially for St. Agnes' a Setting for the Series III Eucharist, which he later adapted for 'Rite A'. George's last Sunday at St. Agnes' was a very happy one for him. He had been 'off colour' a few days before and only at the last minute felt well enough to play the organ. As it was the Sunday in St. Agnes'-tide, the Parish Mass was held at 11.00 a.m. and was followed by a Family Lunch in the Hall. Afterwards George told me how much he and his wife had enjoyed the Mass and the following lunch. During the late afternoon he began to feel unwell and was admitted to Hospital a couple of days later where he died on the Friday. The body was brought into Church on February 3rd and next day the Church was well filled for the Requiem and funeral. The preacher was the Revd. F.C.T. Lancaster, former Vicar of All Saint's, North Ascot.

Mrs. L.V. Bridges passed to her rest at the end of August 1982 after a lingering last illness. Her body was brought into St. Agnes' on August 25th and Vespers of the Dead was recited. The Requiem Mass and funeral followed the next day and there was a good congregation present to bid farewell to one who had given herself unstintingly in the service of God and His Church in Spital.

There have been, besides numerous deaths, numerous births in the last few years, but perhaps I may be forgiven for singling out one in particular - Louise Elizabeth Bonham who was born in Heatherwood Hospital on November 8th, 1976.

A number of memorials and gifts have been given to the Church in recent years. Some have taken the form of bequests to the Restoration Fund but others have taken a more tangible form.

Mrs. Clara Taylor left a bequest which the St. Agnes' Committee decided to use for obtaining new candlesticks for the High Altar. Mr. Percy Yabsley of Walsingham made these from cedar wood from the Shrine Garden. Also in 1976, the large Crucifix which stands in the East Window was renovated and repainted by Mrs. Jones of Clarence Crescent and mounted on a new Cross by Mr. Donald Ashworth. This renovation was done in memory of Mrs. Sarah Squibb from her sister, Miss Bess Reid.

In 1978 a new vestment press was bought in memory of Alfred Giles, Barbara Bridges' father, and also in memory of Phyliss Richardson. A new lamp for the statue of Our Lady was bought with the balance from the memorial fund for Phyliss Richardson. Also in 1978, Miss Rose Campbell gave thanks for twenty years as Parish Worker at St. Agnes' and marked the occasion by giving new carpet runners for the aisles and a new carpet for the Sanctuary.

1979 saw improvements to the altars thanks to various benefactors. An altar cloth made by Mrs. Elsie Crossland and embroidered at the Community of St. John the Baptist with the legend 'Ecce Agnus Dei' (Behold the Lamb of God), was given for the High Altar by Barbara Bridges in memory of her mother, Dorothy Giles. A legacy from Jim Cramer enabled the purchase of a new Tabernacle and various donations enabled a matching set of Crucifix and four candlesticks to be obtained for the Lady Chapel Altar.

The vestments have been improved largely through benefactions. A new set of white vestments were bought in memory of Sidney Hunt by his widow, Susan, and sister-in-law Elsie Maxwell. Following Mrs. Hunt's death, Mrs. Maxwell has enabled the seventy year old red vestments to be expertly restored at the Convent of St. John the Baptist workroom. The red cope which dates from the same time has also been restored partly through donations and partly through funds raised. Other new vestments have been obtained through donations of money as thankofferings.

People no longer need entertainment laid on as in the 'old days' so that organised groups have difficulty in obtaining members. A case in point has been the Ladies Group which is how the Wives Group re-named themselves in 1975. In October 1981 at their Annual General Meeting the Ladies Group took the courageous step of dissolving their organisation and re-forming as the "St. Agnes' Fellowship." This was to be open to all, men and women alike, as a spirtitual and social extension of our Fellowship together in the Church. Membership of the Ladies Group had been dwindling for a number of years so that it was becoming increasingly difficult to obtain outside speakers. The Fellowship so far has proved successful with an average of twenty-five at the meetings.

Oddly enough most fund-raising activities prove to be valuable social events! The Saturday Markets attract a local clientele who rarely come to services but like to support the fund-raising and obtain a few bargains. Other corporate activities such as the sponsored knits and the Sponsored Walk, which Mrs. Joan Eagle organised in May 1982, have brought the congregation together in a new way. There are social activities in the more accepted sense too, of course. The 'Sunday Coffee' after the 9.30 a.m. Mass provides a market place for conversation and is always a lively gathering. The annual Family Lunch on the Sunday in St. Agnes'-tide is a happy time for all - thanks to the hard work of a few devoted ladies, chiefly Joan Fletcher, Vi Roderick, Barbara Saunders and Thelma Harland.

My own memories of 'our time' at St. Agnes' will be for the most part happy ones. Of course, there have been sad, anxious times, but the joy will always outweigh it. Whilst writing this book I have come to 'know' the people in it irrespective of whether they are alive to-day or whether they died fifty years ago! They are more than just names, they are people who have worked for the same end as I am working. I believe that those who have gone to their rest are still supporting us all with their prayers, and I was never more conscious of it than in the dark days of early 1980 when it looked as though St. Agnes' would close. I am convinced that we owe it as much to those who have gone before us to look after this Church which is our inheritance, as we owe it to the next generation to see that there is a Church for them to worship in. In the words of Fr. Stanton, that great priest who loved St. Agnes'; "For life is one and indivisible and we live again in those who are gone before, and they in us."

Every priest who has been at St. Agnes' has made his mark upon it for good or ill, and there are people in Spital who still talk of Charles Farr and William Brook as if they left only yesterday. We are still reaping in 1982 the seeds sown in their time. We are still reaping the seeds sown by Henry Ley when he built the Church Hall at his own expense. Without that Hall built in 1884 there could have been no Church Restoration in 1980. We hope and pray that the seeds of Faith sown in the ministry of Fred Bonham will still bear good fruit in future decades. One thing is certain - that without a loyal and faithful congregation a priest can do nothing. St. Agnes' Spital has been blessed with such throughout her years.

And so past, present and future come together to form an indistinguishable, inextinguishable Present Moment. In the words of T.S. Eliot:-

> "Time past and time future
> What might have been and what has been
> Point to one end, which is always present."
>
> FOUR QUARTETS: BURNT NORTON.

## Appendix 1

## Torpor and Torrent

At the beginning of the nineteenth century the Church of England was at a very low ebb. Spiritual life was almost dead. For over a century the view had been held that the State was the final authority in religious belief. Not without reason has the Church of England been called the "Tory Party at Prayer."

Inadequate training frequently produced clergy who cared little for the cure of souls but rather followed such pursuits as hunting and shooting.

It was not unusual for a clergyman to hold three or four livings at one time, and there was no guarantee that he would supply a curate to those parishes in which he was non-resident. More often than not, daily services were unknown, and the Eucharist would only be celebrated about three times a year. In 1807 out of 11,164 parishes only 4,412 had resident priests.

The state of the parochial clergy was to a large degree a result of the worldliness of the Episcopate. The Bishops regarded themselves as officials of the State rather than Princes of the Church. A few were non-resident in their dioceses, the most notorious example being Bishop Watson of Llandaff from 1782-1816, who lived in Westmorland on the shores of Lake Windermere where he occupied his time planting trees and in agricultural improvements. In some dioceses Confirmations were held only every seven years. There were no Theological Colleges in the modern sense, and after passing through Oxford or Cambridge men wishing to seek ordination were often given only a token verbal examination. This was particularly so in cases of sons of the aristocracy.

Clerical income was equally scandalous. At the episcopal end of the scale, the Diocese of Winchester was said to be worth £50,000 per year and London £10,000, whilst many small country livings were worth less than £150. Curates were paid a pittance for taking duty in parishes where the incumbent was non-resident. Where patronage was in the hands of the Bishop preferment often went to their own sons and sons-in-law. Many incumbents grew wealthy on the fruits of plural benefices and of pew rents.

With so many non-resident clergy and so few church services, inevitably the Church buildings suffered and fell into decay. Belief in the Church of England as a Living part of the Catholic Church had become obscured and likewise belief that the Church building was God's Sanctuary. Attention had become focused on the pulpit rather than on the altar; Churches had become preaching halls.

The time was ripe for change. Politically the Tory Party was on the rocks. In 1828 the Tory Government had been forced to repeal the Test and Corporation Acts which had hitherto barred Non-Conformists from holding State and Municipal office. 1829 saw Catholic Emancipation which was regarded, particularly in Oxford University, as a betrayal of the Established Church. Then in 1832 came the Parliamentary Reform Act which re-shaped Parliamentary representation. By 1833 the Whigs were in power and the outlook for the Church seemed bleak. In 1833 an Act was passed reducing the twenty-two Irish bishoprics to twelve, and this aroused fears that similar suppressions would follow in the English Church.

It was in view of this impending danger that on July 14th 1833 John Keble, Fellow of Oriel, preached a sermon on 'National Apostasy' before the Assize Judges, in the University Church at Oxford. The Sermon made no vast stir at the time but many years later Newman wrote, "I have ever considered and kept the day as the start of the religious movement of 1833." On September 9th the first of the "Tracts for the Times" was issued. Others followed, some written by Newman, others by equally brilliant and zealous men who wished to see the Church re-affirm its belief in its Catholic heritage and tradition - John Keble, Richard Hurrell Froude, Edward Bouverie Pusey, to name but a few. The Tracts soon gave a name to the movement.

The Tracts re-kindled a fire which had never completely died out during the previous one hundred and fifty years. The eighteenth century had seen the rise and fall of the Evangelical Movement within the Church, which had its roots in Oxford with Wesley and Whitefield. Some of the adherents of Evangelicalism remained in the Established Church after the severing of the Methodists although they had lost much of their 'fire'. There was also a remnant of clergy belonging to the old High Church Party (not to be confused with the modern notion of 'High Church' commonly attached to ceremonial practices). They took as their model the seventeenth Century Caroline Divines such as Lancelot Andrewes, Thomas Ken and Jeremy Taylor, and provided oases of an ordered, though somewhat staid, religious observance. Thus there were embers waiting to be stirred, and the Tracts for the Times kindled a fire which has not ceased burning.

The Oxford Movement continued to flourish despite the secession to the Roman Catholic Church of Newman in 1845, and others, chiefly Archdeacon Manning, in 1851.

The secessions dealt a deep blow to those left behind for they were deeply humiliated and felt betrayed by their one-time companions in the cause. Many people had feared that there was a Romanizing tendency in the Movement and these fears now appeared to be justified. Furthermore, there was a general anti-papal feeling in the country which was aggravated by the establishment of the Roman Catholic hierarchy in 1850.

At first the Tractarians had simply emphasized the importance of Catholic doctrine, particularly concerning the Sacraments, but as these ideas spread and Eucharistic worship was revived, the emphasis turned to ceremonial. "Ritualism' as it came to be called was not considered important by the early Tractarians. In time the crucial doctrine came to be that of the "Real Presence" in the Eucharist, and the second generation of the Oxford Movement revived ceremonial in order to emphasise this truth. They held fast to the 'Ornaments Rubric' in the Book of Common Prayer which stated that the vestments and furnishings ordered by the first Prayer Book of Edward VI (1549) were lawful. Difficulties arose with attempts to interpret the Rubric, for no-one was sure exactly which vestments and furnishings were in use in 1549. The issue gradually crystallised into the 'Six Points' - Eucharistic vestments; Eastward position of the celebrant at the altar; the mixed chalice (wine and water); wafer bread; lighted candles on the altar; and incense.

If a section of the public had been alarmed at the early Tract writers, they were certainly alarmed at the younger generation of ritualistic clergy. From both inside and outside the Church the "No Popery" cry was revived with renewed vigour. In 1850 rioting began in London - the hunt was on, and soon many faithful priests were hounded before the Courts. The Bishops were against them and so was Parliament. In 1859 Bishop Tait of London referred to the wearing of vestments as "this childish mimicry of antiquated garments." One of the greatest opponents of the ritualists was Lord Shaftesbury, ardent Evengelical and philanthropist, who in the field of social welfare and industry did much to relieve the distress and hardship of the working classes. This section of the population was also very close to the hearts of many of the persecuted ritualist clergy, for by now the Movement had spread away from its academic birthplace out to the parishes, and many of these were the slum parishes of London, the big industrial centres of the Midlands and the North, and the naval and military garrisons. In 1865 the Church Association was formed to harass the Ritualists and to bring cases before the Courts. The Association soon became known as the "Persecution Company Limited." Five years previously the English Church Union had been formed to uphold and defend the doctrine and discipline of the Church of England and to assist all persons, clerical and lay, who were being harassed or persecuted for their faith.

The ecclesiastical court was the Court of Arches, but if an appeal was to be made then the Judicial Committee of the Privy Council dealt with it. They frequently reversed Judgement from one case to another, so that ceremonial which was legal at one time might suddenly be declared illegal by the same Court!

1874 saw the passage of the Public Worship Regulation Act, due mainly to the efforts of Disraeli and Dr. Tait, who was now Archbishop of Canterbury. The object was in Disraeli's words "to put down Ritualism." A new Court was set up, presided over by Lord Penzance, an ex-divorce court judge. In the ensuing law suits five priests, were sent to prison for contempt of court because they defied the Court's ruling, and many more were either suspended from duty or deprived of their benefices. The defendants claimed that the new Court was a secular court and had no authority on spiritual matters. (The five priests were Arthur Tooth of St. James' Hatcham; Thomas Pelham Dale of St. Vedast, City of London; James Bell Cox of St. Margaret's, Liverpool; R.W. Enraght of Holy Trinity, Bordesley, Birmingham; and Sidney Faithorn Green of St. James', Miles Platting, Manchester)

The strife was not confined to Eucharistic ceremonial. There was another practice to which the Protestant agitators were opposed - private Confession to a priest. Bishop Blomfield of London once described it as "the source of unspeakable abominations." The height of the controversy came in 1870 when a privately published manual for confessors called 'The Priest in Absolution' fell into the wrong hands and passages were quoted from it, out of their context, in the House of Lords. For a time the popular press had a field day printing prurient 'ghastly revelations' from the Confessional, and the 'Punch' cartoonists and other satirists depicted leering priests asking intimate questions of seemingly innocent young ladies, but then the controversy died down.

The incident which did more than anything to make a dead letter out of the Public Worship Regulation Act was the persecution of Dr. Edward King, Bishop of Lincoln in 1888. A Saintlier man would have been difficult to find; he was loved and revered by all throughout his diocese, and the Church Association at last over-reached itself. Many supporters of the Association had already withdrawn after Fr. Tooth of St. James', Hatcham was sent to prison in 1877. In their minds suspension from duty or even deprivation was one thing, imprisonment was quite a different matter. Dr. Benson, Archbishop of Canterbury, intervened in the "King affair" and decided to try the case himself with five Bishops as assessors. The decision, given in 1890, was in Bishop King's favour on all but two points. Although the Act remained on the Statute Book until its repeal in 1962, it was rendered practically ineffective by the outcome of what came to be known as the 'Lincoln Case'.

The ceremonial for which so many priests were persecuted and for which they were prepared to suffer suspension, deprivation, even imprisonment, can be seen in most Anglican Churches nowadays. Much of it would no longer be classed as 'extreme' for most of the ceremonial is accepted as part of the normal trappings of worship. The victory won by the Ritualists was one of Liberty - the right to teach the Faith and express it in worship with such ceremonial as is thought fitting for the Mysteries of God.

## Appendix II

### Rectors of Clewer since 1844

| | |
|---|---|
| Thomas Thellusson Carter, M.A. | 1844-1880 |
| Roland Errington, M.A. | 1880-1899 |
| Arthur Thomas Carnsew Cowie, M.A. | 1900-1925 |
| William Elwell, M.A., C.F. | 1925-1931 |
| Gerald George Payne-Cook, M.A. | 1932-1942 |
| Cyprian Dymoke-Marr, M.A. | 1943-1971 |
| Denis Shaw | 1971- |

### Priests of St. Agnes', Spital

| | |
|---|---|
| George Hervey Swinny | 1874-1876 |
| Henry Ley | 1882-1893 |
| George Jones | 1894-1900 |
| Herbert Burges Hunt | 1900-1903 |
| Walter Saunders Hulme | 1903-1904 |
| Charles Farr | 1904-1911 |
| Marsh Kirkby | 1911-1913 |
| William Brook | 1913-1935 |
| Richard Evelyn Beer | 1936-1939 |
| Hubert Thornton Trapp | 1939-1942 |
| Alban Caldicott Morton Howard | 1943-1945 |
| Edward Ashby Dixon | 1946-1949 |
| William Aubrey Pike | 1950 |
| Maurice Whitehouse Hickin | Dec.1950-1954 |
| Brian P. Elliott-Smith | 1954 |
| Arthur Edward Wood | 1955-1959 |
| Frederick John Prebble | 1959-1963 |
| Raymond Guy Hayne | 1963-1967 |
| Graham Alan Friend | 1967-1974 |
| Frederick Thomas Bonham | 1975- |

Plate 1

The Revd. G.H.Swinny, first priest of St. Agnes'

Plate 2

St. Agnes' Spital in 1907 before the extension was added

Plate 3

Clewer Mothers' outing at Boulter's Lock, June 1909.
In the back row, Mrs. Cowie stands between the Revd. Charles Farr on her right and the Revd. Arthur Cowie, Rector, on her left. Mrs. Emma Uglow stands at the back next to the two women with the two babies.

Plate 4

Choir and Servers in 1911.

Standing left, not robed: A.W.Weston.
Back row in robes: 5th from left, George Uglow, jnr; extreme right, Hugh Garner.
Middle row in robes: 3rd from left, Sydney Pert; 4th from left, Philip Foreman; 5th from left, Alfred Clarke; holding Cross, James Clarke; 3rd from right, Mr Squelch; extreme right not robed, George Uglow, snr.
Seated: 3rd from left, Alfred Kelsey; 4th from left, George Bridges; 5th from left, Victor Myddleton Biddulph; Revd. Charles Farr; 5th from right, William Clarke; 2nd from right, Mr. Upton. The dog belonged to Victor Biddulph.

Plate 5

Memorial card from the Mission of December, 1912.

Plate 6

Choir and Servers, c. 1914.

Back row, men standing: 1st left, Thomas Rosier; holding Crucifix, William Clarke; Mr. Upton; George Uglow snr.
Second row, boys standing: 1st left, William Wilkins; 2nd left, Cecil Upton; 5th from left, Jim Merrifield; 7th from left, Charles Wilkins.
Men seated: From left to right: Mr. Doe; Arthur Thomas; Alfred Clarke; Revd. William Brook; James Clarke.
Sitting on grass: 1st, Harry Grant; 2nd Master Bampton.
The photograph was taken in the field behind St. Agnes'. In the background can be seen the Mission Rooms and Caretaker's Cottage on the left and the three cottages adjoining which have since been demolished.

Plate 7

5th Windsor (Clewer St. Andrew's) Scouts in the early 1920's.

Back row: 1, Bartholomew; 2, Joe Chamberlain; 3, Moore; 4, Scothern; 6, Reg Wilkins.
Middle row: 1, Liddiard; 2, Ernie Rixon; 3, Don Webling; 4, Alfie Harberd; 5, Parker; 6, Cyril Leppard; 7, Victor Harberd; 9, Harry Fowler.
Front row: 1, Jack Merrifield; 3, Ted Merrifield;
5, Scoutmaster Reg Cooke; 6, Rowland Garner; 7, Ernest Warner; 8, Parker.
Extreme right on floor: Webling.

The photograph was taken in St. Agnes' Mission Room.

Plate 8

Scouts' Outing, early 1920's. Taken opposite St. Agnes' outside Eton Cottage.

Plate 9

Mothers' Outing, early 1920's. Revd. & Mrs. William Brook next to the driver.

Plate 10

St. Agnes' interior before 1937 restoration.

Plate 11

St. Agnes' as it was from 1937 until 1973. (Drawing by H. Dean from photograph taken by Mr. G. Tyrell.)

Plate 12

Pert's Bakery, Spital, c. 1905. Master Sydney Pert on left, Mr. John Pert on right. Shop still bears name of previous owners, J.N. Hewitt. Demolished during 1960's.

Plate 13

The 'Stag and Hounds', Spital. 1918, or just after.

Plate 14

The 'Royal Standard', Spital, V.E. Day 1945. Building demolished during the 1960's.

Plate 15

Clewer Lodge, Spital, when it was the Headmaster's House, Imperial Service College.